readings in basic management

A. THOMAS HOLLINGSWORTH

Associate Professor of Management,
University of South Carolina

RICHARD M. HODGETTS

Professor of Management,
University of Nebraska – Lincoln

1975
W. B. SAUNDERS COMPANY
Philadelphia • London • Toronto

W. B. Saunders Company: West Washington Square
Philadelphia, PA 19105

12 Dyott Street
London, WC1A 1DB

833 Oxford Street
Toronto, Ontario M8Z 5T9, Canada

Library of Congress Cataloging in Publication Data

Hollingsworth, Abner Thomas, 1939–   comp.

Readings in basic management.

1. Management—Addresses, essays, lectures.
    I. Hodgetts, Richard M., joint comp.   II. Title.

HD31.H615   658.4′008   74–12914

ISBN   0–7216–4753–7

Readings in Basic Management   ISBN   0–7216–4753–7

Last digit is the print number: 9   8   7   6   5   4   3   2   1

*This book is dedicated
to our families*

PREFACE

The purpose of this book is to acquaint the reader with the field of management. This is, of course, not an easy task. A great deal of writing and research in this field has taken place in recent years. As a result, there is currently a wealth of information available on many areas from long-range planning to control and from motivation to leadership style.

Nevertheless, in this volume we have attempted to bring together articles that will provide a basic understanding of management. In most cases, the selections contain the latest thinking and research in the field. In every instance we have assumed that the reader is either a student or a practitioner with a limited amount of exposure to the management literature. It is our hope that these selections will not only familiarize the reader with some of the important concepts and developments in the field but also motivate him or her to undertake further formal study of management.

In designing a logical, easy-to-understand approach, we have divided the book into four major parts. Part I consists of articles designed to introduce the area of management. It contains historical material and is intended to acquaint the reader with how management evolved to its current state. Part II contains selections designed to familiarize the reader with modern management theory and practice. This part of the book is divided into three sections. Section A introduces what is called the "management process school" and contains selections related to planning, organizing and controlling. Section B covers the "quantitative school" and contains articles related to decision making and mathematical techniques. Section C addresses itself to the "behavioral school" and contains selections dealing with communication, motivation and leadership. Part III is designed to present information related to recent developments in the field of management. In particular, articles dealing with management information systems, the computer, technology, modern organization structures, the management of human assets, social responsibility and international management are contained in this part of the book. Part IV presents articles that examine the future of management. Particular attention is given to the professionalism of management and the profile of the manager of the future.

We believe this book can serve as a supplement to any basic management text in the field. For this reason, we have provided a cross-reference table which follows the table of contents. In addition, graduate students and practicing managers wishing to update their knowledge of the field should find this book helpful.

A. Thomas Hollingsworth
Richard M. Hodgetts

ACKNOWLEDGMENTS

We would like to thank the authors and publishers of the articles in this book for their reprint permissions. We would also like to thank John C. Neifert, our editor, for his assistance in gathering the enclosed materials; Henry H. Albers, Chairman of the Management Department, University of Nebraska, for his encouragement and support; Dr. Ronald Johnson, Management Department, University of Nebraska, for his substantive comments on some of our readings selections; John Markel and Tim McConnell, graduate students at the University of South Carolina, for their help in gathering the articles; and Jeanne Maynard and Lynn Galloway for their secretarial assistance in producing this book.

June, 1975

A. THOMAS HOLLINGSWORTH
RICHARD M. HODGETTS

CONTENTS

CROSS-REFERENCE TABLE.
FOR RELATING THESE READINGS TO BASIC MANAGEMENT TEXTBOOKS

CROSS-REFERENCE TABLE. FOR RELATING THESE READINGS TO BASIC MANAGEMENT TEXTBOOKS

	I. An Introduction to Management		II. Modern Management Theory and Practice		III. Recent Developments in Management					IV. Management in the Future
		Management Process School	Quantitative School	Behavioral School	Management Information Systems and the Computer	Technology and Modern Organization Structures	Management of Human Assets	Social Responsibility	International Management	
Albers, Henry H. *Principles of Management: A Modern Approach.* New York: John Wiley & Sons, Inc., 1973.	Ch. 1, 2	Ch. 3, 4, 5, 6, 7, 10, 13	Ch. 15, 16	Ch. 8, 9, 12, 17, 18, 21, 22	Ch. 19, 20	Ch. 14	Ch. 11	Ch. 23		
Dale, Ernest. *Management: Theory and Practice.* New York: McGraw-Hill Book Company, 1973.	Ch. 1, 2, 3, 4, 5, 6, 7	Ch. 8, 9, 10, 12, 13, 17	Ch. 20, 26	Ch. 11, 15, 16	Ch. 24, 25	Ch. 4 (100–104), 13 (312–314)	Ch. 14, 18	Ch. 19	Ch. 21, 22, 23	Ch. 29
Donnelly, James H., James L. Gibson, and John M. Ivancevich. *Fundamentals of Management.* Dallas: Business Publications, Inc., 1975.	Ch. 1, 2	Ch. 3, 4, 5	Ch. 12, 13, 14, 15, 16	Ch. 6, 7, 8, 9, 10, 11		Ch. 10	Ch. 11	Ch. 17 (391–396)		Ch. 17
Filley, Allan C., and Robert J. House. *Managerial Process and Organizational Behavior.* Glenview, Ill.: Scott, Foresman and Company, 1969.	Ch. 1	Ch. 6, 7, 8, 9, 10, 11, 12, 14	Ch. 5	Ch. 15, 16		Ch. 4, 13	Ch. 17, 18			Ch. 19
Flippo, Edwin, B. *Management: A Behavioral Approach.* Boston: Allyn and Bacon, Inc., 1970.	Ch. 1	Ch. 2, 5, 8, 9, 10, 20	Ch. 3, 4	Ch. 6, 7, 11, 12, 14, 15, 17, 18, 19			Ch. 13, 16, 21, 22, 23, 24, 25			Ch. 26

Reference										
Haiman, Theo, and William G. Scott. *Management in The Modern Organization*. Boston: Houghton Mifflin Company, 1974.	Ch. 1, 2, 3	Ch. 5, 6, 7, 8, 9, 10, 11, 12, 13, 14, 15, 16, 17, 28, 29	Ch. 4	Ch. 23, 24, 25, 26, 27	Ch. 14 (212–214)		Ch. 19, 20, 21, 22	Ch. 5 (63–65)		
Haynes, W. Warren, and Joseph L. Massie. *Management: Analysis, Concepts and Cases*. Englewood Cliffs, N.J.: Prentice-Hall, Inc., 1969.	Ch. 1, 2	Ch. 3 (41–52) 6, 7, 11, 12, 13, 14, 17, 18, 21, 22, 23, 24	Ch. 15, 16, 19, 20	Ch. 7, 8, 9, 10	Ch. 25, 26	Ch. 29		Ch. 3 (36–40) 4	Ch. 27, 28	
Hicks, Herbert G. *The Management of Organizations: A Systems and Human Resources Approach*. New York: McGraw-Hill Book Company, 1972.	Ch. 24	Ch. 1, 2, 3, 4, 5, 6, 12, 16, 17, 25, 26, 27, 28	Ch. 29	Ch. 7, 8, 9, 10, 11, 18, 19, 20, 21, 22, 23	Ch. 30	Ch. 31	Ch. 13, 14, 15, 31		Ch. 32	Ch. 32
Hodge, Billy J., and Herbert J. Johnson. *Management and Organizational Behavior*. New York: John Wiley & Sons, Inc., 1970.	Ch. 2	Ch. 4, 8, 16, 17, 18	Ch. 14, 15	Ch. 9, 10, 11, 12		Ch. 1, 5, 6, 7, 13	Ch. 19, 20	Ch. 3		Ch. 21, 22
Hodgetts, Richard M. *Management: Theory, Process and Practice*. Philadelphia, Pa.: W. B. Saunders Company, 1975.	Ch. 1, 2, 3, 4, 5	Ch. 7, 8, 9	Ch. 10, 11	Ch. 12, 13, 14	Ch. 16, 17	Ch. 18	Ch. 19	Ch. 20	Ch. 21	Ch. 22
Kast, Fremont E. and James E. Rosenzweig. *Organization and Management*. New York: McGraw-Hill Book Company, 1974.	Ch. 1, 2, 3	Ch. 6, 7, 9 (206–229), 17, 18	Ch. 4 (87–99) 15, 16	Ch. 4 (74–86) 10, 11, 12, 13	Ch. 14	Ch. 5, 8, 9 (229–242)	Ch. 19, 20, 21, 22	Ch. 2		Ch. 23
Koontz, Harold, and Cyril O'Donnell. *Principles of Management*. New York: McGraw-Hill Book Company, 1972.	Ch. 1, 2, 3, 5	Ch. 6, 7, 8, 10, 11, 12, 13, 14, 15, 16, 17, 18, 19, 20, 29	Ch. 9	Ch. 25, 26, 27, 28	Ch. 30		Ch. 21, 22, 23, 24	Ch. 4		

Table continues next page

CROSS-REFERENCE TABLE. FOR RELATING THESE READINGS TO BASIC MANAGEMENT TEXTBOOKS (Continued)

	I. AN INTRODUCTION TO MANAGEMENT	II. MODERN MANAGEMENT THEORY AND PRACTICE				III. RECENT DEVELOPMENTS IN MANAGEMENT				IV. MANAGEMENT IN THE FUTURE
	Management Process School	Quantitative School	Behavioral School	Management Information Systems and the Computer	Technology and Modern Organization Structures	Management of Human Assets	Social Responsibility	International Management	
Longenecker, Justin G. *Principles of Management and Organizational Behavior.* Columbus, Ohio: Charles E. Merrill Publishing Company, 1969.	Ch. 1	Ch. 2, 4, 5, 6, 8, 9, 10, 11, 12, 24, 25, 26	Ch. 7	Ch. 15, 16, 17, 18, 19, 20, 21, 22, 23		Ch. 3 (63–71)	Ch. 13, 14	Ch. 3 (50–58)	Ch. 3 (58–63)	Ch. 27
McFarland, Dalton E. *Management: Principles and Practices.* New York: Macmillan Publishing Co., Inc., 1974.	Ch. 1, 2, 3, 25	Ch. 5, 6, 8, 14, 15, 16, 17	Ch. 12, 13	Ch. 18, 19, 21, 22, 23, 24	Ch. 4	Ch. 7, 9	Ch. 10, 11, 20	Ch. 26	Ch. 27	
Newman, William H., Charles E. Summer, and E. Kirby Warren. *The Process of Management—Concepts, Behavior, and Practice.* Englewood Cliffs, N.J.: Prentice-Hall, Inc., 1972.	Ch. 1	Ch. 2, 3, 4, 5, 16, 17, 18, 19, 24, 25, 27, 28	Ch. 11, 12, 13, 14, 15	Ch. 7, 8, 9, 11, 20, 21, 22, 23, 26	Ch. 6 (114–117)	Ch. 6	Ch. 10		Ch. 29	

Reference										
Richards, Max D., and Paul S. Greenlaw. *Management Decision Making.* Homewood, Ill.: Richard D. Irwin, Inc., 1973.	Ch. 1	Ch. 9, 12, 13, 14, 15, 16	Ch. 3, 17, 18, 19	Ch. 5, 6, 7, 10	Ch. 4, 13	Ch. 8	Ch. 10, 11	Ch. 2		
Sisk, Henry L. *Principles of Management: A Systems Approach to the Management Process.* Cincinnati: South-Western Publishing Company, 1973.	Ch. 1, 2	Ch. 3, 4, 5, 6, 9, 10, 11, 12, 13, 20, 21, 22	Ch. 8	Ch. 15, 16, 17, 18, 19	Ch. 7		Ch. 14			
Terry, George R. *Principles of Management.* Homewood, Ill.: Richard D. Irwin, Inc., 1972.	Ch. 1	Ch. 3, 10, 11, 12, 13, 14, 15, 16, 17, 23, 24, 25, 26	Ch. 6, 7, 8	Ch. 9, 18, 19, 20, 21			Ch. 22			Ch. 27
Reeser, Clayton. *Management Functions and Modern Concepts.* Glenview, Ill.: Scott, Foresman and Company, 1973.	Ch. 1, 2, 3, 4, 5	Ch. 9, 10, 11, 12, 13, 14, 15, 16, 17, 18, 20, 21, 22, 23, 24, 25, 30, 35, 57, 58, 59, 60, 63, 64	Ch. 7, 61, 62	Ch. 6, 26, 27, 28, 44, 45, 47, 48, 49, 50, 51, 52, 53, 54, 55, 56	Ch. 8, 65, 66, 67	Ch. 19, 20, 29, 31, 32, 33, 34, 36, 37, 38, 39, 40, 41, 42, 43, 46		Ch. 68		
Belasco, James A., David R. Hampton, and Karl F. Price. *Management Today.* New York: John Wiley & Sons, Inc., 1975.	Ch. 1	Ch. 7, 8, 9, 10		Ch. 2, 3, 4, 5	Ch. 11		Ch. 6	Ch. 12, 13, 14		Ch. 15

I AN INTRODUCTION TO MANAGEMENT

Management entails getting things done through people, and as such, its history can be traced back thousands of years. Today it is coming under close scrutiny, as researchers and practitioners alike ask, precisely what is management?

The purpose of Part I is to provide the reader with a basic understanding of the term *management* by placing it within its historical context. Two important articles will show that modern management has evolved through a series of changes. Beginning in the post-Industrial Revolution era, attention was focused on the economic side of enterprise. Profit, loss, supply and demand became topics of consideration. Emphasis then shifted to the mechanical side of enterprise via time and motion study and scientific management. Next, attention began to be focused on the administrative side of enterprise. Classical theorists concerned with effective management practices and organization structure began to arrive on the management scene. Finally, in the late 1920's, the human relationists made their appearance and attention turned to the human side of enterprise. Modern management owes a debt of gratitude to all who contributed to its evolution.

The first article in this introductory section is "Contemporary American Management" by Robert T. Hof. In this article, Mr. Hof notes that America's greatest resource is its managerial skill, which has served as a catalytic agent in developing all our other resources. His discussion traces the evolution of modern management and culminates in an identification of the manager's job: planning, organizing, motivating and controlling.

The second article in this section, "What About Management Theory for Managers?" by William M. Fox, examines the

1

current "state of the art" of management theory. Professor Fox notes that various management schools of thought have emerged in an attempt to explain what management is. He believes that these schools can be synthesized via an eclectic approach that draws the best ideas from each school in solving pragmatic problems. Professor Fox concludes his article by encouraging management theorists to begin moving toward this objective immediately.

1 Contemporary American Management

Robert T. Hof

Greek historians tell us that in ancient Egypt it took 100,000 men to build the great pyramid of Khufu. The builders used 2,300,000 limestone blocks—each weighing 2½ tons. The pyramid was almost as high as the Washington Monument . . . and its base would cover 8 football fields. It took 20 years to build—and that was 5,000 years ago. These ancient people had no machines and no computers—just manpower, motivation, and management.

I mention the Great Pyramid to make the point that management has been with us a long time. And management is what this article is going to discuss—not the management of ancient Egypt but contemporary American management.

We talk a great deal about mineral resources, agriculture, industry, and human resources. We talk about science and technology, and economics and finance, and such things as the gross national product of nations. There is a golden thread that runs through the discussion of all these subjects. That golden thread is *management*.

Perhaps the greatest resource of all in the United States is management skill. Other nations marvel at it. It is perhaps our most important export. In World Wars I and II and the Korean War, the American Economy astonished our allies and confounded our enemies—with the management ability to mobilize industry in support of the war effort. Management was the hero of the logistics efforts.

Putting aside the war record for the moment, let's look at the peacetime record. The United States has only 6 percent of the world's population and 7 percent of the land. Yet the United States produces one-half of the world's output of energy, and Americans consume one-third of all the world's goods and services.

Today, we accept as commonplace things that 50 years ago were not even visible in the fortune teller's crystal ball: nuclear-powered submarines, space vehicles transmitting close-ups of the moon, aircraft operating at more than twice the speed of sound, and even the everyday household items—air conditioners, television, and frozen foods. Of course, all these things are the brain children of scientists and inventors, and these men are entitled to the highest praise for their work. However, these achievements did not come out of a garage or basement workshop. These are the products of large business—and sometimes government enterprises—with men in charge called managers.

MANAGEMENT AS A RESOURCE

Management is an important economic resource. Management starts with man. Man is a *social* animal. He

This article originally appeared in *Business Perspectives,* Winter 1967, pp. 5–10, 30, and is reprinted with permission.

lives and works together in groups. He specializes in his work. He exchanges the goods and services he produces for other goods and services which other men produce. He is *not* self-sufficient. He has learned that well-being comes about through specialization of labor and through trade.

On the face of the earth, there are still tribes who avoid trade with the outside world—who produce their own food and clothing and very little else. They find subsistence hard and death comes early.

But men who have joined together in enterprises, exchanging the fruits of their labor with the outside world, have grasped the meaning of a better life for themselves and for their children.

To make the cooperative efforts of men work and prosper *is* the task of management. Someone has to have the vision to conceive the need for an enterprise, the skill to mobilize the means of production, the determination to control the enterprise, the leadership to guide people toward objectives, and the financial genius to meet the bills when due. That someone is called a manager. The quality of management spells the difference between success or failure for a business enterprise or for a society.

In the 1920's General Motors was just one of more than 50 automobile manufacturers. Its product had no unique advantages, yet it emerged as the dominant company in the automobile field. The difference was in the quality of management.

We are accustomed to think of management in terms of industry, but every enterprise—government, national defense, the church—calls for management. History records many great management achievements that were not of a private business nature: Columbus was a manager, our founding fathers were managers, General Goethals who built the Panama Canal, Eisenhower's international team which planned the Normandy Invasion, and

the government-industry team which has put men into space, were all managers. And, of course, our Federal government is the largest manager of all.

The Federal budget has grown "a little" since the turn of the century. In 1901, the budget was half a billion dollars. Today, it is about $100 billion and about half of that goes for defense. And the number of employees has grown from 350,000 to five million. Government is certainly big management.

So you see that when we talk about management theory and practice we are talking about concepts that apply to government—including defense—as well as to the industrial segment of the economy.

WHAT IS MANAGEMENT?

At this point, perhaps we should ask ourselves: What *is* management? Is it an art? . . . or a science? A formal definition is "Management is a process of organizing and employing resources to accomplish pre-determined objectives." Another definition is that management is the art of getting things done through people. For this latter definition, we are indebted to Mary Parker Follett, who was a social worker back in the 1920's. In a day of highly autocratic management practices, she made the statement that you can get more work done by exercising power *with* people—rather than power *over* people. She interjected the human element—which we will write more about a little later.

There is, I think, an even better way of describing American management. Someone has said that one opinion is worth 1,000 definitions. Let me give you an opinion on American management as expressed by a group of British businessmen who visited the states a short while ago. They said

If there is one secret, above all, of American achievements in productivity, then it is to be found in the attitude of American management. American management engenders an aggressiveness which believes that methodical planning, energetic training and enthusiastic work can solve any problem.

They attributed this American attitude to four factors:

The legacy of the frontier.—A spirit that has fostered a sense of opportunity pervading American industrial and community life.

Faith in business and the individual.—A faith reflected in the high esteem with which the businessman is regarded in the American national community.

The ideal of competition.—An ideal which leads even those companies, not operating in a highly competitive community, to run their enterprises as though they were.

Belief in change.—A belief whereby a successful experiment is *not* allowed to crystallize into accepted custom . . . whereas an unsuccessful experiment is accepted as an occupational risk and is set against the experience that has been gained.

THE MANAGER EVOLVES

Having heard that outside opinion, and before we plunge into theory and practice, let's take a brief look at the evolution of the American manager himself. This man is a product of change. One hundred years ago, he was the owner-manager of a small business. The largest businesses of those days were tiny compared to today's giants.

Starting about 1880, the captains of industry appeared. They still owned the business but businesses were getting much, much bigger. Some people called them "robber barons." Some of them deserved it. They were ruthless in dealing with the customers, the public, and each other. But let's give credit where it is due. They founded many of our basic industries. They

built industrial empires and railroad and communication systems that joined the East and the West. The old captains or robber barons didn't die—they faded away early in this century, under the onslaught of public opinion and the anti-trust laws and because their business just grew too big for them to handle.

They were followed by the financial managers—the financial wizards, some people called them. Big businesses had grown too big for one-man or one-family ownership. Ownership came to be spread widely among stockholders. The financial wizards ran the business for the stockholders. Unfortunately, many of them were speculators and plungers. Sometimes personal fortunes were made while stockholders lost their collective shirts. This is not to say there were no ethical financial managers; but neither were there many controls over their activities. After the '29 crash, public indignation and government regulation put an end to the heyday of the financial managers.

And then a new man entered the scene—the professional manager, pretty much as we know him today. He is a career man in business. Usually, he doesn't expect to own any large part of the enterprise and he is likely to see more in his career than just making a living. By background and training, he is keenly aware of his stewardship over other people's financial resources and he recognizes responsibilities to employees and to the general public as well as to the stockholders. It is not uncommon for him to seek elective or appointed public office or the job may seek him: Romney of Michigan comes to mind, and there is a man named McNamara.

Now, it is time that we discuss the theory of management. There are two of what I shall call "mainstreams" of modern management theory and one important tributary theory. The mainstreams I shall call, "scientific management" and "human relations." The tributary, I call "the mathematical school," and along with it I will comment on computers.

SCIENTIFIC MANAGEMENT

To begin, scientific management is sometimes called the traditional school. Other people call it "Taylorism," after Frederick Taylor who is known as the father of the movement. Taylor was a foreman at the Midvale Steel Works in Philadelphia back in the 1880's. He later rose to chief engineer. Two things appalled Taylor: inefficient use of manpower and low wages. He was determined to get a full day's work out of every man on the payroll, to streamline operations, and to raise wages.

The first thing he did was to break each job down into its simplest parts so that each man could specialize in a simple task. Then he experimented with production standards and set quotas for each job. Last, he put the jobs together in a smooth flow of work, anticipating the production line.

Taylor achieved resounding success. He began with the pig iron handlers, and the coal and iron shovelers. He reduced the number of shovelers from 600 to 140 and he raised the output per man from 16 tons a day to 59 tons a day. He cut labor costs from 7 cents a ton to 3 cents a ton. *But mark this:* wages went up from $1.15 a day to $1.85 a day! So, he accomplished everything he had set out to do.

"Taylorism" caught on fast. It marked the end of an era—the end of craft workmanship. It paved the way for the assembly line and mass production. The scientific approach was taken up by the railroads and other industries. Henry Ford was a Taylor man. He believed in job simplification, the assembly line, quotas, and higher wages. Taylor's enthusiastic followers introduced industrial engineering complete with time and motion studies. Scientific management is still with us. Taylor's spirit lives on in the person of every manager who takes a logical approach to getting work done more efficiently. It is implicit in the rapid development of labor-saving devices. Many authorities see automation and electronic data processing as a natural evolution of the scientific management theory.

But Taylor's followers back in the 1920's and 1930's got so enthusiastic about job simplification, work flow charts, and time motion studies that they overlooked people. They figured that pay would take care of people. As Professor Dale of Cornell has said "They took it for granted that human beings will act rationally . . . in their own best economic interest." This has been called the theory of the economic man—or simply, that man does live by bread alone. This neglect of people was a major factor in the rise of labor unions. If Taylor was the father of scientific management, he was also at least an uncle of the labor unions.

HUMAN RELATIONS MANAGEMENT

However, something happened in the early 1930's that was destined to shake scientific management to its very roots. The human relations school of management was born in Chicago. The obstetrician in this case was a man named Elton Mayo, a psychiatrist by profession. Mayo conducted a series of experiments at the Hawthorne Works of the Western Electric Company in Chicago. They have become famous as the "Hawthorne Studies." The experiments took place in the relay assembly room—where girls wired telephone relays together. The experiments started out along traditional scientific management lines. They were to study the effects of fatigue upon production workers. In this case, management wanted to find out if they could increase production by improving working conditions. The first thing that Mayo did was to improve the lighting in the relay room. Sure enough, the girls increased production of relays. Then, to verify his results, Mayo reduced the lighting. Guess what! Production went up again.

Mayo tried several other things. He made working conditions better, then worse. He even changed the rules for going to the powder room. No matter what he did, production went up! Mayo asked himself what this meant— this change to the lights and working conditions in relation to production. He concluded that it meant absolutely nothing. The experiment was a bust! But something *had* happened. There *was* an answer to why production went up in the relay room. I think any woman reader can tell us. The girls in the relay room were getting a little attention! Men were asking them serious questions. They were part of an experiment! They felt wanted. Mayo was not a lady, but he was a scientist. He knew he had something.

This is what scientists call serendipity—the wisdom to discover something good you are not looking for. This is how we got penicillin. And this is how the Human Relations School of Management was born. They discovered that Mary Parker Follett had been right all along.

Human relations brought into the management field, at least in an advisory capacity, a wave of social scientists: psychiatrists, psychologists, sociologists, and anthropologists. Needless to say, management has never been the same. The school of human relations is people-oriented as opposed to scientific management which was work-oriented. Human relations has been defined as the science which studies the activities, attitudes, and interrelationships among people at work. It recognizes that work is done by people—usually in groups. It teaches us that the organizational chart is fiction. It is like a turtle's shell. It covers up what is actually going on inside

the animal. It teaches us that the informal organization is a fact with which managers have to cope. Managers may set production quotas—but the informal group sets the production rates.

The human relations school says that managers must seek ways to get people committed to organizational goals. They say that one way to do this is communication, from the bottom up, as well as from the top down —and laterally. They say that participation is another way. People should be allowed to participate in the setting of goals and work standards and decision-making. Hopefully, if we do all these things, individual and organizational goals will be integrated.

We should mention something that the human relations school has done to organizations. It is the genesis of committees as a management technique. Committees are regarded by many people with mixed emotions. For example, when Mr. McNamara took over as Secretary of Defense, he abolished 400 joint committees. In fact, he is reputed to have said that the ideal committee consists of 3 members: one at the North Pole, one at the South Pole, and one at work. However, we still have committees in the Department of Defense. And no one has been able to abolish them in industry. The committee as a management technique appears to be here to stay.

Not all managers accepted the human relations theory with enthusiasm. Some said it gave them schizophrenia. They wound up with split personalities. On the one hand, they tried to be "do-work" managers, with stop watches and production quotas. This manager's motto is, "Get to work or get out!" On the other hand, they tried to be "do-good" managers. Their motto is "Keep warm. Be happy!" Well, perhaps human relations did go too far.

At any rate, in the past decade, the pendulum has swung back to scientific management. Not all the way of course, but to a sort of middle position. This, too, has been supported by experiment. In the early 1950's, the famous Michigan studies (named for the University of Michigan) demonstrated, among other things, that the happiest group is not necessarily the most productive group. (Which should come as no surprise to parents and teachers.)

However, human relations has become part and parcel of contemporary American management theory. The social-psychologist may not have replaced the efficiency expert—but he certainly has joined him.

Today, it is generally accepted that the most successful managers are both work-oriented and people-oriented— even at the risk of schizophrenia. And the combination appears to be profit-oriented.

MATHEMATICAL MANAGEMENT

The basic theory is that all management processes are logical and, therefore, can be expressed in mathematical symbols. This, of course, makes the theory a natural for use with a computer.

The mathematics school takes in such esoteric terms as operations research, linear programming, queueing theory, and model building.

Operations research usually means a balanced team of researchers who make a detailed analysis of military or business problems. They may use computers and they may use models, queueing theory, etc.

By a balanced team, I mean that, depending on the problem, the disciplines represented may include mathematics, chemistry, physics, psychology, and even, believe it or not, business.

Queueing theory, or "waiting line" theory, has been very useful in planning the correct or optimum number of toll booths on turnpikes, the number of tellers' windows in banks, the number of gasoline pumps in filling stations. It has been used to plan the number of loading and unloading docks at transportation terminals and maintenance docks at airports. It is even useful for making up bus schedules.

Without going into all the mathematics involved in linear programming, let me say that it is most helpful in determining the optimum mix of scarce resources—whether they be weapons systems or men or machines.

Model building implies simulation and that is what it is useful for. Mathematical models can be built to resemble a business, an industry situation, or a battlefield. A year's business transactions can be simulated in a minute. A computer can fight 100 land, air, or sea battles in an hour—or at least, simulate them.

Mathematical models are a great aid to business and to military planning, provided numerical values assigned to things like sales projections and casualty rates are valid.

In the Department of Defense we use the whole gambit of these techniques in a process called "systems analysis."

All of these techniques make use of the computer. So, let's talk about the computer. Some people do not appreciate the results obtained from the computer, and it does have its limitations. But, the computer is here to stay.

Computers have vastly increased the amount of information we can store, they recall this information almost instantaneously, and they perform the most complicated mathematical calculations in the twinkling of an eye. There is no question that computers, plus high speed communications, have made a tremendous contribution to the practice of management.

In industry, they have been credited with a major contribution to the current, unprecedented cycle of prosperity. Manufacturers have been able to hold inventories to a minimum while accelerating deliveries. And unprofitable operations can be discovered before serious losses occur. The airlines are using computers to handle reservations much, much faster and more accurately than people ever could do it. Computers are handling payrolls and personnel records centrally, for companies whose operations are spread across the country. In doing this, they read the records, compute the pay, make the deductions, and print and mail the checks. In some cases, computers are running automated factories. This is particularly true of oil refineries which have processes that lend themselves to automatic controls and computer-programmed operations. Tiny computers guide our space satellites in flight.

All of these things they do much faster and much more accurately than people can.

Where the machine extended man's muscle-power, the computer has now extended his brainpower. And, just as we had scientific management and human relations enthusiasts, now we have mathematics and computer enthusiasts. Already some people claim that computers will replace vice-presidents and factory managers.

But those who know the practical application of computers are quick to point out three critical limitations of computers. *First* is the difficulty, and, in some cases, the impossibility, of treating with things that cannot be quantified—things that cannot be dealt with mathematically, such as morale, customer behavior, reaction of business competitors, or the reaction of the Red Chinese for that matter. *Second* is a lack of creativeness. Computers cannot create new ideas or new solutions to new problems. *Finally,* there is a computer's inability to accept responsibility. This third limitation is certainly its most critical.

Even if ways can be found to treat with the first two limitations, only when a computer can be made responsible for success or failure, when it can be fired, will we consider using it to replace our managers.

So now, we are at the point of leaving management theory, the mainstreams of scientific management and human relations plus the wonderful new tools of the mathematical school. It is time to venture into more down-to-earth matters—the practice of management.

THE PRACTICE OF MANAGEMENT

When our bright young men who know all about computers do become managers they will find that they have four major functions to perform: planning, organizing, leading, controlling. These functions, on which there is general agreement, sometimes with minor variations, are a distillation of centuries of experience of men who have had to lead large organizations: prime ministers, governors, princes of the church, generals, admirals and businessmen. As an example, Von Clausewitz's *Vom Krieg (On War)* is almost a textbook for the practice of management.

As we said, the first major function of the management process is planning. Planning is making decisions about the future. The late Charles Kettering once emphasized the importance of planning with an analogy. He said, "One composer can keep 10,000 fiddlers busy."

Setting objectives is the most crucial part of planning. Corporations, governments, armies (and the people in all of them) have to know what their goals are. Objectives or goals range from capturing a larger share of a market or sending a man to the moon down to subgoals such as calling on more customers each month. One thing is certain: people have to have goals. For example, a friend of mine once hired a laborer to dig holes in his front yard. He had him dig one hole, then another, then another. The holes were not in a line or circle—they were scattered around. When my friend asked the laborer to dig another hole, the man said: "I quit. I'm not going to waste my time just digging holes." My friend then explained that he was trying to find a drain pipe that was clogged up. The laborer said, "Why didn't you say so?" and he went back to work.

Short run goals are steps, like the steps of a stairs, leading to the long-run goals at the top. Goals lead to two other kinds of plans: standing plans and single-use plans.

Standing plans simplify the work process and the decision-making process because they decide in advance the what and how of a variety of operations. They are essential for smooth operations. They are called by many names—policies, procedures, standing operating procedures, standard methods, etc.

Standard plans tell us *how* to make up a payroll, *how* to control inventories, *how* to select a mode of shipment; and incidentally, these are the kinds of jobs that are most readily translated into the language of computers.

Standing plans make it possible for managers to spend their most creative efforts on single-use plans.

Under single-use plans we include strategic or long-range plans and all major programs—opening a new plant or buying a new missile system. And here we should note that a program of any magnitude needs to be broken up into time-phased steps. We have to determine the resources needed for each step—men, money, and materials. And we have to assign responsibility for accomplishing each step.

In essence, a well-conceived program covers all actions needed to achieve a specific goal and it shows who does what, and when. For large complex programs, such as planning an annual model change in the auto industry or developing a missile system, there is a hierarchy of supporting programs. And programs, of course, must be

priced out. And when you do and put them all together you have the finance plan.

The first year's slice of the financial plan is the budget. In other words, the budget is the sum total of your standing and single-use plans for the next year, expressed in dollars. Or, as the financial experts say, it is next year's profit and loss statement—you hope.

Some people include innovating under planning. Actually, it applies throughout the planning process and the entire management process. If a man just keeps on doing what he always did or what somebody else always did, the competition will pass him by.

Decision making and innovating go together. They both touch all the other parts of planning. Between them they are responsible for Henry Ford saying, "A manager doesn't re-act—he *acts!*" A manager is a man who makes things happen by innovating and decision making.

And the next major step is, of course, *organizing*. Organization has been with us a long time. The Bible, for example, tells us that Moses "chose able men out of all Israel, and made them heads over the people, rulers of thousands, rulers of hundreds, rulers of fifties, and rulers of tens." "And they judged the people at all seasons: the hard cases they brought into Moses, but every small matter they judged themselves."

The problem that faced Moses was the same problem of organization that faces all managers. He had to divide up the work. Moses chose to form a simple line organization—the pyramid of authority. A line organization in industry might look like this. The chain of command runs straight up and down. Each man reports straight up or gives orders straight down—like the rulers of tens, the rulers of hundreds, the rulers of thousands of Moses' organization.

This straight line organization might work in a small business, but, as the business grows in size, the work of the boss has to be divided up too. So, we add a staff to divide up some of the boss's work.

This is the familiar line and staff organization. The church and the military—both large organizations—have used it for centuries. When business got big, it copied the line and staff organization. The role of the staff is to extend the special knowledge required by the executive and to advise and assist him on such matters as sales, engineering, production, finance, and anything else that is required.

The staff has an advisory capacity toward the line managers—outside the command channel. Theoretically, the staff cannot give orders to the line. Staff men are supposed to get things done by persuasion. But staff men are usually selected for their expertise and their intelligence. Such people are likely to be ambitious, and they have the boss's ear. So there is an eternal power struggle between line and staff. But, bear this in mind, no one has found a solution.

Everyone agrees that an organization needs both line and staff. Each needs the other. They are like some married couples you might know—they can't get along without each other—but when they are together, life is apt to be a series of donnybrooks. A few years ago someone hit upon another kind of organization in an attempt to resolve this age-old problem. Here each staff officer has a command line, but only for his own specialty. The plant manager might be responsible to one staff man for marketing, another for production, another for budgeting, another for quality control—and on and on. He has no direct line to the president.

So after planning and organizing we are ready for the next major function of the management process—what Henri Fayol, writing in 1916, called "command." Since that time it has gone through a semantic evolu-

tion. In turn, it became "direction," then "coordination," then "leading." And finally, nowadays, most writers refer to it as "motivation." Well, what's in a name?

Call it what you will. It means that after all your planning, all your organizing, it still takes people to get the work done, to make the plans come true. This takes leadership—or motivation. You will recall that we discussed motivation of people under the human relations theory and we concluded that the most successful leadership is both work-oriented and people-oriented.

Our discussion of planning, organizing, and motivating leaves only the fourth major function of the management process.

Controlling.   This is the report card! the howgozit chart! the thermometer! Under planning, we talked about goals. *Control mechanisms* tell us how we are moving toward them. We set standards, we pick control points, we measure and we watch—we do this for each area that impacts on our goal. We do it for sales, costs, quality, profits, and all other major areas. And finally, if we are not moving forward as we planned, we take corrective action. The phrase "management by exception" has come to be associated with this. In other words, we don't worry about everything. We let our control system pick out only those things that are going badly (the exceptions) and we find out why, and then we do what needs to be done. Computers again have been a big help in this area, particularly in large complex programs, such as the development of new weapons systems.

As a matter of fact, control is the essence of a system known as PERT—which is the acronym for Program Evaluation and Review Technique. You will recall that I said a well-conceived program covers all actions required to achieve a goal and tells who does what when. PERT uses computers to control all these actions, in the vast hierarchy of plans involved in developing new weapon systems.

The outstanding case has been the development of the Polaris ballistic missile submarine system. Admiral Raborn brought this program to completion 2 years ahead of schedule using PERT with computers for control. The Admiral told a congressional committee that he could not have done it without PERT.

Well, there you have it all, the process of management—planning, organizing, leading, and controlling.

CONCLUSION

In closing let's make one final comment on the manager and what *we* derive from *his* process. We *depend* on him to run our business and our government. We *look* to him for continued prosperity. We expect him to mobilize the resources needed to support our effort in Vietnam—or any other conflict we may get into—as he has done so well in the past. And we depend upon the mightiest array of destructive might the world has ever known . . . which this man's team put together. And we depend on the organization of scientists, engineers, and construction workers (military men and civilians) which this man leads and manages to put Americans on the moon and beyond—before the end of this decade.

He is the contemporary American manager!

2   What About Management Theory for Managers?

William M. Fox

Theory-building may provide stimulating diversion and challenge to the theorist as ends in themselves; however, practicing managers look to theory for intelligent explanation and creative innovation. Practitioners are not interested merely in descriptive data (how things are), but in normative data (how they should be). They want theory that will produce criteria with which to appraise conditions in any type of business organization and at any stage in its growth so that they may improve upon existing practice. Reasonably, they expect that good theory will draw upon an ever-increasing body of research findings in a number of fields to arm them with concepts and techniques which will strengthen significantly their ability to cope with new as well as old business problems. Certainly, they expect that useful theory will have to be based upon research designs and theorizing which reflect sufficiently the real world in which we live and in which they must solve their problems.

Have we management theorists delivered? If not why not? And what can we do to increase the usefulness of our contributions now and in the future? These are important questions and an

This article originally appeared in *The Southern Journal of Business*, November 1972, pp. 47–62, and is reprinted with permission.

attempt will be made to answer them in this article. First, an attempt shall be made to ascertain the "state of the art" by examining certain strengths and weaknesses associated with some of the more influential approaches or schools of thought which have contributed to present-day management theory. Then, consideration shall be given to a type of opportunity available to us now for dealing with that part of the promise yet unfulfilled.

ECONOMICS AND THE ECONOMISTS

It is encouraging to note that some economists are becoming conversant with the wealth of data flowing from important behavioral research, but there are still few if any departments of economics today which see behavioral theory as a *basic requirement* in the development of the professional economist.

It would appear that from the first beginning of their discipline, most economists have been striving for the status and security of an "exact" science. They have come to realize with increasing clarity that realistic incorporation of the vagaries and irrationalities of behavior into their theories will detract from the desired appearance of scientific precision. So, in the name of science, certain simplifying assumptions were introduced and continue to be maintained. Among these, the "economic man" concept of human motivation has survived longer than anyone might have expected and has had the effect of rendering much economic theorizing irrelevant to the real world.

Of course, at the level of macro or aggregate analysis much more has been accomplished than at the levels of individual firm or industry analysis. But economic theory remains essentially at odds with the bulk of findings in the behavioral sciences. As E. D. Kemble of General Electric wrote:

There is need for confronting the fact that most managers see but very little operational usefulness in what is generally understood as economic theory . . . managers expect that economic theory which will be valid and useful for management theory will directly relate to individual responsibilities and accountabilities in a corporation, rather than foreclosing them by resorting to anthropomorphization of a mechanistic model . . . An obvious and logical conclusion which can be reached from such mechanistic models is that "things" would be much better if someone just operated the mechanism.[1]

And a perceptive professor of economics points out that:

Other social sciences and psychology frequently refer to such things as aspirations, goals, and goal objects. Economists define goods as *anything* capable of satisfying wants, and then (usually without explanation or apology) proceed to ignore all goods which are not exchangeable through markets . . . Perhaps because economists have studied transactions in more detail than other social scientists, there is a widespread impression that transactions occur only in marketable goods[2] . . . Economic theory has for years talked glibly of profit maximization, as if this were some sharply definable goal which businessmen work for. But Boulding observes that this quantity which is supposed to be maximized does not really exist, and (as was presented earlier) it was suggested that maximizing one value in a multidimensional context is an illusory goal.[3]

The beauty and reassurance of logical consistency still seem to readily displace pressing matters of more real-

[1] E. D. Kemble, "What the Practicing Manager Expects From Management Theory and Research," in Harold Kootz (editor), *Toward A Unified Theory of Management* (New York: McGraw-Hill, 1964), pp. 162, 168, and 165.

[2] For dramatic and witty evidence to the contrary, see Eric Berne, *Games People Play* (New York: Grove Press, 1964).

[3] Alfred Kuhn, *The Study of Society: A Unified Approach* (Homewood, Illinois: Richard D. Irwin, 1963), pp. 262, 376, and 455.

istic premises and empirical verification of theory for many economists.

THE SCIENTIFIC MANAGEMENT MOVEMENT

The scientific management movement came on strong in the latter part of 1910. Harrington Emerson testified in November of that year before the Interstate Commerce Commission that the railroads of the United States might save a million dollars a day by devoting attention to efficiency in their operations.

When scientific management was applied to the simple operation of loading a railway car by hand with pig iron, the performance of the individual worker increased from 12½ to 47 tons per day. When applied to shoveling coal, it doubled or trebled the performance of the shoveler. In machine shop work it developed in certain operations increases in production ranging from 400 to 1,800 per cent. In bricklaying the day's accomplishment rose from 1,000 to 2,700 bricks. And, when applied in the manufacture of machinery, 75 men in the machine shop with 20 in the planning department did two or three times as much work as 105 men in the machine shop had done previously. These results were due largely to the successful separation of *planning* functions from *doing* functions and to the systematic study of business problems by *specialized* personnel.

Frederick Taylor, the "father" of the movement, was tireless, self-demanding in his work, and of unquestioned integrity, but he was somewhat quick-tempered and diffident in his dealings with others. Like many managers of his day who had had difficulty in coping with large doses of frustration and employee-management conflict, Taylor seemed to long for the security of a "logical" business environment devoid of error, inefficiency, and human conflict. After all, the scientific ap-

proach had been so successful in the physical sciences, would it not also rationalize human relationships and somehow dispense with the need for negotiation and compromise in industry? Pursuit of this idea created increasing distrust on the part of labor and led to drastic revision in the logics of the movement later on.

Generally, Taylor and the other pioneers did not know how to translate effectively their ideals into practice. Their first error was in claiming that theirs was an "exact science." In his testimony before a congressional committee in 1912 Taylor pointed out that "both sides must recognize as essential the substitution of exact scientific investigation and knowledge for the old individual judgment or opinion, either of the workman or the boss, in all matters relating to the work done in the establishment."[4] Frank Gilbreth claims that Taylor told him that the "instruction card can be depended upon to carry the work of the master or the manager without a line of translation in the way of the human element."[5]

These are typical of the comments made by many of the early leaders. The difficulty, of course, is that in industry instances in which fact may be substituted for judgment are far fewer than these men believed. Even if restricted to such specific procedures as time and motion study, methods analysis, and job evaluation, such statements remain misleading, for these activities are far from being based upon an "exact science."

In the scheme of scientific manage-

---

[4]"Testimony Before the Special House Committee," p. 31, in Frederick W. Taylor, *Scientific Management* (New York: Harper and Brothers, 1947). (This is a reprint of public document, *Hearings Before Special Committee of the House of Representatives To Investigate the Taylor and Other Systems of Shop Management Under Authority of H. Res. 90*, Vol. III, pp. 1377–1508).

[5]Louis D. Brandeis, *Scientific Management and the Railroads* (New York: Engineering Magazine Company, 1911), p. 11.

ment there was little protection for the employee against unreasonable supervisors and little basis for employee participation in, or identification with, the work of the organization. And the need for participation became more pronounced as the planning room displaced the worker as the custodian of job knowledge—knowledge that was to be "returned" to the worker only piecemeal.

It was natural, then, that this movement gave impetus to "paternalism" in industry: the giving of benefits, bonuses, and gifts of employers, with the hope that they would get unquestioning obedience, hard work, and nonunion shops in return. If a worker grumbled openly, he was a "bad egg," to be sternly disciplined or dismissed. After all, the rationality of scientific management *assured* the satisfaction and well-being of *normal* employees.

It is easy to see how unscrupulous employers who wished to exploit scientific management by using it to take advantage of their workers encountered little opposition. Organized labor was not strong enough to combat them, and labor legislation at that time gave little protection. And the public of that day embraced the laissez-faire philosophy with the notion that if an employee did not like a particular situation, he could move on to another or set up shop for himself.

THE LESS SCIENTIFIC "CLASSICISTS"

In addition to Frederick W. Taylor there were such outstanding traditional or "classical" theorists as the Gilbreths, Henri Fayol, Henry Dennison, Mary Parker Follett, Oliver Sheldon, Pierre du Point, Alfred Sloan, Donaldson Brown, James F. Lincoln, Henry Nunn, Charles McCormick, Allen W. Rucker, and Ralph C. Davis. The nature of this roster indicates the inappropriateness of the label "classical." Most of the ideas of these theorists

are hardly obsolete . . . in fact, it is amazing how *many* "modern" concepts are directly attributable to them.

Take, for instance, that leading example of "classical-modern" firms, General Motors. Many point to this company today as the epitome of what is best and up-to-date in sound organizational practice. It is one of the few firms which did not experience one quarter of loss during the Great Depression and among only a handful which have grown many-fold without major reorganization. When did this viable, "linking-pin" type of organization with decentralized profit centers take form? This scheme has not changed in its essentials since it was conceived in the early Twenties. Nor is this an isolated instance . . . Standard Oil of New Jersey and du Pont evolved G.M.-type organizations during the Twenties, also. And James F. Lincoln established many of the ultra-modern practices of the Lincoln Electric Company even before the First World War.

As a matter of fact, it has been sound "classical" theory, with certain modifications through time, which has provided the primary guidance to practicing managers in America and has made them the ones to emulate in the world of international business. But there is little question that the movement has been short on behavioral knowledge and most traditional management theorists have sorely neglected the kind of research required to add to, or simply to validate, that which they have "known" or hypothesized. In this regard, the traditionalists have very little leg to stand on when they criticize the presumptuous inroads into their private and sacred preserves by the johnny-come-lately behavioral scientists.

Often it has been charged that classical theorists are wholly insensitive to or indifferent to the human element. On this score read Fayol's *General and Industrial Management,* written in 1916; one will not find much there which is inconsistent with sound, current behavioral theory. A more legitimate criticism is that there has been an overemphasis on attempts to understand and work through egoistic needs and too little attention to social needs and the interrelationships between the two types.

What is sound in traditional theory needs substantiation and enrichment from the wealth of modern behavioral knowledge and research technique. The effective synthesis of the new with the old is an important task still before us.

TAYLOR VS. WEBER AND THE SOCIOLOGISTS

There is little question of the dramatic contribution to management practice made by Taylor and his associates via the scientific management movement. Despite very real limitations, it did provide a systematic approach and greatly improved measuring techniques for investigating worker production activities and their associated physiological constraints. Modern management science clearly has evolved out of the foundation laid by the scientific management movement. Can the same thing be said for the initial and subsequent utility of sociological theory based on the theories of Max Weber? Many practicing businessmen may feel that only they have missed the point, the esoteric value of such theorizing. It may come as somewhat of a surprise to them to learn that a number of behavioral scientists share their skepticism as to the practical value of such work.

George Strother writes:

Hierarchy, order, rationality, impersonality—these are the essentials of Weber's model . . . Weber's model fails to deal with the individual psychological factors which have caused concern among other sociologists who have dealt with the likelihood or even inevitability of dysfunctional developments in an ideal bureaucracy . . . Yet, despite considerable criticism, Weber's model dominates the approach of sociologists to organization and is accepted by most as the point of departure.[6]

Blau and Scott also hit the unreality of Weber's scheme pointing out that "by concentrating on the officially instituted aspects of bureaucracies, (it) neglects the ways in which these are modified by informal patterns and thus excludes from analysis the most dynamic aspects of formal organizations."[7] They go on to point out that Parsons and Gouldner have called attention to an implicit contradiction in Weber's conception of bureaucracy; in Gouldner's words, "On the one side, it was administration based on expertise; while on the other, it was administration based on discipline."[8]

Surely, it may be argued, that subsequently, sociologists have adequately compensated for the deficiencies in Weber's analysis and their lack of contact with the real business world. Elton Mayo for one did not feel that this had happened by mid-century when he wrote that: "Sociology is highly developed, but mainly as an exercise in the acquisition of scholarship. Students are taught to write books about each other's books . . ."[9]

Robert Merton wrote in 1957:

. . . one must admit that a large part of what is now called sociological theory consists of general orientation toward data, suggesting types of variables which need somehow to be taken into account, rather than clear, verifiable statements of relationships between specified variables. We have many concepts but few confirmed theories; many points of view, but few

[6]George B. Strother, "Problems in the Development of a Social Science of Organization," in Harold J. Leavitt (editor), *The Social Science of Organizations* (Englewood Cliffs, New Jersey: Prentice-Hall, 1963), pp. 11, 12.

[7]Peter M. Blau and W. Richard Scott, *Formal Organizations* (San Francisco: Chandler Publishing Company, 1962), p. 35.

[8]*Ibid.*

[9]Elton Mayo, *The Social Problems of an Industrial Civilization* (London: Routledge and Kegan Paul, 1949), p. 19.

theorems; many approaches but few arrivals. Perhaps a shift in emphasis would be all to the good.[10]

There have been significant contributors in the field of sociology, of course . . . such notables as Alexander Leighton (*The Governing of Men*) and George Homans (*The Human Group*). And Blau and Scott sound a note of encouragement with the observation that "recently, however, the gap has been narrowed between the methodologically naive students of social organization and the theoretically naive rigorous researchers."[11] But the fact remains that only a small proportion of what has been written by sociologists is directly relevant and valid for the practicing manager, and managers should not too readily permit themselves to be placed on the defensive in trying to assert this.

OTHER BEHAVIORISTS GET INTO THE ACT

Unfortunately, many other behavioral scholars who have rushed into the "new" field of organizational study lack the sophistication, and knowledge of business organizations possessed by Roethlisberger, Mayo, and other pioneer researchers. Many of them remain unaware of the proper role of behavioral knowledge in successful management. They lack the perspective which would result from an appreciation of other important dimensions to management art and science—the valid economics of enterprise and the interdependencies of organization theory, the role and impact of quantitative techniques, and specialized knowledge about functional areas. The typical behavioral scientist has been slow to realize that a business organization is a "contrived" one with

many unique ramifications which is deserving of intensive study and research in its own right.

Good examples of this are afforded by the following comments on business operations made by a prominent psychologist:

While it is a little extreme, it is perhaps not too much to say that there is no reason, in the operation of the modern corporation, to believe that equity entitles one to any voice in management.[12]

May it be reasonably inferred that he would favor purely inside boards patting their alter egos on the back, "reviewing" their performance, and setting their salaries and executive bonuses? To date, the fact of proprietary interest appears to remain the best motivation for the conservation and prudent disposition of assets.

His observations continue:

. . . It seems to me that the tendency to internalize the ultimate seat of authority will go on in the corporation and that it will shift farther and farther inside . . . The final source of authority will be the authority of the work group. The final control will be self-control; the self-control will come from the individual's commitment to the organization, and the individual's commitment will come from his integration into the general goals and activities of the organization.[13]

The final authority will be the work group . . . and where will the entrepreneurship and capital for the creation of such an organization come from? And what about the determination of how the firm may create and distribute salable utilities competitively so that it may survive . . . such decisions will flow up from the workers to their bosses? It is interesting that the direct appointment and removal of superiors has been turned over to

---

[10]Robert K. Merton, *Social Theory and the Social Structure* (New York: The Free Press of Glencoe, 1957), p. 9.

[11]Blau and Scott, *op. cit.,* p. 13.

[12]Mason Haire, "The Concept of Power and the Concept of Man," in George B. Strother (editor), *Social Science Approaches to Business Behavior* (Homewood, Illinois: The Dorsey Press, Inc., 1962), p. 167.

[13]*Ibid.,* p. 169.

subordinates on a number of occasions . . . and with disastrous results (for examples, in the Prussian army several centuries ago, and the Alabama National Guard in more recent times).

Personal motives should be accommodated to the extent that this leads to and does not interfere with the accomplishment of the firm's goals, but in such a scheme what will keep personal goals from *dominating* the organization? Chester Barnard, a man of extensive experience in top management positions, wrote that "a long catalogue of non-economic motives actually condition the management of business, and nothing but the balance sheet keeps these non-economic motives from running wild."[14]

Unfortunately, many behavioral scientists seem to abandon standards for effective research when they investigate business organizations. A large number of the research designs and models which they use to generate "prescriptions" for management problems are so unrealistic and defective that they would be rejected out of hand if proposed for research in their own disciplines.

Part of the difficulty is pointed up quite clearly by Lawrence L. Ferguson, former Manager of the Behavioral Research Service at General Electric. He reports:

Several years ago when we sought to apply available social science findings to solve specific personnel administration problems, we consistently found that the social science information available then was of little help to us. Why? Largely because the data were derived from non-industrial subjects in laboratory or other highly individualistic situations. This made the research results of questionable value for direct application to problems involving adults in normal industrial environments.[15]

This same point is made by George Strother:

Much of the work on small groups (for example, Bavelas . . . and Leavitt . . . [in their research with communication nets]) is, in fact, the study of [the smallest unit elements within a complex organization]. Findings based on studies of such unit organizations cannot be automatically extended to complex organizations, since the assumption that complex organizations are homogeneous structures is in the face of it untenable.[16]

And the following are the observation of another behavioral scientist based upon research and contact with business organizations:

Moreover, we may have overshot, in condemning Taylorism, by *appearing,* at least, to be condemning any *differentiation* of organizations that separates out planning functions from performing functions. We have urged more participation, more involvement, but we have not been very explicit about how far we want to go toward the extreme of having everyone participate in everything all the time . . .

Does participative management mean, in its extreme form, equal distribution of power throughout the organization? If not, then how should power be distributed? What is a "democratic" distribution? What is an autocratic one? I fear that none of us has satisfactorily resolved these questions. We have made some soft statements, pointing out that participation does not mean that everyone does the same job, and that the president ought still to be president. But our specifications have not been clear and consistent, and we have never made a very good theoretical case for any optimal differentiation of power within an organization . . . One way of setting these beliefs into a different perspective may be, I submit, by viewing large organizations as differentiated sets of subsystems rather than as unified wholes. Such a view leads us toward a management-by-task kind of outlook—with the recognition that many subparts of the

[14]Chester I. Barnard, *Organization and Management* (Cambridge, Massachusetts: Harvard University Press, 1948), pp. 14–15.

[15]"Social Scientists in the Plant," *Harvard Business Review,* May-June 1964, p. 135.

[16]"Problems in the Development of a Social Science of Organization," in Harold J. Leavitt (editor), *The Social Science of Organizations* (Englewood Cliffs, New Jersey: Prentice-Hall, 1963), p. 27.

organization may perform many different kinds of tasks, and therefore may call for many different kinds of managerial practices.[17]

Support for the latter view has been provided by the work of Lawrence and Lorsch and others. Their research data clearly suggest that all larger, more complex organizations must, first, differentiate into specialized subsystems and, then, somewhere along the line, integrate these often conflicting subparts into a unified whole. They have found that what is an appropriate level of participation in various parts of an organization is far more dependent upon technical and innovative requirements than upon ideological considerations.[18] We are only now just beginning to collect "hard" data with which to better understand these relationships.

THE CRUEL ORGANIZATION SCHOOL

A few behavioral scientists have concentrated intently upon what they see as the dehumanizing impact of the powerful business organization which at best denies the individual self-fulfillment and at worst causes him to regress to infantile levels of behavior. This thesis represents a rather surprising attempt to "homogenize" workers into an idealized stereotype which in the name of science may well represent the projected values of the professor-researcher. Levinson, Price, Munden, Mandl, and Solley (a team of clinical psychiatrists and social scientists) write that:

Both McGregor and Argyris have discussed problems of dependency in in-

dustrial organizations. The latter has summarized a wide range of studies. Argyris has argued that business organizations by their very nature foster dependency. Such critics consider any form of dependency detrimental to the "self-actualization" of the person, or his ability to become fully what he is capable of becoming. These criticisms fail to recognize that dependence on others is constant, universal, and necessary in some degree for personal growth. It is found in all spheres of human activity.[19]

And George Strauss points out that, ironically, some of those most concerned with the tyranny of the organization would substitute for it the tyranny of the participative group; that a broad range of people do *not* seek self-actualization on the job and that, in any event, the importance of the job—as opposed to the community or the home—has been overstressed as a source of need satisfaction.[20] He states:

Others are as skeptical as I am regarding the theory of increased alienation. In his conclusion to a survey of job-satisfaction studies, Robert Blauner questions "the prevailing thesis that most workers in modern society are alienated and estranged. There is a remarkable consistency in the findings that the vast majority of workers, in virtually all occupations and industries, are moderately or highly satisfied, rather than dissatisfied with their jobs" . . . True, some people seek much broader limits than do others, and some are not too upset if the limits are fuzzy. However, there are many who feel most comfortable if they work in a highly defined situation . . . What psychologists call the *theory of dissonance* suggests that sudden attempts to increase their sense of auton-

---

[17]Harold J. Leavitt, "Unhuman Organizations," *Harvard Business Review*, July-August, 1962, pp. 92, 96, and 98.

[18]See Paul Lawrence and Jay Lorsch, *Organization and Environment* (Homewood, Illinois: Richard D. Irwin, 1969) and Paul Lawrence and Jay Lorsch, *Studies in Organization Design* (Homewood, Illinois: Richard D. Irwin, 1970).

[19]Harry Levinson, Charlton R. Price, Kenneth J. Munden, Harold J. Mandl, and Charles M. Solley, *Men, Management, and Mental Health* (Cambridge, Massachusetts: Harvard University Press, 1962), p. 43.

[20]"Some Notes on Power-Equalization," in Harold J. Leavitt (editor), *The Social Science of Organizations* (Englewood Cliffs, New Jersey: Prentice-Hall, 1963), pp. 48, 49.

omy and self-determination might be quite disturbing.[21]

One might go even further and suggest that many people would be quite lost and apprehensive without the reassuring and predictable time filler of well structured work. Of course, some do prefer less structuring. But as Strauss observes: "Professors place high value on autonomy, inner direction, and the quest for maximum self-development . . . yet there are many misguided individuals (perhaps the bulk of the population) who do not share the professor's values and would not be happy in the professor's job."[22]

It would seem that far too much emphasis has been placed on only *one manifestation* among many of the conflicts between the individual and society. Business organizations are hardly the basic cause of the conflict nor are they, for that matter, necessarily the most important expression of it.

THE HAPPINESS SCHOOL

Many "human relationists" have created a normative never-never land of organizations and people which never was nor can be of this planet. Permissiveness is their keynote with sweetness and light conquering all. As George Strother observes:

. . . human relations, in resolving the Hawthorne paradox, has created its own. The portrait of the happy, productive, socially related worker which emerged from the studies of the late 1940's and early 1950's has not always been supported by recent more analytic studies. The happy, unproductive worker and the unhappy, productive worker have been discovered; permissive and employee centered supervisors have not always bossed the most productive groups; and consultation

with workers has often created more problems than it has solved."[23]

The idea that organizational goals can always be meaningful to employees, that leaders can enjoy popularity at all times, that most employees have the capacity and desire to participate at the drop of a hat, that there are no individuals who will deliberately subvert an organization and its leaders, that only abnormal or neurotic people will steal from the organization, that the organization reflects little if anything of the head man, and that fighting trim and high standards of performance will somehow evolve automatically from group cohesiveness— these are assumptions which may cheer us, but they have little to do with the real world in which we live.

There is little question that positive motivation is superior to negative motivation when the necessary *time, rapport, leadership skill, group environment* and *individual receptivity* are present to make it possible. But negative motivation is certainly superior to *no motivation* or a laissez-faire approach. This deserves emphasis because there are well-meaning extremists who suggest that positive motivation is the only kind that should be employed in virtually all situations. No one will deny that the employee who conforms to a policy because he believes in it, or the student who learns a particular thing because he is interested in it and can relate it to his needs, is better motivated than those who respond because they have to. But the conflicting demands of life and our own human limitations make the use of negative motivation essential for coordinated action, individual growth, and the protection of the organizational or majority interest. Actually, our rebellion is not against negative motivation, per se, but rather to *unnecessary* or *inappropriate* negative motivation.

Douglas McGregor describes quite

[21]George Strauss, *op. cit.*, pp. 50-51. For further evidence, see A. C. MacKinney, P. F. Wernimont, and W. O. Galitz, "Has Specialization Reduced Job Satisfaction?," *Personnel,* January-February 1962, pp. 8-17.

[22]George Strauss, *op. cit.*, pp. 47, 48.

[23]George Strother, *op. cit.*, p. 14.

effectively the kind of illusion which has been held and nurtured by far too many social scientists:

> . . . Before coming to Antioch (as president) I had observed and worked with top executives as an adviser in a number of organizations. I thought I knew how they felt about their responsibilities and what led them to behave as they did. I even thought that I could create a role for myself which would enable me to avoid some of the difficulties they encountered.
>
> I was wrong! It took the direct experience of becoming a line executive and meeting personally the problems involved to teach me what no amount of observation of other people could have taught. I believed, for example, that a leader could operate successfully as a kind of adviser to his organization. I thought I could avoid being a "boss." Unconsciously, I suspect, I hoped to duck the unpleasant necessity of making difficult decisions, of taking the responsibility of one course of action among many uncertain alternatives, of making mistakes and taking the consequences. I thought that maybe I could operate so that everyone would like me—that "good human relations" would eliminate all discord and disagreement.
>
> I couldn't have been more wrong. It took a couple of years, but I finally began to realize that a leader cannot avoid the exercise of authority any more than he can avoid responsibility for what happens to his organization. In fact, it is a major function of the top executive to take on his own shoulders the responsibility for resolving the uncertainties that are always involved in important decisions. Moreover, since no important decision ever pleases everyone in the organization, he must also absorb the displeasure and sometimes severe hostility, of those who would have taken a different course.[24]

Adequate attention must be given to meaningful performance standards as well as to the significantly varying needs of individuals and situations. At times we may even have to *destroy*

strong informal group cohesiveness when it represents a jelling of values and performance standards which are basically opposed to the best interests of the organization. And we may have to drop those individuals who even after effective consultation cannot buy the direction which top management must move in to maintain a viable and successful organization. An experienced and well-traveled executive, Cameron Hawley, suggests that the "one big happy family" complex on the part of many American top executives has sapped the capacity of their organizations for coping with European competition.[25]

The fact that McGregor's Theory Y over-homogenizes people and situations just as much as his Theory X is brought home forcefully by the important research of Fiedler,[26] Woodward,[27] Lawrence and Lorsch,[18] Chandler,[28] and many others. They show that realistic conceptualization of the dynamics of effective leadership and of viable organization structure is far more complex than has been suggested by previous theorizing. Their data indicate that the issues are not simply autocracy vs. democracy, centralization vs. decentralization, or formality vs. informality . . . but rather the need to determine what is appropriate and productive for a particular set of circumstances. There is little question that these imaginative researchers have opened the door to a new era of investigation and practice, and that the provocative character of their findings helps to explain why so many practicing managers have felt uneasy about accepting and applying

---

[24]Douglas McGregor, "On Leadership," in John Glover and Ralph Hower, *The Administrator: Cases on Human Relations in Business* (Homewood, Illinois: Richard D. Irwin, Fourth Edition, 1963) p. 719.

[25]See his article, "The Quality of Leadership," *Personnel,* May-June 1960.
[26]See Fred Fiedler, *A Theory of Leadership Effectiveness* (New York: McGraw-Hill Book Company, 1967).
[27]See Joan Woodward, *Industrial Organization* (London: Oxford University Press, 1965).
[28]See Alfred Chandler, Jr., *Strategy and Structure* (Cambridge, Massachusetts: The M.I.T. Press, 1962).

the naive "solutions" of so much of conventional theory.

THE SCIENTIFIC MANAGEMENT SCIENTISTS

As was pointed out earlier, Frederick W. Taylor and other early pioneers of scientific management claimed that theirs was an exact science. However, instances in industry in which fact may be substituted for judgment are far fewer than these men believed. Even when attention is restricted to such specific procedures as time and motion study, methods analysis, and job evaluation, discretion and collaborative judgment are still essential for success in any particular application.

The advent of operations research techniques during and after the Second World War spawned a group of modern "scientific managers" who like to show their disdain for the spurious claims and scientific pretensions of their forebearers by substituting the term "management science" for "scientific management." Their procedures are far more valid and their claims for accuracy far more modest, but important limitations remain. Like many economists, O.R. men usually do an excellent job of processing inputs coherently, but often are quite naive and seemingly indifferent as to the relevance and soundness of the *premises* upon which the inputs and their interrelationships are based. And too many show little if any concern with regard to planning for and helping with the effective implementation of their proposals.

In dealing with inventory, design, production scheduling, and other problems where model building can, for the most part, ignore the behavioral element, the management scientist can come up with surprisingly effective prescriptions. But when confronted with important human factors in a situation the management scientist has a strong economist-like urge to over-

simplify away the threat to his rational formulations. In listening to papers presented by operations researchers at various meetings one is struck by the amount of questioning devoted to the processing of data or the consistency of the model and the relative absence of concern with the basic validity of the model as it relates to behavioral realities.

Some of these students of management have actually *encouraged* a lack of regard for the role of behavioral skills in management by claiming that management is simply a decision-making process. Until the day arrives that *intended outcomes* are synonymous with *actual achievement* this will be a most unfortunate and misleading characterization. Certainly, problem-solving and decision-making are important functions of management, but so are those skills and activities required to accomplish that which is planned.

Many management scientists are not quite as impartial and rational as they would have us believe . . . what they label as creativity in themselves is likely to "degenerate" into deplorable intuition when they see it in the manager. Churchman and Schainblatt observe that:

The scientist may abhor what he takes to be either dishonesty or at least self-deception in the managerial process. But he ought to realize, as we have said, that his own way of arranging his affairs is little different. Science knows very little about its basic decision making: the creation of new ideas, the trends in research effort, the debates that go on to establish a line of attack on a new problem, the resistances set up to radical ideas.[29]

And Stafford Beer of SIGMA in

[29]C. W. Churchman and A. H. Schainblatt, "Researcher and Manager: A Dialectic of Implementation," *Management Science*, February, 1965, p. B-83. Also, see the series of articles and rejoinders on ineffective collaboration between scientists and managers in industry in *Management Science*, starting with February 1965 issue.

England underscores this when he suggests that:

The manager's shortcomings are that he is not trained to look for systematic structure within the situation he has grown to govern, and that he has no formal means of quantifying such structure anyway. His strengths are knowledge and experience, leading to an intuitional grasp of what to do. It is high time we researchers recognize intuition as a strength, instead of branding it as a weakness—which it becomes only when it is obsessively pursued.[30]

OPPORTUNITY FOR SYNTHESIS

What could be more natural or desirable than the bringing together of students of management from various disciplines for the purpose of identifying important areas of agreement and disagreement, so that they and others could share and build upon the common ground identified and all could more effectively focus their future efforts where they would do the most good? A number of interdisciplinary seminars have been held . . . why have they not produced much to date?

Too often, it would seem, the absence of a procedure which encourages commitment to specific, operational tasks had virtually precluded the possibility of effective search for common ground and basic differences. Those who have planned such conferences evidently have been too generous in their assessment of an interdisciplinary group's capacity for self-discipline and rational discussion in the type of atmosphere which has been created. When theorists from various fields and persuasions simply are brought together—no outside constraints imposed—many of them will be more concerned with attention-getting cliches, the justification of a particular approach in which there is a proprietary interest, or with the classification and labeling of colleagues . . . than with the announced purposes of the conference.

Things might go differently were participants required to commit themselves more fully to common cause *before* being accepted as participants and were seminars structured to place more personal responsibility upon participants to stick to the business at hand and to produce.

Support for these assumptions is provided by Robert Tannenbaum in his observations about the 1962 UCLA Seminar:

An experience in one group is, I think, worth highlighting, for it suggests one possible answer to our difficulty with semantics. The first half of this group's discussion was on a very general and abstract level. When the discussion was at this level, the members of the group had great difficulty in understanding each other. The second half of the meeting dealt with a case that was presented by one of the practitioners. After this case was presented and everyone began focusing on specific data and a specific problem area, a much more useful and meaningful vehicle was available to the diverse group members for reaching some common ground.[31]

It is quite possible, then, that when individuals with varying backgrounds *get down to cases*, they have a good chance of avoiding many of the problems that have frustrated past synthesizing efforts by interdisciplinary groups. Consequently, why not invite representative people from our universities and industry to participate in seminars requiring individual written case analyses from them *prior* to each conference? This would force personal commitment to the cause at the outset on the part of each partici-

---

[30]Stafford Beer, "Researcher and Manager: Commentary," *Management Science*, October, 1965, p. B-11.

[31]Robert Tannenbaum, "Observations on Large Group and Syndicate Discussions," in Harold Koontz (editor), *Toward A Unified Theory of Management* (New York: McGraw-Hill Book Company, 1964), pp. 93-94.

pant (and discourage attendance for inappropriate purposes), would help to channel everyone's efforts toward the specific tasks at hand, and, hopefully, would generate the kinds of data which could be analyzed and evaluated productively at the seminar itself.

Such seminars could make significant contributions to the validation and dissemination of useful theory, focus on areas of genuine disagreement and promote a more truly interdisciplinary approach in research as well as everyday management practice.

CONCLUSION

In a very real sense we management theorists have *not* delivered. We need to substitute hard data for the often inadvertently biased and naive assumptions and theorizing of colleagues who have never been forced to deal face-to-face with the challenges and rich complexity of real-life organization environments. We have not, it would appear, properly identified, integrated and exploited the valid concepts which we do have. We have not lived up to the expectations which practicing managers can reasonably make of us, nor to those suggested by the abundance of research findings and resources available to us. However, we may be able to alter this situation now, if we only organize ourselves properly for the collaborative task at hand.

II MODERN MANAGEMENT THEORY AND PRACTICE

The purpose of Part II is to introduce the reader to modern management theory and practice. This part of the book is divided into three sections, and in each section one of the three major schools of management thought will be examined. The first of these is the management process school; the second is the quantitative school; and the third is the behavioral school.

These "schools" are an outgrowth of the different ways in which individuals view management. Some practitioners and theoreticians see management as a process of interrelated functions. These people belong to the management process school. Others believe management entails choosing the best alternative from among those available. Many of the individuals who feel this way rely on mathematical models and processes, and they can be grouped under the heading of the quantitative school. The other major group of theorists sees management as a psycho-sociological process; the manager gets things done through people by relying on inter-and intrapersonal relationships. These people belong to the behavioral school of management.

In each of the three sections that follow, readings related to these schools will be presented. Before reading them, however, the reader should realize that none of these three major schools of thought is without its shortcomings. At the present time, however, management theory is in the "schools phase," and there is disagreement regarding an overall theory of management. Perhaps in the near future there will be a synthesis of the views of all three; currently, however, this is not the case. Therefore, to understand modern management theory and practice, one must travel all three roads: process, quantitative and behavioral.

The Management Process School

The management process school grew out of the work of individuals such as Henri Fayol, Mary Parker Follett and James Mooney. It is not, however, a school of thought that can be simply classified by time. There are a number of contemporary writers who could also be placed in this school, including Harold Koontz, Lyndall Urwick and Rollin Simonds, to name but a few. In essence, advocates of this school see management as a process of interrelated functions. The three most commonly cited functions are planning, organizing and controlling, with which the selections in this section are concerned.

The first article addresses itself to the function of planning. Professors Cohen and Cyert describe what they consider to be the nine major facets in the strategic planning process. These are: formulating goals; analyzing the environment; assigning quantitative values to the goals; formulating strategic plans; comparing projected performance against desired goals; searching for new strategies to achieve desired goals; selecting strategic alternatives; implementing the strategic program; and providing for measurement, feedback and control. The authors feel that this process will lead to more internal research for improving managerial decisions. They also stress that this process of strategic planning is frequently forgotten or ignored because of day-to-day problems, even though it is a primary determinant of a firm's long-run success.

The second selection concerns the organizing process. The management process school has placed strong emphasis on the traditional scalar organization in which authority equals responsibility at all levels of the organization. Professor Wright discusses this concept, emphasizing that as authority is delegated downward, it tends to decrease relative to responsibility. When this is the case, Professor Wright recommends a more realistic appraisal of the authority-responsibility concept. He advocates a shared authority approach demonstrating mutual dependency between authority levels. This modification is more realistic than the old simplistic "authority equals responsibility" concept. It also points out some of the problems in trying to apply management principles in a simplistic manner.

The final article in this section deals with control. Professors Daugherty and Harvey discuss the traditional reasons underlying budgets: control, efficiency, feedback, pressure exertion and motivation. They illustrate the dysfunctional aspects of the traditional budgeting process such as padding, deficit spending, intentional distortion and effort duplication. The article outlines a program to alleviate these dysfunctions. In particular, the program includes active participation necessary in establishing the budget, which must be coupled with improved reporting systems. The authors also point out that budgets should be realistic and function as motivators rather than as pressure devices.

3 Strategy: Formulation, Implementation, and Monitoring

Kalman J. Cohen and Richard M. Cyert

The study of corporate strategy within graduate schools of business has been under way for many years. With the growing complexity of the world and with the increased size of business firms, the need for planning and the development of a corporate strategy has become recognized in the business firm. While many areas of management have been subjected to scientific analysis, the strategy area continues to be characterized by a commonsensical, judgmental approach.

This paper is an attempt to impose structure upon the various problems inherent in the process of formulating, implementing, and monitoring corporate strategy in modern business firms. We begin by identifying the relevant considerations in the strategic planning process and then discussing the manner in which formal models can prove useful to executives in dealing with various subproblems. The paucity of valid, normative propositions in the corporate strategy literature indicates the need for a more scientific approach to this important field.

The nine major steps that constitute the strategic planning process are as follows: (1) formulation of goals; (2) analysis of the environment; (3) assigning quantitative values to the goals; (4) the microprocess of strategy formulation; (5) the gap analysis; (6) strategic search; (7) selecting the portfolio of strategic alternatives; (8) implementation of the strategic problem; (9) measurement, feedback, and control.[1] This

[1] These nine steps into which we have subdivided the strategic planning process are consistent with some viewpoints expressed in the current literature. They are not, however, specifically taken from any single source. They represent our characterization of the problem based upon our knowledge of the literature, discussions with corporate executives, and participation in the process itself. Some other attempts to present a conceptual framework for the strategic planning process are presented in George A. Steiner, *Top Management Planning* (New York: Macmillan Co., 1969), chap. 2.

Reprinted with permission of the authors and publisher from *The Journal of Business,* July, 1973, pp. 349–367. ©1973 by the University of Chicago. All rights reserved. Published January, April, July, October 1973.

paper will review these nine steps and present selected ideas that demonstrate how the strategic planning process could be improved through use of analytical procedures. The nine steps should not be viewed as a once-and-for-all process of strategic planning, but, rather, as a continuous, ongoing process.[2] The whole procedure is a dynamic feedback process that has neither a beginning nor an end; it is merely for expository convenience that we label the first step as formulating corporate goals.

I. FORMULATION OF GOALS

The first step in the strategic planning process can be viewed as the development of the arguments in the corporate utility function.[3] This specification is made by the coalition responsible for the top-level management of the corporation.[4] Corporate

goals must stem from participants within the organization.[5] The goals of a small firm under control of a single entrepreneur are determined solely by him. The goals of a large corporation under control of professional managers are determined by a coalition which typically includes the chairman of the board, the president, and a select group of the more important vice presidents. The group is characterized as a coalition because no one dominates it in the way that a single entrepreneur may dominate his organization.

The final set of arguments in the utility function for the corporation must be accepted by the individuals who are responsible for implementing the policy of the corporation. This acceptance can be induced in a variety of ways that have been characterized by organization theorists as "side payments."[6] At this stage, the goals are specified in qualitative rather than in quantitative terms. Some goals relate to measurable entities such as earnings per share, total sales, share of market, return on investment, rate of growth in sales, rate of profit growth, and so forth. Other goals represent management aspirations which are more difficult to measure: for example, a desire to be the most advanced electronics firm in the United States, a desire to be a leader in community improvements, a desire to be ecologically responsible, and so forth.[7]

In the formulation of corporate goals, the relationships between those goals and the goals of the participants in the organization should be considered by the coalition. If all participants had the same goals and the same

---

[2]This point is aptly illustrated in H. Igor Ansoff, "Toward a Strategic Theory of the Firm," in *Business Strategy*, ed. H. Igor Ansoff (Baltimore: Penguin Books, 1969), esp. fig. 6. That planning should be viewed as a continuous, ongoing process is clearly stated in the following quotation "Guide to Business Planning," A brochure printed in 1969 (primarily for internal use) at Westinghouse Electric Corporation: "Planning . . . must be a continuous process of evaluations, decisions, and actions. That does not mean that management must continually recycle the whole formal planning process, or that constant revision of data is required. But management must be continually sensitive to changes that can significantly affect previously planned actions. . . . a *continual review* is required to assess the potential impact of current events and current decisions on future performance; but that will not be done if only one short span of time within the year is preserved as 'planning time.'. . . sustained efforts—in reviewing data, reevaluating plans, and assessing performance—are required throughout the year" (p. 7).

[3]A model of discretionary managerial behavior based on the notion of a corporate utility function has been developed in Oliver E. Williamson, *The Economics of Discretionary Behavior: Managerial Objectives in a Theory of the Firm* (Englewood Cliffs, N.J.: Prentice-Hall, Inc., 1964), chap. 4.

[4]See Richard M. Cyert and James G. March, *A Behavioral Theory of the Firm* (Englewood Cliffs, N.J.: Prentice-Hall, Inc., 1963), chap. 3.

[5]This statement does not imply that the goals of the corporation are necessarily identical with the goals of any participants in the organization. See, e.g., H. A. Simon, "On the Concept of Organizational Goal," *Administrative Science Quarterly* 9, no. 1 (June 1964): 1-22.

[6]Cyert and March, pp. 29–32.

[7]A detailed discussion of the variety of goals pursued by business firms is provided in Steiner (n. 1 above), chaps. 6–7.

perception of the means to achieve them, then there would be no problem in formulating a goal structure for the organization. Similarly, if all participants completely accepted the goals of some single individual (such as the chief executive), the organizational goal structure could be easily understood. However, most organizations consist of individual participants having sets of personal goals that are different from each other's and from the organization's goals. It is clear from even casual observation that there is no formal weighting process by which the goals of each participant are incorporated into the goal structure in a systematic fashion. Further, it is also clear that each individual does not have an equal vote in determining the goals of an organization. Nevertheless, if the organization is to function effectively, its goals must in some sense be an amalgam of the goals of the participants.

A frequent phenomenon in organizations is the formation of subunits and of subunit goals. These subunits, which are usually work groups, become the object of the participants' identification. Group norms arise and may exert more influence over the individual than the organizational goals. The norms of the group may at some time be in conflict with the organizational goals and the subgroup actions contrary to the interests of the total organization. Still the individual may, in fact, substitute the goals of this subunit for the organizational goals. Hence, in formulating organizational goals, the coalition should consider the effect that they will have on subunit goals and on the potential formation of subunits.[8]

Clearly the corporate goals must be viewed from the standpoint of the social values that are held by members of the coalition. It is necessary to differentiate between the social goals that are proper for the organization to hold and those that are proper for the individual participant to hold. For example, there may be a conflict for some firms between pollution control and profit. This conflict becomes particularly strong when the society has not passed the appropriate laws which embody its social values and the corporation is left with the problem of voluntarily reducing its profit in order to contribute to some social goal. It is not clear whether the organizational coalition can properly take actions that reduce the profit of the organization in order to achieve a set of social goals that the coalition itself holds. Most corporation executives take the position that they do not have the right to impose their own social values on stockholders, but they do have a right to fight as individuals for particular kinds of legislation even though the effect of the legislation is to reduce the corporation's profit. There are also an increasing number of attempts to get stockholder approval of particular strategies that will achieve social goals. In the final analysis, however, business firms are profit-seeking organizations, and society depends on them to seek profit as a means of achieving the optimum allocation of resources.[9]

In summary, we have stressed the fact that goal formulation is a process of determining the arguments in the corporate utility function. The particular set of goals that the corporation selects must take into account the personal goals of the members of the organization and the goals of subunits. The coalition must also consider the problem of social goals and the extent to which they are going to be represented in the corporate goal structure. In this first step of the strategic planning process, no attempt is made to assign quantitative values to the set of elements in the goal structure.

[8]See Richard M. Cyert and Kenneth R. Mac-Crimmon, "Organizations," in *The Handbook of Social Psychology,* Gardner Lindsey and Elliot Aronson, eds. 2d ed. (Reading, Mass.: Addison-Wesley Publishing Co., 1968), 1:591–93.

[9]*Social Responsibilities of Business Corporations* (a statement on national policy by the Research and Policy Committee of the Committee for Economic Development, New York, June, 1971).

II. ENVIRONMENT AND THE FIRM[10]

The organization and the environment are parts of a complex interactive system. The actions taken by the organization can have important effects on the environment, and, conversely, the outcomes of the actions of the organization are partially determined by events in the environment. These outcomes and the events that contribute to them have a major impact on the organization. Even if the organization does not respond to these events, significant changes in the organizational participants' goals and roles can occur.[11]

Most organizations attempt to learn from interaction with the environment and respond to changes caused by the environment. Both the learning and response are easiest when the environment is disjoint. In such cases, the causal links among the sectors of the environment are relatively short and events in one sector are likely to have only minor effects on events in other sectors. The organization can then usefully partition such a disjoint environment and consider the sectors in isolation. For example, a multinational firm selling products under different brand names in each of several countries can change policy in one market and analyze the effects without considering interactions with other markets. The learning and response are more difficult for the organization when the environment is complex and long chains of causal links and events in one sector have profound effects on other sectors. In such an environment, the organization must consider the

whole sequence of possible effects of any action it takes. For example, large steel companies must consider the effects that a price increase will have on various sectors of the environment—on labor unions, competitors, consumers, and government.

The parts of an environment that are relevant differ according to the type of organization. For the business firm, economic conditions are of prime importance. When the economy is in an expansionary period, many possible actions can yield the necessary resources to allow the firm to survive and grow. Conflict with other organizations in the environment will be minimized since all organizations can readily meet their basic resource requirements. Conflict within the organization will also generally be reduced because the preferences of the various coalition members can be more easily satisfied. An expanding economy not only makes it relatively easy for the firm to attain its current goals, but also offers the possibility for the firm to expand its goal set. The degree to which the goal set is expanded depends on the expected duration of the favorable economic conditions. Such a change in goals may lead to some internal conflict as the various coalition members assert their own preferences. However, these internal conflicts will not be seriously disruptive, since the firm's increased resources permit all coalition members to achieve higher levels of utility.

In contrast, when economic conditions are unfavorable, goal attainment becomes more difficult and the firm will devote increasing attention toward its goal set. Continued failure to meet its goals without any apparent possibility of increasing resources generally results in a reduction of goal values. In the face of economic adversity, typical firm responses are to tighten operations by postponing expansion plans, engaging in cost-cutting drives, reducing the number of participants, and so on. The extent of these actions depends on the amount of slack in the organization. At the beginning of un-

[10]Some of the material in this section has been directly taken or paraphrased from Cyert and MacCrimmon, pp. 593–602.

[11]An extended discussion of the manner in which roles and tasks within an organization should be influenced by the environment is presented in Paul R. Lawrence and Jay W. Lorsch, *Organization and Environment: Managing Differentiation and Integration* (Boston: Division of Research, Graduate School of Business Administration, Harvard University, 1967).

favorable economic conditions, the organization will usually have considerable slack accumulated during more favorable times. If economic conditions continue at a low level for an extensive period of time, it becomes increasingly difficult to remove slack without reducing services that were previously considered essential. Eventually this set of events will lead to changes in the organizational structure. Some roles may be eliminated completely and other roles may be extensively modified. Serious internal conflict among the individual participants will occur and will result in participants leaving the organization both voluntarily and involuntarily.[12]

The impact of changing economic conditions is reduced if the organization is prepared for them. Thus, organizations attempt to plan ahead: as a basis for planning, forecasts must be made of future changes in economic conditions. These forecasts are, of course, more accurate when the economic environment is relatively stable over time. The organization has more difficulty in learning the structure of the environment and accurately predicting its future states when the environment is highly volatile. Unfortunately, these are the circumstances when forecasts are most essential.

For whatever planning horizon the firm uses, it is necessary to make predictions for the entire planning period. In particular, it is necessary to make predictions of various aggregate economic variables which are relevant for the firm. These aggregates include GNP, price indices, unemployment rates, and similar measures of the state of the economy at benchmark dates during the planning period. It is desirable that these predictions be made at the corporate level and transmitted to the operating units of the firm as a basis for their specific planning. In this way, all planning activity of the firm is conducted under a uniform set of predictions. The predictions will not necessarily be single-valued estimates. The firm may find it useful to develop several plausible alternative economic scenarios and to require its operating units to formulate plans for each alternative.[13]

In addition to aggregate economic predictions, it is necessary for the firm to make predictions about future conditions in the industries and markets in which it operates. An industry forecast is usually made in terms of the total dollar sales expected for the industry. From such forecasts, the firm can predict its future sales over the planning period by making assumptions about the market shares that it will obtain. In making these assumptions the firm must make predictions about the behavior of its present and potential competitors.[14] Estimates must be made

---

[12]Examples of the manner in which adverse economic circumstances can lead to extensive organizational changes have been described in Williamson, chap. 6. A more detailed example of the disruptive influences that a sudden adverse economic environment can have on an organization is the impact of the crisis of 1920 on General Motors. This point is dramatically illustrated in the following quotation from Alfred D. Chandler, *Strategy and Structure: Chapters in the History of the American Enterprise* (New York: Doubleday, 1966), ". . . the automobile market had collapsed . . . but, by the end of October [1920], the situation had become so serious that many General Motors managers were having difficulty finding cash to cover such immediate needs as invoices and payrolls. . . . during the crisis, the prices of General Motors stock plummeted. Then came Durant's disasterous attempt to sustain the price by buying General Motors' stock on credit which led to his financial difficulties and his retirement as president on November 20, 1920. Ten days later, Pierre du Pont took over the presidency. . . . once he agreed to serve, Pierre acted quickly and firmly. The day after he took office, he began a systematic review of the corporation's position and problems. And one of his very first acts *was to approve the plan worked out by Alfred Sloan which defined an organizational structure for General Motors*" (p. 157, italics added).

[13]For a survey of various approaches to forecasting the future environment, see Steiner (n. 1 above), chap. 8.

[14]The importance of analyzing competitors is stressed in S. Tilles, "Making Strategy Explicit," in Ansoff (n. 2 above), pp. 186–90.

of the prices competitors will charge, of their advertising policies, and of the product changes competitors will make. In this regard it is highly useful for firms to maintain an elaborate information system on their competitors. Relevant information on competitors can be obtained from public sources such as financial statements, from information gathered from the firm's salesmen, and from executives who meet rival executives at professional meetings. All of these sources can be utilized to build up a data base on each of the firm's major competitors.

III. ESTABLISHMENT OF QUANTITATIVE TARGETS

After goals have been qualitatively formulated and after the environmental analysis has been completed, the firm's coalition is in a position to establish quantitative targets.[15] Quantitative targets essentially impute quantitative values to those previously formulated goals that are capable of being stated in quantitative terms. These quantitative targets are often usefully established for planning purposes in terms of rates of growth. Thus one goal may be that the firm's profit should grow at some specific annual rate over the planning horizon. Part of the process of establishing quantitative targets also involves weighting the importance of the various targets. Thus, the firm conceivably might weight achievement of its sales goal more than achievement of its profit goal. This weighting is important when the firm may be in a position to achieve some but not all of its goal set. Given the weighting it is then possible to specify strategies which are appropriate when it is impossible to attain all the various targets. Goals

stated in terms of absolute levels rather than rates of change require target dates to be specified. It is generally necessary for a plan to have values for the relevant goals specified for various benchmark dates. This is frequently done, permitting the firm to project *pro forma* balance sheets and profit and loss statements for the individual years within the planning horizon.

One useful heuristic for planning is the process of "backward induction."[16] This approach requires that a specific set of desired values be established for the various goals for the final period of the planning horizon, for example, 5 years from now. The planners specify, for instance, the values the firm should have for sales, profit, capital investment, and so on during the fifth year. On the basis of these specifications, the planners work backward to see where the firm must be in the fourth year if it is to achieve the goals in the fifth year and so on back to the first year of the plan. This process of backward induction is a useful addition to the planning process. It enables the planner to establish a viable plan for the entire planning horizon. Several iterations may be required, and, in this process, goals may be modified.

We have discussed the establishment of quantitative targets from the perspective of the corporation as a whole. Frequently, however, it is also desirable to establish quantitative targets for various collections of operating units within the corporation, for example, groups or divisions, by disaggregating the previously established corporate-wide targets.

This description of the first three planning steps completes the macrophase of the planning process. The next step is to have each operating unit within the firm formulate its own set of plans.

---

[15]Cf. Russell L. Ackoff, *A Concept of Corporate Planning* (New York: John Wiley & Sons, Inc., 1970), chap. 2.

[16]An explanation of backward induction is presented in Morris H. DeGroot, *Optimal Statistical Decisions* (New York: McGraw-Hill Book Co., 1970), pp. 277–78.

IV. THE MICROPROCESS OF STRATEGY FORMULATION

The fourth major step in the planning process can be referred to as "the microaspects of strategy formulation." Each operating unit in the corporation formulates its own strategic plan over the relevant time horizon. The time horizon chosen for strategic planning will vary depending upon the nature of the firm, but 5 years is a typical time horizon for strategic planning in business organizations. It often will be desirable for some qualitative aspects of the strategic plan to be formulated over a 10- or 20-year horizon, even though detailed quantitative projections may be made only for an intermediate-term time horizon such as the next 5 years.

Before each operating unit can develop its own strategic plan, it is necessary for the senior executives of the corporation (or their staff members) to provide the managers of the operating unit with some background information.[17] This centrally provided information should consist of at least the following items:

a) Some guidelines concerning the nature of the strategic planning process should be provided. The emphasis should be put on actively involving relevant executives in the planning process in order to focus their attention on strategic considerations. Especially at the level of the operating units, there is a tendency for managers to worry primarily about immediate problems. A formalized planning process is necessary to induce managers to think seriously about long-term strategy for the operating unit.

b) The relevant goals that top management wants the operating unit to be concerned with should be explicitly stated.

c) All operating units should be pro-

vided with the results of the broad analysis of the economic environment undertaken in corporate headquarters. To the extent that relevant technological or product-market forecasts were centrally made, these should also be transmitted to appropriate operating units. There may be economies in having some of the technological and product-market forecasts made centrally even though they are relevant only to particular operating units in the corporation.

On the basis of this corporate information, each operating unit should develop its own strategic plan, in both qualitative and quantitative terms. A major activity which each operating unit must undertake in developing its strategic plan is a critical, thorough analysis of the environment for its own particular mix of products and markets. A reasonably broad definition of the operating unit's product-market mission needs to be adopted for this purpose. Given this broad view of its product-market posture, the operating unit must attempt to analyze its external environment to discover significant economic, market, and technological developments. As part of its environmental analysis, the operating unit must identify its major present and potential competitors. In addition, the operating unit should make an internal analysis to uncover those areas in which it has had problems and successes in the past in order to diagnose hitherto unrecognized strategic obstacles and opportunities. In the light of these external and internal analyses, the operating unit must then determine where its comparative advantage exists.

This analysis should result in a set of recommended strategic programs for each operating unit. Several types of recommendations may be relevant. These might involve pricing strategy, product-line strategy, marketing strategy, programs of cost reduction for existing products and markets, new products to be developed, new markets to be entered, major research

---

[17]An interesting discussion of one procedure for coordinating the planning done at various levels in a corporation is provided in Ackoff, pp. 133–37.

and development expenditures, major advertising campaigns, and major physical investments. In proposing the operating unit's diversification into additional products and markets, recommendations should be made as to whether this diversification should be accomplished by means of internal growth or through external acquisition. Enough detailed information should be given in the verbal discussion and the quantitative projections so that executives at higher levels in the corporation can independently determine the impact of undertaking, postponing, or rejecting each element in the recommended strategic plan.

V. THE "GAP ANALYSIS"

The fifth major step consists of aggregating upward the strategic plans formulated by each operating unit to obtain aggregate strategic plans for the corporation as a whole and for any relevant subdivisions. This upward aggregation of the specific quantitative projections made by each operating unit for the next 5 years can readily be done by a process of simple summation. Equally important, however, is the upward aggregation of the qualitative, verbal aspects of each operating unit's strategic plan. The hierarchical pattern utilized in the upward aggregation process should be carefully chosen to make the most logical sense for the particular corporation. It might first involve consolidating the operating units into departments, then consolidating the departments into divisions, then consolidating these divisions into groups, and, finally, consolidating the groups into the corporation. Of course, the number of levels present in this upward aggregation process, and the particular labels attached to each level of consolidation, will differ from firm to firm.

The immediate aim of the aggregation is to enable a "gap analysis" to be performed at higher organizational levels in the firm.[18] This "gap analysis" might be made only at the corporate-wide level, or, instead, preliminary gap analyses might be made at each of the "collection points" at lower organizational levels (for example, initially at the departmental level, then at the divisional level, and finally at the group level) prior to the corporate-wide gap analysis.

Regardless of the organizational level at which the gap analysis is performed, the procedural aspects of it are much the same. In particular, the projected performance for the corporation as a whole (or for whatever organizational subdivision the gap analysis is being performed) is compared to the quantitative targets which have been established for the corporation (or the appropriate subdivision). Since the corporation generally has multiple goals, the gap analysis should be done for each goal. Thus for each goal of importance to the corporation, the projected figures will be subtracted from the targets established for that goal in order to develop a perceived gap. For any particular goal, for example, earnings per share, this perceived gap can be expressed as a function of time (for example, year-by-year over a 5-year horizon). Thus, the gap analysis process can be usefully viewed as developing a "perceived-gap matrix," as illustrated in Table 1. The rows in this matrix designate the various corporate goals, for example, total sales, earnings per share, some measure of geographical dispersion, and so forth. The columns of this matrix correspond to various points of time within the planning horizon, for example, years one, two, three, four and five. The entries in this matrix are the perceived gaps along each goal for each particular point of time. The manner in which this perceived-gap matrix can be

[18]A different approach to the gap analysis is discussed in H. Igor Ansoff, *Corporate Strategy* (New York: McGraw-Hill Book Co., 1965), chap. 8.

TABLE 1. AN EXAMPLE OF A PERCEIVED-GAP MATRIX

CORPORATE GOALS	TIME PERIODS IN THE PLANNING HORIZON				
	Year 1	Year 2	Year 3	Year 4	Year 5
Total sales revenue (million $)	+2.5	−7.3	−10.9	−18.7	−28.3
Earnings per share ($ per share)	+0.05	−0.11	−0.31	−0.80	−1.35
Index of geographical dispersion (percentage)	−15	−13	−9	−7	−6

used to initiate strategic search will be discussed in connection with step six below.

VI. STRATEGIC SEARCH

A gap between the goals specified at the corporate level and the predicted achievement developed through the microanalysis stimulates the firm to search for new strategies in order to achieve its goals.[19] The strategic search process generally first focuses on internal activities. For example, the firm may begin its search by reviewing its price strategy to see whether it can achieve its goals by raising prices. More broadly, the firm may review its entire marketing strategy. Another area for search is the cost structure of the firm with a view toward establishing a strategy for cost reduction. Still another area for internal search is research and development. All of these areas, and others which may be undertaken, fall into the category of internal search.

If the measures discovered by internal search do not entirely close the gap, the firm then turns to external search. In this phase the firm begins to examine the environment with a view toward bringing new resources into the firm to enable it to achieve its goals. Frequently this is accomplished through a strategy of acquisition of other firms. In general, the firm searches for acquisitions which would result in economies of scale or positive externalities. An economy of scale would result from an acquisition that would enable the firm to use some of its resources more intensively, for example, by producing or distributing a new product with already existing facilities or manpower. Positive externalities would result from a new (complementary) product whose scale would increase the sales of the firm's present products, from elimination of overlapping facilities (such as branch or headquarter offices), from the acquisition of new technical talent, and so forth. A frequent source of economies resulting from acquisition is the more intensive utilization of capable managers. It is clear that in any economy, including the U.S. economy, there is a significant shortage of good managers.[20] Thus, firms which have capable managerial talent may be able to benefit from acquisitions that do not appear to be a synergistic fit. However, because of the ability of the acquiring firm to supply good management, these acquisitions may prove highly successful.

There is at present in the United States much evidence that legal power will be invoked to restrict the acquisi-

---

[19]A general discussion of the empirical process of search behavior within an organization is presented in James G. March and Herbert A. Simon, *Organizations* (New York: John Wiley & Sons, 1958), esp. pp. 173–74, 180. A discussion of search behavior which focuses more directly on issues of corporate strategy is contained in Ansoff, *ibid.*

[20]Marvin Bower, *The Will to Manage* (New York: McGraw-Hill Book Co., 1966), pp. 92–94.

tion policy of firms.[21] This development reduces the efficacy of external search and increases the importance of internal search. This change in turn emphasizes the need to develop organizational policies that will permit managers with entrepreneurial ability to advance within the firm. Thus it is important that planning activity not restrict initiative by developing inflexible policies; instead, the planning process should induce division managers to feel responsible for developing new business ideas as part of the strategic plans for their own divisions.[22]

VII. SELECTING THE PORTFOLIO OF STRATEGIC ALTERNATIVES

In the sixth step of the strategic planning process, the perceived-gap matrix was used to trigger several different types of strategic search. The purpose of this search is to develop a strategy set that consists of possible strategic actions. Each of the members of this set is a strategic action that might be undertaken by the corporation as a whole (or by appropriate subdivisions).

For example, a strategy set might include proposals for changes in pricing policy, major cost-reduction campaigns, changes in product design, new market introduction plans, diversification into specific new product-market alternatives, major investments in physical facilities, and the acquisition of particular products or of entire firms.

The fact that a set of possible strategic actions has been developed does not imply that each action will be adopted as part of the strategic plan. From the strategy set, management selects a particular portfolio of strategic actions; this portfolio constitutes the corporation's new strategic plan.[23]

The seventh step of the strategic planning process, as we have described it, focuses on the way in which corporations should develop a strategic plan. Because of the rather casual manner in which strategic planning is approached in most corporations, however, little emphasis is placed on the portfolio aspects of the problem. The usual approach is to judge each proposed action as it is uncovered in the search process strictly on its own merits. If the proposed action proves acceptable at this point, then the action is adopted as part of the new strategic plan. When enough proposed actions are adopted in this manner to close the perceived gap (or if the gap is closed by lowering the goal values), strategic search is terminated and the new strategic plan has been formulated. One deficiency in this typical approach is that management fails to evaluate interactions among possible strategic actions. A more complete analysis from a portfolio viewpoint will often lead to a different evaluation of a particular proposed action because of interaction effects. A second deficiency of the usual approach is that strategic search may be prematurely terminated.

[21]U.S., Congress, House, Committee on the Judiciary, Antitrust Subcommittee, *Investigation of Conglomerate Corporations,* 92nd Cong., 1st sess., June 1, 1971. On p. 5 of this report, the following statements are presented: "This public attention, notoriety and industry demand sparked unprecedented attention at the national level to the problem of corporate mergers. In the first 6 months of 1969, at least 8 major investigations were under way at the national level into Federal questions concerning mergers and acquisitions by conglomerate corporations." On the same page, Chairman Celler is quoted as stating: "It may be that the traditional standards of the antitrust laws against mergers and corporations which 'may be substantially to lessen competition, or tend to create a monopoly' need reevaluation in the light of economic and political effects of conglomerate mergers."

[22]Litton Industries is one corporation which was able to obtain this type of behavior by their division managers under their "opportunity planning" process. This is described in Edmund P. Learned et al., *Business Policy: Text and Cases,* rev. ed. (Homewood, Ill.: Richard D. Irwin, Inc., 1969), pp. 833–39.

[23]See E. Eugene Carter and Kalman J. Cohen, "Portfolio Aspects of Strategic Planning," *Journal of Business Policy* 2, no. 4 (Summer 1972): 8–30.

The nature of the strategic search process in organizations often prevents an objective evaluation of proposed actions. When a potential action is advocated by a coalition member, he thereby becomes identified with the action. When this identification becomes close, the coalition member may view the ultimate adoption or rejection of the proposed action as a measure of his personal power position within the coalition. The strategic planning process would be far more effective if the proposed actions could be divorced from individual sponsorship. Typically, however, this is difficult to accomplish because proposed strategic actions are brought to the attention of the coalition through a chain of successive sponsorships within the organization. In this chain, each manager in the hierarchy attempts to convince his immediate superior of the merits of the proposed action and sponsorship of the proposal passes upward with acceptance.[24]

The difficulty of the coalition's making an objective evaluation of proposed actions is further complicated by the loss of information as proposals filter upward through the organizational hierarchy. So many details concerning proposals are eliminated in "the selling process" that it becomes virtually impossible for coalition members to analyze interaction effects even if they so desired. Thus, each coalition member sponsoring a proposal becomes an "uncertainty absorber" with respect to the proposed actions that he advocates.[25] This situation effectively forces the coalition into the necessity of making personal judgments concerning the competence of its members in the guise of selecting a strategic plan. In order to minimize personal conflict among coalition members, the coalition frequently adopts rules of thumb to allocate strategic resources among organizational subunits in some objective but nonoptimal manner, for example, budgeting research and development expenditures in proportion to sales and authorizing automatic reinvestment of depreciation charges.

VIII. IMPLEMENTATION OF THE STRATEGIC PROGRAM

Once a portfolio of strategic alternatives has been established for the corporation (as well as for each group, division, department, and operating unit in the corporation), the next step in the strategic planning process is implementation of the program.[26] We will focus on the implementation problem from the standpoint of overall corporate strategy, but analogous considerations also apply at other levels in the organizational hierarchy.

In order to develop an operational procedure for implementing the agreed-upon strategic program, it is necessary to decompose the broadly stated strategy into a time-phased sequence of plans regarding such actions as new product developments, new market introductions, external acquisitions, capital investment projects, management development, manpower recruitment, and so forth.[27] The vari-

---

[24]This process has been analyzed in E. Eugene Carter, "A Behavioral Theory Approach to Firm Investment and Acquisition Decisions" (Ph.D. diss., Carnegie-Mellon University, 1969).

[25]Cf. March and Simon (n. 19 above), p. 165: "Uncertainty absorption takes place when inferences are drawn from a body of evidence and the inferences, instead of the evidence itself, are then communicated. . . . through the process of uncertainty absorption, the recipient of a communication is severely limited in his ability to judge its correctness."

[26]An overall discussion of some problems involved in implementing strategic plans is contained in Steiner (n. 1 above), chap. 11.

[27]Decomposition of the broadly stated strategy into a time-phased sequence of plans is analogous to some of the steps involved in the planning-programming-budgeting system that was developed during the 1960's in the Department of Defense. See Charles J. Hitch, *Decision-making for Defense* (Berkeley, Calif.: University of California Press, 1967), pp. 21–39.

ous activities necessary to implement any particular strategy should be defined in terms of each type of resource required. It is common practice to reduce this specification of resource requirements to monetary terms. Unfortunately, in many firms, the underlying detail is then lost and only the dollar budget for the strategic program remains as a permanent control document. With this loss of detail and transformation into monetary terms, a subtle change in attitudes also occurs. In place of the inspiration and imagination displayed in the development of the plan, management has merely a set of monetary constraints within which it must operate. This primary emphasis on monetary considerations has the effect of replacing the manager's entrepreneurial spirit with a bureaucratic attitude. The long-term goals of the strategic plan are displaced by the short-term goal of operating within budget.

In arguing that the financial budget should not be the sole form to which the strategic plan is reduced, we nonetheless acknowledge that financial budgets are essential. The various forms of short-term plans and budgets should be consistent with the strategic plan. Such interaction can be accomplished by initially defining the plans and budgets for the coming year as the first-year components in the quantitative projections developed as part of the 5-year strategic plan. If necessary, of course, these initial figures for the coming year can then be further disaggregated in the short-term planning and budgeting process.

It is obvious that any attempt to forecast the future (especially several years ahead) is bound to be subject to errors. Unfortunately, however, many planning and budgeting systems place undue reliance upon the accuracy of the underlying forecasts. More realistically, strategic plans and their accompanying operating budgets should be formulated on a contingency basis. Some type of decision-tree analysis may be a useful planning aid for this purpose.[28] At a minimum, operating budgets for the next year as well as strategic plans for the next 5 years should be in a variable budget format, rather than the more usual fixed budget format. To the extent possible, however, various major contingencies should be envisioned and probabilities of occurrence assigned to each one. Alternative plans of actions can then be developed for each contingency having a sufficiently high probability of occurrence. Obviously, in this regard, some type of computerized planning and budgeting model would be extremely helpful in developing suitable contingency plans.

In order to implement any specific strategic program successfully, it is necessary to obtain enthusiastic cooperation from executives at various levels of the corporation. One way of achieving acceptance of the strategic plan by lower-level executives is to have these executives actively participate in the planning process. The approach to strategy formulation that we have described requires such participation in the process of developing the plan (especially in the microprocess of strategy formulation and in strategic search).

It is critical as part of the implementation process to examine the formal organizational structure.[29] Although major changes in structure will occur relatively infrequently, it is nevertheless important to determine whether minor modifications will in-

---

[28]For an example of the use of decision-tree analysis, see Harvey M. Wagner, *Principles of Operations Research* (Englewood Cliffs, N.J.: Prentice-Hall, Inc., 1969), pp. 18–20.

[29]An appropriate framework for this purpose is presented in Ackoff (n. 15 above), chap. 5. An interesting analysis of the manner in which a firm's organizational structure should be adapted to match the product-market portfolio defined by its overall strategy is presented in E. Raymond Corey and Steven H. Star, *Organization Strategy: A Marketing Approach* (Boston: Division of Research, Harvard Business School, 1971).

crease the likelihood of achieving the goals specified by the strategic plan. By organizational structure we mean the particular description of the roles of the organization, the allocation of decision-making power, and the placing of responsibility. There must be a matching of the structure with the requirements for decision making, coordination, and control emanating from the plan.[30] Generally changes in organizational structure are made along the centralization-decentralization dimension. The strategic plan should be analyzed to determine whether the organizational structure should be shifted in either direction. For example, if the firm acquires a new product that has little relationship to the current product mix, it may be desirable to decentralize decisions relating to the new product. Such decentralization places decision-making power in the roles where appropriate information and knowledge exist.

Speaking more generally, the main factors affecting the degree of decentralization of an organization are its size, the environment (benign or hostile), subunit interdependency, and technology.[31] As an organization grows larger, the cost of maintaining centralized control increases. If the environment is hostile (in the sense that mistakes will be easily exploited by competitors), there will be an increased tendency toward centralization. Similarly, if there is a high degree of interdependency among subunits, more centralization is often necessary. If the technological changes associated with the firm's activities require large investments in order to exploit them, the tendency to centralize is increased. Technological changes that reduce the costs of communications provide an impetus toward decentralization. In order to relate the strategic plan effectively to the organizational structure, management should determine whether there will be any significant changes in size, environment, subunit interdependency, and technology resulting from the plan. If so, modifications of the organizational structure should then be made as part of the implementation process.

IX. MEASUREMENT, FEEDBACK, AND CONTROL

An essential component in the strategic planning process is the development of operational measures of the extent to which the corporation and appropriate subunits thereof are in fact adhering to the agreed-upon plan.[32] Additional information should also be developed to help management determine whether the strategic plan may no longer be appropriate. Corporate targets have already been specified in operationally measurable quantitative terms (see Section III above). It is, therefore, relatively simple to obtain periodic measurements of corporate performance (or subunit performance), and to relate these in a time-phased manner to the targets.

It must be recognized, of course, that any attempt to measure performance and to provide feedback on the degree of goal attainment is an evaluation process which introduces possible pitfalls.[33] Once the "rules of the game" have been laid down, the players can be expected to alter their behavior so

---

[30]For a brief discussion of organizational design problems, see Herbert A. Simon, *The New Science of Management Decision* (New York: Harper Bros., 1960), pp. 12–13.

[31]See Cyert and MacCrimmon (n. 8 above), pp. 584–85.

[32]For a discussion of some common approaches to the measurement, feedback, and control aspects of strategic planning, see Kenneth R. Andrews, *The Concept of Corporate Strategy* (Homewood, Ill.: Richard Irwin, Inc., 1971), chap. 7.

[33]A discussion of some pitfalls that may arise in the measurement and feedback system associated with long-range planning is provided in E. Kirby Warren, *Long-Range Planning: The Executive Viewpoint* (Englewood Cliffs, N.J.: Prentice-Hall, Inc., 1966), chap. 5.

as to "look good" according to the "scorecard" which is kept on them. Therefore, it is essential that the summary evaluative measures conform as closely as possible to the important corporate goals. It also is important that the detailed measures used for ex ante decision analyses are exactly the same as (or at least consistent with) the corresponding measures for ex post performance evaluation. Otherwise, one would expect serious biases to be introduced into strategic decision making and implementation in order to make the performance evaluations look good, often at the expense of the desired corporate objectives.

Dangers inherent in the measurement and feedback process are intensified when attention is focused solely on one type of summary figure, for example, ROI (return on investment), defined as the income after taxes allocated to a profit center divided by the total funds (or investment) utilized by that profit center. Most strategic expenditures are of such a nature that they produce net cash outflows in their early years, accompanied (hopefully) by net cash inflows in later years. If the short-term return on investment measure is in jeopardy at a particular profit center for a given year, it would appear easy for the manager of that profit center to eliminate or reduce strategic expenditures this year, in order to have a better short-run performance evaluation. The emphasis on short-run performance is aggravated in organizations where the profit-center manager can expect to hold that particular organizational role for only a few years.

By having many dimensions of performance on which measurements are made and feedback provided, it is less easy for executives to find ways of arbitrarily "winning the game" at the expense of the long-run corporate objectives. In particular, if the various actions required to implement the profit center's strategic program are clearly spelled out (manpower requirements, research and development projects, physical investments, and so forth), then the profit center manager should be required to explain deviations from the various actions specified in the strategic plan.

X. SUMMARY

In this paper we have outlined the nine major steps which comprise the strategic planning process. Our discussion of strategy formulation, implementation, and monitoring is primarily intended as a normative, rather than as a descriptive, presentation. We would expect that the actual process in a few firms which have concentrated on strategic planning would be generally similar to the framework that we have sketched. We have not, however, made any conscious attempt to describe the manner in which this process is conducted in any particular firm. Unfortunately, we do not believe that most firms approach strategic planning in the serious, logical manner that we have advocated. Thus, this present paper must be regarded as being normative in nature, rather than an empirical description of the strategic planning process in real organizations.

The nine major steps into which we have divided the strategic planning process can be usefully grouped into three phases: formulation, implementation, and monitoring of strategy. Strategic planning should be viewed as being a repetitive, cyclic process. Any firm should repeat this entire process periodically, for example, annually.

The first seven steps together constitute the formulation phase. A prerequisite to any serious attempt to undertake strategic planning is the specification of the overall goals of the organization. This is normally the responsibility of the coalition comprising the top management of the firm. Although initially the goals are stated in qualitative terms, it is ultimately necessary to formulate goals in quantitative terms, for example, as a sequence of target values over several time periods. Before quantitative targets can be meaningfully assigned to the goals, however, it is necessary to analyze relevant portions of the environment in order to determine the type of performance that may generally be feasible. For a business firm, one of the most significant aspects of the environment is the general condition of the economy. Aggregate economic predictions must also be transformed into more specific predictions concerning the various industries and markets in which the firm operates. After specific quantitative goals have been established at the corporate level, it is then critical for the various operating units independently to establish their own strategic plans. A corporate-wide aggregation of the plans produced by each operating unit then provides a prediction of the total corporate performance that would result if no further changes in direction were provided by central management. This implied corporate performance is then compared to the quantitative corporate goals to indicate what gaps there may be in predicted goal achievement. When there are significant positive gaps, that is, when aspirations exceed expected performance, strategic search is initiated both at the corporate level and in various operating units. The objective of strategic search is to discover possible new strategic actions that will improve the performance of the firm beyond that implied by the aggregation of the previously prepared microplans. The senior executives in the firm are then responsible for selecting a particular portfolio of strategic actions from the set of possible strategic actions uncovered in the strategic search process. This portfolio constitutes the new strategic plan for the corporation, thus ending the strategy formulation phase.

Implementation of the strategic plan constitutes the second major phase of the strategy process. The basic problem of implementation is to put the strategic plan into effective action. One of the critical steps in implementing the strategy is to decompose the broadly stated plan into a time-phased sequence of specific action programs. This basically is a specification of the various types of resources that will be required at particular dates in order to achieve the planned strategy. Another critical aspect of the implementation process involves considering possible changes in the organizational structure of the firm if these will increase the likelihood of achieving the plan.

The final phase in the strategy process involves monitoring the extent to which the plan has been effectively implemented and remains appropriate. This requires that various relevant aspects of performance be measured and compared with corresponding aspects of the plan. The behavioral effects of any measurement, feedback, and control system need to be considered to avoid inducing types of motivation that lead to undesirable forms of behavior.

It is our view that the framework we have suggested for the strategic planning process can lead to formulation of serious research efforts that will develop techniques for improving the effectiveness of strategic planning. Such research efforts can be expected to proceed in at least two different directions. On the one hand, some aspects of the strategic planning process can be formulated in rigorous quantitative terms, and the power of management-science techniques and computer systems can be brought to bear to help improve those aspects of the process where the relevant issues can be sharply and definitively stated. On the other hand, some other aspects of strategic planning, which typically have been viewed in qualitative terms and approached solely on the basis of judgment, wisdom, and experience, can be subjected to a more rigorous scientific analysis by the use of the behavioral sciences. We are not maintaining that strategic planning will ever be reduced to a fully automated process in which executive judgment is unnecessary. We do believe, however, that further research efforts will put into clearer focus those areas where executive judgments are essential, thus enabling executives to perform better those tasks in which they have a comparative advantage. This will be possible only when other aspects of the strategic planning process (the ones in which quantitative models, computer-based information systems, and behavioral science concepts possess some comparative advantage) are more rigorously analyzed and understood. The end result will be an improved process of strategic planning, in which the judgment, wisdom, and experience of executives are combined with the judicious use of quantitative and scientific concepts in a manner which effectively exploits the comparative advantages of each component and participant in the process.

Even without waiting for further research efforts to be successfully completed, however, most firms can greatly improve the effectiveness of their strategic planning process by adopting the framework that we have outlined in this paper. Such a framework does not necessarily involve the use of sophisticated quantitative models and computer techniques. Rather, it requires only that the executives in a business firm devote some serious efforts to the strategic planning process and recognize the critical problems inherent in it. Most executives are fully capable of participating effectively in this process if they only take the time to do so. Preoccupation with short-term operating problems unfortunately reduces the attention that most executives pay to strategic planning. It is clear, however, that for the well-being of particular firms as well as our entire economic system, major attention must be paid to produce more effective strategic planning systems in most American corporations. It is only by having effective strategic planning processes that the American economy will have the ability to provide the innovations and adaptations which are necessary to produce an efficient allocation of economic resources in the dynamic society in which we now live.

4 The Myth Inherent in Responsibility Center Management

Robert Granford Wright

The concept of responsibility center management may be merely a collective wish by managers to affix accountability for results. The organizational arrangement conveniently fulfills a superior's need to hold subordinates accountable, but may fail to fulfill the more pervasive needs of the

Robert Granford Wright, "The Myth Inherent in Responsibility Center Management," pp. 49–58, *MSU Business Topics,* Spring 1972. Reprinted by permission of the publisher, Division of Research, Graduate School of Business Administration, Michigan State University.

overall enterprise for integration and control.

Superiors generally believe that they give subordinates sufficient authority to make decisions and to take action, but subordinates also commonly believe that they have insufficient authority to really run their operations. When the views are brought together, they seem to be contradictory. Divergent viewpoints lead in turn to inconsistencies between expectations and results, even in enterprises that generously delegate authority to responsibility centers. Herein lies a dilemma faced by today's managers.

In earlier, less restive times, firms were organized in a way intended to establish durable, economically efficient means of production. Specialization was narrowly defined, channels for the downward flow of communications and authority were carefully drawn, spans of management were set to insure conformity and control, top managers held the authority to tie together functionally specialized parts of the enterprise, and the classical pyramidal structure emerged. It served well as man's response to production oriented, efficiency centered needs in an environment that was changing at a comfortable pace.

Now, with accelerated change, firms must be organized to adapt to the vagaries of dynamic external forces, yet designed to assure accountability for economic efficiency in the development, production, marketing, and distribution of products and services. In response, managers look to organizational arrangements that provide the means for the integration of related specialized activities into self-sufficient components; channels of communications; upward and lateral, as well as downward, authority flows to permit decentralized action and control; and broader spans of management to encompass interrelated functions. The present structure with decentralized cost centers, or profit centers, was formed. Responsibility centers were designed to decentralize authority so that semi-independent decisions could be made and semi-autonomous actions could be taken, and to affix accountability for results.

The Problem

Today many companies have moderated their earlier emphasis on functional departments; total operating departments of manageable size have come into vogue. Problems of cooperation had largely reduced the relative benefits from efficiencies gained from further functional specialization. Problems of adaptability by precariously tall, large, functionalized firms suggested the need for flatter structures of smaller, largely self-contained operating units. And problems of centralized direction of far-flung, often diversified, operations became less practical in an era of rapid change.

But perhaps most important, the idea of decentralized centers of responsibility promised to fulfill a collective wish by managers: the desire to affix accountability for results *absolutely* at particular positions throughout the enterprise. The apparent panacea was responsibility center management, which made specific individual managers accountable for attaining subdivided corporate goals.

Benefits from this form of decentralized operation were quickly recognized—smaller operating units ease communications and coordination. They are more easily managed because they are less diverse and less complex than large, highly centralized companies. They can react and adapt more quickly to changing conditions than multitiered and often unwieldy functional structures. Managers of decentralized units can give appropriate attention to problems that might appear relatively unimportant at the headquarters level. The managers of semi-independent units can see the results of their efforts, which can give a stimulating boost to morale. Control becomes effective because accountability is clear-cut. If results are poor, the cause is pinpointed to the manager, who must take corrective action. If results are good, the cause is also isolated so that the manager can be rewarded. And finally, decentralized and multifunctional units provide a rich training ground for general administrative experience.

It was perhaps inevitable that responsibility center management would become the key concept in the reorganization of many large concerns. General Motors Corporation led the way, followed by such firms as the General Electric Company, Johnson & Johnson, and General Telephone & Electronics. Nonprofit organizations (governments, churches, charities, and so forth) followed the leaders by using the concept, at least in modified form.

Enthusiasm for the concept of responsibility centers diminishes if it appears that accountability is delegated but *comparable* authority is not. This is the major problem in the management of responsibility centers, and it has led today's managers into ambiguous reactions to decentralization.

In Practice

To make a responsibility center work, a manager must have the ability *and authority* to take the initiative on matters that affect the success of his unit. Instead of relying upon someone at the home office or an intermediate superior to keep him out of trouble, he must be able to make all decisions concerning his department and use the resources of his unit to get results. This type of responsibility is made possible only through acceptance of several crucially important assumptions. First, the manager must be kept aware of the direct and in-

direct impact of his actions on other units and the overall firm. Second, he must be given "hands-off" treatment by top management after the broad guidelines have been set. And third, he must be given authority to make decisions and to take action proportionate to the degree of his responsibility.

But often these conditions are difficult, if not impossible, to fulfill. The manager of a decentralized unit is usually conditioned by training and experience to concentrate on his specific unit; he loses the overall view of the business as an integrated whole. It is therefore probably unreasonable to expect him to be fully aware of the impact of his actions. Furthermore, his superior is uncomfortable under a hands-off policy; after all, most top managers attained their positions through aggressive, positive, decisive action. And it worked for them. Hence it is understandably disconcerting for them now to adopt a laissez-faire attitude—one in which teaching, rather than telling; patience, rather than impatience; passive, rather than active behavioral patterns emerge. And finally, under decentralized operating conditions, the attempt to delegate coequal shares of authority and responsibility, when ultimately the superior is held accountable for the actions and results of responsibility centers, produces anxieties.

The purpose here is to illustrate that responsibility centers clearly are not responsible to the degree upper management had expected and hoped they would be when they were established. Further, it will be argued that it is unreasonable to hold even self-sufficient, semiautonomous units fully accountable for results. The belief in the myth of full accountability appears to stem from a basic misunderstanding about the use of authority and responsibility, coupled with an apparent disregard for the needs of the overall enterprise.

THE BASIC FALLACY

The straightforward logic behind the demand by leaders for authority commensurate with responsibility led authorities to accept the notion that authority and responsibility *should be* coequal. The idea seems so irrefutable that managers commonly assume that authority and responsibility *will be* and *are* coequal. The assumption is responsive to the needs of upper managers; it affixes definite points of accountability, assures discretionary decision making and action, and stops buckpassing.

The organization, however, also has needs, needs for integration, cohesiveness, continuity, and control. Devices to fulfill these requirements, albeit mandatory for the good of the overall enterprise, are not necessarily compatible with arrangements designed to satisfy managers. Managers would opt for coequal authority and responsibility, but organizational realities call for superior-subordinate relationships in which authority is clearly less than responsibility. The needs of managers must bow to the greater needs of the organization for unity. Disproportionate authority-responsibility relationships result. The coequality premise is open to serious question—and it is the Achilles' heel of responsibility center management.

Shrinking Authority Concept

It is well known that institutional authority is delegated downward in diminishing amounts required to accomplish activities of narrowing scope and lessening importance to enterprise goals. The process creates the so-called tapering concept of authority. I propose, however, that there is also a shrinking of *authority related to responsibility* as delegation flows from top management to first-level supervisors. The phenomenon might be termed the *shrinking authority concept;* authority diminishes at an increasing rate compared to responsibility as it is delegated downward to subordinate levels of management.

At the level of the board of directors, for example, assume that authority and responsibility are effectively equal. The board sets goals, policies, and strategies. Within those limits, the chief executive is charged with the responsibility to run the firm. And the first step in eroding authority has been taken. The president then redefines the mission and the activities required for its attainment. He in turn charges his immediate subordinates with their particular area of responsibility. But at this second step additional authority is necessarily withheld to coordinate the now more specialized activities and fragmented subgoals, which are all vying for the resources of the company. At the third step in the delegative process specialization proliferates; more finely drawn guidelines are needed; budgets limit resources; procedures limit discretionary action; schedules limit random timing; and controls grow more pronounced and stringent to assure integration and coordination of major divisions of activities. Following the process to its ultimate end, the first-level supervisor's authority *over his section* is circumscribed by limits on resources, fixed production processes, preset technology, standards, procedures, and routines. These constraints on his authority are imposed by superior authorities.

Figure 1 presents the range of constraints that effectively usurp from lower managers the authority to make discretionary decisions and to act independently. It is clear that each level of authority from top to bottom is increasingly bound by predetermined sets of regulations. Withholding authority not only has a chain reaction sequence, but also has a snowballing effect that produces the shrinking authority concept.

Viewed in another way, Figure 2 illustrates the effect of increasing con-

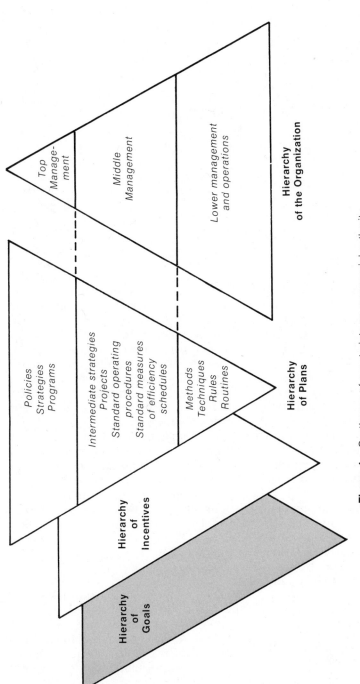

Figure 1. Continuum of constraints on managerial authority.

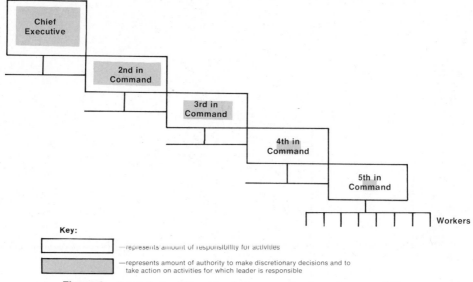

Figure 2. Estimated relationships between authority and responsibility.

straints on authority as they relate to responsibility downward over a chain of management. Although the chart only estimates the relative impact of withheld authority, it depicts the basic concept of shrinking authority as it relates to responsibility. Scopes of responsibility are functionally related to groupings of interrelated activities. Scopes of authority, however, are not regulated by activities for which a line manager is responsible. Authority is withheld by preset limits on resources, procedures for role behavior, and programs for control.

The actions of lower management *are* constrained by regulations imposed from above, and these constraints impinge more stringently as they emanate downward from the top through the chain of management.[1]

As a result, lower managers feel the pressures for performance but sense the futility brought about by the lack of means to control results. They are charged with full responsibility for the activities of their units, but because they do not have sufficient authority, they must gain support from their immediate superiors to fulfill their responsibilities.

It becomes evident that a person in a first- or second-level position without such support would join the chorus of lower management complaints: "Around here, we have abundant responsibility, but we have insufficient authority to do the job as it should be done."

Implicit Recognition

Even companies that staunchly support and devoutly practice management by responsibility center recognize that no manager over any unit within a firm can be granted coequal authority and responsibility. To do so would provide the means for *complete* autonomy of subordinate units. Yet failure to understand this fact causes managers in all types of enterprises to chafe under what appear to be unreasonable constraints on their free-

[1]The momentum generated by these types of constraints is somewhat related to the situation of providing special reports to top management, as seen from the viewpoint of a first-level supervisor. A chief executive requests a report in two weeks. His subordinate, allowing a margin for review, error, and so forth, requests the data in ten days. His subordinate cuts the follow-up to one week. The deadline is tightened as the request moves downward until it is received by the first-level superior—who must provide the information—and it was effectively needed yesterday.

dom to operate. This reality of organizational life is clear. No subdivision of any enterprise can be given so much authority that its activities cannot be tied into the overall goals of the firm by upper management.

Therefore, implicit recognition *is* given to the inequality of authority and responsibility. When responsibility centers are discussed, high-ranking managers refer to them as being "semiautonomous" and "reasonably self-sufficient"; that is, they imply that the units are dependent upon higher authority for support, and that authority for results is withheld. The qualifying terms *semi* and *reasonably* suggest the degree of authority missing from decentralized units. Yet, when results are not achieved, the manager of the wayward unit is held accountable as if he had the full authority to produce.

Needs of Managers and Organizations

It is clear that the inequality between authority and responsibility is not an insidious plot by superiors to impose unreasonable demands on subordinate managers. Instead, the condition stems from a clash between opposing needs—needs of managers and needs of organizations.

The manager needs to know that subordinate managers of units under his direction will perform; to do so, he must first isolate each subordinate's area of responsibility. He must then ensure that in these areas each subordinate has adequate authority to make fast, on-the-spot decisions to cope with changing local conditions. He must provide sufficient authority so that initiative can transfer itself into positive action. When done, the manager feels that he must then hold the lower managers accountable for the success of the semiautonomous units because he has given them the means to perform.

But the overall enterprise also has functional needs that must be satisfied

if it is to be efficient and effective. Authority must be withheld in increasing degrees at each descending level to assure that each unit throughout the company is somewhat dependent on the next higher level of authority. Viewed in reverse, each ascending level is, of course, also partially dependent on the immediate lower levels.

The process of interdependence among essential organizational units fuses activities to bring about unification and integration. Changes in units can be adapted to by other units, resources can be allotted proportionate to subunit goals, and schedules can be designed to integrate otherwise disintegrated activities. In sum, an overlapping of authority provides certain of the means to fulfill enterprise needs for cohesiveness, viability, and balance.

The paradox brought on by these opposing needs is apparent—accountability is achieved through autonomy, integration through dependence. Its resolution, as with most paradoxes, is compromise. A manager gives semiautonomy to affix partial accountability. He holds subordinates semidependent to attain integrated effort. But in so doing, he *must* recognize that lower managers are *not* totally responsible for the results of their respective units because they lack the authority to totally manage their units to attain results. The paradox is at the root of the myth that a manager of a responsibility center is somehow fully responsible for the performance of his unit.

New Conceptual Basis

A brief review of the operating conditions that affect the establishment of responsibility centers will provide the basis for considering how these elements influence the functioning of decentralized centers of activity. It will then be possible to present a new conceptual foundation for forming and managing responsibility centers.

Generally speaking, responsibility centers are established under the following essential conditions:

Decentralized decisions and actions are required to obtain results. Authority is delegated to provide a higher degree of viability and to make certain that sufficient attention is given to local problems.

Accountability for clearly stated goals is required. It is placed on the managers of each decentralized unit.

The manager in charge of a subordinate who manages a responsibility center holds him fully responsible for his unit's performance.

But authority to decide and act must be substantially withheld from the responsibility center manager so that the activities within his unit are tied in with related units and the overall operation. (As has been stated, activities are commonly regulated by such preset devices as budgets, manpower schedules, goals, procedures, physical layouts, and technologies.)

The manager of a responsibility center is aware of the full measure of his responsibility. He also senses that part of the authority required to fulfill his responsibilities has been withheld by his boss. He will, of course, attempt to manage his unit independently because he is fully charged with the responsibility, even though the means to produce are jointly shared with his superior. His boss, however, may believe that the manager actually has coequal authority and responsibility. If this view is held, the superior can, when things go wrong, divorce himself from the actions of this errant subordinate and eliminate himself as a factor in the cause of the problem. Here, in essence, is the dilemma brought on by the "mythical responsibility center."

A new, more realistic way of thinking is needed as a basis for forming and managing responsibility centers; one in which the needs of the superior over the responsibility center manager, the needs of the company, *and*

also the needs of the responsibility center manager are considered.

Since some degree of authority needed to get the job done must be withheld by the boss of the manager of a responsibility center, full responsibility for the unit's performance is jointly shared by the boss and the responsibility center manager. Hence, the valid responsibility center includes the unit of activity, its leader, plus the leader's immediate superior.

Figure 3 shows the influence of this arrangement. The overlapping brought on by mutual dependency between superior and subordinate causes a fusion of responsibility centers with the next higher level, and consequently, the overall firm. Control, coordination, and continuity can thereby be brought about. Enterprise needs for integrated effort toward common goals are fulfilled. By frankly and explicitly admitting the codependence of the manager of a responsibility center with his boss, final accountability for a unit's performance rests with the superior of the manager of the decentralized unit. Affixing accountability at this level is logical because only through the use of this manager's authority can the subordinate leader over the responsibility center obtain desired results.[2] Managerial needs to hold subordinates accountable for performance are thereby fulfilled—but in such a way that the nature of the interdependence between superiors and subordinates is outwardly recognized.

_____

[2]If authority is withheld by higher-level managers, or their staff personnel, accountability will be diffused further. For example, if line managers are ostensibly held responsible for certain activities, yet restrictions are imposed by superiors on the use of resources and compliance to procedures, accountability for results will, of course, be shared by line managers and the sources of superior influence on their operations. Holding any specific line manager totally responsible becomes highly tenuous, if not unreasonable.

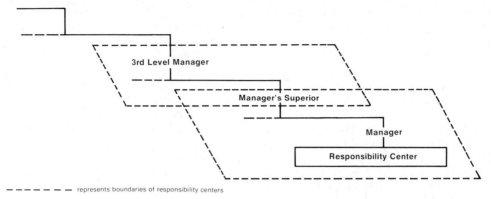

- - - - - - represents boundaries of responsibility centers

Figure 3. Actual responsibility centers.

Here then is the nature of the true responsibility center. It can provide the structure that will make the firm viable, efficient, and cohesive. In addition, the reconceived arrangement modifies thinking about the scope of responsibility, yet fulfills the widely held need among managers to affix accountability at various positions. But by acknowledging the mutuality of relationships among line managers, the tactical behavior between superiors and subordinates may change substantially as a consequence of a newly found awareness that "we are indeed in this thing together," and perhaps more important, "we sink or swim together."

CHANGES IN BEHAVIOR

Certain changes in behavior that might be reasonably expected as a reaction to reconceiving a responsibility center as a component include (1) a unit of activity, (2) its leader, and (3) the leader's immediate superior. Primary concern will be given to behavioral changes between the responsibility center manager and his boss. Changes in behavior would touch nearly every important aspect of managerial activities. The following areas are of particular importance: (1) setting objectives (as well as other parts of planning and organizing); (2) de-

cision making; (3) delegation; (4) controlling; (5) accountability; and (6) evaluating leadership performance.

Changes in managerial behavior will emerge because of newly found roles, role expectations, and role interrelations in which a cooperative tone sets the stage for human interaction. Both boss and subordinate will frankly recognize that an inseparable codependence exists that requires a new spirit of cooperation. This interrelatedness of contiguous authority levels is one of the most crucial elements to bind an enterprise into a cohesive, unified, goal-seeking whole.

Setting Objectives

The illusion that this thing or that lies in a subordinate's area and that therefore the boss must hold him totally responsible will fade into obscurity. The myth will lack support, not because it is not desired by the boss, but rather because he now knows that the authority required to get the job done is jointly shared.

Similarly, other myths have fallen into disrepute. Ptolemy's hypothesis that the earth is stationary with celestial objects revolving around it was a comforting idea that had gained universal support for 1,400 years. Though rejecting the notion in favor of the Copernican system removed a certain calm assurance (one which was zealously defended by Christian scholars), the new way of thinking later made clear the untenable complication of the Ptolemaic system and led to a more adequate explanation of astronomy. Today's myths, like all misconceptions, fall when more suitable explanations of beliefs are discovered.

Codependent authority levels lead to a need for cooperative pursuits. The boss and the subordinate leader directly over a unit together would develop goals for the unit, and plan and organize the means to reach the goals. The overall analysis required for such joint planning and organizing is particularly important since aspects of work—quantity, quality, time use, and costs—are mutually dependent and in balance. Thus if resources are fixed, when goals are changed or added, these aspects of work will be thrown into imbalance. Some elements of activity will gain emphasis to the deemphasis of others, and a new point of balanced effort must be reached. Since responsibility for the conduct of all aspects of work is jointly shared, both boss and subordinate must pool their authority to decide what balance of activities is most appropriate. As a result, the worn approach that holds the subordinate leader totally accountable for attaining goals, and superiors responsible for setting them, will diminish and (it is to be hoped) disappear.

Decision Making

Recognition of codependent authority levels encourages contributions by subordinate leaders to the decision-making process. Participative decision making will increase, not only for its apparent strengths that engender involvement if not commitment, or for its ability to infuse the process with new conceptual and technical insights, but also because the authority to decide and to act *is* jointly shared by boss and subordinate.

A certain degree of authority has been divested by the boss to be invested in a subordinate in charge of some segment of activities. This authority is used to make decisions and to take action on the operating activities of the subordinate's unit. It seems unreasonable that if dealing with more *intensive* decisions this authority would then be withdrawn by the next higher authority; rather, it would be more reasonable to assume that since the success of carrying out the decision lies in large measure with the subordinate leader, he *must* be most intimately involved.

Delegation

Recognition of the mutual dependence of authority levels would foster delegation in varying degrees based upon the particular merits and frailties of each subordinate leader. That is, the boss would give broad latitude for discretionary decisions and actions to each subordinate in his particular areas of competence, but would withhold authority from a subordinate who lacked competency in a given area. This behavior is consistent with the premise of mutual involvement.

When authority had to be withheld, the boss would strive to strengthen the subordinate in the weak area; first, so that the subordinate could carry his full measure of responsibility, and second, because if the subordinate is unable to handle some necessary activity, that work reverts to the boss.

Controlling

When responsibility centers are thought of as including only a unit of activity and the manager over that unit, standards for performance are set largely by the unit manager. Then, feedback relating actual performance to standards flows to him so that appropriate action can be taken on items where discrepancies exist. When responsibility centers are reconceived to include the superior over the unit manager, standards are jointly set so that they fit in with the overall endeavor. Comparative reports on standards and actual performance would thus flow to both the unit manager and his boss. Remedial action would be jointly agreed to by superior and subordinate managers. This gives the superior the opportunity to reallocate resources if this tack is appropriate, and a chance to avoid corrective measures that mitigate a problem in one area of activity but that create imbalance, if not neglect, elsewhere with related activities. Action to reward outstanding achievement also should be jointly agreed to by a unit manager and superior.

The control system would interlock superior and subordinate managers in encouraging joint programs to arrest undesired performance and to applaud desirable results. The resulting interaction is mandatory because the action needed to bring on control will often require the authority held in reserve by the superior manager. In addition, he alone possesses the broader organizational perspective required to decide if a given reaction for control is indeed appropriate.

Accountability

The ultimate accountability for a responsibility center would shift from the manager immediately in charge of the unit up to his boss. This arrangement is consistent with the concept of diminishing authority in that only at this next higher level is authority potentially equal to responsibility.

Thus, when difficulties develop in a given responsibility center, top management must look to the manager of the center and to his boss for positive action to correct the problem. Accountability is shared, authority is shared, and indeed, they become effectively a "team." When superior achievement results, top management also must recognize that sound management stems from effective relationships between a line manager, his subordinates, *and* his boss. Again, accountability is shared, authority is shared, and in this instance, success is shared.

Evaluating Leadership Performance

Today a leader is commonly judged on his individual ability to get results. Such an approach to evaluation recognizably supports the traditional notion of the self-made man, the Horatio Alger dream, and the entrepreneurial idea. Yet it can also spawn wasteful competition, harmful infighting, and intolerable singleness of purpose among managers. A business, after all, is an integrated system of units of activities. Managers over these units are rarely, if ever, privileged to take free-wheeling, or unconstrained, action. They are dependent upon subordinates, peers, and especially superiors to get results.

Therefore, a boss in charge of managers of responsibility centers may come to be judged not solely on the individual achievements of his units, but also on the processes through which he reached these achievements. It is this demonstration of effective managerial processes that get results that are truly a relevant measure of the boss's effectiveness. Otherwise, the boss may be rated in some way simply because happenstance has placed strong or weak subordinate leaders under him. By evaluating how results were attained, superiors get a better feel for a boss's potential value, gain insights into management processes being applied that may work in other units, and acquire an awareness of the degree to which a boss is developing his people.

Knowing the true nature of responsibility centers, leadership techniques must be tailored to be consistent with a setting in which the authority necessary to get results is jointly shared. Thus a manager would be evaluated on his ability to get results through such procedures as joint goal setting, participative decision making, mutually designed programs for employee development, and jointly initiated evaluations of employee performance. These leadership techniques are consistent with the real setting wherein mutually shared responsibility and authority require cooperative pursuits among managers on contiguous levels.

The factors necessary to encourage constructive competition are not throttled by these cooperative processes; only the ambiguous and thus wasteful competition is removed, and stronger human interaction and involvement are constructed. Through these strengthened relationships the most valuable of business assets, human resources, can be developed to their fullest potential.

CONCLUSION

In summary, there is a single theme that extends from the basic thesis developed. The manager of men approaches his task in a way that is consistent with his assumptions about the way organizations work and, thus, the way a manager must operate. If he perceives the organization as one in which units are individuated to operate autonomously, he assumes that line managers possess a coequality of responsibility and authority to get results. In turn, the boss will assert his role and role relationships with subordinates in a way that supports these basic notions.

A behavior pattern would emerge, for example, in which a superior readily would point to the wayward subordinate when things go wrong, and at the same time, remove himself from blame as a factor causing the problem. To be consistent in his behavior, the boss would necessarily disqualify himself from credit when things go right. Yet this behavior is unrealistic. The superior is obviously intimately involved in the success or failure of subordinate leaders.

In reconceiving the basic nature of an organization, a basic misunderstanding can be removed about the way responsibility and authority really work. Assume that an upper manager believes that the organization is designed to provide lower managers of subordinate units with a certain autonomy, but also a degree of dependence; that semiautonomous units are required to provide accountability, yet integration of effort. He rejects the idea of coequality of authority and responsibility among his subordinate leaders in favor of the concept of authority shared between boss and subordinate. As a result, he becomes aware that a manager of a responsibility center, or profit center, is not totally responsible for results in his unit. The boss had to withhold a certain degree of authority; therefore, boss and subordinate are mutually accountable.

A new pattern of behavior would develop because of this newly found awareness that codependence is the true name of the game. Knowing this, superiors would behave in a way that is more consonant with organizational realities. Mutual dependence between superiors and subordinates would lay the foundation for the emergence of supportive management processes. Processes would be designed to assure joint goal setting, participative decision making, mutually charted programs for subordinate evaluations and development, and other leadership techniques internally consistent with a manager's new definition of the situation.

Thus the manager of a responsibility center and his superior are empowered to manage more effectively because they are managing more appropriately in light of valid organizational relationships. Instead of merely *implicit* recognition that a responsibility center is "semiautonomous" or "reasonably self-sufficient," mutual dependency between superior and subordinate is accorded the *explicit* recognition it rightly deserves.

5 Some Behavioral Implications of Budgeting Systems

William Daugherty and Donald Harvey

The motivational impact of budgeting has often been neglected or ignored, as Robert Townsend has suggested:

Budgets must not be prepared on high and cast as pearls before swine. They must be prepared by the operating divisions. Since a division must believe in the budget as its own plan for operations, management cannot juggle figures just because it likes to. Any changes must be sold to the division or the whole process is a sham.[1]

There has been a tendency to emphasize the negative or punishment aspects of budgets, which has tended to reinforce the use of budgetary systems as pressure devices. A recent survey by the authors suggests that budget systems may actually operate as a negative motivational force in many organizations.

The results of the survey suggest that the budgeting process may involve unintended consequences that stifle change and innovation, restrict managerial initiative, induce inappropriate pressures, and tend to reinforce management leadership by the rule book. All of these behavioral consequences tend to have dysfunctional results in terms of overall organizational objectives.

Clearly, these findings lead to an increasing realization of the pervasiveness and significance of the human component and the importance of recognizing the behavioral implications that are inherent in planning and control systems. Therefore, it is the purpose of this article to examine briefly the multiplicity of objectives and models within the budgeting process, to identify some behavioral consequences of planning and control systems, and to suggest some directions for developing more effective systems.

THE MULTIPLICITY OF BUDGET OBJECTIVES AND MODELS

Budgets are now used extensively as an essential element in organiza-

---

[1] R. Townsend, *Up the Organization* (New York: Knopf, 1970).

This article originally appeared in *Arizona Business*, July 1973, pp. 3–7, and is reprinted with permission.

tional planning and control systems by almost all major organizations. Budgeting is the process of taking management's plans and expressing these plans in dollars and cents, allocating or factoring total system resources into a set of subsystem plans, and providing a common language for communicating a description of planned operations and activities for a given period of time.

Generally, with regard to initiation of budget objectives, budget systems fall into one of two general categories or some combination thereof: "top down" where the targets and goals are determined by top management and sent down to lower departmental levels, or "bottom up" where departmental goals and objectives are defined at subordinate levels and integrated with other departmental plans at higher levels. Many organizations combine the two approaches. This involves the determination of guidelines at the higher level of management and actual budget preparation by lower level units.

The survey conducted by the authors revealed a multiplicity of budget functions and budget models used in major organizations. Among the different functions of the budget systems were the following:

1. *Promotion of Efficiency.* In this aspect, the budget is seen as a tool to make operations more efficient; an important measure of managerial performance is the ability of a manager to conform to the budget. An entire operating division's efficiency is usually measured in terms of its performance in relation to planned performance as set out in the division budget.

2. *Control.* The budget is often mentioned as a measurement tool, which management uses in the control of cost by comparing actual costs to budgeted targets and by investigating significant variances.

3. *Planning, Information, and Feedback.* The budgeting system is used to provide information and feedback to management at many organizational levels as an aid to the decision-making process. In this sense, the budget is used to determine where and why the organization is spending time, resources, and dollars.

4. *Pressure-exertion.* Budgets are often used as an instrument for putting pressure on operating supervisors to increase productivity and efficiency. In this sense, the budget is often used as a threat or coercive force.

5. *Motivation.* Budgets are used to present a goal or a challenge for operating units; that is, something to shoot for or a goal to achieve.

From previous studies, in line with this multiplicity of functions, at least three different models of the budgeting process may be derived:

A. *Pressure-oriented Budget Model.* Evidence from a number of studies[2] indicates that most individuals and groups perform more effectively under certain degrees and types of pressure, but on the other hand, that inordinate or unrealistic pressures tend to result in performance deterioration. DeCoster and Fertakis[3] reported research on the relationship between budgetary pressures and leader behavior. They found a positive relationship between budget-induced pressure and supervisory behavior in both directive and considerate leadership styles.

B. *Aspiration Level Model.* The aspiration level is that level of future performance in a familiar task that an individual, knowing his level of performance in that task, explicitly undertakes to reach. Andrew Stedry[4] conducted research into the motivational aspects of budgeting and re-

[2] See, for example, R. Kahn and D. Wolfe, et al., *Organizational Stress* (New York: Wiley, 1964).

[3] D. DeCoster and T. Fertakis, "Budget-Induced Pressure and Its Relationship To Supervisory Behavior," *Journal of Accounting Research,* Autumn, 1968.

[4] A. Stedry, *Budget Control and Cost Behavior* (Englewood Cliffs: Prentice-Hall, 1960).

ported that performance is affected by the type of budget chosen, the conditions of administration, and the way in which aspiration levels of a task are determined. Since the aspiration level represents the manager's internal goal, then a budget goal that significantly varies from this level will tend to have adverse consequences upon managerial behavior.

C. *Participative Model.* A frequently suggested solution to motivational problems is that of active participation in budget preparation. Participation has been defined as "the process of joint decision making by two or more parties in which the decisions have future effects on those making them."[5] The use of participation involves sophistication on the part of the supervisor and an increased inner security in his ability to delegate portions of his own decision-making powers. Participation also usually requires increased time commitments. Consequently, many firms have substituted "pseudo-participation"; that is, the appearance of participation but without giving up decision-making powers to subordinate members or units.

Chris Argyris[6] conducted a study examining the human relation problems of budgets, and found that finance people often tended to view their function as primarily *controlling* and *criticizing* the performance of operating managers. His finding emphasized the need for participation of all key organizational members in establishing budgetary parameters. Becker and Green[7] arrived at similar conclusions; that is, a successful participative budget induces proper motivation and acceptance of specific goals and pro-

vides information that makes it possible to associate reward and punishment with performance.

In comparing these models, it may be noted that the evidence suggests that budgets do have a significant influence on behavior and motivational levels. Although the models differ in their basic assumptions about the motivational consequences, the participative systems appear to be more successful in reinforcing positive motivation. Consequently, this multiplicity of functions and objectives in models of budgeting systems often leads to dysfunctional behavioral consequences as a result of the approach that is emphasized.

SOME DYSFUNCTIONAL BEHAVIORAL CONSEQUENCES

The preceding sections have pointed out some of the behavioral consequences of administering budgeting systems. Often for every pressure applied from above, subordinate levels devise countermeasures to offset the pressure. Consequently, budgets tend to lose their control, information, and motivational functions, and become one of the games managers play. These consequences include the following:

Padding the Budget or "Building in Fat." This tactic is often used where organizational management (or any other decision group) reacts to budget requests by "trimming the fat" out. Over a period of budget reviews, the operating groups learn to anticipate the amount of trimming necessary to satisfy the reviewing body. This will probably be a percentage, and is usually expressed in some ingroup slogan such as "Every budget has X percent of fat in it."

Therefore, in order to perform well against the budget goals, the manager builds X percent into his budget so that in effect he is building into his estimates an amount that he antici-

[5] S. Becker and D. Green, "Budgeting and Employee Behavior," *Journal of Business,* Oct., 1962.

[6] C. Argyris, *The Impact of Budgets Upon People* (New York: Controllership Foundation, 1952).

[7] Becker and Green, *loc. cit.*

pates will be cut out. Consequently, his expenditure level can be reduced and he will come out with what he really wanted in the first place. Another consequence is that the manager who submits a realistic budget (but who also suffers the percentage reduction) is forced to work under a handicap. The system then, tends to reward defensive budgets and to penalize realistic estimates.

Refill the Empty Tank or "Oil the Squeaking Wheel." Another tactic managers often utilize is the forecast based upon past use plus a growth factor. In this situation, future allocations are based upon past consumption, therefore, a wise manager strives for a deficit. For example, the allocation of fuel to military units is based upon the previous year's expense. If the unit is underrunning the allocation, usage levels are raised to use up the budget. It is not unusual to find a high increase in flight time in May and June at the end of the fiscal year. No budget negotiator wants to go in with an unused allocation for any item—advertising, manpower, supplies, travel costs, because the budgeted targets tend to decrease. This in effect is a Parkinsonian Law: *Expenditure rises to fill the amount allocated to it.*

Put Off Till Tomorrow, What Could Be Charged to Today. It is not unusual for budget managers to learn to manipulate the budget variables, and in a sense, defer the bad news. This is done by either manipulating the recording of sales between periods, or deferring cost items from period to period. The result, of course, is to distort the budget in a favorable direction. If done adroitly, this may be continued for years, and a real gamesman can gain a promotion on the basis of his fine performance, and then hand the whole mess to a new man. It will probably take the new manager six months to a year to find out why he is in such big trouble. Further, when he understands what has hap-

pened, he is motivated to continue the game to avoid an adverse effect on *his* performance.

Underground Operations or "Midnight Research Supply." This game is usually concerned with R & D Management. Here the game involves subsidizing one activity by hiding it or burying it in another, usually larger, more ambiguous budget section. This usually occurs when scientists feel they have a better knowledge of where R & D efforts should be expended than does top management. Therefore, they operate a subterranean research project on some other budget. For example, they might "sell" some engineering budget for a product that actually has already been designed, then apply it to their *pet* project. If it succeeds, it is approved, if it doesn't, no one outside is aware of the losses.

Counterbudget Systems or "Do Unto Others Before They Do Unto You." Another consequence of the budget game, as we have already suggested, is the use of evasive tactics requiring increased information gathering and control systems. This in turn tends to create the development of counterbudget groups. These are staff people who gather information for the operating level manager to support his budget demands. Consequently, he is able to go into budget negotiations armed with supporting data. Trend analysis, ratios, and percentages are generally assembled on flip charts to back up and "sell" his budget demands. Obviously such systems themselves introduce a significant cost factor into the budget and into the overhead costs.

Our preliminary survey suggests that these counter strategies often introduce added costs and cause dysfunctional reactions because budgets become too arbitrary, too rigid, and unrelated to the real world at the operating level. When this happens, participation by managers in the budgeting process may become a perfunctory ritual, devoid of operational significance.

IMPLICATIONS

There is evidence that the human component plays a significant and important part in the effectiveness of planning and control systems. Unwise use of budget systems or ignoring of behavioral implications can have dysfunctional consequences upon organizational effectiveness. It appears that these problems are often the unintended consequences of using the budget as a pressure device. Although the budgeting system appears to be an effective and efficient tool of management, when the underlying attitudes of managers and the effectiveness of budget systems are critically analyzed, it is often found that dysfunctional reactions result from the budgeting process because the human component has been ignored or neglected.

The proposed solution to this problem includes:

Active Participation in the Preparation of the Budget. Considerable evidence indicates that participation tends to provide better plans, increased understanding of goals, and especially, increased acceptance of and commitment to these goals throughout the organization.

An Improved Reporting Structure. An initial step in determining behavioral consequences involves an examination of the reporting structure to identify its weaknesses and shortcomings in providing for the needs of operating managers. This should include isolation of critical factors for both short-term results and for long-term growth and competitive strength. These critical factors may then be utilized in implementing management by objectives or participative budget programs. Each executive or manager must receive the feedback he needs to control his own performance parameters.

Increased Responsibility and Accountability for Realistic Objectives. Once an effective system of reporting and setting budget objectives is attained, management information systems should feed back information about actual performance results in relation to these objectives. The key words here are *realistic budget objectives.* Our survey data indicates that too often unrealistic budget targets are set. After a few months, this type of budget is no longer an effective motivator because it lacks any correspondence to individual aspiration levels or performance measures.

The Use of Positive Motivations That Appeal to Higher Level Needs of Organization Members. Behavioral science research indicates that the most important factor in motivating managers today is a sense of accomplishment in the achievement of challenging goals, and recognition for these achievements. Consequently, it seems reasonable to assume that the human factors in budgeting systems must be given as much consideration as is currently given to the financial and technical aspects.

Given the multiplicity of budget system functions and models, it appears that more research needs to be aimed at determining the relationship between these dimensions and the impact of budgets upon the behavior of organizational members. For example, more needs to be known about the relationship between planning groups and operating groups, the effects on future performance of success and failure to meet budget goals, and the consequences of pressure-oriented systems.

Modern managers cannot be expected to be experts in the psychology of human behavior. It is not unreasonable, however, to expect them to have an awareness of the behavioral implications of the budgeting process and to use the budget wisely in administering their organizations. Clearly, the behavioral consequences can result in increased success for managers who are aware of the human factor in budget systems.

The Quantitative School

The quantitative school is really a basic extension of scientific management. However, the tools and techniques employed by the modern manager are far more sophisticated than those used by Frederick Taylor and his associates.

In essence, the quantitative school is primarily interested in scientific decision making. As such, advocates of this school are particularly concerned with choosing the *best* alternative from among those available. In the last twenty years there has been a marked increase in the number of quantitative decision-making tools and techniques available to the manager for attaining this objective. For example, the computer and the development of mathematical models for solving problems related to areas such as resource allocation, economic order quantity and the balancing of waiting times and service have all proved very helpful.

As a result, the quantitative, or management science as it is sometimes called, school has emerged. To a large degree, individuals who subscribe to this school are greatly interested in applying the scientific method to decision making. It is also common to find them evaluating their decisions according to economic effectiveness criteria.

In this section, the topic of quantitative decision making as related to management will be examined. The articles have been carefully chosen to provide the reader with a basic understanding and appreciation of mathematical decision making without confusing him or her with the use of either esoteric terminology or complicated equations.

In the first article, Professor Ruch points out a fact that many managers already know—there is a need to understand mathematics as a language, but the manager does not have to be a mathematician to utilize decision science concepts. However, the manager must understand some of the more basic mathematical concepts so he can communicate with those helping him solve sophisticated mathematical problems, i.e., mathematicians, researchers, economists. In addition, Professor

Ruch points out that the manager must make certain that the solution applies to his or her problems. In the final analysis, the mathematical model is only useful to the manager if it helps him make the *right* decision.

In the second article, Professor Mali describes the use of decision trees to display events and risks. The decision tree reduces abstract thinking to a logical visual display. The tree approach offers an analysis of the impact of future decisions, uncertainty and varying payoffs facing a decision maker. It also provides a measurement of risk and demonstrates the sequence of events and tasks that must be accomplished to attain the payoff set. This accounts for the increased use of decision trees among practicing managers.

The third selection, "Do Managers Find Decision Theory Useful?" by Professor Brown, demonstrates that although decision tree analysis is a beneficial tool, it is only one of many tools available through decision theory analysis (DTA). In the article he examines the executive input needed in decision theory analysis: the stipulation of alternatives to be considered, the assignment of probabilities to areas of uncertainty, the quantification of possible consequences and the attitudes regarding these consequences. He also cites a number of instances when DTA has been utilized in specific companies. In addition, he cites the major items of analysis to be considered with DTA—cost-benefit analysis. Only when costs incurred are less than benefits attained does it make good managerial sense to utilize DTA. In closing, Professor Brown notes that the value of DTA will depend upon the desire of business to improve the quality of its decision making.

6   Quantitative Decision Making

William A. Ruch

Every time you make a decision, you take a risk. If your objectives were completely clear and you knew all the ramifications of every course of action open to you, you wouldn't have to make a decision. The comparative consequences of various alternatives would dictate what should be done—and any sane supervisor would do it. Unfortunately, however, only in the most

Reprinted by permission of the publisher from *Supervisory Management,* January 1974. © 1974 by AMACOM, a division of American Management Associations.

routine matters can the consequences of a decision be entirely predictable.

Knowing the risks you face, how can you make the best decision—in other words, choose the best alternative available to you? Not long ago, supervisors had to rely heavily on their intuition, feelings, and imagination in making decisions. It was their single most creative act. Management used to be more an art and less a science. Today—as a result of advances in quantitative decision making—the supervisor can reduce his intuitive judgment with mathematical formulations that help him make rational decisions. He still has to provide input and interpret answers—but the outcome involves far less risk.

Decisions that once took days in the minds of managers may now take nanoseconds in the core of a computer. But this shouldn't make *your* day any shorter. The hours saved by using quantitative decision-making techniques can now be spent on problems that are not readily quantifiable—problems such as worker satisfaction, increased productivity, ecology, and safety. The less time you spend on low-level problems, the more time you can spend on higher-level management problems. But before you can solve these higher-level problems, you should learn how to solve more quantifiable problems with mathematical techniques.

WHAT IS MATH?

Quantitative decision making is based on mathematical concepts. Before you can understand quantitative decision making, you should have a basic understanding of the mathematical processes involved. You don't, however, need to become a mathematician in order to give a systems analyst or a mathematician enough information for them to help you solve a problem. You simply have to understand exactly how much information they need and in what form. To do this, you should understand the nature of the math involved—but not necessarily how to perform it.

Unlike chemistry and physics, mathematics is a language—not a science. Chemistry and physics are sciences because they deal with properties of the real world—and knowledge of these fields can be expanded through scientific investigation. Although mathematics is used in scientific investigation, the discipline itself exists only in symbolic representations and in the minds of those who practice it. It is based on a set number system and definitions of operations that this system can perform.

Thus, math is a system based on man-made premises. Think of it as the language that scientists use to quantify and test knowledge—and to communicate this knowledge to others.

When you were in school, did you learn that arithmetic, algebra, geometry, and calculus were all part of a single system called "mathematics"? Some people didn't get that message. Several years ago, for example, a state legislator (who shall remain nameless) proposed a bill to make *pi* (π) equal to exactly 3.0 in order to simplify calculations. Although he had apparently used *pi* at some point in his life, no one had ever told him that it was the ratio of the circumference of any circle to its diameter.

Educators today are trying to make more of an effort to teach mathematical *understanding* as well as knowledge. In the new math, for example, children are taught not only what to do but *why*. They develop a sound mathematical perspective. If you ask a youngster today, for example, whether one plus one equals two, he or she might tell you that one plus one does equal two—except in a binary system where one plus one equals ten. And this isn't blasphemy. The common decimal system (base ten) is only one of an infinite number of systems that can be used for calculating numbers. Although few people do calculations in a binary system, most computers work on a binary system and translate to a decimal system only for the convenience of those who read the output.

Most people are comfortable with the fact that two plus two equals four. They won't readily admit that this may not always be true—or that they don't know what this equation really means. Take the example of the father whose eight-year-old daughter asked him, "What's the difference between a number and a numeral, Daddy?" When he shrugged his head in ignorance, she explained that a number is a concept, like "twoness," and that the numeral is simply the symbol that represents that concept—like the Arabic "2" or the Roman numeral "II."

Children today are able to understand complicated mathematical processes that only a few years ago were reserved for graduate students—because they think of math as a second language, not a rigid set of magical and awesome laws. Don't despair if you're still stuck at the multiplication-tables or long-division school of mathematical understanding. Math is simply a set of symbols that almost anyone can understand. Try to think of it as a foreign language. When you read a mathematical section of a text book, journal article, or report, think of yourself as being bilingual.

Law students do not have to understand ancient Roman culture in order to understand the Latin phrases in their law books. Like a law student who must understand *some* Latin, accept the fact that you may have to read, write, and manage in two languages. If the meaning of a word or a symbol is not clear in either language, figure out the meaning from the context. If that fails, consult a reference book. Most dictionaries have sections explaining mathematical notations, and there are now many specialized books on mathematical symbols and formulae.

THE MANAGER AND THE MATHEMATICIAN

Once you can communicate and interpret some of the more basic mathematical concepts, you will be better able to work with mathematicians—who may include systems analysts, economists, or researchers working in your company. Why mathematicians? Because when you have a problem, they will be able to help you find a solution. If you can learn how to tap their knowledge, you will be able to make better decisions in half your usual time.

Let's look at the five steps in the decision-making process to see how a manager and a mathematician can work together to solve a problem. Here are the steps:

1. Identify and define the problem.
2. Develop a criterion measure.
3. Construct a model.
4. Derive a solution.
5. Implement the solution.

In certain problems, steps three and four may be: (3) Develop alternatives, and (4) choose one alternative.

You must perform steps one and two because (1) you are the only one who can recognize the problem and (2) you are responsible both for solving it and for choosing how the solution will be measured—whether in cost, time, man-hours, or some other criterion.

Then the mathematician comes into the picture. You will need his services for the third and fourth steps. Although you cannot give him carte blanche with the problem (you're still responsible for finding the solution), you should respect his expertise—as you would that of a corporate attorney or a family physician.

If you can define the problem well enough to communicate it to the mathematician, he will be able to develop a model from which he can derive a solution. Note that this is a solution to the *model,* and not to the problem. Only after the mathematician finds a solution to the model can you translate the model solution into organizational or departmental terms—temper the solution with judgment, implement it, and follow through.

BEDAZZLED

Some unfortunate supervisors cannot tell the difference between the solution to a model and the solution to a problem. Often the victim of this ailment, according to Herbert Simon in his book on the science of management decisions, is "so dazzled by the beauty of the mathematical results that he will not remember that his practical operating problem has not been solved."

Whenever you use the services of a technical expert in making a decision, don't lose sight of the importance of the interchanges between steps two and three and between steps four and five. You must be able to translate from one language to another and from one discipline to another. First you must be able to encode the problem so that the mathematician can understand it and, later, you must decode the model solution so that *you* can understand it. If you can't make the transition between steps four and five, you won't be able to use the mathematician's results to help you make a decision.

Both you and the mathematician should share the responsibility for communicating these transitional phases. A failure to communicate cannot be blamed on only one person. Doctors, for example, accept the responsibility for communicating their highly technical language so that their patients can understand it. Similarly, both the manager and the mathematician should make an effort to understand each other's language.

A CASE IN POINT

Here's how one supervisor used the services of a mathematician to help him solve an important problem:

Production manager Fred Halloway had to make a production schedule for the coming week. He asked one of the operations-research people for some help. This is how he phrased the problem: "The B-26 turret lathe is down and the QC (quality-control) boys have frozen the last shipment of castings so that they can do some additional testing. Since we can't use those castings, we can switch over to the base plates for the McElwain contract, catch up on our housings production, or finish the X-101 gear covers. Should we try to do some of each to keep the sales department off our backs?"

The operations-research analyst didn't know what Fred was talking about. "Look, Fred," he said. "Let's sit down and try to work this thing out. Could you explain it in a different way?" After discussing the problem with the mathematician, Fred came up with this definition: "The company must allocate scarce resources (labor, materials, machines) to meet several competing needs (products) in a way that will maximize the total contribution—first to overhead and then, after overhead costs are met, to profit."

To Fred, it was a production problem; to the mathematician, a problem in linear programming. After receiving pertinent data from Fred, the operations-research analyst translated the problem into these symbols:

Max $Z = 5.00A + 2.00B + 1.00C$

Subject to:

$$R: 3A + 5B + 4C \leq 2700$$
$$S: 1A + 1B + 0C \leq 1800$$
$$T: 3A + 2B + 0C \leq 3000$$

Solution: $Z = \$4600$

A = 800	R = 0
B = 300	S = 700
C = 0	T = 0

Fred, of course, didn't understand the mathematician until he translated the symbols into Fred's language. The mathematician explained that A, B, and C were the real products, which contributed \$5.00, \$2.00, and \$1.00 per unit to overhead and profit. R, S, and T were the available resources, expressed as 2,700 hours of labor,

1,800 square feet of material #1, and 3,000 gallons of material #2.

The equations expressing the restraints imposed by the available resources also indicate how much of each resource is used in making each product. So, $3A + 5B + 4C \leq 2700$ means that each unit of Product A requires 3 units of labor; each unit of Product B, 5 units of labor; each unit of Product C, 4 units of labor; and that the total labor used must equal or be less than 2700 units. This is information that Fred gave the mathematician.

The solution to the *model*? Producing 800 units of Product A, 300 units of product B, and none of product C would yield the highest profit contribution: $4600.00. All labor and all of material #2 would be used, but 700 square feet of material #1 would be left over.

Fred carefully considered this infor-mation. Then he decided to produce a minimum 100 units of product C because of a special order that was coming in, adjusted the rest of the production schedule accordingly, and released it to the shop.

Neither Fred nor the operations-re-search analyst could have solved the problem alone. Each made a contribution to the problem-solving process—Fred at the beginning and end, the mathematician in the middle. The critical links in the process—where the operation came closest to failure—were the points at which the language of one discipline were translated into the language of the other.

Fred's approach to mathematics from the viewpoint that it was a special-ized discipline, written in a foreign language, minimized much of his irra-tional—but natural—aversion to using math in solving managerial problems.

7   Management Climbs the Decision Tree

Paul Mali

How valid is the MBO plan? How much confidence can we place in it?

Determining objective validity may well be the most important step in the strategy of MBO, or managing by objec-tives.

Unless validity is shown, the man-ager implements his objectives with little confidence and at high risk of not getting what he wants. The process of validating objectives requires firming up the expected end results by tracing, both forward and backward, the man-ner in which resources and activities have been organized. Which brings us to decision trees.

The concept of using decision trees is a novel approach for validating fu-ture commitments. It is a concept that examines which objectives are most likely to be reached, and the associated risk. The approach includes as many variables as necessary to provide a concrete background for decision-

This article originally appeared in *Administrative Management*, January 1973, pp. 63–65, and is reprinted with permission.

making on a proposed venture, and helps to anticipate faults that may occur in a proposed set of objectives before the objectives have completely committed.

Decision trees employ a unique structure for displaying events, the degree of risk in each event, the likelihood of potential problems, and contingency actions to minimize such problems. Decision-trees reduce abstract thinking to a logical visual pattern of cause and effect through a series of logical possibilities. They also are known as proba-

bility trees, shorthand for the likelihood of a chain of events occurring when certain decisions are made. The trees, whatever their classification, display choices, risks, objectives, and decision criteria from one point to another, as illustrated at left. They are made up of a series of nodes and branches.

At the first node, on the left, the manager is faced with setting an objective for productivity improvement. He has three choices: install new equipment, schedule overtime, or hire more workers. Each branch of the tree repre-

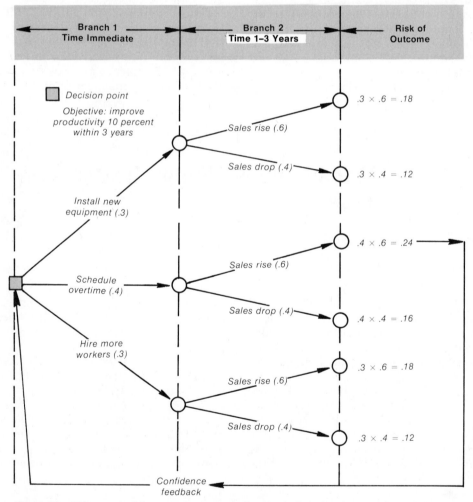

Figure 1. Using a decision tree to analyze the alternatives for the stated goal (improving productivity) enables the manager to evaluate his risk of outcome in each situation.

sents an alternative course of action or an alternative decision. At the end of each alternative is another node representing a chance event—for example, whether sales will rise or drop. Each subsequent alternative course going right represents an alternative outcome of this chance event. Probabilities are assigned for each branch, stated in value running from 0 (absolute impossibility) through 1 (absolute certainty), or in percentages from 0 through 100 percent.

Thus, if we assign the probability P = 0.5 to some event E, such as reaching the largest share of the market, it means we think the event has a 50 percent chance of actually occurring. A probability assignment is an expression of the level of confidence and risk. High probabilities mean high confidence and low risk. Low probabilities mean low confidence and high risk. Probability assignments can be made on the basis of verifiable data from the past, with weights based on statistics, correlations, or other reliable survey information. Probability assignments can also be made on the basis of subjective judgment—that is, personal opinion supported by the individual's experience with similar types of problems or situations. To say that a new business venture has an 80 percent chance of success, can identify a subjective level of confidence in the new venture.

Decision trees allow us to go through a trial run of likely events. A simulated feedback is obtained to check and recheck the original decision. The objective in the illustration is to improve productivity 10 percent in three years. The tree graphically and simply shows the alternatives possible after the decision to pursue this objective is made. The risk factor of 0.24 reveals the highest feedback confidence; thus, out of all the alternatives, a sale rise has the greatest chance of occurring as a result of scheduled overtime. Venture analysis using a decision tree enables management to take a more precise,

confident, and direct account of the following:

The Impact of Possible Future Decisions. A tree's branching and its spreading chain of events can clarify potential barriers, changes, and problems. The analyst can probe a variety of effects on his model tree by deliberately imposing faults and critical conditions to foresee their impact.

The Impact of Uncertainty on Confidence. Layout of the events in a tree structure makes more visible the alternatives that may occur. Risk-factor assignments or probabilities give a better insight to, and confidence in the future effects of, a decision made in the present.

The Impact of Varying Commitments of Payoff. Trying a variety of tentative objectives in a decision tree can reveal comparative advantages and disadvantages. These can be analyzed in a payoff table for criteria such as present or future profits. This validation procedure can frequently lead to restating the objective or selecting a new one.

The Sequencing and Interrelations of Tasks and Events. The schematic display of starting events, secondary and terminating events, allow for insights into input/output relationship and start/stop phasing as branching is extending into the future. Priorities can be established from the difficulties, complexities, and time requirements suggested by each path.

The Measurement of Risk. Each path of the decision tree contains, in addition to the elements of the paths, an assigned risk factor. This is the estimated likelihood of occurrence of the terminal event in the path. How probable the outcome?

The basic point to decision-tree analysis is in gauging the probable outcomes of a decision toward an objective. The possibility of building a new production facility may be structured into an objective, and a decision tree may be developed to see outcomes of main, secondary, and tertiary branches, as illustrated in the drawing at left.

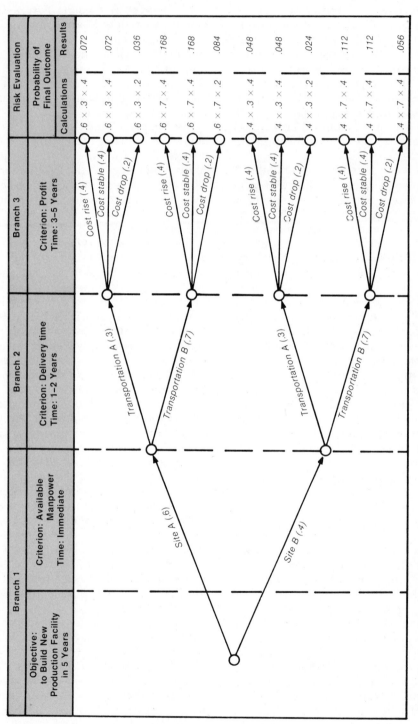

Figure 2. A decision tree with branches enables the manager to see main, secondary and tertiary outcomes from a stated objective. In this way, expected profitability to the company of an immediate decision toward this objective can be evaluated.

Expected profits over a long period can be evaluated as a result of an immediate decision. Each branch of the tree would have one or more criteria to establish the likelihood of an event's occurring. A future time period makes the analysis realistic in terms of a long-term proposed commitment. Profit plans usually cover a three-to-five year time span. Examining the factors involved in site determination, transportation systems, and development costs for future time spans helps in determining the likelihood of profits. Feedback of risk factors strengthens or diminishes the original decision to build a new production facility, and may give some insight to other possible objectives which might be pursued.

8 Do Managers Find Decision Theory Useful?

Rex V. Brown

For thousands of years, businessmen have been making decisions in the face of uncertainty about the future. Such decisions have often served to separate "the men from the boys" in business—and perhaps always will. In recent years, however, the problem executives face has been altered by the introduction of a set of techniques of quantitative analysis which I shall refer to here as Decision Theory Analysis (DTA). These methods are familiar to HBR readers,[1] and they have, in fact, stimulated widespread attention, both critical and laudatory, in the business world.

As might be expected when a radically new approach is used, business executives have often found DTA methods frustrating and unrewarding. Nevertheless, there is a steadily growing conviction in the management community that DTA should and will occupy a very important place in an executive's arsenal of problem-solving techniques. Only time can tell if, as some enthusiasts claim, decision theory will be to the executive of tomorrow what the slide rule is to the engineer of today. But clearly, in my opinion, the *potential* impact of DTA is great.

Author's note: I wish to acknowledge the assistance of Paul Vatter, Howard Raiffa, Stanley Buchin, and Robert Buzzell in arranging contacts for the survey discussed in this article.

[1] See, in particular, David B. Hertz, "Risk Analysis in Capital Investment," January–February 1964, p. 95; John Magee, "Decision Trees for Decision Making," July–August 1964, p. 126, and "How to Use Decision Trees in Capital Investment," September–October 1964, p. 79. Ralph O. Swalm, "Utility Theory—Insights Into Risk Taking," November–December 1966, p. 123; and John S. Hammond, III, "Better Decisions With Preference Theory," November–December 1967, p. 123. Many other articles on other methods of quantitative analysis are contained in HBR's Statistical Decision Series, Parts I, II, and III.

The primary purpose of this article, which is based on a survey of 20 companies made in 1969, is to present some of the experiences of practitioners who have been exploring various applications of DTA techniques to management decision making. These experiences should help would-be users to identify particular situations in their own companies where the new technology might greatly benefit them, and to build on the lessons learned the hard way by earlier users.

Executives and staff specialists in the companies provided the bulk of the material. The companies included three organizations with several years of active experience with DTA (Du Pont, Pillsbury, and General Electric): a sampling of corporations that have taken up DTA in the past two or three years and are now quite active in employing it (e.g., General Mills and Inmont Corporation); one or two organizations whose experience with DTA has been disappointing; a few companies (such as Ford Motor and Time, Inc.) where there is a definite interest in DTA but—at least, as of 1969—little application; and a couple of consulting firms with well-known expertise in the area (notably Arthur D. Little, Inc. and McKinsey & Company).

During the course of the survey, particular attention was focused on such questions as the following, which will be discussed in this article:

What tangible impact does DTA have on how businesses are run and on how individual decisions are made?

What areas of decision making is DTA best suited for?

What practical benefits result?

What trends in usage are apparent?

What obstacles and pitfalls lie in the way of more effective usage?

What organization steps should management take to use DTA more effectively?

What remains to be done in developing and expanding the usefulness of DTA?

DTA IN REVIEW

Before turning to the findings of the survey, let us review some of the elements of DTA. (The theory does not, by the way, always go under this name. Sometimes it is called "Personalist Decision Theory" or "Bayesian Decision Theory.")

First, what information does DTA demand of the executive? It requires such inputs as executive judgment, experience, and attitudes, along with any "hard data," such as historical records. In particular, the executive is asked to:

1. Stipulate what decision alternatives are to be considered in the analysis of a problem.

2. Make a probabilistic statement of his assessment of critical uncertainties.

3. Quantify some possible consequences of various actions and his attitudes toward these consequences.

The logically preferred decision can then be derived routinely according to the highly developed statistical theory that underlies DTA, using decision trees, computer programs, and/or other computational devices.

The use of DTA is not restricted to investment, marketing, or other types of business decisions. Potential and actual applications are also to be found in the area of medical, military, engineering, and governmental decisions. The most ambitious application of decision theory yet reported apparently was employed in the hypothetical problem of whether to push the nuclear button if the President receives different kinds of ambiguous evidence of an impending Russian attack on the United States.

The analyst does not need to keep in his head all the considerations that are taken into account, and, indeed, all the considerations do not need to be evaluated by the same person (although whoever makes the decision must *accept* the evaluations). For instance:

The company president might determine the company's attitude toward risk in new product planning.

The vice president of marketing might choose the business decisions to be compared.

The director of research might provide information on development times, likely success in solving technical problems, and so on.

The probable costs might come from the controller's office.

The probable sales might come from a sales manager or forecasting specialist.

Contentious elements in the analysis can be lifted out, and revised assessments substituted for them, without the analyst's having to reconsider every issue.

HOW DTA WORKS

One version of DTA—the "decision tree" approach—lends itself readily to simple manual computations, and can be used to illustrate the general ideas involved in this subject.

All elements which an executive considers important to a decision, however subjective, can be represented on a decision tree. To show how the process of common-sense decision making can be expressed in the necessary manner, let us take an example involving a hypothetical, but realistic, business decision.

Suppose that a New York metal broker has an option to buy 100,000 tons of iron ore from a Far Eastern government at an advantageous price, of, say, $5 a ton. Other brokers have received the same offer, and so our man in New York feels that an immediate decision must be made. He knows he can get $8 a ton for this ore, but he believes there is a 50-50 chance that the U.S. government will refuse to grant an import license. In such an event, the contract would be annulled at a penalty of $1 a ton.

A decision tree, representing what I shall call the initial problem, is shown in Part A of Figure 1. Note that both the "act forks" (labeled in capitals) and the "event forks" (lower case) are represented by branches on the decision tree, and that at each fork there are as many branches as there are alternatives.

The choice between alternative acts (in this case, the decision whether or not to buy the ore) is under the control of the decision maker. On the other hand, the occurrence of a particular event (the approval or refusal of the import license) is beyond his control. He estimates a 50-50 chance of approval. The probabilities are noted in parentheses.

The uncertainty about the license makes it impossible to know in advance what the "best" decision would be. Every path through the tree corresponds to a possible sequence of acts and events, each with its own unique consequence. For example, if our broker decides to buy ore, but his license application is rejected, he stands to lose (assuming a penalty of $1 a ton) $100,000.

In order to reach a good decision, the broker clearly has to take into account the probabilities, as he sees them, of each of the two events, approval or refusal of the import license. Intuitively, it is easy to see that if the broker assesses a high probability of approval, he would be wise to go ahead and buy the ore; but since he actually thinks there is only a 50-50 chance of approval, he is faced with a 50% chance of obtaining $300,000 (his best estimate now of the potential profit) against an equal chance of losing $100,000. His estimates of the gains and losses are shown to the right of the decision tree, in Figure 1A.

Which act should he prefer? His attitude toward possible consequences must be noted. Suppose he has a general policy of "playing the averages" and is not at all averse to taking risks. This can be restated formally as maximizing the "expected" monetary consequences. (By contrast, other people "play it safe" or, conversely, are "gamblers," indicating they like to deviate from the averages.)

Formal analysis begins by computing an "expected" consequence for all event forks at the right-hand edge of the decision tree. This value is treated as if it were the certain consequence of reaching the base of the event fork. Its value is then substituted for the actual event fork and its consequences, as shown in Figure 1B. In this case, there is only one event fork (approval or rejection of the application) on the tree; it is therefore replaced by $100,000—that is, .5($300,000) + .5(−$100,000). If there were several event forks on the right, each would be replaced by an expected consequence.*

Since the event fork is now eliminated, only the act fork is left. The branch which has the highest expected consequence is now selected. That is the "Buy ore" branch with a consequence of $100,000. The analysis of the problem is now complete.

With such a simple problem, it may hardly seem worth going to the trouble of a formal analysis. The real pay-off is likely to occur when the problem has more separable elements than the decision maker can comfortably take account of in his head. Typically, in such cases, there will be more than two "echelons" of forks in a decision tree, and more than one fork at each echelon. By alternating the two methods described for eliminating event and act forks respectively, the origin at the left-hand side of the tree will eventually be

---

* See the examples discussed by John Magee in "Decision Trees for Decision Making," HBR July–August 1964, p. 126, and "How to Use Decision Trees in Capital Investment," HBR September–October 1964, p. 123; see also John S. Hammond, III, "Better Decisions With Preference Theory," HBR November–December 1967, p. 123.

reached, and both the optimum strategy and its expected consequence will be determined.

Although the analysis depicted in Figure 1 could be perfectly adequate in representing our New York broker's first thoughts about his problem, a little reflection may lead him to take into account new considerations whose action implications are less easy to think through informally. For instance, it may occur to him that the acts "Buy ore" and "Don't buy ore" are not the only ones immediately available for consideration. As in most business problems, he may have the option of delaying his decision while he gathers more information. If so, the additional options and the consequences of every set of act-event sequences could be shown on the decision tree, and an optimum strategy determined in essentially the same way. Similarly, he might want to take into account some aversion to risk that he may possess in certain circumstances, the possibility of nonmonetary side effects (like goodwill), or uncertainty about quantities he had previously treated as certain (such as the prices he can get for the ore).

These considerations, too, can be handled in the same format and with very little in the way of additional technique.* However, more ambitious forms of DTA, such as computer simulations, often prove to be more convenient when there is a technical specialist available.

While, in principle, any decision problem *can* be analyzed by DTA methods, this is a very far cry from arguing that it always *should* be. In various instances, traditional decision making may be more economical, practical, and sound than modern methods of quantitative analysis.

Growing Use

Only a few U.S. companies appear to have used DTA in operations for any length of time. Two of these companies are Du Pont, which got started with the approach in the late 1950's, and Pillsbury, which got started in the early 1960's. However, there has been a dramatic increase in DTA activity since about 1964. That is when executive interest began to be stimulated, notably by articles in HBR, executive orientation seminars, and reports of successful applications on the part of pioneering

*See Robert D. Buzzell, Donald F. Cox, and Rex V. Brown, *Marketing Research and Information Systems* (New York, McGraw-Hill Book Company, Inc., 1969), Chapters 9 and 10.

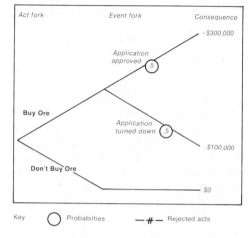

A. The Problem

Key ⬭ Probabilties —#— Rejected acts

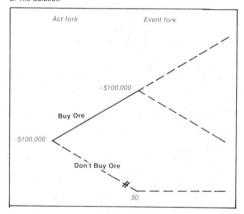

B. The Solution

$ 000 Consequences or expected consequences

Figure 1. An example of decision tree analysis.

companies, and, perhaps most important of all, a steady stream of DTA-trained MBAs who began to enter managerial ranks in substantial numbers. The principal intellectual thrust behind nearly all of these developments was the technical work and teaching of Robert O. Schlaifer and Howard Raiffa at the Harvard Business School.[2]

Stimulated by such developments, executives in a number of companies began to explore the potential applica-

[2] See, for example, Robert O. Schlaifer, *Analysis of Decisions Under Uncertainty* (New York, McGraw-Hill Book Company, Inc., 1969), and Howard Raiffa, *Decision Analysis* (Reading, Massachusetts, Addison-Wesley Publishing Company, 1968).

tions of DTA to their own operations. For example:

General Electric set up an intensive study of DTA by a high-level committee that led to major changes in plant appropriation methods.

Ford Motor and other companies put literally hundreds of their middle and senior managers through training programs varying in length from a few days to several weeks.

Other companies, including General Mills, began to introduce DTA on a project-by-project basis.

IMPACT ON DECISION MAKING

Since the companies in the survey were selected on the basis of their actual or imputed use of DTA, no special significance can be attached to the fact that most of them do indeed use the tools. What is significant, in my opinion, is that even these companies, leaders though they are, do not show drastic changes in their general decision-making procedures as a result of DTA. However, *individual* decisions are often profoundly affected. Examples from the experience of the most active companies interviewed—Du Pont, Pillsbury, GE, and Inmont—give some measure of how DTA is being used by managers.

Application at Du Pont

Substantial DTA activity is going on throughout the Du Pont organization, stimulated by staff groups in the Development Department and elsewhere. Managers in the various departments have shown increasing interest in the staff groups' services (which are supplied for a fee) during the past ten years. Yet, even after all this time, Dr. Sig Andersen, manager of one of the consulting groups and perhaps the most prominent figure in the application of DTA, says he feels that DTA has not yet reached the point where it really has a major impact at the general man-

ager level in Du Pont. J. T. Axon, Manager of the Management Sciences Division, says:

"I think [Andersen and his colleagues] have indeed been pioneers and missionaries on behalf of DTA within Du Pont, and I share with them the conviction that their work has improved the quality of numerous decisions around the company. Their impact has been seriously limited, however, by the absence of appropriate educational efforts aimed at the decision makers. Even at this date, we have in Du Pont, in my judgment, very few key decision makers who are 'alive' to the possibilities of DTA and comfortable in its use. It is this lack that has dragged down the Du Pont effort."

At Du Pont middle and even senior managers increasingly will take action or submit recommendations that include DTA along with more conventional analyses, but the presentation to top management is likely to be supported by more informal reasoning, not DTA. Thus:

In the case of a new product which had just reached the prototype stage at Du Pont, the question before management was: On what scale should initial pilot production be carried out? Critical uncertainties involved the reliability of the military demand for which the prototype had been originally designed, and the amount of supplementary commercial business that would be generated.

DTA was performed on a computer to produce "risk profiles" of return on investment for various plant sizes and pricing strategies. The inputs included probability assessments of demand for each possible end-use of the product (based on market research), as well as assessments of cost and timing. The analysis indicated that, on the basis of the assessments used, a certain price was optimal, and a $3-million pilot plant would have the highest expected rate of return.

When this conclusion was transmitted to top management, it was couched in the language of informal reasoning, not of DTA. Management opted for a smaller, $1-million plant, but adopted —unchanged—the pricing recommendation of the study. It appears that top management, without explicitly disagreeing with the assumptions underlying the analysis, possessed an aversion to risk which was not assumed in the analysis.

Pillsbury's Approach

James R. Petersen, Vice President of The Pillsbury Company and General Manager of the Grocery Products Company, uses decision trees regularly in evaluating major recommendations submitted to him. More than a dozen marketing decisions a year are approved by him on the basis of the findings of detailed DTA. (Many more decisions in his divisions are rendered after first using a skeletal decision tree to clarify the key problem issues.)

Typically, a middle manager in the Grocery Products Company will spend a week or so developing a DTA approach, often with the help of a staff specialist. When the middle manager's recommendation comes to be considered by Petersen, this analysis is the vehicle for discussion. For instance:

In one case, the issue before management was whether to switch from a box to a bag as a package for a certain grocery product. Petersen and his sales manager had been disposed to retain the box on the grounds of greater customer appeal. The brand manager, however, favored the bag on cost considerations. He supported his recommendation with a DTA based on his own best assessments of probable economic, marketing, and other consequences. Even when the sales manager's more pessimistic assessments of the market impact of a bag were substituted for the brand manager's, the bag still looked more profitable. Petersen adopted the recommendation, the bag was introduced, and the profits on the product climbed substantially.

During the course of discussions, some Pillsbury executives urged that the bag be test-marketed before man-agement made a firm decision. The original DTA showed, however, only a one-in-ten chance that the bag would prove unprofitable—and if that occurred, it would probably be not too unprofitable. A simple, supplementary DTA showed that the value of making a market test could not remotely approach its cost. Accordingly, no test marketing was undertaken. Management's confidence in the analysis was later confirmed by the bag's success.

Uses at GE

At General Electric there has recently been a formal head office requirement that all investment requests of more than $500,000 be supported by a probabilistic assessment of rate of return and other key measures. In the wake of this requirement, and largely in the area of plant appropriations, more than 500 instances of computerized DTA have been recorded over the past four years.

Heavy use is made of a library of special DTA programs developed largely by Robert Newman, Manager of Planning Services, who works with managers in other GE operations on a consulting basis. The consulting relationship, no doubt enhanced by Newman's own experience in line management, often has an impact on issues beyond the scope of the originating inquiry, as this example shows:

One GE division was faced with a shortage of manufacturing capacity for a mature industrial product. Using the information and assessments supplied by the division manager (including a suspicion that the product was obsolescent), Newman spent a few hours on a DTA which suggested that the division should not increase capacity, but raise prices. Both the consultant and the manager felt uneasy about this conclusion.

Further discussion yielded new but confidential information that the division was developing a product which promised to supplant the old one. This intelligence, plus various estimates of the probability of success and related matters, led to a new DTA (which employed GE's prepackaged computer programs). This study pointed to the conclusion that research and development expenditures on the new product should be increased by a factor of 20. The recommendation was adopted, the new product went into production two years later, and it achieved highly profitable sales of some $20 million a year.

Inmont's Programs

Although Inmont Corporation's usage of DTA is less extensive than that of the three companies just discussed, James T. Hill, President, comments that he often uses computer simulations in evaluating potential acquisition candidates. Preliminary information available on such candidates is programmed into a model by his assistant. This model is part of a prepackaged DTA simulation program which merges Inmont and the acquisition candidate according to the specific purchase strategy that Inmont is contemplating. The computer prints out detailed information as to the cost to Inmont and the return to the individual shareholders of the acquired company, including a pro forma balance sheet and income statement both before and after conversion of convertible securities.

Once the results are reviewed by Hill and his top executives, any alternative financing schemes that have been suggested can be explored in a matter of minutes in order to determine the best financial plan. Computer terminals are available at strategic decision-making locations in the head office, and the program is designed so as to enable any executive's secretary to put in data for different possible modes of acquisition. It is an easy matter, therefore, for alternative strategies to be evaluated quickly at any stage in the decision-making process.

When the most desirable financial approach has been determined, a second program can be utilized to run projected pro forma balance sheets and income statements for any period into the future. This program uses probability theory to arrive at the "best guess" as to the outcome of various operating strategies. It also enables executives to determine the factors most crucial to the future return on investment of a proposed merger. This "sensitivity analysis" thus focuses on the critical questions with which Inmont's management would have to deal if it were to undertake the acquisition.

This is what Hill says about Inmont's use of the procedure:

The two programs, together, help ensure that the decision as to a potential acquisition is made after a comprehensive analysis of alternatives. It is not necessary to choose only one method of financing or one method of operation, for example. Rather, it is possible to explore, in a very short period of time, numerous strategies to discover that which will maximize the benefits to the merged companies. It is understood that the decision is no better than the reliability of the inputs, including the assigned probabilities.

Various other companies responding to my survey report that they are using DTA on a more-or-less systematic basis for marketing and allied decisions, most frequently in the area of new product selection and development, but also in promotion, pricing, test marketing, and other activities. In fact, about 50 specific applications of DTA to marketing problems are noted—and some of these will be mentioned subsequently in this article.

OBSTACLES AND PITFALLS

Enthusiasm for DTA is very great in many quarters. For example, Robert Newman of General Electric predicts:

Within 10 years, decision theory, conversational computers, and library programs should occupy the same role for the manager as calculus, slide rules, and mathematical tables do for the engineer today. The engineer of Roman times had none of these, but he could make perfectly good bridges.

However, he could not compete today, even in bridge building, let alone astro-engineering. Management is today at the stage of Roman engineering. Needless to say, managers will still use specialists, just as engineers use heat transfer experts.

While Newman's time schedule may be optimistic, my survey findings in no way contradict the substance of his view. However, a number of more or less serious obstacles—many no doubt attributable to inexperience in using DTA—lie in the path of a major revolution such as Newman envisages.

Personal Competence

It is clear that companies will experience only limited success with a new analytical approach like DTA unless they have executives who are alive to its possibilities and use it effectively. While there is a substantial and rapidly expanding number of DTA-oriented executives in positions to influence management decisions, they represent a tiny fraction of the total managerial pool. The momentum of educational processes will remedy this problem in time—but it will take time.

Much the same can be said about the current scarcity of trained technical specialists needed to carry out or advise managers on DTA. After all, the first comprehensive handbook on applied DTA was published only recently.[3]

However, even if there were no manpower shortage, serious obstacles to successful and expanding use of DTA would still exist. Removing them may require more deliberate initiative and research on management's part than will correcting the lack of line and staff training.

Uncertainty Over Return

For one thing, no substantial personal or corporate benefits of using the technique may be apparent to the potential user. Many effective managers have a "show me" attitude toward new decision-making techniques, and as yet there is little to show. Indeed, no firm

evidence is available to prove that DTA *does* have widespread practical value. The evidence from my survey is encouraging, but far from conclusive, enough disappointments have been reported to sustain the doubts harbored by many businessmen. For example:

A central staff team for an international manufacturer of industrial components carried out a sophisticated and competent DTA designed to help a regional subsidiary choose which of several alternative markets to compete in. When the DTA part of the study was presented to the subsidiary's president, however, he perceived it as having little relevance to him in his decision making. He told me that the market forecast and other input data gathered for the analysis were certainly of substantial value to him, but he could not see that the DTA itself added much that was useful. Indeed, while the market data provided a basis for much of the subsidiary's subsequent strategy, no specific action appeared to be traceable to the DTA part of the study (though some people in the company felt that the analysis had some diffuse influence on several decisions).

The managers of the subsidiary are seeking to adapt the DTA to meet their needs, and the prospects look encouraging. Moreover, the staff team from the head office has since introduced DTA to *other* subsidiaries with, it seems, substantial success.

Note that this experience was the first the company had had with DTA. Almost all of the most successful users of DTA have started out with one or more disappointing experiences. What accounts for such disappointments? Let us take the international manufacturer again as a case example. Its experience is typical of that of several other companies I know about:

1. The logic and language of DTA was unfamiliar to the president and his senior executives, and they could not readily and comfortably incorporate it into their normal mode of thinking. A more gradual introduction of the complex technology would surely have been more digestible.

2. The decision options addressed

---

[3]Robert O. Schlaifer, *op. cit.*

by the DTA turned out *not* to be the ones the president was concerned about. (For example, he was more interested in deciding *how* to develop a particular market sector than in *whether* to be in it at all.) Fuller and earlier communication between executive and staff analysts helps to counter this very common problem experienced in applying DTA.

3. The DTA was initiated and performed by "head office" people over whom the subsidiary had no direct control, and the subsidiary president may have felt some threat to his autonomy. Having such an analysis performed or commissioned by his own people would have removed the threat.

4. The subsidiary president told me that the way to make money in his business was to get good data and implement decisions effectively. He had little interest in improved ways of *processing* data to make decisions, which is, of course, the special province of DTA.

Diffused Decision Making

At Ford Motor Company, some 200 senior executives have passed through a brief DTA-oriented program during the past five years; the program has been followed up in some divisions by intensive workshops for junior executives. And yet, according to George H. Brown, former Director of Marketing Research at Ford headquarters, usage of DTA at Ford has been negligible in the marketing area, and the prospects unpromising, at least as of the time of this survey. In his opinion, large organizations with diffuse decision-making processes (like Ford) are not as well suited to the effective use of DTA as, say, the small or one-man organization is.

John J. Nevin, now Vice President of Marketing for Ford, adds the following observations:

I am not sure that there is any reason to be discouraged by the fact that, in many companies, DTA may be far more accepted and far more utilized by middle management. Maybe all analytical tools sneak into general usage through the back door. It does not seem to me to be improbable that the middle management people, who are more comfortable with these techniques and are using them on very specific technical problems today, will, as they grow to top management positions, feel as uncomfortable switching to some new decision-making process as many of today's managers feel in switching to a more disciplined analysis.

He also notes that the average executive has difficulty picking up all of the variables in a complex decision-making problem. He attributes this in large part to the executive's inability to discipline himself to use a new technique.

Nevertheless, several Ford divisions are now exploring DTA applications at their most senior executive levels. Since my survey began, early in 1969, there have been some cases of successful implementation. For instance:

At Ford Tractor, a product policy decision was recently required. In a regional market suffering from competitive inroads, the main options were to reduce prices or to introduce one of several possible new models; a modest DTA was carried out on these choices. Several runs incorporating assessments and modifications advanced by the marketing manager, the assistant general manager, and the general manager were made. The somewhat controversial conclusion to introduce a certain model was presented in DTA form to the general manager, who adopted it and initiated the necessary engineering studies.

Organizational Obstacles

If there is one dominant feature that distinguishes the successful from the less successful applications of DTA, judging from the findings of this survey, it is the organizational arrangements for offering DTA. The most successful appears to be the "vest pocket" approach, where the analyst works intimately with the executive and typically reports directly to him (Pillsbury's Grocery Products Company and Inmont Corporation provide excellent examples of this approach).

At the other end of the spectrum is the arms'-length approach, which is characteristic of much operations research. In this approach the analysis is performed by a staff group which is organizationally distant from the executive being served. In such instances, the executive may feel threatened rather than supported by DTA, and critical weaknesses may thus develop in the communication of the problem and its analyses.

Relation with Consultants

The epitome of the arms'-length arrangement appears in the role of the outside consultant. The survey suggests that consulting firms are doing relatively little DTA work for their clients. (One exception is McKinsey & Company, which reports substantial DTA work in nonmarketing areas.) I find this significant, in view of the facts that potentially, at least, consulting firms are a major resource for companies that want to use DTA, and that leading consultants have done much to explain DTA to businessmen.[4]

It seems that clients often insist on holding some of their cards close to their chests—and effective DTA depends critically on incorporating in the analysis *all* of the elements that the decision maker sees as important. Many clients prefer to limit consultants to performing clearly specified technical or data-gathering tasks with a minimum of two-way communication; executives worry about jeopardizing company security and giving the consultant too much say in their business.

Dr. Harlan Meal, a departmental manager for Arthur D. Little, makes a telling observation concerning the role of consultants and general obstacles to the adoption of DTA:

Many of the executives who hire consultants or who employ expert technical staff do so in order to reduce the uncertainty in their decision making, rather than to improve their ability to deal with uncertain situations. Many of the clients we have want to buy from us information which will make the outcome of a particular course of action

more certain than it would otherwise have been. If all we can do for them is reduce the chance of making an incorrect decision or improve the expected performance of the decision they do make in the face of uncertainty, they are not very interested.

It is on this point that I think the application of decision theory analysis gets stuck nearly every time. Very few executives think of themselves as gamblers or of making the best kind of decisions in a gambling situation. They want, instead, to think of themselves as individuals whose greater grasp of the available information and whose greater insight remove the uncertainty from the situation.

When the information quality is so poor that the assignment of probabilities to outcomes seems an exercise in futility, decision theory analysis can be most useful. Yet most executives in such a situation say that the only thing which really can be useful is their own experienced intuition. The executive is going to behave as though he has information about the situation, whether he has it or not.

Technical Questions

A further obstacle to the widespread use of DTA has to do with the logical underpinnings of DTA. Some potential users, especially in staff positions, take the position that where information about an uncertain quantity is weak, there is no point in *attempting* to measure that uncertainty. This amounts to a rejection of a basic tenet of DTA, viz., that subjective judgment, however tenuous, must be taken into account *somehow* by the decision maker, and that a DTA approach may do the job more effectively than unaided intuition.

In addition, increase in the effectiveness of DTA is to some extent dependent on the state of the art. The development and propagation of economical and quick routines utilizing inputs and outputs that can be readily communicated will no doubt be a major factor. Such routines affect the practicality and appeal of DTA in a management setting. However, it seems clear that purely theoretical developments are not holding up further application of DTA; the frontiers of the technology are way ahead of the applications, in most cases.

---

[4] See, for example, John Magee and David B. Hertz, *op. cit.*

REALIZING THE POTENTIALS

How beneficial is a DTA to a company? Does it lead to "better" decisions than other approaches to decision making? Logic alone cannot give us the answer. However, it seems clear that DTA may *not* be the best approach if:

1. The subjective inputs required for the analysis are inaccurately measured and recorded. (Executives, as Meal suggests in the comment quoted earlier in this article, may not explicitly admit to uncertainty about some critical variable, whereas they may take it into account in their informal reasoning.)

2. The DTA does not incorporate all the considerations which the executive would informally take into account— for example, some non-monetary side effect like goodwill. (Where there is good communication between executive and analyst, the executive often can and does make "eyeball" adjustments for anything that has been left out of the analysis. Sometimes, though, such adjustments are so substantial that they swamp and thereby invalidate the entire DTA.)

Considering all the angles and factors that bear on a good DTA (or any other analysis) is time-consuming and sometimes quite frustrating. Clearly, though, it is one of the prerequisites of making this approach. The following experience should suffice to make the point:

A corporate staff team at General Mills evaluated an acquisition opportunity by means of a DTA computer program that took four months to develop and another two months to run with successively modified inputs corresponding to new assessments and assumptions made by the researchers and executives. In all, 140 computer runs were made before arriving at a recommendation to make the acquisition and to adopt a specific marketing and production strategy. The recommendation was rejected by top management, however, when the company's legal counsel advised against the acquisition on certain legal grounds. The lawyers discovered that a critical consideration had been omitted from the analysis which rendered it unusable for the purpose at hand.

It should be noted that this was the company's first major attempt at applying DTA, and the experience performed a valuable function in exposing line and staff to the scope and pitfalls of DTA. The company's record with DTA since then has been quite successful.

Costs vs. Benefits

The costs of applying DTA are by no means inconsequential. It is true that the out-of-pocket costs for technicians and computers, even for a large-scale analysis, may be relatively trivial. Moreover, these costs can be expected to decline as DTA technology becomes more streamlined. Other, less obvious costs, however, are not trivial and are unlikely to become so. For example:

Critical decisions may be unacceptably delayed while an analysis is being completed. (When General Mills does not use DTA for market planning decisions, this is cited as the most common reason.) A busy executive needs to devote some of his valuable time to making sure that all of the relevant judgments he can make have been fed into the analysis.

Even more serious a "cost" is the discomfort an executive feels as he forces his traditional way of thinking into an unfamiliar mold and lays bare to the discretion of a DTA specialist the most delicate considerations that enter into his decision making. These considerations sometimes include confidential information (as in the GE new product example previously noted), admissions of uncertainty (which often run counter to the prevailing managerial culture), and embarrassing motivations. In one instance of an elaborate analysis of possible locations for a European subsidiary, the actual decision was dominated by the fact that key personnel wanted to be near the International School in Geneva. Somehow, that consideration seemed too noneconomic and nonrational to be fed into the analysis.

However, such costs are by no means prohibitive if management's approach to DTA is sound and thorough. When that is the case, the advantages claimed by users of DTA are material and persuasive:

It focuses informal thinking on the critical elements of a decision.

It forces into the open hidden assumptions behind a decision and makes clear their logical implication.

It provides an effective vehicle for communicating the reasoning which underlies a recommendation.

Many of the executives most satisfied with DTA value it as a vehicle for communicating decision-making reasoning as well as for improving it. My own feeling is that DTA's contribution to the quality of decision making often seems to come more from forcing meaningful structure on informal reasoning than from supplementing it by formal analysis. For instance, in the Pillsbury Grocery Products Company, for every DTA pushed to its numerical conclusion, there are half a dozen cases where only a conceptual decision tree has been drawn. Such a tree is used to focus attention on the critical options and uncertainties, and is then dropped in favor of informal reasoning.

Suggestions for Starting

After reflecting on the experiences of successful and unsuccessful users of DTA, I want to offer some suggestions for the executive intent on trying out DTA in his organization:

Ensure the sympathetic involvement of the chief executive of the company (or operating unit).

Make sure that at least a few key executives have a minimal appreciation of what DTA can do for them and what it requires of them. (This might be done by means of one of the short DTA orientation courses currently available.)

Make at least one trial run on a decision problem—preferably a live one—with the help of a DTA specialist. Use the exercise as a training vehicle for your executives and staffers, without expecting immediate pay-offs.

Plan on recruiting or developing in-house staff specialists to do the detail on subsequent analyses. The specialists should report directly to you, not to part of an organizationally distant operations research group.

Wean yourself and your staff from outside specialists as soon as possible, using them only as residual technical resources.

On any particular DTA, follow the analysis closely enough to make sure that the problem which gets solved is the problem you have, and that you accept *all* of the underlying assumptions. This will probably mean a less sophisticated analysis than would gladden the heart of the typical technician. It will also probably mean you spend more time with the analysis than you think you can afford.

CONCLUSION

What efforts are needed to make DTA a more effective tool for the executive? It may be helpful to think of DTA as in some way analogous to an industrial product and to ask ourselves: What aspects of its "manufacture" or "marketing" stand most in need of attention?

The "fundamental research" and "product design" aspects (corresponding to statistical decision theory and the development of special analytical devices) appear to be in rather good shape. Rare are the instances in which successful use of DTA is held up through shortcomings in the purely technical state of the art. Of course, there are areas where improved DTA techniques need to be developed, such as the extraction of probability assessments, handling risk aversion and non-monetary criteria for action, and accommodating group decision making. But, even so, it is clear that greater use of DTA does not depend on such refinements. The tools that exist are well in advance of the capacity of most companies to use them.

Improvements in "production technique"—i.e., in the ability to deliver competent DTA at an acceptable cost—appear to be somewhat harder to achieve. In one major analysis of a pricing problem, the only reason that subjective probabilities were not introduced explicitly was that the computer cost would have been too high. However, we can be confident that within a few years progress in computer technology will largely eliminate this deterrent.

The manpower costs and delays involved in performing a reasonably complete analysis are usually more intractable. With the emergence and propagation of generalized computer programs of the type developed independently by each of the leaders (notably General Electric) in the DTA field, such costs can also be expected to decline—but the improvement will be gradual during the next five to ten years.

The inadequacy of "production facilities"—that is, the ability of DTA analysts to use available methods and concepts—is another temporary obstacle. Solving this problem will take more formal education and increased awareness of the issues and techniques that others have learned. Certainly help to this end will come from university programs and professional publications. Need for access to physical facilities, such as computer services, does not seem to be a serious limiting factor.

"Promotion" and "packaging" are areas requiring serious attention because they have been more neglected. It is true that the "product awareness" needed to stimulate management demand has been created by publications and executive development programs. But willingness to try the product DTA) requires communicating to a potential user the benefits he can expect. These benefits need to be ascertained and documented in a far more effective way than by incomplete testimonials from satisfied—and not so satisfied—users (as in a survey like the present one).

"Repeat buying" on the part of experimental users requires an attractive and convenient "package" so that an executive can contribute judgments and estimates with less pain and confusion, and also so that the conclusions of a DTA can be presented in a more effective, appealing manner. Confusing computer print-outs and technical reports account for many indifferent receptions to what are otherwise very adequate DTA's.

Somewhat allied to the packaging problem, and still more critical, is the question of how DTA should be *used* in the context of a company's operation. This raises the whole issue of how to organize the DTA function, how to implement recommendations, and how to identify suitable applications. Kent Quisel, a senior analyst at Du Pont, comments that he spends a third of his time on what he calls "user engineering," and that this amount is still not enough. At companies less experienced in DTA than Du Pont is, the proportion of time spent in this way is generally much less than a third, to the almost invariable detriment of DTA's effectiveness.

Possibly the most important area of all for study is "product evaluation." Just how good a product *is* DTA? How deserving is it of intensive development and promotion? The survey findings leave no doubt in my mind that many users are pleased with DTA, and with good cause. What is much less clear is just how important its impact can be on business as a whole. After all, only a very minute fraction of companies have so much as experimented with DTA. Can it really revolutionize management as mathematics has revolutionized engineering? Or will it forever be an occasionally helpful side calculation in a decision-making process that remains essentially unchanged?

The answers are clearly of major importance to businessmen and, indeed, depend in large measure on the businessmen themselves. How eager are they to improve the quality of their decision making? What scope for improvement is there? The answers to these questions are the key to many of the issues raised in this article.

SECTION C

The Behavioral School

One of the criticisms often made against both the management process and quantitative schools is that they give inadequate attention to the human side of enterprise. The behavioral school attempts to fill this void.

Many people feel that the first phase of this school was the human relations movement. This movement grew out of the famous Hawthorne Studies conducted at Western Electric's Hawthorne plant in Chicago. The major contribution of these studies was the interest they generated in human behavior in the work place. As a result, further studies by other researchers were conducted.

This has led to the evolution of the behavioral school. Advocates of this school are interested in the systematic analysis of behavior in organizations. As a result, they rely on the scientific method and the application of psycho-sociological concepts. In contrast to the human relationists who believed happy workers were productive workers, modern behaviorists believe each situation must be evaluated on its own merits. In addition, their interests cover a wide spectrum, including inter- and intraorganizational communication, motivation and effective leadership styles. The articles in this section are designed to provide the reader with a broad perspective of the behavioral school by examining a number of important behavioral concepts.

In the first article, Professor Golightly discusses the complex problem of organizational communication. He points out that "communicating" is not sufficient. What are also needed are criteria to determine what and *what not* to communicate as well as how to do it. He illustrates the importance of honesty and consistency in communicating with employees. He also stresses the importance of face-to-face exchanges. Without this type of interchange, a leader may fail to fully comprehend a particular situation. In the final analysis, organizational communication is a highly personal business, tempered and shaped by the people who use it.

Motivation is the key to productivity in organizations. In the second selection, Professor Vance Mitchell illustrates the complexity of this concept as well as the current "state of the art." He explores the major differences between expectancy x valence and drive x habit theories. The latter is not very explanatory of complex, judgmental behavior, whereas the former, particularly regarding valences, is very difficult to quantify. He also examines the major contributions in the area and concludes with an eclectic model that includes the strong points of each. Professor Mitchell feels that the major problem in this area of motivation is that of operationally defining terms.

The third article of this section, "How to Choose a Leadership Pattern," is a classic in the management field. First published in 1958, it has been revised and updated. In the latest version, Professors Tannenbaum and Schmidt present a continuum of leadership behavior extending from boss-centered leadership to subordinate-centered leadership. However, in contrast to their earlier article, the authors have now expanded their continuum to include forces in the external as well as internal environment. In addition, they note that in choosing a leadership pattern three factors are of particular importance: forces in the manager, forces in the subordinates, and forces in the situation.

In the last article of this section, Professor A. T. Hollingsworth points out that the complexity of organizational decisions and the lack of operationally defined variables do not preclude a manager from the responsibility of making decisions. The decision maker must operate within a framework containing a myriad of variables. Professor Hollingsworth illustrates this by pointing out the plethora of variables, both formal and informal, that have an effect on organizational decisions. He illustrates, through two examples, the importance of an awareness of these variables and their logical use if an individual is to make effective decisions.

---

9   The What, What Not, and How of Internal Communication

Henry O. Golightly

Almost everyone involved in the management of business—whether on a large or small scale—understands the importance of good corporate communications. To underline this importance, virtually every large company

---

This article originally appeared in *Business Horizons* (December 1973), pp. 47–50. Copyright 1973 by the Foundation for the School of Business at Indiana University. Reprinted by permission.

and a high percentage of smaller ones launched programs within the past decade that they hoped would improve communications within their organizations. The goal of these programs was basically to deliver appropriate company information (goals, specific objectives, and policies) to managers and employees at every level and to see that information also flowed in the reverse direction, from employees to management.

But despite all the effort, many such programs never seem to get off the ground. The main reason, I believe, is that, while the initial purpose is commendable, its concept has rarely been developed. Simply "communicating" is not enough. One must consider just what it is that a chief executive (or other leader) should communicate, what he should not communicate, and how he should do both.

Following is an exploration into these areas. A company must explore them in depth before it can launch an internal communications system that will offer the chief executive and his aides the tools they need to convey information effectively to and from their people.

WHAT TO COMMUNICATE

In creating a communications program, the top executive must first consider just what it is he should communicate. Obviously, he should tell his employees about the company's policies, its objective and goals, those jobs he wants done, and the way he wants them done. He should make available to them an outline of the organization's framework and the structure of the communications system, so that employees know how the company and the system work and what they can reasonably expect from both. Each employee should have a clear-cut definition of what his job is and his scope of authority.

The top executive should confide to employees those serious problems and opportunities that affect the company as a whole, especially if the employees can do something about these problems and opportunities. He should also balance the news. If the news is too good too often or too good to be true, it will be doubted. For example, an oil company that claims it has eliminated pollution completely or an aerospace firm that swears good times are just around the corner may find it difficult to achieve credibility. Developments within a company must be evaluated and reported as they really are—or not at all. Is there genuine indication that a company's problem has been solved or is it just a surface improvement?

When there are real accomplishments, by all means, report them. Nothing will renew confidence and hope faster. But be sure first that the progress is authentic.

This leads to the most important point of all—an executive must communicate with honesty. He must tell only those things that are true, and he must be sure before he promises anything that he or his company is able to deliver it. Only then can he convince his audience—the supervisor who did not get a raise, the union member who knows there has been a contract battle, the board of directors that expects dollar returns, his lending institutions who need to have accurate forecasts and performance information—that what is being communicated is worthy of communication.

One further piece of advice to all managers: no matter what the communication is, it must be consistent with other information. The president of one company talked, quite truthfully, to his employees on closed circuit television about serious major problems of the company. At the same time, his top aides were announcing that the company's sales volume was at an all-time high. Who was to be believed? As far as the employees were concerned, no one was. Although both were correct, they were inconsistent from the perspective of the audience.

Or consider a company that goes to great lengths to tell employees about adverse conditions, but communicates little when the sailing is smooth. Be consistent in approach.

WHAT NOT TO COMMUNICATE

On the other side of the coin, the astute executive will sense what *not* to say to his audience. He will not, out of simple respect for his fellow workers, publicly criticize other executives or departments. Nor will he try to influence his employees' political convictions. These actions would be, in a sense, spreading propaganda and infringing upon employees' rights.

If he heads a large company, the chief executive will not be directly involved in day-to-day labor relations. Although he maintains friendly relations with the union, and sees that the policies governing employees are fair, equitable, and competitive, labor relations consume too much time for the chief executive to conduct contract negotiations personally and still run the business. This important activity must be delegated within limits.

Among the matters that he should not communicate are the commonplace, nitty-gritty problems of the normal nature of the business. As I have already suggested, the major problems that affect the entire company are best told to the employees. For one, they may be able to help; two, they may very well have heard an "unreleased" and distorted or exaggerated version, and that version should be challenged by the truth. But everyday worries are different. For the most part, these problems belong to the chief executive alone. Make them public and they will become a source of worry, and ultimately of annoyance, to everyone.

HOW TO COMMUNICATE

While the communication techniques utilized by a company are dictated by its size, the principles of communication remain the same for all companies. The large company, for instance, will have its regularly issued in-house organ; the small company will send out an occasional newsletter. But both of these represent communication by the written word.

The basic and most common way the chief executive communicates—regardless of company size—is formally, through his organizational channels. The good executive knows how to use his chief aides, communicating through them to all parts of his organization, until all appropriate employees have been reached. The efficient company has as few management levels as possible so the company messages downward and upward can move quickly and not be diffused or distorted.

The president may want to extend his message, not only through executive channels, but directly to all employees. Eastern Airlines, for example, recently called a meeting of approximately 800 managers to communicate next year's plans. Pan American is using a similar approach, management workshops, to secure understanding of its new streamlined field organization.

There are various ways to reach many people quickly. One means is through print. The written word is especially effective in conveying important announcements the president wants to be sure are understood. Other methods are radio, film, and closed circuit television. But the most effective and unbeatable method for learning what employees are thinking, what their needs are, and what their problems are that relate to the company's product is to visit personally with employees right down the line. Although no president has the time to rely exclusively on the first-hand, person-to-person method of communication, no president can afford to ignore this method entirely. Nothing else he does will bring him as close to his rank-and-file employees, and nothing else will make his message count for more.

Soon after President Eisenhower took office, I asked one company's vice-president for governmental affairs to comment on the different communication styles of President Eisenhower and President Truman. She told me that President Eisenhower depended almost completely on all news going through regular channels, with each key man giving him a briefing on what was happening. As a result, he had to see very few people.

President Truman, on the other hand, saw practically everyone. People came and went constantly, until it was almost like having Andrew Jackson back in the White House. To the casual observer, President Truman was the most disorganized person in the world. But through his methods, he was able to personally determine the things that were important. He *really* knew what was going on. I believe the same is true for the president of a company who goes out—at least occasionally—to his employees.

However, one point must be considered when a corporate manager decides on his primary means of communication. And that is his personality or style. One executive may be at his best when he is dealing with a small group of aides; another man may shine when he is facing thousands in mass contact; and another is most effective in personal contact with the individual.

But even the president who is not comfortable with throngs of people must still make the effort to get out and see things for himself. He must not, through timidity or other characteristics, abdicate his authority. And this can easily happen if he sits in his office waiting for news to be brought to him rather than going out to gather and give the news himself.

Some executives at all levels suffer from not venturing out of their offices frequently enough. Reports come over their desks, which they peruse carefully every day, but which may not reveal the whole truth. An executive may, for example, go out to see the plant in Albuquerque and discover that the local manager has been painting a rosy glow over a gloomy situation. The plant manager has not actually lied; he has merely stressed what is rosy—and disregarded the rest. Or consider the manager of a hotel that showed a handsome profit but at the expense of ignoring property maintenance.

But there are many companies that have established communications systems that keep the president informed at every level. International Telephone and Telegraph, for example, holds two meetings a month of general managers—one in New York, the other in Europe. Each manager makes his own report. I can venture to say that Harold Geneen knows very well what is going on in his company. In the Norton Simon Company, the president participates in operation board meetings of all subsidiary divisions. He gets reports directly, and his personal statements and attitudes are communicated in turn right down the line. Many years ago, American Airlines eliminated its regional management setup and had major cities report to a general manager. This shortened the lines of communication and reduced the number of employees while increasing the volume of reports.

Corporate communications is a highly useful and mature discipline. But no matter how sophisticated the system is, it still remains highly personal business, tempered and shaped by the man who uses it. In this sense it is, in the final analysis, the president's personality and his allegiance to the truth that can make any system work.

10 Expectancy Theories of Managerial Motivation

Vance F. Mitchell

INTRODUCTION

Behavioral scientists concerned with understanding motivation in the work place have directed their attention in recent years along several different lines. These lines of investigation have been labelled respectively as drive × habit, expectancy × valence, equity, goal, and two-factor theories. Of these, the most fully developed are drive × habit and expectancy × valence theories.

Although we are concerned here primarily with expectancy theories of motivation, it seems appropriate to trace the origins and explain both theories very briefly. The two lines of theorizing will then be compared. The remainder of the paper will be devoted to the current state of expectancy theory and some of the problems that must be resolved for the future development of this approach to explaining managerial motivation.

The origin of both drive × habit and expectancy × valence theories of motivation is found in the ancient Greek philosophy of Hedonism as well as in the work of the English Utilitarians such as Jeremy Bentham and John Stuart Mill (Vroom, 1964; Atkinson, 1964). The central assumption of such thinking is that of the familiar pain-pleasure principle, i.e., that behavior is directed toward pleasure and away from pain. Drive × habit theories of motivation, however, grow directly out of the work of Thorndike (1911) as expressed in his well known Law of Effect. This law may be paraphrased simply as stating that behavior which seems to lead to reward tends to be repeated, while behavior which seems not to lead to reward or to lead to punishment tends not to be repeated.

In common with the Hedonistic principle, the Law of Effect does not explain why certain events are satisfying or dissatisfying, but it does incorporate the notions of past learning and stimulus-response relationships in explaining present behavior.

DRIVE × HABIT THEORY

Modern drive × habit theory, notably as expressed by the psychologists Hull (1943, 1952) and Spence (1956) has evolved from this rather mechanistic point of view incorporating the very extensive body of experimentation on learning and reinforcement that has taken place during the past forty years. In its present form the theory explains behavior as resulting from a combination of drives, habits and incentives.

Drives are seen as energizers and partial directors of behavior in an effort to satisfy basic human needs. Habits are defined as gradually built-up associations between a stimulus situation and a response that influence the type of behavior a drive will energize. Incentives are conceived of as anticipations about future goals that serve to trigger habits established through past learning.

Not withstanding the inclusion of

This article originally appeared in *Academy of Management Proceedings* (1971), pp. 210–220, and is reprinted with permission.

incentives as a variable, the important characteristic of this line of theorizing about motivation is its heavy dependence on past experience and learning as determinants of human behavior. Not surprisingly, it has been found quite useful in explaining and predicting repetitive, production-type work behavior. As Lawler (1971) points out, drive × habit theories have often been cited as support for piece rate types of incentive programs. Applicability of the theory to complex, judgmental behavior usually associated with managerial positions is much more limited.

EXPECTANCY THEORIES

On the other hand, expectancy theories of motivation explicitly take into account our differing preferences for various outcomes or consequences of behavior and our tendencies to develop subjective probabilities or expectations concerning the future.

This line of theorizing may be traced to the work of Lewin and Tolman that had its beginnings in the 1930s. From the work of these psychologists, a number of very similar theories of motivation have been developed. Among the first of these to deal specifically with the question of motivation in the workplace was the path-goal hypothesis advanced in 1957 by Georgopoulos, Mahoney and Jones of the University of Michigan's Survey Research Center. This hypothesis stated that "If a worker sees high productivity as a path leading to one or more of his personal goals, he will tend to be a high producer" and conversely. Path-goal perceptions were conceived as expectancies or psychological probabilities of varying amounts of return or reward as a consequence of certain behavior. As these authors put it, "How much payoff is there for me toward attaining a personal goal while expending so much effort toward the achievement of an assigned organizational objec-

tive?" (Georgopoulos, Mahoney and Jones, 1957, p. 346) An empirical test of the hypothesis by the authors with a sample of production workers yielded confirming results and has served to encourage further development of the expectancy theories.

A more elegant statement of the theory was expressed by Vroom (1964) in his landmark study *Work and Motivation*. Shortly thereafter, Porter and Lawler (1968) provided a somewhat different and more elaborate statement of expectancy × valence theory explicitly directed toward the question of managerial motivation.

Motivation

As far as the motivation segment of both models is concerned, there are three key variables. Porter (1971) has termed these Type I Expectancies or subjective probabilities, Type II Expectancies, and the Valence of Outcomes. Type I Expectancies are those that a given amount of effort will lead to some level of work-related accomplishment. Type II Expectancies are that a given level of accomplishment will lead to particular outcomes or results such as a promotion or increased job security on the one hand or a demotion or getting fired on the other. Vroom terms these Type II Expectancies as Instrumentalities. Valences of Outcomes may be thought of as preferences. That is, how much an individual likes or dislikes the possible outcomes associated with a situation.

Motivation to perform then, in Vroom's formulation is determined by the interaction between the expectation that a given amount of effort will lead to a particular level of performance and the valence or attractiveness of that performance level for the individual. But the valence of a given performance level is in turn a function of the net valence of the several outcomes that are associated with it and the perceived likelihood of these outcomes occurring.

For example, a manager may believe that a great deal of effort on his part can lead to a high level of job performance. However the theory argues that before embarking on this course of action he will consider the possible outcomes associated and the probability of their occurrence. If the probability he attaches to negatively valued outcomes such as a heart attack or possible trouble with his wife should outweigh his expectations of good feelings or a badly wanted promotion, he would not be motivated to work harder.

Porter and Lawler explain motivation somewhat differently. Type I Expectancies that effort will lead to performance and Type II Expectancies that performance will lead to particular outcomes are hypothesized as interacting to form a single variable which they label the effort-reward probability. The nature of the interaction is not specified but is visualized by these theorists as "probably multiplicative" (Porter and Lawler, 1968, p. 20). That is, the probability of effort leading to performance times the probability of performance leading to reward forms the probability of effort leading to reward. The valence or preference for possible outcomes is referred to as Value of Reward. Motivation is described as the product of these two variables, or effort-reward probability times value of reward.

There are two important differences between Vroom's formulation and that of Porter and Lawler. First, Vroom takes into account the possibility of both pleasant and unpleasant outcomes of an individual's performance. While Porter and Lawler recognize the existence of unpleasant outcomes, their model focuses only on those with a positive value to determine their variable value of reward. A second difference lies in the method of combining expectancies and valences which could lead to different predictions of the level of motivation where multiple outcomes of performance exist.

Ability

In addition to motivation, both Vroom and Porter and Lawler hypothesize that an individual's actual performance depends also on his ability or capacity to perform. This distinction between motivation or will to perform on the one hand, and actual ability on the other, and the notion of some form of interaction between these two variables in determining performance has been recognized for some years. An operationally satisfactory definition of task-related abilities however, has been elusive to say the least. Vroom defines a person's ability to perform a task as ". . . the degree to which he possesses all the personal attributes necessary for a high level of performance, excluding those of a psychological nature" (p. 198). Porter and Lawler (1968) are only slightly more helpful. To them abilities are ". . . relatively stable, long term individual characteristics (e.g., personality traits, manual skills, intelligence, etc.) that represent the individual's currently developed power to perform" (p. 22).

Role Perceptions

Porter and Lawler also introduce the concept of role perceptions as an additional determinant of performance. More precisely, this variable is described as the accuracy with which an individual defines his job role. As Porter and Lawler state, "If his perceptions of his role correspond to those of his superiors in his organization, then he will be applying his effort where it will count the most for successful performance as defined by the organization" (p. 24). If his perceptions do not correspond to those of his superiors, then he may try very hard indeed yet fail to reach an effective level of performance as defined by the organization.

To summarize thus far, Vroom explains the level of an individual's job performance as some function of a multiplicative interaction between force to perform or motivation, and task relevant abilities. Porter and Lawler, on the other hand, see performance as a function of a three way multiplicative interaction between motivation to perform, which they term effort, task relevant abilities, and the accuracy with which an individual perceives his job role. The two formulations are depicted in Figure 1.

Rewards

Porter and Lawler go further however by specifying two classes of positive outcomes or rewards that the individual can receive as a consequence of performance. A job well done may lead to intrinsic rewards such as increased feelings of self esteem. The organization may provide extrinsic reward in the form of increased pay or promotion. Either class of reward or both may be associated with an individual's performance. Additionally, the model recognizes that any reward received by the individual will be perceived in terms of its fairness or equity. These two classes of rewards and the perception of equity of reward are seen as intervening between performance and satisfaction and also as feeding back to influence the individual's future perceptions of the probability that effort will lead to reward.

DRIVE AND EXPECTANCY THEORIES COMPARED

At this point let us compare in somewhat more detail the expectancy theories of motivation that have been described with those that are built on the basis of drives and habits. It has already been noted that a major difference lies in the emphasis placed on past learning by the drive theorists as contrasted with the forward-looking focus of expectancy theories. Although drive theories do include incentives, the manner in which this variable is defined fails to provide a satisfactory explanation of behavior that is in-

tended to avoid unpleasant consequences.

Drive theory explains avoidance behavior in terms of generalized emotional reactions such as fear that in turn elicit specific avoidance habits such as refusal to work harder or to undertake high risk courses of action. This does not explain why the manager in our earlier illustration might avoid a high level of effort because of the perception that this effort might lead to a heart attack if he had never experienced such an outcome previously.

Expectancy theory explains avoidance behavior quite simply in terms of disagreeable consequences that are perceived as sufficiently likely to occur that they will discourage an individual from a particular line of behavior. Fear or other generalized emotional response need not be present at all.

On the other hand, expectancy theories have not been at all explicit in explaining how people learn just what behavior is appropriate in different situations. Porter and Lawler attempted to deal with this shortcoming in two ways. First they described the feed-back loop between rewards, or the outcomes of performance and the future perception of the probability that effort would lead to reward. Thus outcomes that are perceived by an individual both as related to his performance and as rewarding would serve to reinforce a particular pattern of behavior. Second, the role perceptions variable in the Porter and Lawler model implicitly takes into account past learning since role behavior is built up over time as a consequence of perceptions and experience. Notwithstanding, the extremely important concepts of learning and habit are not dealt with explicitly in either the Vroom or the Porter and Lawler model.

Expectancy theories have been criticized also for their vagueness about the manner in which individuals formulate their personal expectations about the

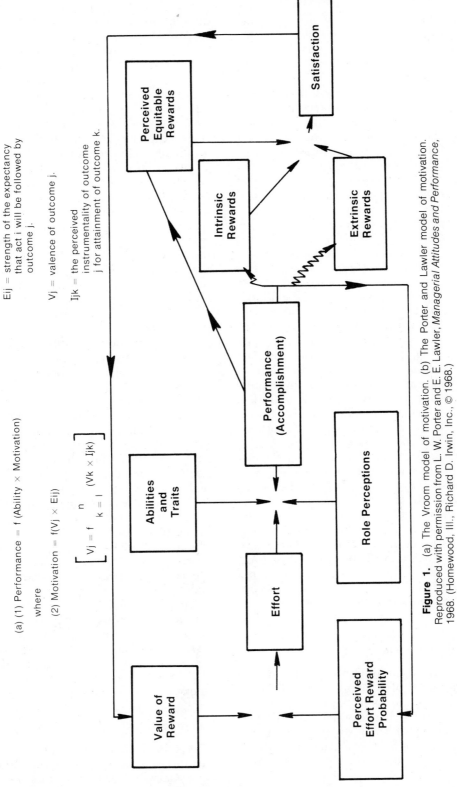

(a) (1) Performance = f (Ability × Motivation)

where

(2) Motivation = f(Vj × Eij)

$$\left[V_j = f \sum_{k=1}^{n} (V_k \times I_{jk}) \right]$$

Eij = strength of the expectancy that act i will be followed by outcome j.

Vj = valence of outcome j.

Ijk = the perceived instrumentality of outcome j for attainment of outcome k.

Figure 1. (a) The Vroom model of motivation. (b) The Porter and Lawler model of motivation. Reproduced with permission from L. W. Porter and E. E. Lawler, *Managerial Attitudes and Performance*, 1968. (Homewood, Ill., Richard D. Irwin, Inc., © 1968.)

likelihood of various outcomes occurring. Drive × habit theory emphasizes associations that are built up over time through experience and reinforcement. But drive theory is silent concerning expectations that can be created quickly by simple verbal statements or assurances that certain outcomes will follow specified types of performance. Neither line of theorizing attempts to account for the rapid changes that occur in the subjective probabilities that individuals attach to certain classes of outcomes.

Still another criticism that has frequently been made of expectancy theories concerns their failure to explain what factors determine the valence of particular outcomes. Porter and Lawler provide a partial explanation by hypothesizing that satisfaction or dissatisfaction with particular outcomes will influence their valence. For example, the satisfaction an individual experiences from the perception of appropriate recognition by his superiors on completion of a difficult task is hypothesized to influence the future valence of recognition. This hypothesis is based on the assumption that one of the ways through which outcomes acquire valence is through their ability to satisfy various needs. On the other hand, drive theory traditionally has been quite specific in describing the ability of objects or physical rewards to satisfy certain primary physiological drives. It is difficult to see, however, how cognitive needs such as autonomy or self-fulfillment could be incorporated into drive theory.

Empirical Evidence

Notwithstanding these shortcomings a number of scholars in the field of organizational behavior have elected to focus their attention on the further development and testing of expectancy theory. In particular, the two theoretical formulations by Vroom and Porter and Lawler have generated considerable interest and research. At least eleven empirical studies have attempted to test portions of one model or the other and a number of others have investigated various expectancy hypotheses. However, these studies will not be reviewed in detail here. Excellent discussions of the published evidence are available in a forthcoming review article by Heneman and Schwab (in press) and in Lawler's careful and scholarly study of *Pay and Organizational Effectiveness* (1971).

It is important to note that this evidence does not provide strong support for either model. There are several excellent reasons why this is so. First, in only one instance has the design of a study conformed to the complete theoretical framework of either of Vroom's or Porter and Lawler's model. The motivation variable has frequently been measured in ways that are inconsistent with the theories. Measures of ability have been omitted from most studies and when included have been inappropriate or perfunctory. The accuracy of role perceptions has been included as a variable in only one investigation. Finally, the analytical techniques that have been employed frequently have been suboptimal.

The evidence does suggest that both Type I and Type II expectancies and the accuracy of role perceptions do influence the level of an individual's performance. On the other hand, the interactions between motivation and ability hypothesized by Vroom or between effort, ability, and accuracy of role perceptions postulated by Porter and Lawler have not been confirmed. It seems appropriate to conclude with Heneman and Schwab (1972) that "The predictive power of the total theory is thus essentially unknown."

Theoretical Developments

At a theoretical level, much more encouraging development has taken place. Campbell, Dunnette, Lawler and

Weick (1970) have developed a hybrid expectancy model that incorporates a number of the ideas of Graen (1967) and Porter and Lawler (1968). However, Lawler (1970, 1971), has elaborated the Porter and Lawler statement of expectancy theory in a way that provides the most appealing answers thus far to several of the criticisms of the theory noted earlier.

Consistent with Vroom's formulation, motivation is described in the Lawler model as determined by the interaction between effort-performance expectations, performance-outcome expectations and valences of outcomes. As in earlier models this interaction is specified as multiplicative. However, several additional variables are included. Past learning and habit are subsumed through the impact on both sets of expectations of an individual's observed and personal experience in similar and identical stimulus situations. Effort-performance expectancies are visualized also as affected by the individual's self-esteem or confidence in himself. Perceptions of the probability that performance will lead to some set of outcomes are hypothesized as influenced by the internal or external nature of the individual's personality (Rotter, 1955). That is, to what extent does he see himself as "Captain of his fate" as opposed to being subject to environmental forces beyond his control.

Needs such as those postulated by Maslow (1954), McClelland (1961) and others are specified as an important determinant of the preference for outcomes as is the perception of fairness of the outcomes seen as likely to result from given levels of effort and performance.

Although not explicitly stated in the model, Lawler does recognize that situational factors may intervene between effort and performance. That is, events beyond the individual's control may interfere with his performance no matter how hard he may try.

The role perceptions variable in the earlier Porter and Lawler model is relabeled Problem-solving Approach which Lawler (1971) describes as the individual's "how to do it approach" and somewhat similar to the drive theory concept of habit (p. 113). The interdependence of the several variables and feed-back relationships specified by Lawler are depicted in Figure 2. Note that performance is hypothesized as leading to rewards. Although the link between performance and rewards is by a wavy line to indicate that rewards may not always follow from performance, use of the term outcomes would have been more consistent with expectancy theory and the remainder of the model.

This theoretical model is much richer conceptually than either of its predecessors. Furthermore, the model substantially narrows the difference between expectancy theory on the one hand, and drive × habit or other theoretical approaches to motivation on the other. Important concepts and findings from these other lines of theorizing have been incorporated to form an eclectic explanation of motivated behavior that has a great deal of intuitive appeal. Learning and habit, individual difference variables, and the whole range of human needs are portrayed as influencing expectations and preferences to determine motivation and the pattern of performance.

PROBLEMS TO BE RESOLVED

Lawler's model provides an excellent basis for further theoretical and empirical development of our understanding of managerial motivation. There are however, some formidable problems to be resolved. Let us examine a few of these.

We need much more information concerning the factors that influence expectations about both the likelihood that effort will lead to performance and that performance will lead to certain outcomes. In addition to the vari-

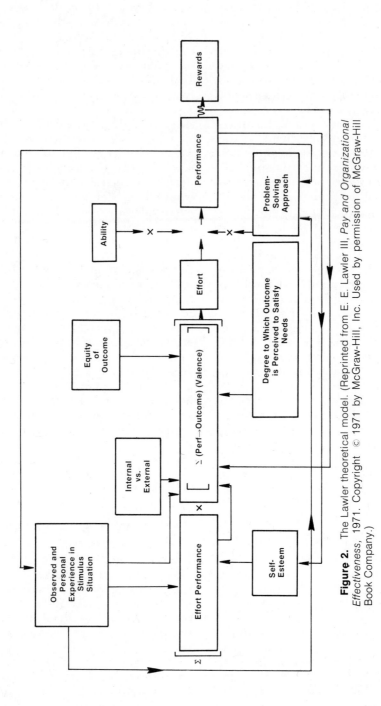

Figure 2. The Lawler theoretical model. (Reprinted from E. E. Lawler III, *Pay and Organizational Effectiveness*, 1971. Copyright © 1971 by McGraw-Hill, Inc. Used by permission of McGraw-Hill Book Company.)

ables Lawler has specified, we do know that an individual's expectations are highly volatile and are influenced in the short run by such factors as his physiological and emotional state. For example, what may at one time seem very feasible or likely may be viewed with much less optimism when one is tired, depressed, or even disappointed by the outcome of some quite unrelated undertaking. Likewise, the work of Rotter (1967) on differences in the level of interpersonal trust suggests that this phenomenon may very well affect one's expectations.

Valences also have been shown to be temporally unstable (Edwards, 1954, 1961). That is, both the relative and absolute magnitude of an individual's feelings toward particular outcomes tend to change from one time period to another. Much remains to be learned about the factors that influence valence and how best to measure this variable. In this regard, Vroom (1964) has identified four alternative methods for measuring valence in addition to the self-report measures that are most commonly used.

Heneman and Schwab (1972) have pointed out the need for further research to identify more accurately the various outcomes of performance that are perceived as possible by individuals in particular job settings as well as the valence they attach to each. Thus far most investigators have preselected a limited number of outcomes, almost invariably limiting these to positive outcomes or rewards. Systematic investigations are needed of the outcomes that are both actually available and perceived as available by individuals in various job situations. These investigations should include both pleasant and unpleasant types of outcomes and seek to learn what performance—outcome expectations have the greatest influence on behavior. How do these outcomes and expectations change as the individual gains seniority in the organization or moves from one function or level to another?

Answers are required to these and many more research questions concerning expectations and valences (for a more complete discussion of research questions suggested by expectancy theories of motivation, see Campbell et. al., 1970.)

Similar problems exist with respect to nearly all the variables in the model. The concept of effort is a particularly difficult one where other than simple physical exertion is concerned. Applied to managers, effort may be thought of as how much of himself a manager devotes to the job out of the total resources of effort and energy available to him. In this sense the term effort would include mental as well as physical effort and such aspects of the individual's energy resources as would be consumed by the enthusiasm, sense of involvement, and feelings of concern he develops in doing his job. Most studies thus far have by-passed this variable and attempted to explain motivational variations in performance entirely in terms of expectancies and valences. Yet, using a relatively crude measure that included these aspects of effort, Mitchell (1967) found a highly significant relationship between self-ratings of effort and supervisors' rankings of performance. Additional studies are needed that will investigate the components of managerial effort and the relationships between expectancies and valences on the one hand and actual effort expended on the other.

Turning now to problem-solving style, there does not seem to be any real difference between Lawler's explanation of this "how to do it" variable and the accuracy of role perceptions variable in the Porter and Lawler (1968) model. Porter and Lawler point out that the role elements that are critical to performance may differ considerably from one job to another. Comparatively little work has been done to identify these inter-job differences or to develop sensitive measures of the agreement between supervisors' and subordinates' perceptions of the subordinates' role (Barrett, 1966; Mitchell, 1967). At the same time, we must recognize that supervisors may differ in their judgments of appropriate role behavior on the part of their subordinates largely because of differences in their basic management philosophy. Further, as managers progress beyond the lower levels of supervision, specifications for the job become more difficult to define and more idiosyncratic to the incumbent. Perhaps then in a number of managerial positions the individual's perceptions of appropriate role behavior may be more valid than those of his supervisors (Gavin, 1970).

While the accuracy of role perceptions has received relatively little attention, the abilities that are necessary for effective managerial performance have been the subject of a great deal of research. The expectancy theorists point to the availability of a wide variety of psychometric instruments. Yet a careful review of a large number of prediction studies shows that correlations between individual difference measures and managerial effectiveness have rarely exceeded .40. The best prediction results have been obtained through a combination of psychometric and clinical assessments that were carefully tailored to individuals, positions, and organizations (Campbell et al., 1970). Future tests of expectancy models should recognize this experience and incorporate only ability measures that have been carefully validated for the situation to be studied.

Comparatively few organizations have undertaken such a program of selection research. On the other hand, where meaningful measures of ability have been identified and adopted, an effective test of the expectancy model could be seriously complicated since a rather restricted range of scores could be expected from members of such an organization.

Finally, students of organizational behavior are only too familiar with the criterion problem, or the difficulties that are encountered in defining and measuring effective managerial performance. Enough has been said on this subject elsewhere to warrant mere reference here of the problems yet to be solved with respect to this variable.

CONCLUSION

In conclusion, the work of the expectancy theorists represents a truly large step away from the dust-bowl empiricism of which industrial psychology and organizational behavior so often have been justly accused. However, a great deal of work is needed to refine the definition and extend our understanding of the individual building blocks comprising expectancy theory. In the process of this work, it seems very likely that additional, essential elements of the theory will be identified.

Our efforts should be directed toward the performance of these tasks, but with a strong Type II expectation that successful performance will lead to outcomes all of us will value highly in the form of increased understanding of managerial motivation.

REFERENCES

Atkinson, J. W. *An Introduction to Motivation.* Princeton, N.J.: Van Nostrand, 1964.

Barrett, R. S. The influence of the supervisor's requirements on ratings. *Personnel Psychology,* 1966, *19,* 375–387.

Campbell, J. P., Dunnette, M. D., Lawler, E. E., and Weick, K. E. *Managerial Behavior, Performance, and Effectiveness.* New York: McGraw Hill, 1970.

Edwards, W. The theory of decision making. *Psychological Bulletin,* 1954, 51, 380–417.

Edwards, W. Behavioral decision theory. *Annual Review of Psychology,* 1961, *12,* 473–498.

Gavin, J. F. Ability, effort, and role perceptions as antecedents of job performance. *Experimental Publication System,* 1970, issue 5, manuscript number 190A.

Graen, G. B. Work motivation: The behavioral effects of job content and job context factors in an employment situation. Unpublished doctoral dissertation, University of Minnesota, 1967.

Georgopoulos, B. S., Mahoney, G. M., and Jones,

N. W. A path-goal approach to productivity. *Journal of Applied Psychology*, 1957, *41*, 345–353.

Heneman, H. G. and Schwab, D. P. An evaluation of research on expectancy theory predictions of employee performance. *Psychological Bulletin*, 1972, *78*, 1–9.

Hull, C. L. *Principles of Behavior*. New York: Appleton-Century, 1943.

Hull, C. L. *A Behavior System*. New Haven, Conn.: Yale, 1951.

Lawler, E. E. Job attitudes and employee motivation: Theory, research, and practice. *Personnel Psychology*, 1970, *23*, 223–237.

Lawler, E. E. *Pay and Organizational Effectiveness: A Psychological View*. New York: McGraw Hill, 1971.

Mitchell, V. F. The relationship of effort, abilities, and role perceptions to managerial performance. Unpublished doctoral dissertation, University of California, 1967.

Porter, L. W. Motivational theory as it relates to professional updating. Paper presented at the XVII International Congress of Applied Psychology, Liege, Belgium, July 1971.

Porter, L. W. and Lawler, E. E. *Managerial Attitudes and Performance*. Homewood, Ill.: Irwin, 1968.

Rotter, J. B. The role of the psychological situation in determining human behavior. In M. R. Jones (ed.), *Nebraska Symposium on Motivation*, 1955. Lincoln: University of Nebraska Press. 245–268.

Rotter, J. B. A new scale for the measurement of interpersonal trust. *Journal of Personality*, 1967, 35, 651–665.

Spence, K. W. *Behavior Theory and Conditioning*. New Haven, Conn.: Yale, 1956.

Thorndike, E. L. *Animal Intelligence: Experimental Studies*. New York: MacMillan, 1911.

Vroom, V. H. *Work and Motivation*. New York: Wiley, 1964.

11 How to Choose a Leadership Pattern

Robert Tannenbaum and Warren H. Schmidt

"I put most problems into my group's hands and leave it to them to carry the ball from there. I serve merely as a catalyst, mirroring back the people's thoughts and feelings so that they can better understand them."

"It's foolish to make decisions oneself on matters that affect people. I always talk thing over with my subordinates, but I make it clear to them that I'm the one who has to have the final say."

"Once I have decided on a course of action, I do my best to sell my ideas to my employees."

"I'm being paid to lead. If I let a lot of other people make the decisions I should be making, then I'm not worth my salt."

"I believe in getting things done. I can't waste time calling meetings. Someone has to call the shots around here, and I think it should be me."

Each of these statements represent a point of view about "good leadership." Considerable experience, factual data, and theoretical principles could be cited to support each statement, even though they seem to be inconsistent when placed together. Such contradictions point up the dilemma in which the modern manager frequently finds himself.

NEW PROBLEM

The problem of how the modern manager can be "democratic" in his relations with subordinates and at the same time maintain the necessary authority and control in the organization for which he is responsible has come into focus increasingly in recent years.

Earlier in the century this problem was not so acutely felt. The successful executive was generally pictured as possessing intelligence, imagination, initiative, the capacity to make rapid (and generally wise) decisions, and the ability to inspire subordinates. People tended to think of the world as being divided into "leaders" and "followers."

New Focus: Gradually, however, from the social sciences emerged the concept of "group dynamics" with its focus on *members* of the group rather than solely on the leader. Research efforts of social scientists underscored the importance of employee involvement and participation in decision making. Evidence began to challenge the efficiency of highly directive leadership, and increasing attention was paid to problems of motivation and human relations.

Through training laboratories in group development that sprang up across the country, many of the newer notions of leadership began to exert an impact. These training laboratories were carefully designed to give people a first-hand experience in full participation and decision making. The designated "leaders" deliberately attempted to reduce their own power and to make group members as responsible as possible for setting their own goals and methods within the laboratory experience.

It was perhaps inevitable that some of the people who attended the training laboratories regarded this kind of leadership as being truly "democratic" and went home with the determination to build fully participative decision making into their own organizations. Whenever their bosses made a decision without convening a staff meeting, they tended to perceive this as authoritarian behavior. The true symbol of democratic leadership to some was the meeting—and the less directed from the top, the more democratic it was.

Some of the more enthusiastic alumni of these training laboratories began to get the habit of categorizing leader behavior as "democratic" *or* "authoritarian." The boss who made too many decisions himself was thought of as an authoritarian, and his directive behavior was often attributed solely to his personality.

New Need: The net result of the research findings and of the human relations training based upon them has been to call into question the stereotype of an effective leader. Consequently, the modern manager often finds himself in an uncomfortable state of mind.

Often he is not quite sure how to behave; there are times when he is torn between exerting "strong" leadership and "permissive" leadership. Sometimes new knowledge pushes him in one direction ("I should really get the group to help make this decision"), but at the same time his experience pushes him in another direction ("I really understand the problem better than the group and therefore I should make the decision"). He is not sure when a group decision is really appropriate or when holding a staff meeting serves merely as a device for avoiding his own decision-making responsibility.

The purpose of our article is to suggest a framework which managers may find useful in grappling with this dilemma. First, we shall look at the different patterns of leadership behavior that the manager can choose from in relating himself to his subordinates. Then, we shall turn to some of the questions suggested by this range of patterns. For instance, how important is it for a manager's subordinates to know what type of leadership he is using in a situation? What factors should he consider in deciding on a leadership pattern? What difference do his long-run objectives make as compared to his immediate objectives?

RANGE OF BEHAVIOR

Figure 1 presents the continuum or range of possible leadership behavior available to a manager. Each type of action is related to the degree of authority used by the boss and to the amount of freedom available to his subordinates in reaching decisions. The actions seen on the extreme left characterize the manager who maintains a high degree of control while those seen on the extreme right characterize the manager who releases a high degree of control. Neither extreme is absolute; authority and freedom are never without their limitations.

Now let us look more closely at each of the behavior points occurring along this continuum.

The manager makes the decision and announces it

In this case the boss identifies a problem, considers alternative solutions, chooses one of them, and then reports this decision to his subordinates for implementation. He may or may not give consideration to what he believes his subordinates will think or feel about his decision; in any case, he provides no opportunity for them to participate directly in the decision-making process. Coercion may or may not be used or implied.

The manager "sells" his decision

Here the manager, as before, takes responsibility for identifying the problem and arriving at a decision. However, rather than simply announcing it, he takes the additional step of persuading his subordinates to accept it. In doing so, he recognizes the possibility of some resistance among those who will be faced with the decision, and seeks to reduce this resistance by indicating, for example, what the employees have to gain from his decision.

The manager presents his ideas, invites questions

Here the boss who has arrived at a decision and who seeks acceptance of his ideas provides an opportunity for his subordinates to get a fuller explanation of his thinking and his intentions. After presenting the ideas, he invites questions so that his associates can better understand what he is trying to accomplish. This "give and take" also enables the manager and the subordinates to explore more fully the implications of the decision.

The manager presents a tentative decision subject to change

This kind of behavior permits the subordinates to exert some influence on the decision. The initiative for identifying and diagnosing the problem remains with the boss. Before meeting with his staff, he has thought the problem through and arrived at a decision—but only a tentative one. Before finalizing it, he presents his proposed solution for the reaction of those who will be affected by it. He says in effect, "I'd like to hear what you have to say about this plan that I have developed. I'll appreciate your frank reactions, but will reserve for myself the final decision."

The manager presents the problem, gets suggestions, and then makes his decision

Up to this point the boss has come before the group with a solution of his own. Not so in this case. The subordinates now get the first chance to suggest solutions. The manager's initial role involves identifying the problem. He might, for example, say something of this sort: "We are faced with a number of complaints from newspapers and the general public on our service policy. What is wrong here? What ideas do you have for coming to grips with this problem?"

RETROSPECTIVE COMMENTARY

Since this HBR Classic was first published in 1958, there have been many changes in organizations and in the world that have affected leadership patterns. While the article's continued popularity attests to its essential validity, we believe it can be reconsidered and updated to reflect subsequent societal changes and new management concepts.

The reasons for the article's continued relevance can be summarized briefly:

The article contains insights and perspectives which mesh well with, and help clarify, the experiences of managers, other leaders, and students of leadership. Thus it is useful to individuals in a wide variety of organizations—industrial, governmental, education, religious, and community.

The concept of leadership the article defines is reflected in a continuum of leadership behavior (see Figure 1 in original article). Rather than offering a choice between two styles of leadership, democratic or authoritarian, it sanctions a range of behavior.

The concept does not dictate to managers but helps them to analyze their own behavior. The continuum permits them to review their behavior within a context of other alternatives, without any style being labeled right or wrong.

(We have sometimes wondered if we have, perhaps, made it too easy for anyone to justify his or her style of leadership. It may be a small step between being nonjudgmental and giving the impression that all behavior is equally valid and useful. The latter was not our intention. Indeed, the thrust of our endorsement was for the manager who is insightful in assessing relevant forces within himself, others, and the situation, and who can be flexible in responding to these forces.)

In recognizing that our article can be updated, we are acknowledging that organizations do not exist in a vacuum but are affected by changes that occur in society. Consider, for example, the implications for organizations of these recent social developments:

The youth revolution that expresses distrust and even contempt for organizations identified with the establishment.

The civil rights movement that demands all minority groups be given a greater opportunity for participation and influence in the organizational processes.

The ecology and consumer movements that challenge the right of managers to make decisions without considering the interest of people outside the organization.

The increasing national concern with the quality of working life and its relationship to worker productivity, participation, and satisfaction.

These and other societal changes make effective leadership in this decade a more challenging task, requiring even greater sensitivity and flexibility than was needed in the 1950's. Today's manager is more likely to deal with employees who resent being treated as subordinates, who may be highly critical of any organizational system, who expect to be consulted and to exert influence, and who often stand on the edge of alienation from the institution that needs their loyalty and commitment. In addition, he is frequently confronted by a highly turbulent, unpredictable environment.

In response to these social pressures, new concepts of management have emerged in organizations. Open-system theory, with its emphasis on subsystems' interdependency *and* on the interaction of an organization with its environment, has made a powerful impact on managers' approach to problems. Organization development has emerged as a new behavioral science approach to the improvement of individual, group, organizational, and interorganizational performance. New research has added to our understanding of motivation in the work situation. More and more executives have become concerned with social responsibility and have explored the feasibility of social audits. And a growing number of organizations, in Europe and in the United States, have conducted experiments in industrial democracy.

In light of these developments, we submit the following thoughts on how we would rewrite certain points in our original article.

The article described forces in the manager, subordinates, and the situation as givens, with the leadership pattern a resultant of these forces. We would now give more attention to the *interdependency* of these forces. For example, such interdependency occurs in: (a) the interplay between the manager's confidence in his subordinates, their readiness to assume responsibility, and the level of group effectiveness; and (b) the impact of the behavior of the manager on that of his subordinates, and vice versa.

In discussing the forces in the situation, we primarily identified organizational phenomena. We would now include forces lying outside the organization, and would explore the relevant interdependencies between the organization and its environment.

In the original article, we presented the size of the rectangle in Figure 1 as a given, with its boundaries already determined by external forces—in effect, a closed system. We would now recognize the possibility of the manager and/or his subordinates taking the initiative to change those boundaries through interaction with relevant external forces—both within their own organization and in the larger society.

The article portrayed the manager as the principal and almost unilateral actor. He initiated and determined group functions, assumed responsibility, and exercised control. Subordinates made inputs and assumed power only at the will of the manager. Although the manager might have taken into account forces outside

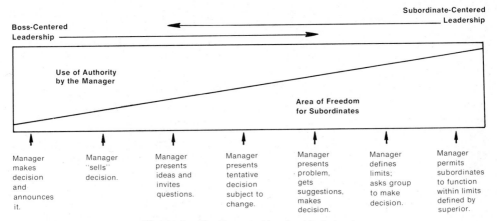

Figure 1. Continuum of leadership behavior.

himself, it was *he* who decided where to operate on the continuum—that is, whether to announce a decision instead of trying to sell his idea to his subordinates, whether to invite questions, to let subordinates decide an issue, and so on. While the manager has retained this clear prerogative in many organizations, it has been challenged in others. Even in situations where he has retained it, however, the balance in the relationship between manager and subordinates at any given time is arrived at by interaction—direct or indirect—between the two parties.

Although power and its use by the manager played a role in our article, we now realize that

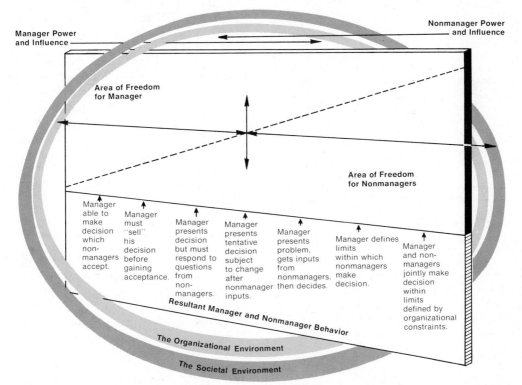

Figure 2. Continuum of manager-nonmanager behavior.

our concern with cooperation and collaboration, common goals, commitment, trust, and mutual caring limited our vision with respect to the realities of power. We did not attempt to deal with unions, other forms of joint worker action, or with individual workers' expressions of resistance. Today, we would recognize much more clearly the power available to *all* parties, and the factors that underlie the interrelated decisions on whether to use it.

In the original article, we used the terms "manager" and "subordinate." We are now uncomfortable with "subordinate" because of its demeaning, dependency-laden connotations and prefer "nonmanager." The titles "manager" and "nonmanager" make the terminological difference functional rather than hierarchical.

We assumed fairly traditional organizational structures in our orginal article. Now we would alter our formulation to reflect newer organizational modes which are slowly emerging, such as industrial democracy, intentional communities, and "phenomenarchy."* These new modes are based on observations such as the following:

Both manager and nonmanagers may be governing forces in their group's environment, contributing to the definition of the total area of freedom.

A group can function without a manager, with managerial functions being shared by group members.

A group, as a unit, can be delegated authority and can assume responsibility within a larger organizational context.

Our thoughts on the question of leadership have prompted us to design a new behavior continuum (see Figure 2) in which the total area of freedom shared by manager and nonmanagers is constantly redefined by interactions between them and the forces in the environment.

The arrows in the exhibit indicate the continual flow of interdependent influence among systems and people. The points on the continuum designate the types of manager and nonmanager behavior that become possible with any given amount of freedom available to each. The new continuum is both more complex and more dynamic than the 1958 version, reflecting the organizational and societal realities of 1973.

The function of the group becomes one of increasing the manager's repertory of possible solutions to the problem. The purpose is to capitalize on the knowledge and experience of those who are on the "firing line." From the expanded list of alternatives developed by the manager and his subordinates, the manager then selects the solution that he regards as most promising.[1]

The manager defines the limits and requests the group to make a decision

At this point the manager passes to the group (possibly including himself as a member) the right to make decisions. Before doing so, however, he defines the problem to be solved and the boundaries within which the decision must be made

An example might be the handling of a parking problem at a plant. The boss decides that this is something that should be worked on by the people involved, so he calls them together and points up the existence of the problem. Then he tells them:

"There is the open field just north of the main plant which has been designated for additional employee parking. We can build underground or surface mutilevel facilities as long as the cost does not exceed $100,000. Within these limits we are free to work out whatever solution makes sense to us. After we decide on a specific plan, the company will spend the available money in whatever way we indicate."

The manager permits the group to make decisions within prescribed limits

This represents an extreme degree of group freedom only occasionally encountered in formal organizations, as, for instance, in many research groups. Here the team of managers or engineers undertakes the identification and diagnosis of the problem, develops alternative procedures for solving it, and decides on one or more of these

---

* For a description of phenomenarchy, see Will McWhinney, "Phenomenarchy: A Suggestion for Social Redesign," *Journal of Applied Behavioral Science*, May 1973.

[1] For a fuller explanation of this approach, see Leo Moore, "Too Much Management, Too Little Change," HBR January–February 1956, p. 41.

alternative solutions. The only limits directly imposed on the group by the organization are those specified by the superior of the team's boss. If the boss participates in the decision-making process, he attempts to do so with no more authority than any other member of the group. He commits himself in advance to assist in implementing whatever decision the group makes.

KEY QUESTIONS

As the continuum in Figure 1 demonstrates, there are a number of alternative ways in which a manager can relate himself to the group or individuals he is supervising. At the extreme left of the range, the emphasis is on the manager—on what *he* is interested in, how *he* sees things, how *he* feels about them. As we move toward the subordinate-centered end of the continuum, however, the focus is increasingly on the subordinates—on what *they* are interested in, how *they* look at things, how *they* feel about them.

When business leadership is regarded in this way, a number of questions arise. Let us take four of especial importance:

Can a boss ever relinquish his responsibility by delegating it to someone else?

Our view is that the manager must expect to be held responsible by his superior for the quality of the decisions made, even though operationally these decisions may have been made on a group basis. He should, therefore, be ready to accept whatever risk is involved whenever he delegates decision-making power to his subordinates. Delegation is not a way of "passing the buck." Also, it should be emphasized that the amount of freedom the boss gives to his subordinates cannot be greater than the freedom which he himself has been given by his own superior.

Should the manager participate with his subordinates once he has delegated responsibility to them?

The manager should carefully think over this question and decide on his role prior to involving the subordinate group. He should ask if his presence will inhibit or facilitate the problem-solving process. There may be some instances when he should leave the group to let it solve the problem for itself. Typically, however, the boss has useful ideas to contribute, and should function as an additional member of the group. In the latter instance, it is important that he indicate clearly to the group that he sees himself in a *member* role rather than in an authority role.

How important is it for the group to recognize what kind of leadership behavior the boss is using?

It makes a great deal of difference. Many relationship problems between boss and subordinate occur because the boss fails to make clear how he plans to use his authority. If, for example, he actually intends to make a certain decision himself, but the subordinate group gets the impression that he has delegated this authority, considerable confusion and resentment are likely to follow. Problems may also occur when the boss uses a "democratic" facade to conceal the fact that he has already made a decision which he hopes the group will accept as its own. The attempt to "make them think it was their idea in the first place" is a risky one. We believe that it is highly important for the manager to be honest and clear in describing what authority he is keeping and what role he is asking his subordinates to assume in solving a particular problem.

Can you tell how "democratic" a manager is by the number of decisions his subordinates make?

The sheer *number* of decisions is not an accurate index of the amount of freedom that a subordinate group enjoys. More important is the *significance* of the decisions which the boss entrusts to his subordinates. Obviously a decision on how to arrange desks is of an entirely different order from a decision involving the introduction of new electronic data-processing equipment. Even though the widest possible limits are given in dealing with the first issue, the group will sense no particular degree of responsibility. For a boss to permit the group to decide equipment policy, even within rather narrow limits, would reflect a greater degree of confidence in them on his part.

DECIDING HOW TO LEAD

Now let us turn from the types of leadership which are possible in a company situation to the question of what types are *practical* and *desirable*. What factors or forces should a manager consider in deciding how to manage? Three are of particular importance:

Forces in the manager.
Forces in the subordinates.
Forces in the situation.

We should like briefly to describe these elements and indicate how they might influence a manager's action in a decision-making situation.[2] The strength of each of them will, of course, vary from instance to instance, but the manager who is sensitive to them can better assess the problems which face him and determine which mode of leadership behavior is most appropriate for him.

Forces in the Manager. The manager's behavior in any given instance will be influenced greatly by the many forces operating within his own personality. He will, of course, perceive his

leadership problems in a unique way on the basis of his background, knowledge, and experience. Among the important internal forces affecting him will be the following:

1. *His value system.* How strongly does he feel that individuals should have a share in making the decisions which affect them? Or, how convinced is he that the official who is paid to assume responsibility should personally carry the burden of decision making? The strength of his convictions on questions like these will tend to move the manager to one end or the other of the continuum shown in Figure 1. His behavior will also be influenced by the relative importance that he attaches to organizational efficiency, personal growth of subordinates, and company profits.[3]

2. *His confidence in his subordinates.* Managers differ greatly in the amount of trust they have in other people generally, and this carries over to the particular employees they supervise at a given time. In viewing his particular group of subordinates, the manager is likely to consider their knowledge and competence with respect to the problem. A central question he might ask himself is: "Who is best qualified to deal with this problem?" Often he may, justifiably or not, have more confidence in his own capabilities than in those of his subordinates.

3. *His own leadership inclinations.* There are some managers who seem to function more comfortably and naturally as highly directive leaders. Resolving problems and issuing orders come easily to them. Other managers seem to operate more comfortably in a team role, where they are continually sharing many of their functions with their subordinates.

4. *His feelings of security in an uncertain situation.* The manager who releases control over the decision-making proc-

[2] See also Robert Tannenbaum and Fred Massarik, "Participation by Subordinates in the Managerial Decision-Making Process," *Canadian Journal of Economics and Political Science*, August 1950, p. 413.

[3] See Chris Argyris, "Top Management Dilemma: Company Needs vs. Individual Development," *Personnel*, September 1955, pp. 123–134.

ess thereby reduces the predictability of the outcome. Some managers have a greater need than others for predictability and stability in their environment. This "tolerance for ambiguity" is being viewed increasingly by psychologists as a key variable in a person's manner of dealing with problems.

The manager brings these and other highly personal variables to each situation he faces. If he can see them as forces which, consciously or unconsciously, influence his behavior, he can better understand what makes him prefer to act in a given way. And understanding this, he can often make himself more effective.

Forces in the Subordinate. Before deciding how to lead a certain group, the manager will also want to consider a number of forces affecting his subordinates' behavior. He will want to remember that each employee, like himself, is influenced by many personality variables. In addition, each subordinate has a set of expectations about how the boss should act in relation to him (the phrase "expected behavior" is one we hear more and more often these days at discussions of leadership and teaching). The better the manager understands these factors, the more accurately he can determine what kind of behavior on his part will enable his subordinates to act most effectively.

Generally speaking, the manager can permit his subordinates greater freedom if the following essential conditions exist:

If the subordinates have relatively high needs for independence. (As we all know, people differ greatly in the amount of direction that they desire.)

If the subordinates have a readiness to assume responsibility for decision making. (Some see additional responsibility as a tribute to their ability; others see it as "passing the buck.")

If they have a relatively high tolerance for ambiguity. (Some employees prefer to have clear-cut directives given to them; others prefer a wider area of freedom.)

If they are interested in the problem and feel that it is important.

If they understand and identify with the goals of the organization.

If they have the necessary knowledge and experience to deal with the problem.

If they have learned to expect to share in decision making. (Persons who have come to expect strong leadership and are then suddenly confronted with the request to share more fully in decision making are often upset by this new experience. On the other hand, persons who have enjoyed a considerable amount of freedom resent the boss who begins to make all the decisions himself.)

The manager will probably tend to make fuller use of his own authority if the above conditions do *not* exist; at times there may be no realistic alternative to running a "one-man show."

The restrictive effect of many of the forces will, of course, be greatly modified by the general feeling of confidence which subordinates have in the boss. Where they have learned to respect and trust him, he is free to vary his behavior. He will feel certain that he will not be perceived as an authoritarian boss on those occasions when he makes decisions by himself. Similarly, he will not be seen as using staff meetings to avoid his decision-making responsibility. In a climate of mutual confidence and respect, people tend to feel less threatened by deviations from normal practice, which in turn makes possible a higher degree of flexibility in the whole relationship.

Forces in the Situation. In addition to the forces which exist in the manager himself and in his subordinates, certain characteristics of the general situation will also affect the manager's behavior. Among the more critical environmental pressures that surround him are those which stem from the organization, the work group, the nature of the problem, and the pressures of time. Let us look briefly at each of these:

TYPE OF ORGANIZATION. Like individuals, organizations have values and traditions which inevitably influence the behavior of the people who work in them. The manager who is a newcomer to a company quickly discovers that certain kinds of behavior are approved while others are not. He also discovers that to deviate radically from what is generally accepted is likely to create problems for him.

These values and traditions are communicated in numerous ways—through job descriptions, policy pronouncements, and public statements by top executives. Some organizations, for example, hold to the notion that the desirable executive is one who is dynamic, imaginative, decisive, and persuasive. Other organizations put more emphasis upon the importance of the executive's ability to work effectively with people—his human relations skills. The fact that his superiors have a defined concept of what the good executive should be will very likely push the manager toward one end or the other of the behavioral range.

In addition to the above, the amount of employee participation is influenced by such variables as the size of the working units, their geographical distribution, and the degree of inter- and intra-organizational security required to attain company goals. For example, the wide geographical dispersion of an organization may preclude a practical system of participative decision making, even though this would otherwise be desirable. Similarly, the size of the working units or the need for keeping plans confidential may make it necessary for the boss to exercise more control than would otherwise be the case. Factors like these may limit considerably the manager's ability to function flexibly on the continuum.

GROUP EFFECTIVENESS. Before turning decision-making responsibility over to a subordinate group, the boss should consider how effectively its members work together as a unit.

One of the relevant factors here is the experience the group has had in working together. It can generally be expected that a group which has functioned for some time will have developed habits of cooperation and thus be able to tackle a problem more effectively than a new group. It can also be expected that a group of people with similar backgrounds and interests will work more quickly and easily than people with dissimilar backgrounds, because the communication problems are likely to be less complex.

The degree of confidence that the members have in their ability to solve problems as a group is also a key consideration. Finally, such group variables as cohesiveness, permissiveness, mutual acceptance, and commonality of purpose will exert subtle but powerful influence on the group's functioning.

THE PROBLEM ITSELF. The nature of the problem may determine what degree of authority should be delegated by the manager to his subordinates. Obviously he will ask himself whether they have the kind of knowledge which is needed. It is possible to do them a real disservice by assigning a problem that their experience does not equip them to handle.

Since the problems faced in large or growing industries increasingly require knowledge of specialists from many different fields, it might be inferred that the more complex a problem, the more anxious a manager will be to get some assistance in solving it. However, this is not always the case. There will be times when the very complexity of the problem calls for one person to work it out. For example, if the manager has most of the background and factual data relevant to a given issue, it may be easier for him to think it through himself than to take the time to fill in his staff on all the pertinent background information.

The key question to ask, of course, is: "Have I heard the ideas of everyone who has the necessary knowledge to make a significant contribution to the solution of this problem?"

THE PRESSURE OF TIME. This is perhaps the most clearly felt pressure on the manager (in spite of the fact that it may sometimes be imagined). The more that he feels the need for an immediate decision, the more difficult it is to involve other people. In organizations which are in a constant state of "crisis" and "crash programming" one is likely to find managers personally using a high degree of authority with relatively little delegation to subordinates. When the time pressure is less intense, however, it becomes much more possible to bring subordinates in on the decision-making process.

These, then, are the principal forces that impinge on the manager in any given instance and that tend to determine his tactical behavior in relation to his subordinates. In each case his behavior ideally will be that which makes possible the most effective attainment of his immediate goal within the limits facing him.

LONG-RUN STRATEGY

As the manager works with his organization on the problems that come up day by day, his choice of a leadership pattern is usually limited. He must take account of the forces just described and, within the restrictions they impose on him, do the best that he can. But as he looks ahead months or even years, he can shift his thinking from tactics to large-scale strategy. No longer need he be fettered by all of the forces mentioned, for he can view many of them as variables over which he has some control. He can, for example, gain new insights or skills for himself, supply training for individual subordinates, and provide participative experiences for his employee group.

In trying to bring about a change in these variables, however, he is faced with a challenging question: At which point along the continuum *should* he act?

Attaining Objectives. The answer depends largely on what he wants to accomplish. Let us suppose that he is interested in the same objectives that most modern managers seek to attain when they can shift their attention from the pressure of immediate assignments:

1. To raise the level of employee motivation.

2. To increase the readiness of subordinates to accept change.

3. To improve the quality of all managerial decisions.

4. To develop teamwork and morale.

5. To further the individual development of employees.

In recent years the manager has been deluged with a flow of advice on how best to achieve these longer-run objectives. It is little wonder that he is often both bewildered and annoyed. However, there are some guidelines which he can usefully follow in making a decision.

Most research and much of the experience of recent years give a strong factual basis to the theory that a fairly high degree of subordinate-centered behavior is associated with the accomplishment of the five purposes mentioned.[4] This does not mean that a manager should always leave all decisions to his assistants. To provide the individual or the group with greater freedom than they are ready for at any given time may very well tend to generate anxieties and therefore inhibit rather than facilitate the attainment of desired objectives. But this should not keep the manager from making a continuing effort to confront his subordinates with the challenge of freedom.

CONCLUSION

In summary, there are two implications in the basic thesis that we have

---

[4] For example, see Warren H. Schmidt and Paul C. Buchanan, *Techniques that Produce Teamwork* (New London, Arthur C. Croft Publications, 1954); and Morris S. Viteles, *Motivation and Morale in Industry* (New York, W. W. Norton & Company, Inc., 1953).

been developing. The first is that the successful leader is one who is keenly aware of those forces which are most relevant to his behavior at any given time. He accurately understands himself, the individuals and group he is dealing with, and the company and broader social environment in which he operates. And certainly he is able to assess the present readiness for growth of his subordinates.

But this sensitivity or understanding is not enough, which brings us to the second implication. The successful leader is one who is able to behave appropriately in the light of these per-ceptions. If direction is in order, he is able to direct; if considerable participative freedom is called for, he is able to provide such freedom.

Thus, the successful manager of men can be primarily characterized neither as a strong leader nor as a permissive one. Rather, he is one who maintains a high batting average in accurately assessing the forces that determine what his most appropriate behavior at any given time should be and in actually being able to behave accordingly. Being both insightful and flexible, he is less likely to see the problems of leadership as a dilemma.

12   An Approach to Organization Theory For The Practicing Manager

A. Thomas Hollingsworth

INTRODUCTION

This article will present a heuristic framework which will aid a practicing manager in making decisions concerning his human resources. The first 2 sections of the article will deal with the organization as a total system, consisting of both formal and informal sets of behavior norms. The third section of the article will illustrate how the formal and informal aspects of the organization are interrelated. The final section will demonstrate the usefulness of the conceptual framework to the practicing manager. The latter will be accomplished by the use of 2 incidents observed within industrial organizations.

FORMAL ORGANIZATIONS

An organization is an "open-dynamic system; that is, it is characterized by a continuing process of input, transformation, and output."[1] The goal of organizations in this society is to produce useable sets of out puts. It is this

---

[1] Robert L. Kahn, et al., *Organizational Stress: Studies in Role Conflict and Ambiguity* (New York: John Wiley & Sons, Inc., 1964), 12.

This material appeared originally as an article in Volume XX, Number 3, of the *Business and Economic Review,* Bureau of Business and Economic Research, College of Business Administration, The University of South Carolina, Columbia, South Carolina.

useable set of outputs which justifies each organization's existence.

The formal organization specifies formal lines of authority which, in turn, designate spheres of activity for organizational members and constraints on the use of their authority.[2] This authority carries with it the right to utilize all of the positive sanctions (rewards) or negative sanctions (punitive measures)[3] available. These sanctions are applicable, however, only within the authority constraints of a particular position in the formal structure. The typical organization chart illustrates these lines of authority.

The formal organization is, of course, not merely a set of blocks and lines represented by an organization chart, but, more realistically, a series of linked roles, each being defined by how it is linked to other roles in the organization.[4] The formal role is only 1 of many associated with a particular position.

There are a number of formal aspects to organizations which cannot be readily seen on a typical organization chart.

Figure 1 illustrates many of the control variables found within the formal constraints of an organization. These variables are controlled directly by the formal authority system which determines such factors as objectives, division of labor, coordination, and job activities. Figure 1 also depicts some of the exogenous variables affecting management in its determination of internal controls.

Operating within these formal parameters, managers have the authority to force changes on the total organizational system which they feel will remedy problems within a subsystem. By initiating these decisions, managers assume that organization members will readily accept such changes. They act as though the "real" organization is the one defined by the formal organization chart. It is the objective of this article to emphasize the contrary, i.e., that while attempting to attain equilibrium in a subsystem, the manager may actually cause disruptive consequences in other subsystems. Before

---

[2] Herbert A. Simon, *Administrative Behavior* (New York: The Free Press, 1957), 147–148.
[3] Kahn, *Organizational Stress,* 197.
[4] *Ibid,* 388–389.

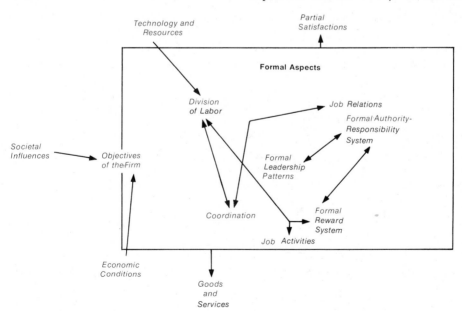

Figure 1. The formal organization.

there can be any intelligent discussion of the dysfunctional aspects of rigid adherence to a strict formal definition, there must be an understanding of the informal facets of the organization. These latter are considered in the following section.

INFORMAL ORGANIZATION

The term "informal organization" refers to personal relations within an organization which affect internal decisions but which either are omitted from the formal scheme or are not consistent with the scheme.[5] The informal organization specifies norms of behavior, leader-follower relations, communication channels, shared values, and status rankings of members.[6] It also assists in maintaining the cohesiveness of the formal organization.[7]

---

[5] Simon, *Administrative Behavior,* 148.

[6] Joseph A. Litterer, ed., *Organizations: Structure and Behavior* (New York; John Wiley & Sons, Inc., 1963), 140–142.

[7] Chester Barnard, *The Functions of the Executive* (Cambridge, Mass.: Harvard University Press, 1938), 122.

Figure 2 illustrates these informal variables and their interrelatedness. There are, obviously, a number of factors affecting sentiments within the informal organization, and an understanding of these sentiments is important to any decision maker since they are the determinants of the informal set of norms. The term "sentiments" is admittedly general, but the model allows a decision maker to observe the variables related to it. These variables and their importance to the informal organization must be constantly reviewed and reevaluated by a decision maker in each situation if he is to operate at peak efficiency.

INTERACTION BETWEEN THE FORMAL AND THE INFORMAL ORGANIZATIONS

It is, as stated above, important for the decision maker to be aware of all of the variables in a decision situation, of their interdependency, and of their utility value to those people affected by the decision maker's alteration of these variables. The variables in a total

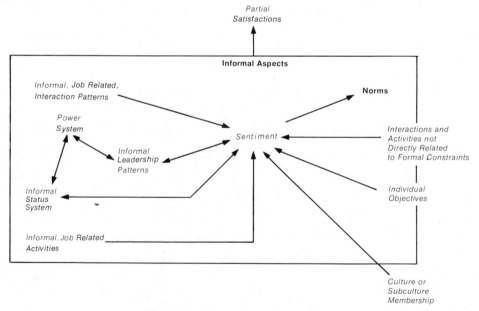

Figure 2. The informal organization.

organization context are presented in Figure 3.[8] The set of variables presented there is not a collectively exhaustive set of the variables themselves or of their interdependencies, but only an example of the multifaceted effects which organizational decisions may have.

The model in Figure 3 introduces 3 conceptual areas not shown in Figures 1 and 2: (1) cohesiveness of the organization, (2) leadership styles, and (3) motivational systems within the organization. The model points out that these 3 variables are affected by both the formal and informal aspects of the organization, but that they do not belong to either one exclusively.

Figure 3 depicts a number of areas in which the formal organization interfaces with the informal organization. It also shows the probable direction of the interaction between variables.

The formal organization affects the informal organization by specifying job content, which is the control the worker may exercise over his job; by designating job relations involved in the interdependency between jobs as well as the social distance between jobs; and by specifying the interrelatedness of jobs, which designate required interactions, work flows, and initiation of work.[9] The informal organization sets norms of production, establishes an informal status or reward system, and affects job satisfaction, absenteeism, and attrition rates.[10] These informal variables, particularly variables such as sentiments and norms, cannot be controlled directly by the formal decision maker. They can, however, be influenced by the formal decision maker.

An interactionist approach yields a viable description of the interaction between formal and informal organiza-

tion for a decision maker. The problem with this approach is the problem inherent with any general approach; that is, the variables are broad and difficult to operationalize. However, the approach does yield a methodology that will aid the practicing manager in determining the strategic variables in his decision model. The interactional model in Figure 3 offers a method through which the decision maker may view the variables in any decision problem, separate them as controllable and noncontrollable, and examine the interaction patterns between the variables.

The model demonstrates the complexity of decisions made within the total organization. A worker brings his entire personality to the organization. This is exemplified by the concept of sentiments and its many determining factors. The worker then is affected by numerous variables in the work situation, both formal and informal. For example, an attempt to motivate individuals strictly through monetary wages illustrates, in many cases, that management is not aware of the total organization.

OPERATIONALIZING THE CONCEPTS

The usefulness of behavioral model building for the practicing manager can be shown by utilizing actual industrial cases and by demonstrating how behavioral models can be used to isolate strategic variables and, thereby, act as decision making guides. This will be done in the following sections.

The first incident, "Always Blame Quality Control," will be utilized to demonstrate how important it is for a manager to recognize the formal tools that he can employ to affect formal behavior patterns directly. The second incident, "The Wayward Work Group," will be utilized to demonstrate some of the problems involved when *only* formal behavior patterns are considered by the

[8] Litterer, *Organizations*, 207 (initial idea for this type of model).

[9] *Ibid.*

[10] Peter M. Blau and W. Richard Scott, *Formal Organizations* (San Francisco: Chandler Publishing Company, 1962), 94–95.

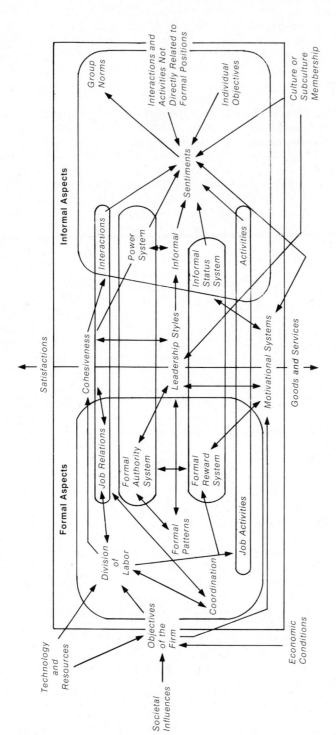

Figure 3. The total organization.

Group Cohesivensss = f (size, stability of membership, division of labor)

Leadership Style = f (leader, subordinate, work situation)

Motivational Systems = f (organizational objectives and individual objectives)

decision maker. The implicit decision model of the manager involved will be explained, and then a normative model will be given which offers a more logical approach to the problem.

"Always Blame Quality Control"

This first incident occurred in a multiplant automobile manufacturing corporation. The company was established with each plant acting as a separate profit center. Quality, always a constant problem along a production line, had deteriorated to the lowest point both in the company's history and in the industry.

To rectify the situation, top management hired a new Quality Control Manager to occupy the position of a Staff Assistant at the divisional level (see Figure 4). The new "Assistant's" primary function was to improve the quality of the company's products. His initial move was to establish a team to check the quality at various plants. The results showed that quality was equally poor at all plants, and that incoming raw material inputs were at acceptable quality levels in all plants, but, that there were no rigidly-defined standards of quality utilized on a company-wide basis.

The Divisonal Quality Control Manager then interviewed the Quality Control Managers at the company's various plants and found the turnover in their ranks to be extremely high: there was a 60 percent attrition rate of Quality Control men at the plant level. Of these, approximately 60 percent requested transfer, while the other 40 percent were dismissed by the Plant Managers. The Quality Control Managers at the plant level were administratively responsible (for raises, bonuses, etc.) to the Plant Managers and functionally responsible to the Divisional Quality Control Manager.

During the interviews, the Divisional Quality Control Manager learned that there was a reluctance on the part of the local Quality Control Managers to pull too many cars off the line. The reason for this was that it would cause the line to shut down, and this would not be allowed by the Plant Managers, as they were judged on their plant's profitability which was measured solely by the number of cars produced.

The new Quality Control Manager then began interviewing Plant Managers. The latter were very quick to point out that the poor quality was obviously a result of divisional quality control and a lack of rigid standards. The Plant Managers also revealed that they had repeatedly dismissed incompetent Quality Control men at the plant level, but that they had no control over divisional quality control.

The new Divisional Quality Control Manager finally examined all the data which he had gathered regarding the problem and (referring to Figure 1) decided that the primary causes of the quality control problem were within the parameters of the formal organization. The variables which he felt to be important causal factors were (1) a lack of work standards, (2) a break-down of authority-responsibility relationships—relative to company objectives, and (3) an inefficient system of reporting quality deficiencies. These problems seem obvious; however, it must be noted that for at least 18 months prior to the hiring of the new Divisional Quality Control Manager, the Quality Control Managers at the plant level had been used as "scape-goats" for the company's quality levels.

A 3-part solution then was proposed and accepted: (1) that rigid quality standards be established, (2) that an improved method of reporting quality deficiencies to line management be designed, and (3) most importantly, that the authority-responsibility role of the Plant Managers be redefined. The latter were made responsible for both quantity and quality, and the formal reward system was modified to reflect this quality responsibility. Hence, Plant Managers would be judged on profitability based on sales revenue less cost of

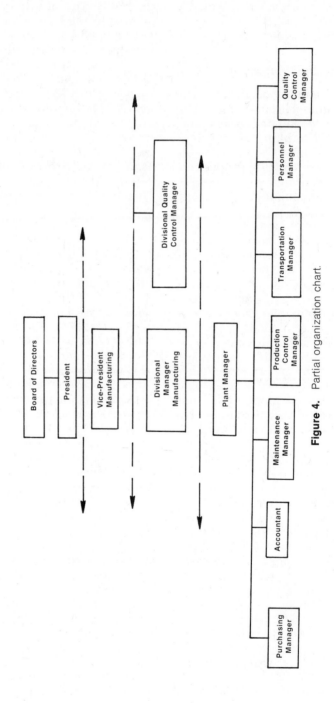

Figure 4. Partial organization chart.

rework needed on their products. Again, Figures 1 and 3 demonstrate how a theoretical construct can be utilized in a pragmatic situation.

The previous solution resulted in higher quality levels and a decrease in the turnover of Quality Control Managers at the plant level. It also resulted however, in a short-run increase in turnover of Plant Managers!

The previous solution was effective because the implementation agent (a recent MBA graduate) analyzed the situation within the theoretical constructs of the formal organization. He then utilized his controllable variables to establish a workable solution in a pragmatic situation.

It is important to note, however, that solutions which can be applied only within formal constraints are not the only ones of which managers must be aware. Many times solutions to organization problems will call for a combination of both formal and informal constructs. This type of problem will be illustrated in the following incident.

"The Wayward Work Group"

The incident under consideration here occurred in an operating division of a large utility company. His division was responsible for maintaining electrical service within its area and utilized approximately 17 crews ranging in size from 6 to 12 members to handle the operations. These crews were responsible for maintenance and also for small installations. Each Foreman in the division handled 4 work crews, with each crew working in a different geographical area. The Foremen reported to an Assistant Distribution Manager who, in turn, was directly responsible to a Distribution Superintendent.

The problem under discussion was brought to the attention of the Distribution Superintendent by his assistant. One of the work crews, a 6-man crew, was constantly "goofing off." This group had a tendency to take extra long coffee breaks and to quit early, and had

even, on occasion, been caught by their Foreman sleeping in their truck. They had been warned by both the Foreman and the Assistant Distribution Manager, but to no avail.

The Distribution Superintendent, upon hearing this report, unilaterally decided that the problem was being caused by the close proximity of the crew members, that is, their formal job relations. Based on this simplistic premise, he broke up the crew and assigned each of the 6 crew members to a different crew in his division. This decision model is represented in Figure 5. It graphically illustrates the fact that the decision maker, in attempting to solve this problem, chose S_4 and implicitly assigned a high probability to Θ>.

Unfortunately, this was not the case; in fact Θ_3 had the highest probability given S_4. The result, therefore, was not as the Distribution Superintendent had anticipated. Of the 6 men moved, 4 had seniority rights in their new crews, and, therefore, gained access to their respective crew's trucks. They could now meet for coffee at some central location to which 4 of the 6 men could drive, taking turns picking up the other 2 members. This increased the cost to the company, for now transportation costs as well as other crews were involved.

The final result was the decision of the Distribution Superintendent to fire 3 of the 6 men. As shown in Figure 5, this caused extreme discontent among workers and eventually generated union problems within the division. Obviously, these were not the results that had been anticipated after the initial decision had been made, or the decision maker would have selected S_2 as his initial strategy.

The decision maker, in this case, utilized a simplistic model on which to base his decision. He assumed that formal job relations were directly and singularly the cause of the problem. What he failed to understand was the number of variables, as shown in Figure 3, that affect the informal group's sentiments and norms. He should have

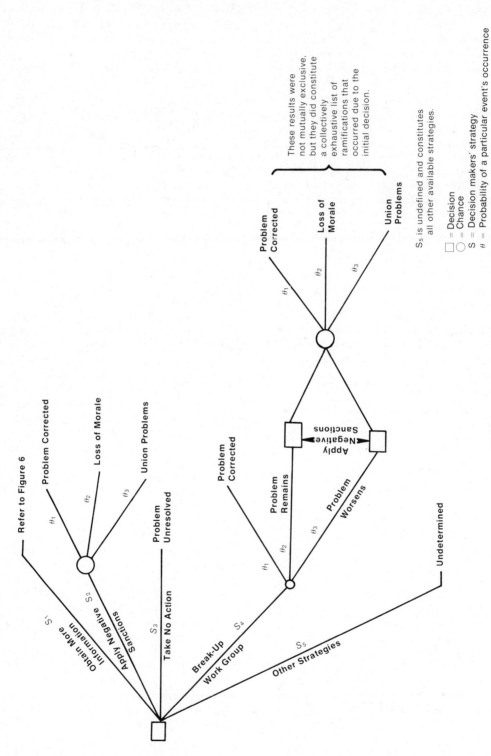

Figure 5. Actual decision.

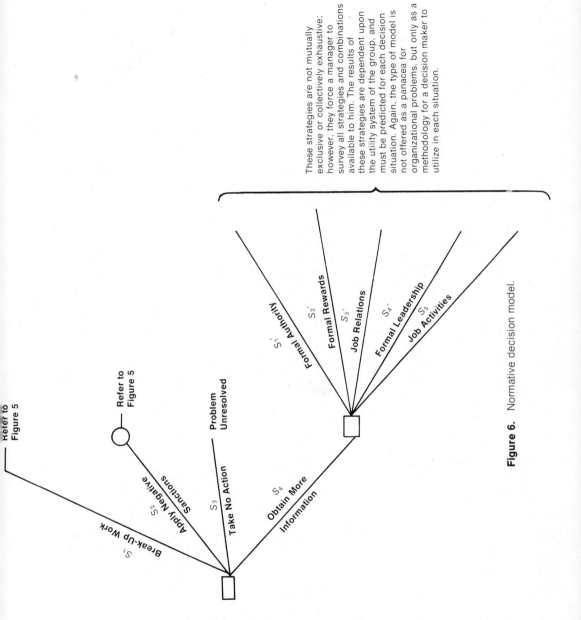

These strategies are not mutually exclusive or collectively exhaustive; however, they force a manager to survey all strategies and combinations available to him. The results of these strategies are dependent upon the utility system of the group, and must be predicted for each decision situation. Again, the type of model is not offered as a panacea for organizational problems, but only as a methodology for a decision maker to utilize in each situation.

Figure 6. Normative decision model.

attempted to assess all the variables rather than just the most obvious, formal role relations. Had he been aware of the interfaces between the formal and the informal organizations, he could have solved the problem where it occurred—in the informal organization.

The normative model is presented in Figure 6 with S_4 being the recommended strategy. In this case, historical data could have been utilized to gain some insight into the workers' potential behavior. These men were all from the same rural community, and they socialized off the job as a group. The formal and informal organizations interfaced far beyond the constraints of the formal organization as shown in Figure 3. Cultural or subcultural membership should have been investigated. The Distribution Superintendent did not take this into consideration when he made his decision. He only utilized the constructs shown in Figure 1 which were not sufficient to explain the actual situation.

Figure 6 offers alternative methods of positively affecting the informal norms. For instance, there could be a modification of the reward system, coupled with a change in job activities. This would certainly be a long-run solution, but it would seem a better answer than the final result of firing, coupled with union problems. By not correctly assessing the situation, the decision maker caused inefficiencies in the formal organization, which could have been either planned for or avoided by utilizing an improved decision model.

The decision maker acted as though the formal constraints were the only determinants of the norms of the informal organization. Obviously, they were not. He made the decision from his formal position, utilizing his utility system and not that of his subordinates. He assumed that the variables that were most important to him were also those most important to his workers. The deterministic approach, therefore, was not as effective as the heuristic approach presented here.

SUMMARY AND CONCLUSIONS

The purpose of this article has been to investigate the manner in which organizations affect the behavior of their members, both directly and indirectly. A general approach was used, but it demonstrated the interrelatedness of the 2 spheres of an organization. This type of approach allows a decision maker an opportunity to divide the variables in a decision situation into 1 of 2 types: controllable or noncontrollable. The controllable variables are those which managers can control through a formal organization. The noncontrollables can be divided further into 2 subcategories: variables which can be influenced by the decision maker and variables which cannot be influenced by the decision maker. These noncontrollable variables are operative within the informal organization.

An effective decision maker understands how he can utilize his controllable variables to affect the total work situation, that is, both the formal and informal aspects of the situation. The list of variables utilized in the models in this article does not constitute a collectively exhaustive set of all variables affecting human behavior. The purpose of utilizing these particular variables was to emphasize the fact that there are numerous variables affecting human behavior in organizations.

A manager must recognize the fact that there are many variables present in organizational situations. He may weigh these variables differently, and he may weigh the probabilistic outcomes of his actions differently; but the effective manager will be aware of all these variables when making decisions concerning human resources. Only through this understanding can he correctly assess situations, define problems, and make decisions in the best interest of attaining organizational goals.

III RECENT DEVELOPMENTS IN MANAGEMENT

The purpose of Part III is to examine recent developments in the field of management, and this part of the book has been divided into five sections: (a) management information systems and the computer, (b) technology and modern organization structures, (c) management of human assets, (d) social responsibility and (e) international management. These are all rapidly developing areas that are of paramount concern to the modern business firm. They also share a number of common elements, so some overlap is inevitable. It is extremely important, however, to remember that organizations are integrative by nature, and the five sections of Part III should be viewed in terms of their contribution to an understanding of the total organization.

Management Information Systems and the Computer

The purpose of this section is to examine systems theory from the manager's viewpoint, and both the human and the mechanistic aspects of systems will be discussed. In particular, attention will be focused on management information systems and the role of the computer in the modern organization.

In the first article, by W. A. Fredericks, the impact of the systems construct on today's managers is examined. Mr. Fredericks stresses that management must be aware of the interlocking effect of the systems approach and the fact that this approach must be specifically engineered for each firm. This is in keeping with the previous idea that models must provide pragmatic rather than theoretical solutions. Mr. Fredericks describes how the management information system (MIS) should be established within an organization, again stressing that each organization requires a unique system. He concludes by demonstrating that any system's approach must add more to profits than to costs or it is either an improperly designed system or not needed by the firm.

The second article, by Professor Irwin H. Derman, describes MIS as a tool for helping management operate more effectively. MIS supports decision makers, but it cannot unilaterally decide what information is to be collected or who are to be the recipients of MIS reports. The MIS is only a tool, although many times it is thought to be more than simply a tool. When this occurs, neither the managers' nor the customers' needs are fulfilled. Professor Derman's comments on the computer are well taken. A manager must demand an explanation from the data processing people when he becomes confused with jargon. He must not make decisions out of fear of the computer, but rather because he understands the message. The author goes on to point out that fear of computers is rooted in an ignorance of its functions. The latter part of the article discusses important topics such as how to judge whether one's MIS has outgrown its usefulness and how to develop an MIS from scratch. As might be expected, cost-benefit analysis is emphasized as a determining factor.

In the last article in this section, Professors Ronald and Charlotte Seaberg present a synopsis of how Xerox of Canada Limited has begun utilizing a computer-based MIS in the planning processes.

The underlying rationale for the program is that planning can be improved through better information handling. In Xerox a modular approach was used, so that a number of modules were created which combined to form the entire planning process. This allowed more aspects of the model to be "seen" by user managers so that needed changes could be more easily recognized and implemented. As a result, the decision maker was highly involved with the initial modeling process and the use of the system remained within his control. The entire article concentrates on the practical applications of computer-based decision systems.

13   A Manager's Perspective of Management Information Systems

Ward A. Fredericks

A plethora of seminars, speeches, articles, and scholarly books extolling the virtues of MIS (management information systems) has descended upon the business community. *On-line, real-time, data base,* and *teleprocessing* have become part of the "compleat" manager's vocabulary, albeit with less understanding of meaning than usual. In fact, management has accepted the reality of the concept of MIS with open arms, trusting that the types of key decisions which have to be made daily will somehow become easier when the promised data appear in precisely organized formats.

Major companies have mounted massive efforts aimed at designing MIS with results ranging from disaster to partial success. It is still appropriate to say that well-designed and operating MIS are much easier to find in the pages of technical and management journals than in real life.

In order to look at the concept and the application of MIS, an appropriate starting point is to look at management and its most fundamental actions and processes to see what role systems can play in aiding managers in the attainment of their objectives.

The term *top management* as used in this article will cover those members of management whose perspective must include the operation of the entire company—typically the president and executive vice-president in centralized companies, and division general managers in decentralized companies.

Textbooks list planning, controlling, organizing, and so on, as the major functions of management. In an on-

Ward A. Fredericks, "A Manager's Perspective of Management Information Systems," pp. 7–12, *MSU Business Topics,* Spring 1971. Reprinted by permission of the publisher, Division of Research, Graduate School of Business Administration, Michigan State University.

going business enterprise, however, top management makes key decisions relating to certain aspects of the business which determine the size, character, and long-term viability of the organization. These decisions are made in every company, regardless of size, and represent the most difficult part of the management process. They set the tone for the entire enterprise. To simplify the perspective in these key decisions and actions, a five-way categorization would be: (1) decisions and actions which affect pricing, (2) decisions and actions which affect volume, (3) decisions and actions which affect overhead or structural cost, (4) decisions and actions which affect product (or service) cost, and (5) decisions and actions which affect asset turnover.

In every business enterprise it is the interaction of the decisions made in each of the above categories which determines the viability and profitability of the organization. Any MIS effort, then, should address, both in cause and effect terms, the impact of having systems which can influence the outcome of these various decisions and actions.

PROFITABILITY: A COMPLEX RESULT

In order to put proper emphasis upon the complex interaction of the five main areas for management action just listed, let us investigate the "anatomy of a profit." Profit is certainly one of the major objectives of business enterprise, although not the only objective in today's complex society. Continued existence of the enterprise is dependent upon the generation of acceptable profit, however, and therefore management thrust must be directed toward this result.

Management action aimed at producing profit in an ongoing business enterprise may be looked at in terms of the four parts to the profit equation below:

$$1)\ (P \times V) - PC - SC = PROFIT$$

$$2)\ \frac{Profit}{Assets} = Return\ on\ Investment$$

Simply stated, price times volume equals gross revenue for the enterprise, from which is subtracted product cost and structural cost (or overhead). Profit-oriented management action must be aimed at impacting one or more of the variables in the equation to have a favorable effect on the result. Return on investment of the enterprise is a function of profit, certainly, but turnover of assets involved in the business plays a major role in determining the resultant rate of return.

It is prudent to begin an analysis with simple truths in order to follow the flow of logic to the desired end. In terms of the actions of management and the impact of various kinds of decisions on profitability and return on assets employed, the "truths" exposed above are certainly simple and both mathematically and judgmentally provable to the most practical manager.

Where does the impact of various elements of the MIS come into the picture? Basically, operating systems in any company form the basis for the information system, and these operating systems impact the profit equation by their very existence.

SYSTEMS IMPACT ON THE PROCESS OF THE BUSINESS

Perhaps the easiest way to visualize the interrelationships between the business, operating data processing systems, and the overall MIS is to visualize the total enterprise as being made up of intertwined key processes. Then it can be seen that the planning, control, and administration of these key processes constitutes the overall management of the company.

The major interacting processes which together make up the entity called the company include:

The financial analysis and control process.

The market research—product definition—product introduction process.

The sales planning—forecasting—and monitoring process.

The purchasing—provisioning—manufacturing—and finished product distribution process.

Each one of the four processes needs to be managed at strategic, tactical, and operational levels. In order to properly manage each process, an information system must exist which provides data to the manager which is a symbolic representation of the process itself. The information system needs to provide the *planning, control,* and *administrative* data necessary to constantly evaluate and take appropriate action upon the process to bring it under control. Therefore, in each area or department of the business, management must go through a disciplined thought process in order to: (1) define the process (or processes) for which the function is responsible; (2) define the information necessary to plan, control, and administer the process; (3) design the operating and/or information systems which will provide operational assistance and reports necessary to plan, control, and administer the process; (4) determine the level of cost which the present and proposed techniques will require to carry out the process; and (5) determine what changes in the method or technique of handling the process are required to minimize costs or allow for greater volume at minimum expenditure.

Let us take the process of acquiring raw materials, transforming them into finished product, and distributing the product, as an example. Let us examine it at operational, tactical, and strategic levels, and then look at the implications. Table 1 summarizes the aspects of the process.

It is evident that in the development and implementation of information systems in a company, when we view the problem as one supporting the planning, control, and administrative functions of a major process, we must define the operational, tactical, and strategic requirements and considerations which permit management of that process on a continuous basis under constantly changing circumstances.

Conversely, when we are looking at the strategic, tactical, and operational management needs of the corporation, we have to take into consideration and formalize the planning, control, and administrative systems necessary to manage the major processes.

It is obvious that with this approach we are no longer talking about *the* MIS, as if it were some mythical beast like the unicorn; we are talking about an interlocking, coordinated set of management systems designed to optimize the planning, control, and administration of specific processes operationally, tactically, and strategically. Modularity is essential in our approaches to management concepts and to system design.

A SENSE OF STRATEGY: MIS

Management information systems don't just happen, they have to be uniquely constructed to fit the enterprise they are to serve.

We have already seen that the management perspective of MIS implies that there are operational elements as well as tactical and strategic planning elements in the hierarchy of systems which together make up an MIS.

From a strategic standpoint, development of an MIS must start with development of operational systems which have immediate benefits to the enterprise in terms of reducing overhead costs or some other major variable in the profit equation.

Information to be used in MIS originates at the operating levels within the company, and in the marketplace. In order to develop an MIS one does not set out to design one, but one should set out to design specific opera-

TABLE 1. ASPECTS OF THE BUSINESS LOGISTICS PROCESS

Functions	Operational Level	Tactical Level	Strategic Level
Planning	a) Plan the receiving and progress chasing schedule for next day's schedule of material deliveries. b) Plan releases on suppliers to be processed next day. c) Plan machine shop schedule for next day. d) Plan next day's assembly schedule. e) Plan inspection, packing, and shipping schedule for next day. f) Plan minimum/maximum in-process inventories (short lead items).	a) Forecast of sales in detail of each specific product within lead time of material acquisition. b) Translation into future build program. c) Determination of sourcing pattern. d) Planning of inventory levels of raw material, work in process, and finished goods. e) Planning of purchasing quantities and orders on suppliers. f) Planning and scheduling of utilization of existing facilities and available labor. g) Planning of requirements for cash to finance any seasonal needs.	a) Determine future product line requirements and strategies. b) Estimate long range demand for existing and planned products by demand region. c) Determine production and warehousing facilities requirements. d) Plan management, administrative, labor, and other resources required for planned growth. e) Determine capital requirements and financial conditions for successful growth.
Control	Control all activities (processes) against documented plan prepared yesterday; report and take appropriate action on variances.	Monitoring of accuracy of all forecasts up to cut-off point determined by lead time of materials and components. Continuous feedback in response to market changes and production achievement, modifying tactical plan on a continuous basis.	Control against predicted performance to adjust strategic plans on a continuous basis in response to: economic trend changes, inflationary changes, political situations, industry and competition, technological developments, and current performance accomplishment.
Administration	Prepare and communicate all operational control documentation and capture for future analysis and extrapolation of historical performance. (Receiving documentation, machining orders and instructions, scrap reports, assembly tallies, packing instructions, shipping documentation, production volume data, and so forth.)	Maintenance and communication of all tactical planning and feedback information. Acquisition, maintenance, and extrapolation of historical data.	Maintain continuously updated planning data base containing feedback from the tactical control system and monitoring of external environment.

tional and control systems required for the on-going management of individual processes and functions in the company. Further, each operational and control system in a given functional area consisting of a series of specific applications needs to be evaluated and brought into being only after identifying the business goals of the system and performing initial cost/benefit analysis prior to expenditures on design and installation.

In terms of a basic strategy of systems development, one of the key management goals in a manufacturing company is the control of cost of goods sold. In a situation where material is the dominant element of the total cost of finished goods, a key system to be developed would be a manufacturing and logistical control system primarily oriented toward optimizing work in process and raw material inventories, and toward optimization of assets used in the production process, machine tools, toolage, and so forth. Justification of such a system would lie in increased utilization of assets, reduction of inventories in relation to throughput, and, in general, increased throughput through the factories for a given level of investment.

Similarly, in the marketing area as far as control of the flow of finished goods from factory door to retail is concerned, information on order status through the distribution system leads to better information on product mix and volume. Relating production mix to demand mix makes lower inventories in the distribution pipeline possible for any given level of sales activity. This again leads to conservation of assets employed in realizing a given level of revenue.

We find that if we define and implement an information system designed to control the process which has to be carried out (such as purchasing, production control, machining, assembly line scheduling, wholegoods warehousing, wholegoods distribution, and so forth), the data which have to be maintained to do so almost automatically include information needed to control costs—to account for the operation, and to develop historical data for statistical and forecasting purposes. It is really right at the basic level of operational control data that a computer-aided MIS is anchored, because it is at that level that facts for planning, extrapolation, and monitoring of progress have to be captured.

These examples are given in an attempt to illustrate the point that the foundation of an MIS is in the information and operating systems designed to control and support operations in the manufacturing, distribution, marketing, financial, and logistics areas.

BACK TO THE BASICS

We began this analysis with a discussion of the basic tools open to the manager and of the arena in which he could take actions to increase profits. Where then, does the construction of an MIS aid him in the manipulation of the variables which determine the result of his efforts? Let's look again at the variables and indicate where the elements of an MIS impact each and what abilities the manager has with operating management systems which he would otherwise forego:

1) *Structural Costs (Overheads)*. Perhaps the most difficult group of decisions made by top management revolve around the ongoing costs of administering the company. Early EDP (electronic data processing) applications typically address segments of this expense in terms of mechanizing payroll, accounting, and billing. The key decision factors in mechanizing these areas are those which relate to the relative simplicity of accomplishing the EDP application and the high level of predictability that savings in overhead will, in fact, occur as a result of the mechanization effort. Order processing, warranty claim processing, purchase order preparation, and work in process in-

ventory status are all applications which form the most basic parts of an overall MIS, and which, if properly conceived and executed, should provide for a reduction in overhead cost at expected levels of volume.

Many technical writers bemoan the fact that companies tackle the administrative and accounting applications first rather than some abstruse decision-making types of functions. Business logic and the realities of commercial life strongly suggest that these applications are, in fact, the most appropriate bases upon which to build a MIS effort.

2) Price and Volume. It is in the marketing and sales area of price and volume that creativity in systems design can pay off for the knowledgeable businessman. The customer of any company is looking for a supplier and a product which minimizes his total cost of doing business. Development of systems which make it easier to do business with your company than with competitors can provide opportunity to maximize price without attendant loss of volume. Providing the customer with an inventory control system and maintaining his inventory records allows for reductions in his costs while giving sales management useful information on product movement.

Price and product cost analyses with the kind of detail possible by use of EDP systems may suggest different pricing approaches where basic models of the product are sold at low margin while typical add-ons carry higher profit. In addition, the relatively fixed nature of the cost of mechanically handling administration activities may make it possible to go after incremental volume at less than fully absorbed price when circumstances are appropriate.

3) Product Cost. While product cost may be reduced by better scheduling of manpower and assets utilized in the company, many other opportunities also exist to employ EDP-generated intelligence to minimize costs. Product-by-product cost/price analysis will invariably show up specific products where inflation and other factors have seriously deteriorated margins. Decisions can then be made on pricing action or product phase out. Purchasing systems which analyze bought-out materials by commodity type, vendor, frequency of usage, commonality of usage, or multiple vendors in various geographic locations are relatively straightforward systems applications which typically yield profitable results. These applications will often provide summarized data which establish different make/buy situations than had been previously recognized.

4) Asset Turnover. The critical elements which lead to improved asset turnover are summarized in the ability to tightly and precisely schedule usage of assets, and in the ability to react to changes in need for assets quickly enough to avoid acquisition of unnecessary dollars of inventory. Sales analysis and forecasting systems can provide intelligence on shifts in needs for inventory and production. Combined with appropriate production control and material provisioning systems, lead times to react to market changes may be reduced by months. The ability to react to change should, in fact, be the over-riding objective in design of material and production control systems, since an overly precise result which cannot be changed quickly in the face of market shifts will straitjacket management instead of providing the flexibility necessary to maximize results.

THE MANAGEMENT QUESTIONS

We have seen that an MIS is not one system but a series of interrelated operating elements which support different ongoing process of the business. How then does operating top management select and determine priorities of effort in the systems area, and how does the management know when the efforts it is sponsoring are paying off?

Basically, there is a set of questions to which management needs to know the answers in order to effectively run the business. The questions are simple, their answers straightforward, and their interrelationships obvious. They are:

Q. What are we selling?—Product and dollars.

Q. Where are we selling it?—Geography and product mix.

Q. What will we be selling and where?—Forecast—units and dollars.

Q. What do we own?—Company inventories—product and dollars and age.

Q. Where is it?—Locations of inventory.

Q. What are we producing for sale?—Production schedules.

Q. When will it be ready for sale?—Future product availability.

Q. What will it cost us?—Product cost.

Q. What should we be producing and selling tomorrow?

Any MIS which is truly responsive to the needs of top management should provide the answers to these questions—accurately and quickly. The system will be composed of a number of sub-systems which address certain aspects of one or more questions—and which are used by operating personnel as an inherent part of their activities. The answers to the questions will provide management with data indicating whether action needs to be taken in the arena of price, volume, structural cost, product cost, or asset turnover—and should indicate the basic area for action. And it should be paying for itself, in reduction of structural costs or product costs; the MIS benefit should be a product of the "gestalt" equation where $2+2=5$.

If the EDP systems in a company can answer the questions posed above then they represent truly an MIS.

It is managements' responsibility to ask "why not?" if the systems efforts in their company do not appear to produce the desired end results. If systems in a company do not provide answers to the key questions, then management hasn't been providing enough input to the systems development process and the technicians have been practicing their own brand of footwork. One can consider the projects currently underway in any systems group and determine if they meet *all* the tests of relevance contained below:

Will existence of the system being designed help to answer one or more of the nine key top management questions about the business?

Has the system been cost justified by the operating area which is to use it?

Are the systems people working with (and for) the staff of the operating area of the business which is the sponsor of the effort?

Are there explicit time targets for the systems people to meet in order to finish the project?

Does overall systems management know and recognize where this systems effort will fit into the total information system needs of the company?

If systems efforts in a company can meet the tests of relevance, chances are good that an overall MIS is coming into being. If not, management is not being served, and whatever is to be produced by the systems effort will not aid in making the kinds of decisions necessary to produce profits.

It remains up to management to produce an MIS which will produce profits instead of costs for the company. The final product of management is, after all, profits.

14   Do You "Mis" Understand?

Irwin H. Derman

Management Information System (MIS) is the circulatory system of a business; its function is to transmit information for use in decision making. This article examines the strengths and pitfalls of information systems, and addresses the particular usefulness of one of those systems, the computer-based MIS. There is no magic in MIS. It is the formalization of a business function that has operated since the Florentines.

It is easy to assume that MIS has a life of its own. However, MIS has no right to exist beyond its obligation to provide management with useful, timely information. When systems considerations dictate how a business should be run, management has lost sight of the relationship between the business and the MIS. But, if we can accept the need for information in its true light, then the formalized MIS is reduced to its realistic status—a tool to help management operate effectively. In this way, the need for information will dictate the kind of MIS to be used.

One manager we know has an excellent information system; he circulates among his staff and he asks the right questions. His information system is almost flawless. Top management at most companies, however, rightfully feel that they cannot personally collect data, and they spend millions of dollars to develop an MIS that will gather information on a corporate-wide basis.

MIS problems are compounded by the diversity of management relationships. For example, the purchasing-receiving-inventory-payment cycle is handled in a variety of ways in different companies. Because MIS systems depend greatly on how business has been conducted in the past, each one becomes unique, and there is little or no possibility of transferring specific experience or information from one company to another.

Some of the premises of a management information system are the following.

MIS does not determine:

  a. The information to be collected

  b. The combination of raw data into reports

  c. The distribution of reports

  d. The use of reports by recipients.

MIS does exist:

  a. To satisfy a specific business need

  b. To support decision makers with the information they need or want to know.

THE PROBLEMS OF AN INSTITUTIONALIZED MIS

The size of most companies precludes having the decision maker, himself, collect the information he needs to make a decision. These companies must systematize the data collection through the controller's office, the computer center, the MIS group, and so on. Typical problems exist in any institutionalized information system whether or not a computer is involved. The problems special to a computer-based MIS will be covered in a separate section. First, we will discuss MIS difficulties that are common to both the manual and the automated systems.

This article originally appeared in *Business Horizons* (October, 1972), pp. 55–64. Copyright 1972 by the Foundation for the School of Business at Indiana University. Reprinted by permission.

Institutionalized MIS Seems to Have a Life of its Own

How many times have you wanted to do something even a little unusual with an information system, only to be told "It can't be done!"? This is a clear indication that your MIS is second rate. A system, even a computerized one, should not be a limiting factor in information handling. The system is virtually useless if its design does not take exceptions into account or allow processing of an unusual request. The following transaction is a case in point.

A colleague wanted to change the billing date for his credit card account with a large bank. First, he was told that it couldn't be done. "Our system is designed to bill the M people on a specific date." But, the same bank branch had recently switched the billing of all people in that office to a common date. "Why can't I do the same thing? Do all of the people in your branch have last names beginning with the same letter?" he asked. Finally, a vice president said the request could be handled very simply and immediately.

Alas, the story continues: To make the change, it was necessary to close out the previous account and open a new one that would "fool" the system, so that it would "think" our colleague's name began with a different letter. During these machinations, service charges accrued on the old account; and our colleague received billings on both the old and new accounts. A few more phone calls and a few months of interest compounding finally satisfied what should have been a simple request.

If the original system had been designed correctly, this kind of problem could have been avoided. The platitude "garbage in, garbage out," applies principally to data; we suggest a new one as the slogan of poor systems analysis: "intransigence in, intractableness out." When a company allows hardware limitations or inherent laziness or stupidity on the part of an analyst to dictate its system design, it risks having a system similar to that described above.

Lower Echelon Employees Design MIS

It is not possible for any more than a handful of executives to understand completely all the functions in today's complex company. Yet, these same executives frequently shun the task of designing the information systems that they will use and they relegate its development to a $15,000-per-year man—a systems analyst or an assistant controller.

Lower echelon employees are required, then, to institutionalize a system based on plans and assumptions that are never fully communicated to them. Ask a representative sample of people in your company what are the company's goals, objectives, and strategic plans. How many would be able to tell you? This is the situation that too often prevails during MIS implementation activities.

Top management involvement in the planning process is a prerequisite for successful MIS design and implementation. In most cases, they are involved in the early stages, but even when top management takes a continuing interest in MIS development, the employees at the operating level must fully participate. Top management's influence must be balanced with that of the operating personnel.

It is critical to top quality systems development that only people with a wide knowledge of operations and plans be assigned to the MIS team. Unfortunately, those assigned to work with systems planners are not always the most knowledgeable. A company is inclined to assign members to its MIS team on the basis of current availability and immediate productivity, to avoid "overhead" charges. A system planned by qualified personnel is superior in many ways to one designed by "available" personnel. First, the planning itself will be more thorough. Second, the system will be more readily accepted by the company. Third, the system will function as it should.

MIS Designers Are Vulnerable Politically

What is your concept of "business"? Is it an entity that exists to maximize profits? Or do you see a fortified castle doing battle for the money and loyalty of something called a consumer? Maybe by taking a more analytical view you see that people in the castle perform functions included currently in your company. Most people, though, tend to view an organization built almost exclusively to allow them to do their thing. Since this is a normal individual viewpoint, it is almost impossible to find a definition acceptable to everyone. How then can an effective MIS be designed—when the individual functions of the employees and the overall objectives of the company cannot be defined in a manner satisfactory to either those who will be designing the information system or to those who will be using it?

Too frequently, the system designer becomes enmeshed in definitional and organizational infighting, and people problems become more acute during MIS planning. Lines of demarcation between functions become fuzzy when people are bargaining for control. Because organization structures break down a function into discrete parts that are necessarily interdependent, the system designer often finds himself involved in jurisdictional disputes. He must determine, at times arbitrarily: (1) his data source (2) how the information will be used by a company not really organized to optimize its activity.

Even these difficulties could be overcome if the designer were to identify the correct incentives for cooperation. Incentives for cross-functional cooperation, however, are usually placed too high in the organizational structure. Group managers in decentralized organizations are not judged by the cooperation they exhibit as much as they are judged by the amount of money appearing on their report cards—the profit and loss statement.

In addition, people installing an MIS are educated in the latest, business-oriented, computer techniques and they are anxious to carry out a successful implementation program. Their enthusiasm compounds the problem of poor communication between departments; they face the "youth/age" barrier. The systems analyst, symbolically a threat to the security of all management, is grudgingly accepted by those who want the MIS and skillfully thwarted by those who do not. Many young analysts have not yet developed the finesse to "field" the people problems; their interests are primarily "thing" oriented, wherein lies their competence. The MIS team is confronted, therefore, with the problem of utilizing the expertise of younger team members—without creating major disputes among company personnel.

$500,000-a-Year Monster

When the prestige of installing an ambitious MIS outweigh the cost, a company is practicing one-upmanship. One-upmanship takes on more than one dimension; often, company decisions are based on who swings the most weight rather than what activity will be most instrumental in meeting the company's goals. Even after an MIS has been selected as a study project, the desire of some managers to obtain control over a greater number of activities may motivate an expanded effort beyond what is economically justifiable. As long as people run business, such occurrences cannot be avoided, but they must be controlled.

MIS development is a long, costly process. Even small systems are difficult to develop and involve a long planning and development process. Top management, impatient for results, exhibits frustration and often causes the MIS manager to panic and look for ways of showing short-term, tangible benefits. This leads to incomplete systems and hastily assembled subsystems, compounding rather than reducing communication problems. Such poorly executed exercises, in turn, drastically reduce top management's commitment to future MIS efforts. Until an understanding is reached of the investment needed for a good MIS, all MIS implementation programs will fail to elicit the cooperation of those who will benefit most.

Worse than a poor system design effort is the inability of the MIS team to admit to errors in system implementation. Rather than expend effort in justifying poor work, it would be more sensible for MIS teams to correct the portions of a system that have proved inadequate. Often, the personnel responsible for implementation feel that they must justify what has been done, instead of learning from the experience during the system's operation to recommend sensible changes. An example aptly illustrates this point.

A company with a 10,000-product inventory decides to computerize inventory control. A study determines the size of the machine required, and the implementation and transfer of the manual system to the computer are accomplished. As the number of items controlled by the computer increases, the computer becomes inadequate to operate the system efficiently. A larger computer is obtained.

Does this example sound familiar? Instead of evaluating the need to retain all items in the computer-controlled system, the empire-building solution is taken. In instances where an evaluation of the control system is made, it is generally found that a large number of small-activity items are taking up valuable processing time and storage space. It is easier to add new items to the control system than it is to remove old ones.

Is your company more interested in the prestige of having its entire inventory in the computer, or in the efficiency of controlling only items that should be computer-controlled? Realistically, a computer-based system need not be an all-or-nothing proposition. One of the most common symptoms of a poorly organized MIS is the executive who receives, each morning, 200 pages of computer printout. The odds are good that he seldom refers to at least 90 percent of that information.

Summary

Every decision maker needs information. In a few cases, all the information he needs can be obtained by a quick trip through the shop and a few key questions asked of trusted employees. In most cases, the volume of the information required is such that a separate department exists to collect, process, and report that information. The rapid overview and the dedicated department are both valid forms of an information system, whether or not a computer is involved. However, even if a whole MIS department is producing reports, the reports and the department that created them are justified solely to the extent that they are useful to the decision maker.

THE ROLE OF THE COMPUTER IN MIS

The use of a computer for MIS is justifiable only when the information cannot be produced manually in time to be useful, or at a reasonable cost. If, in response to an urgent customer inquiry, three days were to elapse before scheduling could tell marketing that a job could be handled in seven days, a manual system would lack adequate response time. The rapid response requirement is typified by the payroll services offered by metropolitan banks. Only by using computers can they offer the service economically. There is virtually no way that even the lowest-paid clerk-typists can do the same job at the same cost.

We have pointed out some of the common problems unique to the computer. For example, "alphabet soup" may occur:

Setting:—Friday, 4 pm
Manager (angry): "Why were the payroll checks late today?"

DP (data processing) Manager (apologetic): "Because my request for 2314s was disapproved last spring!"

Manager (regrouping): "Oh."

The DP Manager could just as easily have said his Fragistan was on the fritz. The DP Manager is engaged in the well-known "alphabet-soup" game; using such phrases as "Hasp," "RJE," "2701," and so on. DP managers have found this an effective technique for avoiding both criticism and a decrease in next year's budget.

Any general manager who receives a memorandum filled with computer jargon should demand an English translation. After all, if a salesman said he didn't get the Jones' contract because the "moon was in the seventh house," you would probably fire him. On the other hand, if he said that Jones was feeling lousy the day of the presentation, you would probably understand.

Fear and Misunderstanding

Have you seen a newspaper cartoon depicting the computer as anything other than a bumbling, overbearing, ridiculous monster? NO. People are basically afraid of computers and they find an outlet for their fear by laughing at the machines. Even the enlightened manager, not computer oriented, cannot help but feel personally threatened when systems and computer people are evaluating his job. He does not speak their language, and they seldom miss an opportunity to point it out (alphabet soup). Not all analysts are condescending in their manner, but enough are to alienate even the most conscientious managers. Instead of developing a unifying force to view the problem being investigated, the analyst who is smug in his knowledge and the manager who is fearful in his ignorance accomplish little more than to convince the manager that the cartoons are probably right.

The Computer Is No Panacea

Shifting to computer processing is no substitute for knowledge of a company and its problems. It is easy to forget that a computer is nothing more than a machine and that it alone cannot make decisions or solve problems. Programmers themselves tend to forget that the computer is not human; instead of asking if the computer is running, many programmers ask how the computer is "feeling." The humor is soon forgotten, and the computer is thought of as a living entity.

It is understandable that programmers and other computer-oriented personnel are inclined to personify the computer. In fact, haven't you known at least one person who adopts the same attitude toward his car, or his boat, or some other meaningful object in his daily life? In all honesty, more than just one person?

But the extent of such feelings isn't limited just to those most closely associated with the piece of machinery in question—not when that instrument is a computer; nor are those feelings always felicitous. Where computers are concerned, the view is accentuated for those who have no idea of what "goes on in that THING!" This personification can be seen in the following example.

In one well-known company the planning department system was computerized. As part of the system's error checking procedures, all input into the system was coded with a number identifying the source planner. When errors were detected, the name of the planner who had furnished the incorrect data was retrieved. This check was not meant as a punitive measure, but to speed up the correction cycle. Within one week of its operation, the identification check was deleted from the system at the request of the planning department supervisor. It seemed that his men were upset that the "monster" could identify them by name. To this day, there are probably 23 planners who still do not understand how the computer could point its accusing "finger" at their work.

The "Older" Manager Problem

The men managing American industry today are predominantly in their

50s and 60s. They received their training in various disciplines and have progressed through the management hierarchy; each has his own style, his own expertise, and his own staff to complement and supplement his talents. Few have a working knowledge of computer functions or the changes that take place when a computer is used to augment their skills.

When a computer-based MIS is considered, we are asking these men to trust a system developed because of the computer's increased capacity to process information. How many managers are really able to accept the required dependence on a system that is foreign to them? Managers who really do not trust the machines are not likely to give their complete support to the installation of MIS. Using a manual system, it may take some time to receive the information he has requested; but, when he does, he knows where it came from and how it was processed. Replace the manual methods by a computer-based MIS and the "Black Box" aspect may very well prove the demise of the system. The manager's background and training do not lend themselves to the blind acceptance of information without knowledge of the source. Thus, top management introduces fear into an MIS study because they do not understand what is involved in the proposed system, and they have not developed a plan to educate themselves and their managers.

Pave the Way with Education

An automated MIS does not in itself create a need to teach managers how to do business or how to utilize information. With a computer-based MIS, the manager should receive exactly the information he has *requested*—no more and no less. But, a computer-based MIS may be able to provide managers with timely information to which they have not previously had access.

A need does exist, though, to educate managers to the extent of the computer-based MIS' capabilities so that the manager can take full advantage of the new tool. By feeling comfortable in his knowledge, he will actively support efforts to implement the automated system.

Computer people do speak a special language—and so do many of the recent business school graduates. To communicate with these people and to understand their potential, top management is forced to learn computer technology. Very little is done, however, to educate down-the-line management—where greatest resistance is evident. No system plan is complete without a clearly defined educational program to provide managers with an understanding of systems analysis and computer hardware and software to a sufficient degree that they feel comfortable with the techniques involved.

Visibility of Cost

A computer-based MIS in itself is not expensive. It should be cheaper than alternative means of doing the same job; if it is not, maybe you should consider removing the computer. But, computer-based MIS costs are highly visible. The computer is often housed in a glass-enclosed room in the main lobby. In some companies, it may be the only department that is air conditioned.

The computer, the computer room, and the computer group are much in evidence in most companies, both organizationally and physically. During cost-cutting periods, they are a tempting target for attack. Because MIS is so visible, it is frequently a convenient scapegoat for bureaucratic injustices. If the same MIS activities were carried out by a number of clerks in obscure cubbyholes throughout the plant, the system would still exist—maybe more costly, maybe less—but the target would no longer be obvious. Cost-cutting experts would not be confronted by seemingly monumental costs emanating from one centralized area.

HOW TO COPE WITH AN OVERGROWN COMPUTER-BASED MIS

Do you as a manager:

a. Receive stacks of computer print-out you never read or use?

b. Feel that the MIS group has built an uncontrollable empire?

c. Feel that you are not getting as much from MIS as you would if the same money were spent on advertising, new equipment, or lower prices?

If the answer to any one of these questions is "yes" your MIS should be pruned because it has grown too large to be useful. There are many ways of cutting down a computer operation. When reduced to essentials, they fall into two categories: (1) systematic reduction and (2) start from scratch.

The Technique of Systematic Reduction

In general, trouble in implementing an MIS arises when companies are not selective about the functions included in, or the extent of their management information systems. The key to systematic reduction is to focus on MIS output costs.

By instituting a system to distribute the entire cost of MIS activity to the budgets of operating managers—in direct proportion to the volume of reports they receive—a company will implement a self-controlling measure to limit MIS costs and reports. The cost distribution approach has proven to be one of the most effective measures of limiting an MIS, since operating managers determine the value of MIS reports to their operations in relation to other uses for their operating funds. If a report no longer proves useful, the manager may exercise his prerogative to cancel it.

Effect on Operating Managers. To optimize this approach, cost allocation should be made to the lowest organizational level at which the manager has a degree of choice in apportioning his budget. Since a manager is judged, presumably, on the quantity and quality of his department's output, he will begin to examine the cost of this information service and judiciously limit his requirements to those that will realize the greatest benefits. He will, in effect, assist in pruning the company's MIS costs.

Effect on the Computer Group. As reports are cancelled, the computer group may choose to: ignore the cancellations, decrease the cost of making reports, or improve the relevance of existing reports and design new ones. Clearly, the first alternative is suicide; if the number of reports are cut but the computer group does not react by cutting costs, the remaining reports become more costly. Eventually, only the payroll or another critical report will be produced, but its cost will be so high that an outside agency could probably perform the same service more economically.

A more rational solution would be to cut computer group costs. Suddenly, the perennial request for a larger machine will disappear, and the computer group will find ingenious ways to economize. They will either do so by themselves, without prodding, or be faced with the situation described above.

If computer group members are truly clever, they will mount a crash program to determine from users how to make reports more useful—and reduce the risk of cancellation. They will interview potential receivers of new reports and, in general, attempt to make their product as useful as possible. They will, in essence, sell their product within the company itself, vying with other uses for a department's funds.

Effect of Charge-Back. The charge-back system has several advantages. First, it runs by itself without top management's supervision or prodding. Second, since the operating manager decides if a report is to be cancelled, there is no risk of stopping a vital report. Finally, it leads either to total elimination of the computer group, or to a reduction of the size and cost of the group.

There are, however, several drawbacks. Operating managers are reluctant to accept the fact that they can alter the reports they receive. After they have made the desired alterations, the computer group will have to restructure its activities to conform to the wishes of the operating managers, which will take time.

In some cases, this process is intolerably long; but once these hurdles are overcome, an effective MIS results. However, if the computerized MIS has become so cumbersome that it causes a serious drain on profits or that it fails to respond to operating needs, the company must perceive the problem and be willing again to "start from scratch."

HOW TO DEVELOP AN MIS FROM SCRATCH

Since many books have been written on this subject, we will not repeat what has become a vast literature. We only wish to point out some crucial elements of an ideal MIS.

Develop a Systematic Information Flow

To have a successful MIS implementation, a company should consider its information flow to be an overall system dedicated to the single objective of providing sufficient information to the managers who must make decisions in the best interests of the total organization. To optimize performance, the information system should not be fragmented for use by each of the unique functional areas. Instead, companies should recognize the need for a system collectively developed and updated by the various functional areas.

To minimize duplication errors and inefficiency, only one source should be designated for a given piece of information and only one person or group of persons responsible for its accuracy and updating. Conversely, wide accessibility to information, except for such sensitive information as personnel data, is mandatory, thus providing information as required to any portion of the organization. A company cannot afford to collect data primarily for use by one area. The same data gathered for financial purposes can and must satisfy the information requirements for inventory management, production scheduling, estimation of future jobs, and so on. As difficult as it may appear, a corporate-wide, one-for-all/all-for-one philosophy is desirable so that each input contributor recognizes the company-wide effect of any neglect in maintaining accuracy and completeness. MIS efforts in many companies were started with good intentions, but they have degenerated into fragmentation because the employees failed to maintain this philosophy.

Beware of a Packaged MIS

MIS supports decision makers with whatever information they want or need to know. Therefore, the first task of the systems analyst is to ask each user to define the reports he wants to receive. The MIS group does not define reports; its role is to produce the reports requested by the decision makers. By definition, prepackaged programs are suspect; economies to be derived from purchasing a packaged program can often be dissipated in attempts to tailor that package to the unique needs of the decision makers.

No two companies are so alike that a generalized MIS package can be developed for one and used without modification by the other. While a company has a legal existence separate from the individuals that constitute the work force, it is those individuals who directly affect the company's stature and the direction of its activity. On a broad scale, a company reflects the expertise of its chief executive officers. On a more refined scale, each area reflects the interest of its manager, who, presumably, is promoted because of his ability in his field.

Take Your Time to Do It Right

The cardinal rule of MIS implementation is: Don't Rush! A company should develop a long-range plan that allows time to create, test, and prove each of the multitude of steps required. An attempt to implement an MIS without taking into account the historical reluctance of businessmen to plan activities is almost doomed to fail. The magnitude of an MIS is such that it must be constructed through a series of building blocks, each of which is essential to the support of the next level. There must be a plan to determine how these blocks should be placed, and progression to each level must not occur until all steps in the preceding levels have been executed.

Fortunately, an MIS can be implemented in relatively small steps compared to conversion to electronic data processing. Each of these steps must be analyzed and evaluated so that relative priorities can be established. The priorities established must then be rigidly maintained to avoid the pitfalls between concept development and implementation. MIS is something to be created, not purchased or legislated into effect.

The value of each block of activity in an MIS must be weighed against the planned time of its implementation. There is little value in developing a report that by its completion time will have passed the payoff point where such information would have been useful to the decision maker. The time in which a user requires information must also be considered. For example, if a system is being designed to provide daily output information, it would be logical to use a cathode ray tube (CRT) device for user inquiry, even though such a device may be too expensive today. A system designed solely to solve today's problem on today's equipment is a waste of a company's resources —time and money.

There are other factors that must be considered when a company is designing a management information system:

a. With the current objectives in mind, design a system for the future.

b. Considering both equipment capabilities and user needs, plan in five- and ten-year increments.

c. Balance the systems capabilities against both the time and the cost of implementation.

d. Maintain adequate documentation for the system. To reduce implementation time by skimping on the documentation is a temptation that faces all organizations. But it is one that must not be indulged in without careful consideration of all factors.

Most companies planning an automated MIS face the task of developing an orderly system from a maze of existing subsystems. Although it may appear to be a duplication of effort, the best way to develop an MIS is to use a group separate from those presently maintaining the system. To attempt to integrate MIS development into everyday activities will be far more costly in the long run than creating a separate responsibility. In addition, it is important to realize that investing money in MIS development will be far less costly today than tomorrow, next month, or next year. Developing an MIS by patching together existing subsystems or by shifting existing systems to more advanced computer equipment is also more expensive than attacking the problem directly. Within an overall plan, the MIS must be structured from the bottom up with no subsystem sacred, no information flow fixed, no output unchangeable, and no preconceived restrictions on equipment usage or human resources.

Caveat Emptor

While the cost of developing and implementing an MIS can be staggering, the cost of not developing one can be even more. This cost must be measured against factors such as the cost of staying in business, or the cost of remaining competitive. It is not sufficient to evaluate MIS expenditures only in terms of the money to be spent for development and implementation; these costs must be weighed against the benefits of having timely and accurate information when a decision must be made. An analysis of costs and benefits will also develop information useful to establishing an implementation schedule that the company can afford—both in time and money.

Justification by ROI

Most companies follow the traditional idea of using cost reductions to justify computer systems, even though experience has shown that such reductions are seldom realized. In evaluating MIS, a new justification must be used, for instance, return-on-investment. An ROI-based evaluation may help management to see that, although the MIS investment may be greater than that made for any system in the past, the potential return may make the expenditure mandatory.

There is no reason why a computer based information system investment should be judged differently from the investment for a factory machine or an office calculator, both capital facilities whose cost justification must satisfy a specified return-on-investment criter-

ion. But the similarity ends there, since the resources committed to a system are not firmly and completely established for the specified development and implementation period.

By using an ROI criterion for MIS, systems management can be measured by return-on-investment and by improvements in operations. MIS can be one of the most valuable company resources, and information can be managed with the same care and planning as the company's manpower, money, and material resources.

With the past year's general business conditions forcing companies to reappraise all aspects of their enterprises, it is fitting that MIS, too, be reevaluated. With the initial excitement of MIS implementation gone, a dispassionate review of the original promise and the structure that resulted will do much to set a meaningful direction for future information systems development. Beware of the solution that calls for junking the MIS and its hardware. If you review your system and pinpoint its problems, you can direct future systems work to respond to existing needs without creating problems. A poor MIS is the symptom; identify the disease before applying the remedy. It is easy to see the out-of-pocket costs of a poor system, but one never sees the opportunity loss of a system that could have been.

15 Computer Based Decision Systems in Xerox Corporate Planning

Ronald A. Seaberg and Charlotte Seaberg

The whole concept of modelling has caught on aided immeasurably by the considerable progress in computer technology. Mini-computers, timesharing systems, remote terminals, and graphical displays have placed computer power directly into the hands of the decision maker.

This paper presents a corporate decision-aiding system, a family of timeshared models, developed for Xerox of Canada Limited (XCL) in an effort to link the functional areas for communication, planning, and control purposes. Using the approaches of statistical forecasting, heuristics, and simulation, the XCL Decision System assists and guides management all the way from deriving product demand forecasts to simulating the day-to-day operations of the firm to formulating divisional financial statements to preparing corporate operating and medium-range plans. Developed in a short time span and at low cost, the system is used extensively in Canada and has been adopted, in part, by U.S. corporate and regional offices.

"Planning is the design of a desired future and of effective ways of bringing it about" (Ackoff, 1970).

1. INTRODUCTION AND PHILOSOPHY

Computers for a considerable time have economically justified themselves in performing data processing tasks such as tracking inventories and calculating receivables and payrolls. Management and management scientists suggest that an even bigger payoff is going to result from the application of computers to management processes especially those concerned with decision making, planning and control.

Our philosophy as to how this can be accomplished is as follows:

A recognition that the management process (including provision for economic and political influences) can be modelled.

The derived models can be computerized.

The computer-based models can be directly executed by functional management to assist them in their decision processes.

A combined "man-model-machine" based system will be economically employed to derive better solutions than those that would have otherwise been made without the contribution of management science and computer technology.

Planning (anticipatory decision making) is the process which determines "Where do I want to go and what steps must I take to get there?" It is the translation of objectives into possible course of action. Planning consists of a series of interrelated processes linked into a continuing and changing system; including Strategic Planning, Operational Planning, and Operations Management (monitoring, variance analysis and corrective action). The planning process must provide for a feedback and control system to track actual to

---

This article originally appeared in *Management Science* (December 1973), Part II, pp. 575–584, and is reprinted with permission.

planned performance. Without this provision, planning degenerates into an expensive theoretical exercise.

The purpose of this paper is to describe how Xerox of Canada Limited (XCL) has implemented computer and management science technology into our planning process, the types of computers and models utilized, adaptation of the models to both a dynamic internal and external environment, and our findings to date on the success of application of computers to decision-making processes.

Some of the basic issues and questions that are addressed in the XCL planning process include:

Market identification and how it is changing over time.

Forecast of revenue and profit plus key factors—market penetration, manpower productivity, pricing trends, cost trends, product line information such as order projections, product trading patterns, inventory requirements, and product life cycles.

Human resource requirements.

The structure and effects of competition.

Other resource requirements such as capital and facilities which are especially critical in view of high growth rate of the firm.

2. SYSTEM DESIGN PROCESS

Our modelling effort developed as a direct result of a primary objective to improve the quality of the planning process. We concluded that such improvement could be accomplished by having direct access to more timely, accurate, in-depth, and logically-consistent information plus a flexible system for coping with a dynamic environment.

We felt that the overriding consideration in the design process was to develop models that would (a) be used, (b) be relevant and responsive to the needs of the user, and (c) be implemented with a minimum of time delay. To assist in this endeavor we attempted to design models around the decision maker. We have done this by our approach to modelling, by the scope and type of models we designed, and by the computer system we utilized.

In the model design phase we at-

TABLE 1. XEROX OF CANADA LIMITED CONTROL REPORT. SAMPLE DATA

| | ACTUAL PERFORMANCE | | | | OUTLOOK (FORECAST) | | | | |
| | June Year to Date | | Current Month | | | | | Full Year Impact | |
	Amount	Percent of Plan	Amount	Percent of Plan	July	August	September	Amount	Percent of Plan
PRODUCT LINE 8:									
Orders	1550	146	130	140	177	146	156	2462	119
Better Than Plan	473		66		20	7	(24)	397	
Better Than PMO	(4)		22		0	(20)	(42)	(149)	
Inventory	273	97	273	97	37	36	36	485	90
Better Than Plan	9		9		7	8	8	56	
Better Than PMO	(31)		(31)		0	1	0	(7)	
REVENUE:									
Product 8	1420	101	233	99	200	198	185	2626	96
Better Than Plan	(11)		2		22	15	36	121	
Better Than PMO	164		(3)		21	12	43	42	
Total Revenue	2037	105	626	131	572	609	657	3692	112
Better Than Plan	91		149		152	191	264	387	
Better Than PMO	37		(18)		5	53	50	150	
EXPENSES:									
Salaries	525	96	130	140	104	100	94	1195	102
Better Than Plan	23		(37)		(14)	(13)	5	(23)	
Better Than PMO	130		(3)		3	(4)	1	(73)	

PMO—Prior Month Outlook (Forecast)

tempted to replicate either the existing decision process or alternative processes as suggested by the functional manager. Involvement in model-development has led managers, in many instances, to view their operation in differing ways. This new insight frequently resulted in improved business operations thereby realizing a major goal of the modelling effort.

We utilized a variety of models with varying degrees of scope of operation and complexity so that the manager does not have to wade through a detailed model if he is only interested in aggregate and/or simplistic solutions. We relied primarily on simulation (case study or heuristic) models rather than optimization (algorithmic or linear programming) models which are restricted to single predetermined objectives. We found that simulation models most closely replicate managerial decision making and are most readily understood by managers as well as being easier to design from a modelling viewpoint. We found that as management became more familiar with the power of models we could begin approaching the incorporation of optimization techniques into our models.

It was our opinion that the advantages a timeshared system has for the decision-making process significantly offset any limitations such as reduced core storage and increased execution time. The program-size limitation was, for the most part, overcome by the development of smaller functional models which could either be run on a stand-alone basis or linked together into a corporate model. We decided to utilize the APL programming language (a very macro-oriented language) because it minimizes time and cost of program development and because knowledge of only a few basic commands allows the user considerable "programming" capability.

The advantages of timeshared computer models has been discussed in the literature [4]. Our experience, which bears favorably upon their conclusions, has shown the following to be significant:

1. *Reduced Information Data Overload.* Planning involves a large number of variables which must be simultaneously considered. Computerized models aid the decision maker by processing information for him quickly and efficiently.

2. *Information Selection.* Key variables, identified within the model-building process, assisted in defining information to be included in a data base. Statistical analysis models were used to perform sensitivity analysis to aid in this selection process in addition to simulation models which allowed the user to vary input variables and observe the results against a "base case."

3. *Economical Solutions.* Models provided answers at low cost and with a minimum of manpower resources by enabling managers to experiment with a variety of alternatives, forecasts, and cases.

4. *Fast Turnaround.* Generally, managers are unwilling to delay the decision process. The timeshared system, since it provided nearly instantaneous information and solutions, allowed the decision models to be explicitly incorporated into the managerial planning process.

5. *Interrelation of Operations and Planning Systems.* Computer-based models facilitated the incorporation of operating results explicitly into the planning process. This was achieved by analysis and control models having direct access to operating and financial data thereby promoting detailed plan, actual and forecast comparisons.

6. *Communication Aid.* A large integrated model, encompassing the functional areas of the business, provided a common language between the areas and enhanced the communication of ideas.

7. *Direct Involvement.* A modelling capability was placed directly into the hands of the decision maker. This allowed him to bypass intermediary obstacles such as coding sheets, keypunching, and programmers.

3. IMPLEMENTATION OF INITIAL SYSTEM

A manually-performed forecast and control activity (referred to in XEROX as the Outlook) was the impetus for the initial modelling effort. The Outlook, which is essentially a rolling 12-month forward look at the business, was considered a prime target for mechanization because (a) it was a major responsibility which incorporated the activities of several functional areas, (b) it was performed monthly, and (c) it required considerable, high-level manpower resources. It was felt that successful mechanization of the Outlook would pave the way for the development of additional man-machine decision systems for such areas as operational and long-range planning.

A major question that arises during the Outlook cycle is the impact of cumulative performance to date upon the full year Operating Plan. All areas of the business are affected—marketing, finance, service, manufacturing and distribution. An answer to this question requires examination and analysis of cumulative and current performance, forecasted trends, and a provision for management action where "gaps" exist or are projected to exist. Computerized analytical and statistical control models provide answers to the first two points. Forecasting and simulation models are utilized by functional managers to assist in providing solutions to the last point.

The initial model, a deterministic simulation model which produced a rolling 12-month forecast of the major areas of the business, required two man-months to develop. Inputs to the model consisted of assumptions, parameters, and strategies; many of which were manager-controlled. Approximately 30 input variables, such as growth rates, various fixed and variable costs, trade assumptions, and inventory parameters, together with the model equations produce about 300 output variables such as sales orders, inventory levels, net profit, produce revenue, expenses and manpower requirements. A schematic of this early system is illustrated below.

A sample report is displayed below.

This sample report could be analyzed in the following way:

Customer installations for product line 8 is currently ahead of plan on a year-to-date basis and is forecasted to maintain this favorable position for the balance of the operating year.

The revenue resulting from this product is below plan indicating the fact that our customer leased inventory of this product is currently and projected to remain below plan. The negative impact of this product is more than overcome by the favorable position of other product lines on total revenue.

The management group may execute additional simulations to determine the impact of various decision alternatives (such as increasing the commission rate, adjusting price, or an extensive advertising campaign) on other product lines in terms of functional department effectiveness and efficiency and the total corporate effect in terms of revenues and profits.

Although the above is highly simplistic in terms of how the system is actually put to use by XCL management it, nevertheless, serves to highlight the types of situations which can be investigated by the system.

The "what if" aspect of the model aided management in deriving solutions to such questions as:

Determine the most likely effect on salesman performance (and productivity) by changes in the compensation plan?

Given current sales trends, what will profits look like 12 months hence? How will this picture be influenced if (a) changes are made to the pricing structure of certain products, and (b) sales manpower is increased by 3%?

How should the manufacturing mix of production be changed to achieve the profit plan given current and projected sales trends?

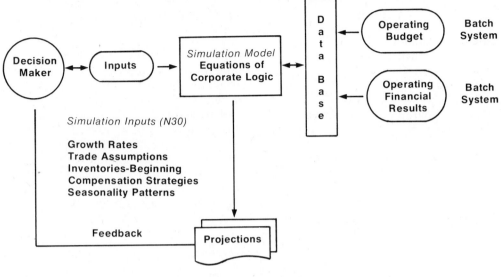

Figure 1.

The above are representative of the types of questions which the model assisted management in solving either at a functional level (finance or marketing) or at the corporate level.

Use of the model resulted in significant time and cost benefits. Each simulation required an average of 8 to 10 CPU seconds with the initial model. Generally, 4 to 6 simulations (performed within an elapse time of two days) were executed to produce each finalized 12-month forecast. Less than 10% of analyst time was required for data manipulation versus 80% in the manual environment.

The manual system had been characterized by:

1. Considerable resource requirements. Approximately 6 man-weeks of analyst-level effort was allocated to this task each month with only one complete forecast being generated.

2. Forecasting logic not rigidly defined. Lack of a universally-accepted logic resulted in non-standardized forecasts.

3. On-the-spot changes. Because of the severe time constraints, adjustments were made to the forecast without consideration of the impact such changes (e.g. increase in sales) might have on other variables (e.g. inventory levels, expenses). As a result forecasts were not always internally consistent.

4. There was insufficient time for analysis. Utilizing worksheets, tab-runs, and calculators, a high proportion of analyst effort and time was spent on number-crunching. Operating plans and budgets (at the time) were outputs of a large batch planning system. This system was operated in a simulation mode; dozens of test plans or simulations were run over a three-to-six month period before the final plan was derived. Extensive input data, manually derived, was a prerequisite for each

simulation. Considerable time (several days in some instances) were required to analyze and transform the data into a suitable format for the batch model. With the manual handling of large quantities of data it was also error-prone in addition to being a slow process. The simulation output had to be manually manipulated if any analysis was required that was not already programmed.

The timesharing capability was initially used to develop the required input data for the batch planning system and to perform user-defined analysis on the output. These initial efforts established a foundation for a series of timeshared planning models which were developed the following year and, subsequently, replaced the batch system.

4. PLANNING AT XCL WITH THE PRESENT COMPUTERIZED SYSTEM

On-line models at XCL have become an integral part of the management planning and control process. This approach has greatly reduced time and manpower resources to accomplish the task and has allowed managers to quickly ascertain the effects of various courses of action in developing plans and/or responding to operating variances.

Planning at XCL begins with top management defining corporate objectives and philosophy (Strategic Planning). Strategic Planning anticipates the future and formulates strategies to foster progress towards goals. It includes the long range conceptualization and forecasting of markets, estimating resources, and developing alternative strategies to achieve these broad corporate objectives. Being a highly intuitive and judgmental exercise, it is generally not quantifiable.

The identification of Key Result Areas (KRA) is an important part of strategic planning. Once KRA (profitability objectives, productivity assumptions) have been defined, models can assist the planner in several ways. Sensitivity analysis helps select those critical operational variables having significant effect on the KRA. Simulation models provide a readily accessible analytical tool to assist top management in the design and development of alternatives to achieve the KRA and to evaluate the effects of various alternatives in terms of a "base case" or specified goals. These simulations then provide the basis for our long range plan.

Operational Planning

Operating and financial plans become the basis for the implementation of decisions and the control of the business. Operational Planning, relying on input from the Strategic Plan, is involved with the detailed development of selected strategies and relies extensively on cost benefit analysis to aid in the alternative selection process. Much of our modelling efforts have been in this area.

The long range plan is a 10-year forward look of the business and focuses on time-phasing our KRA strategic variables at a summarized level by functional area. Simulation models are utilized to identify alternative approaches to achieve the targeted levels. The two-year Operational Plan, on the other hand, is a highly detailed document which provides the first line manager with a set of specified objectives and a financial budget. Financial budget models are used to quickly and economically calculate detailed "chart of accounts" budgets by directly interfacing the output from corporate operational models and other input assumptions (salary levels, travel rates) and special algorithms (depreciation). In addition to the "line item" budgets a set of pro-forma financial operating plan statements are generated.

Short Term Forecasts

Forecasting is the process of saying "Here I am today and this is where I will be tomorrow if I maintain substantially my present course and speed." Although related to planning, it is a different process. At XCL the computer has made a significant impact when applied to forecasting. We have implemented statistical models to analyze and project our key operational and financial variables. These "analysis-control-forecasting" models were designed to be used primarily for estimating the input variables necessary for the planning and forecasting (12-month rolling outlook) simulation models.

The forecasting system, including three exponential smoothing models and a regression model, analyzes current actual data into demand levels, trends and seasonals, and uses these estimates together with past information to project the most likely future level. All products are forecasted by each of the statistical techniques. In addition, the "best" forecasting method (defined as the one that has the lowest mean-absolute-deviation based on historical forecasting) is determined. A forecastability index, serving as a warning signal, indicates which product lines and/or variables are being poorly forecasted.

The statistical forecasts of all critical variables are available within a few seconds. Management has the option of overriding any forecast. This flexibility is critical as frequently the manager has insight into changing events that invalidate statistical approaches and, also, he can often influence and control a variable to achieve particular objectives. The bases for overrides have been (1) a poor forecastability index, (2) a manager in possession of special knowledge not controlled for by the model, and (3) a "what if" position.

The Overall System

It is important to realize that we do not have a planning model as such, rather, we have a series of models (control, forecasting and simulation) which assist in improving our planning and decision-making capability and which are changing over time as we learn more about our business. The entire forecasting and planning system is referred to as the Computer Assisted Outlook and Planning System (CAO/CAP). The classification scheme developed by Little (1970) will aid in understanding the component parts of this decision system which is illustrated below.

The following points clarify events depicted in Figure 2.

1. The data base is updated from two sources.

    (a) Actual operating and financial performance is collected by in-house batch systems.

    Salesman order related activity—MAPS

    Current and historical financial data—General Ledger

    Customer information—MIS

    This information is transferred tape-to-disc from the batch systems to the timeshared system where it is highly summarized and stored "on-line."

    (b) Data, primarily plans and forecasts, is created as output from the various models and is stored on the on-line data base.

2. Management information is made accessible to the models in the following ways:

    (a) Projections of management decision variables are obtained from the statistical/econometric forecasting models and are made available directly to decision tables embedded within the simulation models. The decision maker has the option of overriding any parameter.

    (b) Management assumptions and objectives can be set up in decision tables prior to execution of a model or can be entered "conversationally" during execution.

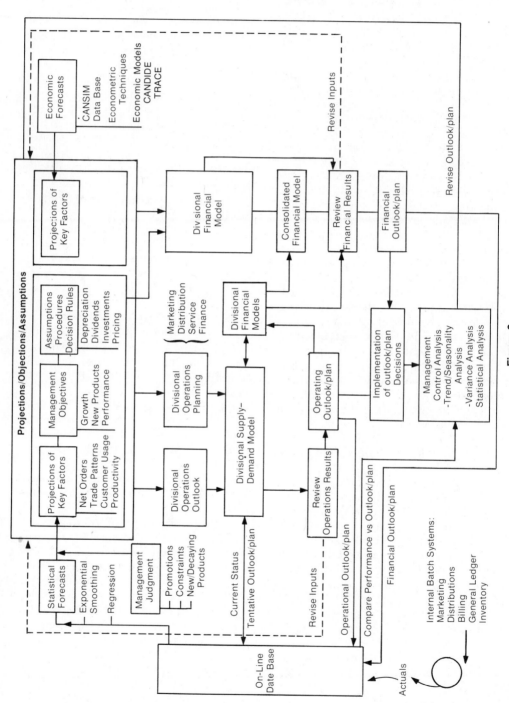

Figure 2.

3. Man-machine interaction occurs at multiple points throughout the system.

    (a) Each activity (module) shown is a computerized process except those denoted as judgment or review.

    (b) Each module contains an interactive model which, in many instances, is comprised of several micro-models. These micro-models, generally possessing a greater amount of detail and complexity, allow the decision maker to examine a problem area independently and in greater depth.

    (c) A module may describe the activities of several divisions such as ISG, CMD, XRC, XRO, Cheshire and Toner Plant. Each of these divisional models may incorporate the activities of several functional areas such as marketing or finance.

    (d) Each manager retains control (execution and updating) of models directly related to his functional area. Information generated by one model automatically becomes available to all other models requiring that information.

    (e) A decision maker is required to execute a series of models sequentially to derive a financial outlook or operating plan. Intermediary information can be retrieved via standard reports or direct data base inquiry with each model.

Information System

The heart of the overall system is the timeshared, on-line data bank. This is a repository of XCL operational and financial data, comprised of actuals, plans and forecasts. The mechanical links (tapes) between XCL operations which reside on in-house batch computers and the information system maintains the timeliness and integrity of the actual/performance data.

The information system can be assessed in two ways. Raw data can be retrieved and manipulated by the analyst, or report generators can be used to output information in a variety of standard formats. The keynote is flexibility in accessing and manipulating the data via the terminal. The functional departments control levels of data access for other functional users and, thereby, maintain data integrity and security.

Simulation System

The simulation models developed to date have been primarily the man-machine type although later models were designed to operate with a minimum of human intervention. The initial simulation model has been expanded and refined to describe in additional detail the operations of the functional areas and the financial procedures of XCL. More complex, integrated models have evolved from this effort for use in forecasting, planning, and simulating procedural changes (operations or financial) and for special one-time or infrequent studies such as pricing reviews, promotional campaigns, and facility locations analysis.

The modelling effort, subsequent to the initial simulation model, has been, for the most part, heavily reliant upon the particular functional area for initiation and support. While this approach resulted in uneven development of models (sophistication and depth) it did assure that each manager had models that were responsive to his needs.

Modelling at XCL has been and is a continuous process. We found that solutions to one problem generally resulted in additional questions or demonstrated a lack of understanding of other processes. Model updates and revisions are processed on an on-going basis by changing, discarding and re-creating, or at the same time both enlarging some models (to account for added complexities) and adding simplifying models for summary level analysis.

Management Control and Analysis

The planning process should provide a timely feedback mechanism to measure how well objectives are being attained, a methodology to investigate deviations to determine their causes and a means for management to correct unsatisfactory performance that is within control or to adjust plans in light of altered external conditions outside control.

As performance data becomes available to the information system, differences between actual results and plan or previous forecast are monitored for varying historical time periods. Specialized techniques are utilized to perform comparative analysis, determine if the differences are statistically significant and interpret the results in a way that is meaningful to management. Trend analysis and variance analysis are two well-used techniques. Trend analysis assists in identifying changing trend levels and seasonality patterns in critical factors. Variance analysis is used to split revenue and expense deviations into rate and volume components.

These "actual-forecast-plan" relationships are made available through routine or exception reporting or by data base inquiry from a terminal. While these "control" models are passive in the sense that they do not trigger action by themselves to correct perceived deviations, they do convey exception information which, when coupled with the simulation models in an on-line environment, provides the manager with an adaptive mechanism for positive action.

Decision System

The decision system is the most important part of the total system. At the core is the decision maker. Since the other systems have been designed to support the decision maker, it is essential that the right individual be in this position otherwise the most elaborate models will be rendered useless. On the other hand, ineffective computer models, regardless of how sophisticated they are, will impede the decision-making process.

The information and simulation systems are under complete control of the functional areas from the initial design stage through routine execution of the system. In no case has decision making been turned over to the computer. With the introduction of the mechanized planning and control systems we have experienced substantially more functional participation in the planning and control activities.

5. CONCLUDING REMARKS

In conclusion, timeshared models have proved to be imminently successful in assisting in the planning process at XCL. They have extended the capabilities of the decision maker by providing him with an instantaneous data retriever, analyzer and projector. The simulation models have been adopted in the U.S. company as well as being adapted to our smallest divisions; a fact which demonstrates that computer-based models are economically viable in small as well as large businesses.

This experience has proved to our satisfaction that (1) the basic philosophy is sound, (2) the key element of the process was the application of the scientific method to the business environment, and (3) the decision maker can be intimately involved in the initiation, implementation and execution of on-line models.

REFERENCES

1. Ackoff, K. L., *A Concept of Corporate Planning*, Wiley-Interscience, 1970.
2. Boulden, J. B., and Buffa, E. S., "Corporate

Models: On-line, Real Time Systems," *Harvard Business Review,* July—August 1970.

3. Gershefski, George, "Corporate Models— The State of the Art," *Management Science,* Vol. 16, No. 6, February 1970.

4. Little, John D., "Models and Managers: The Concept of a Decision Calculus," *Management Science,* Vol. 16, No. 8, April 1970.

5. Seaberg, Charlotte, "Business Applications in APL," Presentation to APL Conference at York University (Toronto) January 1972.

SECTION B

Technology and Modern Organization Structures

Modern technology is having a profound impact on mankind. One effect occurring in our organizations is a trend away from the traditional bureaucratic structure and toward modern flexible designs. This is especially noticeable in organizations operating in high-technology industries. The impact of continuous change is leading these firms to adopt flexible structures that can adapt to this dynamic environment. However, technology is not the only reason for these new structures. Organizations are also finding that many of their people operate more effectively in a nonbureaucratic environment. The goal of the articles in this section is to examine the areas of technology and modern organization structures as they relate to the practicing manager.

In the first selection, Daniel Roman discusses how improvements in forecasting can affect overall strategy. In his article, Professor Roman distinguishes between exploratory and normative technological forecasting. Exploratory forecasting is a logical extension of current scientific development, whereas normative forecasting works backwards, moving from the desired state of technology to the present time, determining the technical gaps that currently exist. In his discussion of technological forecasting, the author cites both advantages and limitations of the process. He also explores the organizational areas affected by this type of forecasting. The purpose of this article is to provide the reader with a heuristic approach to forecasting in a dynamic society.

In the second selection, Professors Shetty and Carlisle point out the need for a flexible attitude in designing organization structures. There is no reason one form of organization is going to be optimally effective in today's society. As a result, the authors advocate a scaling of designs based on a number of variables. In essence, they believe that the major factors to be considered in designing an effective organization structure are: (a) forces in the manager, (b) forces in the task, (c) forces in the environment, and (d) forces in the subordinates. Based on these factors, they feel that the organization design will be more effective than one which simply evolves over time.

150

The last article in this section, "Emerging Perspectives About Organization Planning and Development," briefly traces the history of organization structures from the traditional designs to those currently employed by many modern organizations. In this article, Mr. Partin notes the need for organizations to function as open systems and to design structures capable of existing within this environment. In explaining this area, he identifies a number of important subsystems, including goals, values, technology, structure, psycho-social and managerial, all of which play a major role in fashioning the "right" type of structure. In essence, the author not only identifies current organization designs but offers direction for the future as well.

16 Technological Forecasting in the Decision Process

Daniel D. Roman

INTRODUCTION

The New Technology

Companies in the United States are spending billions of dollars each year to research and develop new products. Technological expansion has vital economic, sociological and political implications.

The economic impact of technology is so great that some industries derive most of their current business from products which did not exist 20 years ago.[1] A study of 11 industries indicated that somewhere from 46 to 100 percent of anticipated short-term corporate growth could be attributed to new pro-

ducts.[2] It is now commonplace for major companies to derive 50 percent or more of current sales from products developed and introduced in the past 10 years.[3]

In a dynamic technology there must be recognition of potential human and capital obsolescence. Productive utilization of new knowledge will affect the demand and supply of present skills and new occupations not yet identifiable will emerge. Additionally, it is reasonably safe to assume that technological pressures will encourage increased interdisciplinary communication.

It is difficult to isolate the economic,

[1] *Investing in Scientific Progress, 1961–1970,* Report NSF 61-27 (Washington, D.C.: National Science Foundation, 1961), p. 7.

[2] *Management of New Products,* 4th ed., (New York: Booz, Allen and Hamilton, Inc., 1964), p. 6.

[3] *Ibid.,* p. 2, and *Report of the Joint Economic Committee,* U.S. Congress, 88th Congress, 2nd session, (1964), p. 56.

This article originally appeared in *Academy of Management Journal* (June 1970), pp. 127–138, and is reprinted with permission.

sociological and political consequences of technology. It is obvious that economic and sociological factors could not be disassociated from political factors. It is also difficult to do justice to the full range of economic, sociological and political possibilities in a paper of this nature. However, recognition of the extent and direction of technological expansion can help provide the means to minimize disruption, lead to an orderly transition and assist in maximizing the positive aspects of technology.

The impact of technical developments such as lasers, jet aircraft, atomic energy and communication devices, to name a few, has been significant. On the horizon are such developments as new rapid transit systems, mechanical devices to replace human organs, [4] undersea farming and mining, economically useful desalinization of sea water, new synthetic materials for ultra-light construction, automatic language translators, and reliable weather forecasts. Other major technological breakthroughs are not so remote as to preclude planning for integration of these developments.[5]

As we move into a "post industrial society" phase, science and technology will be a compelling force for change.[6] In some environments managers must be alert and plan to compensate for change; in other situations a prime managerial function is to instigate technological change.[7]

In either case the manager must be aware of technological impact and be sensitive to the need for more precise planning for the future. Technological forecasting has been a response to this need.

TECHNOLOGICAL FORECASTING

Technological Forecasting— A Distinction

Technological forecasting, as distinct from general forecasting activity, has been described as "the probabilistic assessment, on a relatively high confidence level, of future technology transfer."[8] According to Jantsch, technology transfer is usually a complex process taking place at different technology transfer levels. These levels can be segregated into development and impact levels and are composed of vertical and horizontal technology transfer components. Vertical transfer of technology progresses through a discovery phase, a creative phase, a substantiate phase, a development phase and an engineering phase. The engineering phase leads to a functional, technological system that could involve a hardware product, a process, or an intellectual concept. Jantsch feels that the extension of the vertical transfer by substantial subsequent horizontal technology transfer represents technological innovation.[9]

---

[4] In the November 1969 issue of *Industrial Research* there is an interesting discussion of the potential use of glassy materials in product design, specifically glass that won't clot blood which could be used for producing artificial organs.

[5] Olaf Helmer, *Social Technology* (New York-London: Basic Books, Incorporated, 1966), pp. 56–57, and "New Products—Setting a Time Table," *Business Week* (May 27, 1967), pp. 52–61. Bright identifies seven technological trends: (1) increasing capability in transportation, (2) increased mastery of energy, (3) increased ability to control the life of animate and inanimate things, (4) increased ability to alter the characteristics of materials, (5) extension of man's sensory capabilities, (6) growing mechanization of physical activities, and (7) increasing mechanization of intellectual processes. James R. Bright, "Directions of Technological Change and Some Business Consequences," appearing in *Automation and Technological Change*, Report of the Assembly Jointly Sponsored by Battelle Memorial Institute and the American Assembly (May 9–11, 1963), pp. 9–22. Also, P. Michael Sinclair, "10 Years Ahead," *Industrial Research* (January 1969), pp. 68–72. Also, William O. Craig, "The Technology of Space—Earth," *Transportation & Distribution Management* (October 1969), pp. 22–26.

[6] Editorial, "Managing Technology," *Science and Technology* (January 1969), pp. 72–73.

[7] Marvin J. Cetron and Alan L. Weiser, "Technological Change, Technological Forecasting and Planning R&D—A View from the R&D Manager's Desk," *The George Washington Law Review*, Vol. 36, No. 5, (July 1968), p. 1079.

[8] E. Jantsch, *Technological Forecasting in Perspective* (Paris: Organization for Economic Cooperation and Development, 1967), p. 15.

[9] *Ibid.*

Cetron essentially supports Jantsch's definition. He cautions that a technological forecast is not a picture of what the future will bring; it is a prediction, based on confidence, that certain technical developments can occur within a specified time period with a given level of resource allocation. According to Cetron, "the foundation underlying technological forecasting is the level that individual R&D events are susceptible to influence." The periods where these events occur, if they are possible, can be significantly affected by the diversion of resources. Another fundamental of technological forecasting is that many futures can be achieved and the route to these occurrences can be determined.[10]

Exploratory and Normative Forecasting

It is important to recognize the two fundamental types of technological forecasts—exploratory and normative. The exploratory technological forecast starts from the existing base of knowledge and proceeds to the future on the assumption of logical technological progress. Exploratory technological forecasting is passive and primarily an analysis and reporting of anticipations. As a simple illustration, technological development in electronics can be cited. Starting with the post World War II period, transistors have evolved from an expensive and qualitatively unpredictable commodity to a modestly priced, reliable component. If exploratory forecasting were used in the 1940's to target in on this phase of technology, it would have been possible to predict increasing availability, lower price and more extensive use of transistors. The anticipations suggested would have been miniaturization of

electronic systems and the potential for a vast number of new products resulting from application, such as portable radios, home appliances, etc.

It would seem that most industrial firms could effectively use exploratory forecasting. Reasonable identification of emerging technology and analysis of technological implications could provide clues for the firm as to competition, possible expansion of existing product lines, related product lines —which the firm should ease into, and new product areas where a foothold could provide a competitive edge. In short, a look into the future would enable better planning, more effective use of resources and considerable avoidance of human and capital obsolescence.

Normative forecasting represents a different approach; it is mission- or goal-oriented. As distinct from exploratory forecasting, normative forecasting is an active or action-directed process.

In the normative method, future objectives are identified exclusive of the fact that technological gaps may currently exist that might act as constraints to attainment of these technological objectives. Normative technological forecasting can provide incentive to technological progress by focusing on the problems to be surmounted and solved. Perhaps the supersonic transport (SST) can be used to demonstrate normative forecasting. At a given time the state of the art for aircraft technology can be determined. It is decided that a need will exist five years from the base period for an aircraft incorporating the SST specifications. On a logical technological progression using exploratory forecasting some technical advancements can be predicted. However, technical gaps appear which indicate that the SST will not be an evolutionary development by the time the need or market will require the product. There are many problems beyond the technical expertise of this author which must be surmounted but

[10] M. Cetron, "Prescription for the Military R&D Manager: Learn the Three Rx's," unpublished paper presented to The NATO Defense Research Group Seminar on Technological Forecasting and its Application to Defense Research (Teddington, Middlesex, England: November 12, 1968), p. 2.

some examples could be the development of materials necessary to make flying at supersonic speeds economical, safe and technically feasible.[11] Also, ways must be found to cope with sonic booms so the SST can be used over land routes.

In normative forecasting situations, the analyst works backward from the planned mission operational date and determines the technical obstacles. Normative forecasting could act as a directional force to channel effort and resources. In the example used, these resources would be diverted to solving such problems as the sonic boom or developing new materials. Since resources are limited, normative forecasting could be used in deciding priorities and decisions could be made in conjunction with cost effectiveness studies to determine whether the mission requirements are as critical as presented, are possible within the stipulated time and if the ultimate accomplishment of the mission is worth the resource expenditure.

Normative forecasting has been used primarily by the military, but industrial organizations could possibly use it. With the normative approach, the firm could examine the market potential, explore the technical feasibility, look at its expertise in the area, estimate the cost to accomplish product development and then decide whether the project should be undertaken.

Jantsch contends that presently the most difficult technological forecasting problem is establishing the correct time-frame in normative forecasting. In exploratory forecasting difficulty exists in conceiving an end-effect in the future due to the time covered, but it is relatively simple to prognosticate compared to the normative forecast difficulties. In the normative method the forecast is predicated on objectives,

requirements, and sociological factors; the problem is the assumption that present requirements or anticipations are representative of the future.[12]

Methodologies of Technological Forecasting

Technological forecasting methods range from naive intuitive approaches to ultra sophisticated procedures.[13] Most of the methods are academic with limited practical adoption. Essentially, the methods can be refined to intuitive, extrapolative and correlative, and logical sequence or network type techniques.

Intuitive forecasting, the most common method employed, can be done individually by genius forecasting or by consensus. Generally this method represents an "educated guess" approach. It can vary from a very naive approach in a localized situation to a broad sampling and consensus of authoritative opinion. Delphi, the best known method under this classification, was developed by Olaf Helmer of the Rand Corporation.

A plethora of methods exist which are essentially variations of PERT. Relevance trees, graphic models, Planning-Programming-Budgeting Systems (PPBS), Mission networks, Decision Trees and Systems Analysis all use network construction to derive technological forecasts.

If numbers are any criteria it would seem that after some variation of Delphi, the network technique is the most popular avenue to technological forecasting. Networks help in identifying and establishing a logical pattern from an existing point to an anticipated goal. An intuitive method, regardless of in-

---

[11] One such material emerging as a possibility is boron filament which has remarkable strength for its weight. See "Tough Featherweight Plays Hard to Get," *Business Week* (November 15, 1969), p. 38.

[12] Jantsch, *op. cit.* pp. 29–32.
[13] Extensive treatment of technological forecasting methodologies can be found in: M. J. Cetron, *Technological Forecasting* (New York: Gordon and Breach, 1969), Jantsch, *op. cit.,* and J. R. Bright (Ed.), *Technological Forecasting For Industry and Government* (Englewood Cliffs, N.J.: Prentice-Hall, Inc., 1968).

dividual technological perception, might ignore or minimize a significant obstacle to technological attainment. On the other hand, the network system is vulnerable in that all critical events might not be recognized, parallel technology might be ignored or unknown, information may be inaccurate, fragmentary, or misinterpreted (leading to wrong conclusions) and, finally, optimism or pessimism might permeate the forecast.

After examining the multitude of techniques available for technological forecasting, the author is of the opinion that while some methods appear quite scientific on the surface, minute examination almost invariably shows reliance on non-quantifiable and subjective factors before reaching conclusions. Additionally, the rationale of seemingly more sophisticated methods is often difficult to follow and the cost compared to ultimate value of the forecast could also be questioned, all of which might explain the popularity of the Delphi method or its derivatives.

TECHNOLOGICAL FORECASTING AS A MANAGEMENT TOOL

Some General Observations

Technological forecasting as an organized management concept is relatively new. The model depicted in Figure 1 shows how technological forecasting might be integrated into the management process. Objectives which represent the initial *raison d'etre* generally become fluid as the organization moves through its operational life cycle. The degree of modification of objectives and the extent of operational flexibility can be dictated by external and internal factors.

In the model, technological forecasting is shown as a prelude to operational activity. Technological forecasting, depending on the nature of the operation, can encompass the universe or it can be used to focus on a relatively small segment of the universe. It can be used by management in probing the general environment and then be refined to help in determining the im-

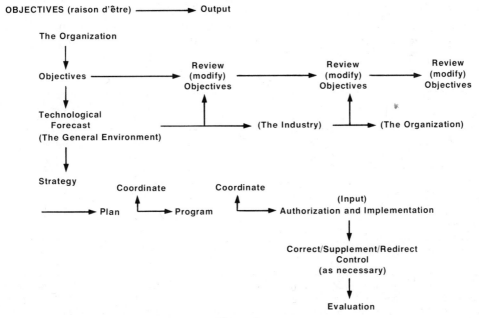

Figure 1.

plications for the industry and the specific organization. As each technological phase is explored, objectives should be reviewed and modified for compatibility with potential accomplishment. From this, procedure strategy can be derived to guide planning, programming, authorization, implementation, control and evaluation.

Advantages and Application

The incorporation of technological forecasting into the process of management is an extension of existing methodology. In the past it would appear that management has often intuitively drifted in this direction. Evidence can be advanced to support this contention from the information in Table 1 which shows a condensation of the time gap from innovation to application.

To be useful, technological forecasting does not have to be precise. If an innovation can be identified, and if the innovation can be translated into constructive action within a reasonable and discernible time frame, it can substantially contribute to the decision-making process.

Often, long-term commitments are undertaken on the basis of short-term technology. In many cases inability to anticipate technology leads to built-in obsolescence. Attendant to obsolescence are high modification costs to update facilities and operations, difficulty in selling change to entrenched interests and failure to exploit market potential.

An illustration of potential benefit from technological forecasting would be in product development. The technological forecasters have not yet developed the precise refinement of being able to localize specific innovations within a technological continuum. However, most technologies follow an "S" shaped curve and evaluation of existing and anticipated status of the technology can be meaningful in the decision to undergo or forego investment in product development. The technical scope, cost and time to develop a new product may be attractive or unattractive after technological forecasting information is assembled.

Generally, technological forecasting can assist management in several ways. It can represent an organized approach to a selective search for information. It can provoke thought by expanding horizons. It can help provide perspective and facilitate interdisciplinary communication. It can encourage operational sensitivity. It can assist management in determining the magnitude of anticipated change and provide a

TABLE 1 *

INNOVATION	YEAR OF DISCOVERY	YEAR OF APPLICATION
Electric motor	1821	1886
Vacuum tube	1882	1915
Radio broadcasting	1887	1922
X-ray tubes	1895	1913
Nuclear reactor	1932	1942
Radar	1935	1940
Atomic bomb	1938	1945
Transistor	1948	1951
Solar battery	1953	1955
Stereospecific rubbers & plastics	1955	1958

*Seymour L. Wolfbein, "The Pace of Technological Change and the Factors Affecting It," *Manpower Implications of Automation,* Papers presented by U.S. Department of Labor at the O.E.C.D. North American Regional Conference on Manpower Implications of Automation (Washington, D.C.: December 8–10, 1964), p. 19.

basis for estimating costs and requirements for people, facilities, equipment, etc. It can aid in giving direction to product development and market penetration. It can assist in recognizing competition and other possible restraints such as natural resources or technological limitations. It can be used to help determine sociological and economic trends.

Limitations

Several limitations to technological forecasting should be apparent to the discerning reader. The fact that limitations exist in technological forecasting just as there are limitations in other techniques should not discourage management; awareness should lead to more critical and productive application.

Information may be the greatest limitation to contributive technological forecasting. The information problem is extensive. For instance: What information is needed? How much information is required? Is the information accurate? Have related and unrelated disciplines been explored for possible information transfer or possible technological fallout?

Information interpretation is a vital ingredient in technological forecasting. No mechanical process presently exists which will evaluate the information in terms of available technical solutions, cost and value, product applicability and market potential. Human judgment is a factor in interpreting information and interpretation can be colored by optimism or pessimism and courage or conservatism. Information analysis can also differ due to the competence of the analyst and his functional orientation. Augmenting the difficulties cited is the fact that often pertinent information may not be available due to security restrictions and trade secrets. The unavailability of essential information may negate the entire process by establishing the technological forecast on incomplete or erroneous premises.

Forecasting is far from an exact science, so much so that standard methods and procedures have not been generally established. Although the literature abounds with methodology, in practice, it appears that variations of the Delphi technique and network construction are most commonly used. More exact and understandable techniques must be developed which are practical and provide management with reasonable confidence in their accuracy. However, a standard method may not be feasible since each organization based on its size and mission must develop forecasting techniques to suit its own operational environment.

Another limitation is that unanticipated discovery can lead to demand for a family of products which were previously inconceivable. Good examples are the transistor and the laser. A major discovery can instigate derived demand for related and supporting products and technology and give rise to satellite industries.[14]

Quinn points out that the interaction of many technological breakthroughs could lead to unforeseen prospects which would have a negating effect on all forecasts. He says,

Similarly, one cannot at present anticipate specifically how biological studies of cellular and molecular coding will interact with extremely high-polymer investigations which are beginning to produce synthetic molecules with many of the characteristics of living organisms. In such advanced areas one can only recognize that there is a strong probability of potential interactions which will increase the importance of both fields, and therefore do more extensive research or monitor such activities more closely.[15]

ORGANIZING FOR TECHNOLOGICAL FORECASTING

Many functions survive in organizations because of defensive manage-

---

[14] J. B. Quinn, "Technological Forecasting," *Harvard Business Review* (March-April 1967), pp. 101–103.
[15] *Ibid.*, p. 102.

ment attitudes. Most managements desire a progressive image and as a consequence may install publicized new techniques without really embracing the concept. Utilization failures can often be attributed to management's unwillingness to get involved with things about which they are not familiar, and subsequently have misgivings about. Contributing to this attitude are the practitioners who lose themselves in technique and take little or no pains to translate their work into understandable terms and useful concepts which management would be willing to implement. This represents a very real threat to expanded management acceptance of technological forecasting.

A review of the literature leaves the impression of enamorment with technique. This can be disastrous if substance is sacrificed for method.

Some Organizational Considerations

There are several factors management must consider before commiting itself to technological forecasting. It must look at the type of operation in which it is involved. Is the organization in a technologically sensitive environment? Is the organization a leader or follower in its operational environment? Are operations large and diverse enough to justify commitment to a technological forecasting activity? How extensive a commitment should be made in terms of people, facilities and budget? Would management want sporadic technological forecasts on an informal basis or would there be formal reviews at set intervals? The answer to the last question could dictate the extent of commitment management is willing to make and the type of people it will have to train or recruit. In line with the aforementioned, management will have to select people with compatible skills to achieve technological forecasting objectives. Does management want a group of specialists in a range of technical areas? Does management want a group composed of multi-viewed individuals with broad perspective and minimal functional allegiance? Or is a combination of generalists and specialists more desirable? The range of possibilities is not exhausted because management can use in-house functional specialists in concert with management types to act as a technological forecasting advisory board. Finally, management may not want any internal commitment and may prefer to use outside specialists or consulting organizations to bring in fresh views to reconcile against internal prognostications.

Organizational Location

Technological forecasting can be a function or an activity within a function. Several organizational affiliations appear logical such as placement in long-range planning, marketing, materials management or in the research and development group. Technological forecasting can also be elevated to functional status with independent identity.

There are no clear cut answers or universal solutions to organizational location of technological forecasting. Strong arguments can be advanced for affiliation with each of the functions indicated or for independent status. The ultimate answer of placement might be dictated by factors such as functional utilization of the technological forecast or management's orientation. Functional affiliation may lead to high utilization but it can also mean that the technological forecasting activity is functionally captive and narrow in its perspective. A danger in this situation is that technological forecasting may be slanted to support the functional parent rather than provide general direction more compatible with the objectives of the total organization.

There are some compelling advantages to having technological forecasting as an independent operation and functional entity if the size and scope of the organization warrants technological forecasting. As a noncaptive operation it can be used by management for organizational checks and balances and as a directional force in assessing the validity of long-range planning and objectives. It can help in determining what emphasis to place in research and development and to give management insight into the reality of marketing goals. What must be guarded against if technological forecasting has functional independence is excessive cost generated by operational practice inconsistent with the organization's need and capacity.

CONCLUSIONS

Several significant theories and techniques have been incorporated into management practice in the past quarter of a century. Often these ideas have been accepted without critical examination. Adoption without adequate evaluation has, in many instances, initially led to disillusionment and obscured the true value. Uncritical acceptance and overcommitment frequently can be attributed to the disciples of innovations who oversell a concept. The fact that all tools are not applicable in all situations, or, where applicable, have differing degrees of utility should not minimize the potential contribution. Management must recognize that no single panacea exists and must judiciously exploit ideas with

consideration of the operational environment.

Technological forecasting as a formal concept can be traced back to the mid-1940's. Its present structure and direction took shape around 1960.[16] To date the greatest application and methodology development has been military-oriented. The military services have had encouraging success and indications are for intensification of effort in this area.

The idea of technological forecasting is relatively unknown in business circles. Professor Bright has probably been the most active disciple in promoting technological forecasting to industry. Indications are that inroads are being made. There has generally been enthusiastic reception from those industrial executives exposed to technological forecasting.

Technological forecasting in proper context should seriously be considered as an addition to the management process. As Jantsch so aptly stated,

Technological forecasting is not yet a science but an art, and is characterized today by attitudes, not tools; human judgment is enhanced, not substituted by it. The development of auxiliary techniques, gradually attaining higher degrees of sophistication (and complexity) since 1960, is oriented towards ultimate integration with evolving information technology.[17]

---

[16] Jantsch, p. 17.
[17] Jantsch, p. 17.

17   A Contingency Model of Organization Design

Y. K. Shetty and Howard M. Carlisle

Organizations have played an important role in the history of mankind, but attempts to analyze and understand them have progressed very slowly and perceptions about them are often elusive. However, the last decade witnessed a new direction in the study of organizations. Evidence from recent research indicates that there is no one best way to organize an enterprise as was once thought. An organization is not an independent entity, but rather an interdependent system—a result of complex interaction between itself and the environment. A consistent organization style is no virtue if it prevents an organization from coping effectively with its problems and opportunities. The type of organization most suitable in a particular setting depends on its internal and external environment. Basically, this approach is leading to the development of the "contingency model" of organization design. The optimal organization pattern is contingent on the managerial situation. To put it differently, organizational designs appropriate to one technological and market environment may not be appropriate for another. It must be tailor-made for the firm.

This article will examine some of the recent research findings on organizations and suggest a scheme for understanding how different organizational patterns may develop in response to specific combinations of elements in the internal and external environment. Before pursuing this, a brief review of the theories of organization will help provide a suitable background.

Classical Model.   Early in the twentieth century the great German sociologist Max Weber, noting common elements in different types of organizations (business, government, and military), called this form of organization bureaucracy. In his bureaucratic system, Weber placed very heavy emphasis on a hierarchical structure, position, authority, and rules for solving repetitive problems. Functionaries with specialized training learn their tasks better by practice. "Precision, speed, unambiguity, knowledge of the files, continuity, discretion, unity, strict subordination, reduction of friction and of material and personal costs—these are raised to the optimum point in the strictly bureaucratic administration, and in its monocratic form."[1] It could be said that Weber tried to promote efficiency through technical proficiency, a disregard for personal feelings, and governance by rules and regulations. As bureaucracy develops towards perfection, the more it is dehumanized and the more completely it succeeds in eliminating from official business all purely personal, irrational and emotional elements. Weber said that bureaucracy was succeeding because of its machine-like qualities.

---

[1] H. H. Gerth and C. Wright Mills, (eds.), *From Max Weber: Essays in Sociology* (Fair Lawn, N.J.: Oxford University Press, 1958), p. 214.

Around the same time, Frederick W. Taylor popularized "scientific management" in which man is thought of as mechanical and motivated by economic considerations. Though Taylor was primarily concerned with the production aspects of an organization, some of his proposals, such as functional foremanship and separation of planning and doing, had indirect implications to organization structure. The classical organization theory was further developed and refined by Mooney and Reiley, Fayol, Gulick, Urwick and others. They based their theory of departmentalization on the assumption that an organization, given an overall mission, will be able to identify the required tasks, allocate and coordinate these tasks by giving jobs to sections, place the section within units, unite the units within departments and coordinate departments under a board, all in the most economic manner. They thought of an organization as a rational instrument for implementing objectives and policies.

The classical organization theory met with widespread acceptance among many managers and some writers in management. But in recent years the theory has encountered growing criticism. A major criticism is that the classical organization principles are too broad to provide much help in the actual work of designing organizations. The principle of specialization, for example, does not tell the organizer how the tasks should be divided, and to say that an organization needs coordination is merely to state the obvious. It is also claimed that some of the principles contradict others and that, therefore, it is impossible to observe them all. Herbert A. Simon agrees that unity of command is incompatible with the principle of specialization. He concludes that some of the other classical principles are "no more than proverbs," and that administrative theory must be concerned with the weights that should be given to each of the various principles in any concrete situa-

tion.[2] Simply stated, this criticism implies that the classical theory is simplistic, contains contradictory principles, and is "normative" rather than "empirical," (it says what ought to be rather than what is).

The most insistent criticism leveled against the classical organization theory comes from behavioral scientists. They claim the classical theory is too mechanistic and thus ignores major facets of human nature. The rational model has been attacked as an abstraction that overlooks human behavior, the non-rational elements in human conduct and their implications for operators. Some even claim that the theory is incompatible with human nature. This is a serious omission for formal structures are designed solely for the purpose of enabling people to work effectively together for a common goal.

Of late, bureaucracy has been attacked on another count. It is argued that "bureaucracy thrives in a highly competitive, undifferentiated and stable environment . . . A pyramidal structure and authority, with power concentrated in the hands of few with the knowledge and resources to control an entire enterprise was, and is, an eminently suitable social arrangement for routinized tasks. However, the environment has changed . . . which makes the mechanism most problematic." [3]

Behavioral Model. The behavioral theory reacts to the excessive mechanistic structure and argues that an industrial organization should be viewed as a social system with at least two objectives: producing the product and generating and distributing satisfaction among employees (achieving both economic effectiveness and job satisfaction). Hence, an organization should be considered a social system

---

[2] Herbert Simon, *Administrative Behavior* (New York: Macmillan Company, 1957), p. 44.

[3] Warren Bennis, "Beyond Bureaucracy," *Trans-Actions* (July–Aug., 1965), pp. 31–35.

which has both economic and social dimensions.

Behavioralists argue that effectiveness is achieved by arranging matters so that people feel that they count, that they belong, and that work can be made meaningful. The behavioralists do not necessarily reject the classical doctrine, but they feel that more goes into an organization design than rules, regulations and strict rationality. For instance, every member of any organization is unique to some degree, and all actions are not necessarily explained rationally. There is the element of subjectivity to an individual's actions: they are based on his perception and personal value system.

Behavioralists, at least the earlier ones, do not necessarily prescribe any one form of organization structure but believe it can be improved by modifying it in accordance with informal structure—through less narrow specialization and less emphasis on hierarchy, by permitting more participation in decision-making on the part of the lower ranks, and by a more democratic attitude on the part of the managers at all levels.

Organic Model. Recent years have seen the development of a form of organization structure based on behavioral theories called the organic organization—a structure in which there is a minimum of formal divison of duties. According to this view, organizations should be composed of temporary task forces in which membership will shift as needs and problems change. Warren Bennis argues that bureaucracy (the classical structure) is too rigid to be serviceable in the time of rapid technological change and that it will therefore be replaced by the task-force type of organization. He says:

First of all, the key word will be temporary. Organizations will become adaptive, rapidly changing temporary systems. Second, they will be organized around problems-to-be-solved. Third, these problems will be solved by relative groups of strangers who represent a diverse set of professional skills.

Fourth, given the requirements of coordinating the various projects, articulating points or "linking pin" personnel will be necessary who can speak the diverse language of research and who can relay and mediate between the various project groups. Fifth, the groups will be conducted on organic rather than on mechanical lines; they will emerge and adapt to the problems, and leadership and influence will fall to those who seem most able to solve the problems rather than the programmed role expectations. People will be differentiated, not according to rank or roles, but according to skills and training. . . . Though no catchy phrase comes to mind, it might be called an organic-adaptive structure.[4]

ORGANIZATION PATTERNS

The literature on organization shows that organizations can be characterized in various ways, but the degree of specificity of role prescription and its obverse, the range of discretion, seem most appropriate. The resulting dichotomy can be represented by these distinctions: closed system v. open system, formal v. flexible, programmed v. non-programmed, mechanistic v. organic (or organismic), habit v. problem solving, and structured v. unstructured.[5] The mechanistic structure is likely to be less open, more formalized, and so on, while the organic structure is likely to be open and less formalized.

Thus organization patterns can be portrayed on a scale with mechanistic at one end and organic-adaptive at the other. Organic organizations are characterized by less formalized definitions of jobs, by more stress on flexibility and adaptability and by communication networks involving more consultation than command. Mechanistic organizations are characterized by rigid specialized functionalization, and in general define the opposite pole from

[4] Warren Bennis, "Organizational Developments and the Fate of Bureaucracy," *Industrial Management Review* (Spring 1966), p. 52.

[5] D. J. Hickson, "A Convergence in Organization Theory," *Administrative Science Quarterly* (September 1966), pp. 224–237.

an organic-adaptive continuum. In between the poles are various patterns which an organization can display. In general terms, functional organization falls closer to mechanical structure and project organization comes closer to organic structure.

Most organizations are formed through evolutionary processes rather than by design. At certain stages, design or redesign takes place, by codification or modification of the results of the evolution or by reaction to environmental forces. An adequate framework for developing organization theory should make it possible to increase the role of a conscious design process in the development of an organization. Hopefully, the suggested model would provide such a framework. The question of organization design can fruitfully be explored by identifying the diverse forces influencing the structure. Then the question is: What factors or forces should be considered in deciding how to design an organization structure? These are of particular importance:

forces in the manager,
forces in the task,
forces in the environment, and
forces in the subordinates.

The following is a brief analysis of these elements which would indicate how they might influence a company's actions in designing an organization. The strength of each will, of course, vary from instance to instance, but management which is sensitive to them can better assess the problems which face it and determine which mode of organizational pattern is most appropriate for it.

Forces in the Managers. The design of an organization in any instance will be influenced greatly by the many forces operating within managers' personalities. Managers, of course, perceive their organizational problems in a unique way based on their background, knowledge, experience and values.

Management, particularly top management, may be the most important influence in shaping organization structure. They decide initially what industry the organization will enter, how it will compete (for example, price, quality, diversity of product line, service, and so on), where it will be located, the kind of organization it will be, who will be the top managers, and who will directly influence the organization structure. All these decisions have to be made in the context of the relationship between the environment and the managerial philosophy of the entrepreneurs involved. As R. M. Cyert and J. G. March point out, "Organizations do not have objectives; only people do." [6]

Alfred Chandler has clearly shown the relationship between the strategy a business adopts, consciously or otherwise, and the structure of its organization.[7] According to him, different types of organizations will necessarily cope effectively with different managerial strategies. The choice of corporate purpose and the design and administration of organizational process for accomplishing purposes are by no means impersonal procedures, unaffected by the characteristics of the manager.

How strong the manager feels that individuals should have freedom and autonomy in their own sphere of work will have an important influence in organizational design. Douglas McGregor [8] identified the bedrock assumptions about human nature which support markedly different approaches to organization and management—the theories X and Y. The organization structure emerging from the managerial value system implied by the view that man is inherently

[6] R. M. Cyert and J. G. March, *A Behavioral Theory of the Firm* (Englewood Cliffs: Prentice-Hall, Inc., 1963).
[7] Alfred D. Chandler, *Strategy and Structure* (Mass.: MIT Press, 1962).
[8] Douglas McGregor, *The Human Side of Enterprise* (New York: McGraw-Hill, 1960).

lazy and pursues goals contrary to the interests of the company is not the same as that which emerges from the obverse image of human nature. The implicitly held management value system manifests itself in contrasting organizational designs. The manner in which work is organized and decision-making authority is distributed, the span of control, the shape of the organization, and so forth—all depend upon the underlying value system of managers. A theory X value system might lead to a more mechanistic organization, while a theory Y value system might lead to a more organic structure.

Managers' assumptions about the external environment and its relations with the organization will influence the organization structure. If the managers believe that organizations could function effectively by being able merely to adjust to external environmental conditions, then the structural model will be closer to bureaucracy. This is basically a process of equilibrium, rather than change. When managers believe that an organization could not only respond to change but could be an agent of change, then the structure will be closer to organic-adaptive.

Forces in the Task. The task element in an organization situation is the central point of concern in any type of organization design and analysis. The nature of the task will have important influence on how the organization is designed.

Significant empirical literature is emerging relating technology to various organization variables. Joan Woodward, Charles Perrow, James D. Thompson and several others consider technology to be a major determinant of organization structure.[9] In her

<hr>

[9] See Joan Woodward, *Industrial Organization: Theory and Practice* (Fair Lawn, N.J.: Oxford University Press, 1965); also Charles Perrow, "A Framework for the Comparative Analysis of Organization," *American Sociological Review* (April 1967), pp. 194–208; and James D. Thompson, *Organizations in Action* (New York: McGraw-Hill, 1967).

study, Joan Woodward reveals some interesting insights into the relationship between technology and organization structure. She found that organization structure varied according to the type of technology. Let us examine some of the technological variables influencing the structure.

The production technology limits the amount of discretion which subordinates can be given and, hence, influences organization structure. Woodward found that the organization structure varied depending upon the type of technology—different technologies seem to have varying degrees of "management content." Management content is substantially higher in continuous-process technology than in the unit-production technology. Fewer managers supervise more people in unit production than in mass-production or continuous-process technologies. Since unit production technologies have the fewest managers and supervisors in relation to subordinates, it would mean that these technologies also have the wider span of control or "flat" organization structure. If technology can dictate the ratio of managerial personnel it may, therefore, limit the amount of freedom which subordinates can be given.

Also, under unit-production technology, relatively higher levels of skills may be necessary at the worker level in terms of technical knowledge of the job, methods, tools, knowledge about operating errors, inspection skills and control. Under these conditions the employees are more likely to perform effectively when they are given more freedom on the job. Research suggests that skilled workers feel more involved in their jobs and are more anxious for an opportunity to participate in making decisions relating to it than are unskilled workers. This makes it possible to delegate more authority to lower levels in the organization.

Technology may determine the extent to which the job may be programmed, that is, employee behaviors may be precisely specified. The kind of organization required in a low task structure is not the same as that required in a high task structure. It is meaningless to talk of permitting exercise of discretion to assembly line workers; the very nature of technology tends to develop unique interests. While the organic type of work organization has a relatively autonomous task, each member of the group feels responsible for the entire organization. Under such circumstances competent internal coordination and group responsibility develop. In situations where cooperation arises spontaneously out of the structure of the work it is far easier to adopt more flexible structure compared to a highly structured arrangement, where coordination is not so spontaneous.

One of the elements of technology which is also related to the organization pattern is the nature of work flow. The amount of discretion given to subordinates seems to vary according to the type of specialization. Parallel specialization occurs where work flow is organized to minimize the amount of coordination required, that is, the work flow among individuals and departments is at a minimum. Interdependence specialization occurs where the activities of one individual or department are closely dependent on other individuals or departments. Unit production technology is one of the examples of parallel specialization and mass production technology is an example of interdependent specialization.

Interdependent specialization is characterized by lateral relationship in order to obtain effective coordination between specialized groups. At the same time, under this type of specialization, the subordinates have a vested interest in their own typical point of view or approach to problems and are unable to see the impact of their actions on others. Only the personnel at the top would have the interest of the total organization and, thus, be able to see the

overall picture and integrate the efforts of the different parts in order to achieve the overall organizational goals.

Under unit-production, employees see themselves as responsible for a total process, something with an observable output, and are able to see the total efforts rather than a part. For these reasons, under parallel specialization, a more organic type of organization may be appropriate, but interdependent specialization may call for a less organic type of structure and a decreasing delegation of authority to the lower levels.

The size of an organization influences its coordination, direction, control, and reporting systems and, hence, the organization structure. Where an organization is small, interaction is confined to a relatively small group, communication is simpler, less information is required for decision-making and there is less need for formal organization aspects.

Forces in the Environment. The environment in which an organization as a whole functions—its product and supply markets, the field of relevant technical knowledge, its political and socio-cultural environments—has a strong influence on the organization. Recent studies suggest that the most effective pattern of organization structure is the one which enables an organization to adjust to the requirements of its environment.[10] It is argued that the pattern of these environmental requirements over time, particularly with respect to their variability, may create different levels of uncertainty with which the organization has to cope

[10] See Paul R. Lawrence and Jay W. Lorsch, *Organization and Environment* (Boston: Harvard Business School, 1967); also, T. Burns and G. M. Stalker, *The Management of Innovation* (London: Tavistock, 1961); also, F. E. Emery and E. L. Trist, "The Casual Texture of Organizational Environment," *Human Relations* (Feb. 1965), pp. 21–32; and Jay R. Galbraith, "Environmental and Technological Determinants of Organization Design," *Studies in Organization Design* (Homewood, Ill.: Richard D. Irwin, 1970), pp. 113–139.

through its structural arrangements. These different environments will tend to require different structural accommodation.

The market environment that an organization chooses to enter substantially influences the design of an organization. The market environment includes the availability of resources, the type of products or services provided by the company, the nature of competition, the predictability or unpredictability of demand, product innovation, and change, to mention a few. The characteristics of the product or service pervasively influence the entire organization and its component parts.

Lawrence and Lorsch [11] found that organizations operating effectively in different environments had different patterns of differentiation, and had developed different organizational mechanisms to achieve the differentiation and integration required by their environments. They found (from their research of ten firms in three distinct industrial environments) that the environments of uncertainty and rapid rates of market and technological change place different requirements on the organizational design than do stable conditions. They also found that the degree of differentiation among the functional units of the organization was related to the relative certainty of the parts of the environment and their resulting diversity or homogeneity.

The managers in the functional departments of the most dynamic environments had developed a high degree of differentiation in thought and pattern. In the most stable environments there was less differentiation in pattern and thought. Also, for firms in these environments to be effective, they must have developed the required state of interdepartmental integration. A firm's departments must function in unique ways to fulfill their individual purposes, but must also coordinate to be completely effective. Their study strongly

indicates that organizations with less formal structure and widely shared influence (organic) are best able to cope with uncertain and heterogeneous environmental conditions. Conversely, highly structured (mechanistic) organizations will be more effective in stable environments.

According to Burns and Stalker[12], in the science-based industries such as electronics, where innovation is a constant demand, the organic type of organization is appropriate. Lacking a frozen structure, an organic organization grows around the point of innovating success. Studies of communication reinforce the point that the optimal conditions for innovation are non-hierarchical. In an organization not primarily concerned with technological innovation but preoccupied with production problems, however, a mechanistic type of structure is needed to facilitate coordination.

Jay Galbraith[13] used data collected at the Boeing Company to substantiate a similar point. He describes conditions prior to 1964 and then the changes which occurred in the environment in which Boeing was operating. There was an increased demand due to increased air traffic, and there was a very significant change in the market in which Boeing was operating. Their response was mainly to increase coordination. There was more uncertainty in decisions and plans. Boeing had to become much more functional to maintain its position. A liason group was developed between product and process design to reduce uncertainties. Another coordination device was the task force which provided additional interfunctional coordination. Task force members worked full time as long as the task existed. This was a temporary structure change which modified the authority relationship during the periods of high uncertainty. In this case, organizational change followed an environmental change and Gal-

[11] Paul R. Lawrence and J. W. Lorsch, *op. cit.*

[12] T. Burns and G. M. Stalker, *op. cit.*
[13] J. R. Galbraith, *op. cit.*

braith treats the uncertainty of the task as the basic independent variable influencing the design of the organization. On the whole, considerable research has indicated that organizations with low degrees of formal structure could more profitably cope with changing environments than those which have a higher degree of formal structure.

Forces in the Subordinates. There is some research evidence suggesting that a major contribution to organizational effectiveness will derive from adapting the structure to accommodate more adequately the psychological needs of organizational members. Chris Argyris, Frederick Herzberg[14] and others have drawn attention to the conflict which is likely to prevail between a traditional definition of formal organization structure and the needs of psychologically mature individuals. Herzberg has developed a two-factor theory of employee motivation which suggests specific structural adaptation to provide the "job enrichment" to enhance motivation and performance. Therefore, before designing an organization structure, it is necessary to consider a number of forces affecting the subordinate's behavior and performance. The subordinate's desire for independence, skill and motivation for assuming responsibility, need for a sense of achievement, and so forth, will greatly influence the organization structure.

Research suggests that, compared to unskilled workers, skilled workers and professional personnel are more involved in their jobs and are more anxious for an opportunity to have a high degree of autonomy on the job and an opportunity to participate in making decisions relating to it.[15] Studies consistently show that scientists as well as professional employees want autonomy and job freedom. They prefer not to be commanded in the same way as other employees in the organization.

There is also research evidence to suggest that some workers have positive attitudes toward work and can be called "motivation seekers," while others, who seem relatively unaffected by the same conditions, can be called "maintenance seekers." Perhaps the significant difference is that maintenance reaches a state of relative fulfillment at the primary needs level, whereas motivation seekers continue to be motivated by the need for a higher level of social acceptance.[16] This implies that certain forces in the subordinates will have substantial influence in designing an organization structure.

A CONTINGENCY MODEL

The organization structure is a product of many forces: the forces in the managers, the forces in the technology and environment, and the forces in the subordinates. The structure evolves through a complex and dynamic interaction between these forces which can be depicted graphically (see Figure 1).

These simultaneously interacting forces shape the pattern of organization chosen by companies. Every organization is in the middle of varying and complex pressures. They react to the many pressures and demands of environment. The successful organization is one that takes into account the forces suggested above and which is sensitive to individual situational needs. Once a firm adopts this contingency framework, it will begin to look more closely at and analyze more thoroughly the relevant variables. It is a company which identifies the kinds of

---

[14] See Chris Argyris, *Integrating the Individual and the Organization* (New York: Wiley, 1964); also Frederick Herzberg, *Work and Nature of Man* (New York: The World Publishing Company, 1966).

[15] Howard Vollmer, *Employment Rights and the Employment Relationship* (Berkeley: University of California Press, 1960).

[16] M. Scott Myers, "Who Are Your Motivated Workers?" *Harvard Business Review* (Jan.-Feb., 1964), pp. 73–88.

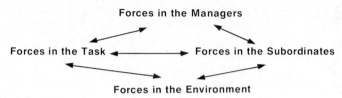

Figure 1. Interacting forces in which organization structure evolves.

conditions which enhance a particular pattern of structure in some situations and impedes its effectiveness in others. It is neither a bureaucracy nor a complete organic-adaptive model, but rather maintains a balance determined by the particular situation in question. The consistent and effective practices of an organization at one level may be of little use in another department having different technological considerations. The organization appropriate in one market-technology environment may be irrelevant or even dysfunctional in another environment. A firm producing a standardized product sold in a stable market may require a pattern of organization altogether different from a company manufacturing a highly technical product for a more dynamic market. There is no one pattern of organization style that is universally appropriate.

CONCLUSION

Organization theory has increased in importance as organizations themselves have become more complex. The production-centered classical theory stressed strict compliance to rules and regulations. The behavioral theory was people-centered and behavioral scientists stressed the worth of the individual, his needs, and the functioning of social groups. Today, the organic approach is gaining strength in a number of technologically advanced firms. Generally speaking, whereas the classical model tended to hold in more stable environments, the organic model is more appropriate to dynamic environments.

A contingency theory is developed which puts the stress of organizing on a number of variables. The theory supports the idea that there is no one best way in which to organize. The design is conditional. An effective organization, it was found, must be designed to fit its managers, market environment, technology and its subordinates. The need to understand the theoretical aspects stems from the need to solve what, at first sight, seem to be low-level operational problems but which on closer examination may turn out to be organizational problems of a higher order.

The authors wish to express sincere thanks and deep gratitude to Dr. S. B. Prasad of Ohio University, College of Business Administration for his comments on the first draft of this paper.

18 Emerging Perspectives About Organization Planning and Development

J. Jennings Partin

Earliest man saw a need for organizations. Anthropologists have documented the nature of human organizations that developed early in the evolution of civilized man. The need for organized groups is no less today than ever before. How they function however is changing rapidly and becoming increasingly more difficult to manage.

The increasing number of meetings on organization planning and development is evidence of increasing interest in the nature of organization in a complex environment. This interest is not based on idle curiosity so much as it is survival in a rapidly changing world.

STATE OF TURMOIL

We live in an age of discontinuity. However, the nature of social change is such that there are always holdovers from the past. These exist alongside new behavior patterns which are established. Still newer ways of viewing things are expressed. The net effect of all this is a state of continual turmoil which is difficult for individuals and organizations to cope with.

First, let us examine some of the underlying assumptions and concepts of prevailing organization theory and note some of the problems they encounter in today's environment. Second, we will examine stages in the evolution of organization design and the values on which they are based.

Third, we will study the process of value formation and its effects on organization. We will then look at the effects of social change on traditional organization concepts. Finally, we will consider an approach to organization which appears to be a viable alternative to traditional models as a means of dealing with the emerging social environment.

TRADITIONAL ORGANIZATION ASSUMPTIONS

The principles of "scientific management" which were articulated by Frederick Taylor are well known. We've all been perplexed by the problems of living with organization objectives, line/staff relationships, chain of command, span of control, responsibility/authority relationships, and other traditional guidelines for organization design and functioning.

These are all based on a rather interesting set of assumptions about what the character of organizations should be. It seems fair to describe the thinking of traditional organization theory in the following ways:

1. The structure of an organization is determined by a rational thought process intended to control the organization in order to achieve its end.

2. The basis for functional designations is commonality of purpose.

3. Objectives and goals are formally

stated in order to openly express the purpose of the organization.

4. Organizational hierarchy presupposes a differential jurisdiction over people and a delegation of specific tasks to a particular unit.

5. Decentralization allows for specialized entrepreneurial functions without loss of efficiency or control.

6. The basic aim of the entrepreneurial functions is the welfare of the organization and its continued viability.

7. The organization is designed to achieve the least cost or greatest return for management/stock holders.

8. Optimal solutions to solving an organization problem can be achieved by discovering a better way to operate the formal model.

9. Organizational tasks are viewed as recurring cycles, viewed in terms of patterns.

10. Checks and balances are imperative.

11. A routine, specialized information system is mandatory.

12. Management action is directly related to information the system provided.

Much more can be said about the typical pyramidal, hierarchical, bureaucratic model that characterizes typical organization models. They are designed for endurance and are a product of the conventional wisdom that prevailed in a much more stable environment than we find in the 1970's.

ORGANIZATION DESIGN DEVELOPMENT

A stable world, however, has never existed. Consequently, organization design was modified through the years as new insights were gained. There appears to be a discernable pattern of design changes that accompanies changes in environment. Organizations can be classified into three categories although variations are found in each type.

Organization According to Function. Centralized or multifunctional organization developed during the 1920's and is still widely used. The basic organizing principle is to group similar activities under major functional managers who, in turn, report to central headquarters (Figure 1).

The next form to appear was a decentralized divisional or multidivisional organization. This idea was pioneered by GM and DuPont. The basic principle of this form is to group activities by related product-markets and not by related activities. Each division is assigned to a manager who has complete responsibility for the strategic, administrative and operational decisions in areas assigned to him.

Increasing problems with the functional and divisional forms has led to some recent adaptations which have in effect created substantially different organization forms. Many companies since World War II and especially in the defense industry have gone to a matrix organization or project management design. The principle behind these designs is to form temporary organizations with sufficient authority responsibility, and resources to serve a specific product-market with a limited life cycle.

The manager of one of these organizations "owns" a number of people of various skills and utilizes others on a temporary basis as needed. The latter remain *functionally* responsible to a manager in another organization but are *administratively* responsible to the project manager during the time of his service there.

Organization design has gone through a number of stages. Each form is suited to certain conditions. Its effectiveness decreases as environmental conditions change. That in short is where the basic source of organizational stress comes from today. Stability is gone. Flux and change are constant.

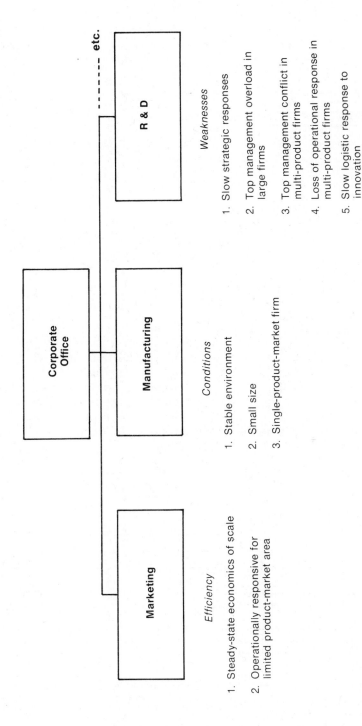

Figure 1. Functional organization design. (From Ansoff, H. I. and R. G. Brandenburg, "A Language for Organization Design," *Management Science*, Vol. 17, No. 12, Aug. 1971.)

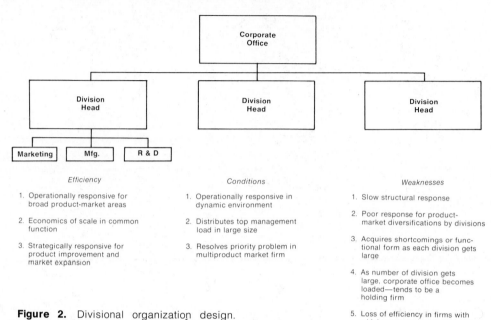

Efficiency	Conditions	Weaknesses
1. Operationally responsive for broad product-market areas	1. Operationally responsive in dynamic environment	1. Slow structural response
2. Economics of scale in common function	2. Distributes top management load in large size	2. Poor response for product-market diversifications by divisions
3. Strategically responsive for product improvement and market expansion	3. Resolves priority problem in multiproduct market firm	3. Acquires shortcomings or functional form as each division gets large
		4. As number of division gets large, corporate office becomes loaded—tends to be a holding firm
		5. Loss of efficiency in firms with widely separated markets for respective product lines
		6. Suboptimal efficiency by logistic function due to conflict of innovative and steady-state actions.

Figure 2. Divisional organization design. (From Ansoff, H. I. and R. G. Brandenburg, "A Language for Organization Design," *Management Science,* Vol. 17, No. 12, Aug. 1971.)

The thrust of our current social upheaval is directed toward the established units of our society.

VALUE BASE

One way to view the current social crisis is in terms of clashing values. Values can be thought of as the fundamental assumptions that people hold about what is good or evil, important or trivial. They are guides to action. Conflicting values evoke personal confrontations at the deepest levels of one's being.

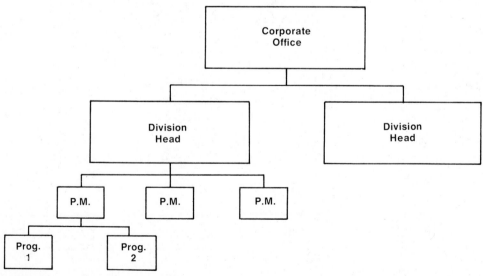

Figure 3. Adaptive organization design. (From Ansoff, H. I. and R. G. Brandenburg, "A Language for Organization Design," *Management Science,* Vol. 17, No. 12, Aug. 1971.)

In organizations, the values of the management affect its style. Values influence policy, the boundaries within which members of the organization may operate without restraint. The values of top management determine organization objectives. They influence the entire human interaction system within the organization. Likewise, the individual values of each member of the organization interact with the prevailing attitudes of the management.

Over time, certain values are viewed as sacred and inviolate by management in traditional organizations. For example, most companies hold the following values in highest esteem:

1. *Activism:* It is better to appear active than idle.

2. *Optimism:* The future will be better than today. We are growing and expanding.

3. *Egalitarianism:* Opportunity is widespread for all. We are an equal opportunity employer (i.e., EEO). There is upward mobility in our company.

4. *Practicability:* Actions should be chosen on a practical basis.[1]

These basic core values are then translated into organization goals, found in various policies, procedures and objectives. These concepts become a part of the very fabric that the management works with in achieving organizational goals. They are the core of the ideal image the company wants for itself, and are often articulated like this:

1. *Effectiveness:* We want to become increasingly effective in successfully coping with organizational problems.

2. *Growth:* We want to grow in size and scope, and continuously improve our technical competence and quality.

3. *Realization of Potential:* We want to realize our potential competence and organizational power.

4. *Productivity:* We want to continuously increase the ratio of output of goods or services to the input of human energy, money, and materials.

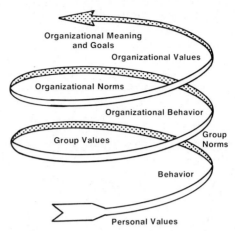

Figure 4. Effects of values and norms in organizations.

5. *Social Image:* We want to be viewed as being socially useful and beneficial to the community (e.g., ecology).[2]

These values are consistent with the Protestant Ethic which gave impetus to the industrial revolution. They are found in every organization. They have a unique configuration in each organization based on the personal values of its members. An interaction occurs between the organization and the individual. The effects of that interaction affect the achievement of both organizational and individual objectives.

Typical pyramidal, hierarchical organizations resist variance from norms. They tend to deny individual differences. In a time of radical change, value confrontations are inevitable.

EFFECTS OF SOCIAL CHANGE

Some basic components of traditional organizations follow. The traditional functional and divisional organization models have rather well-defined methods of dealing with external forces.

They have:

1. A well-defined chain of command.

---

[1] Kuriloff, Arthur H., *Organization Development For Survival,* American Management Assn., 1972.

[2] *Ibid.*

2. A system of procedures and rules for dealing with all contingencies relating to work activities.

3. A division of labor based on specialization.

4. Uniform approaches to individual members.

DISRUPTIVE INFLUENCES[3]

Organizations of this type are threatened whenever one or more of the following happens:

1. Rapid and unexpected change.

2. Growth in size where the volume of the organization's traditional activities is not enough to sustain growth.

3. Complexity of modern technology where integration between activities and persons of very diverse highly specialized competence is required.

4. A psychological threat springs from a change in organizational behavior.[4]

These threats can be analyzed in terms of internal and external forces. The *external* forces have been identified by social scientists. It is difficult for us to understand what is happening to our society because we are too much a part of what is happening. We are at the same time participants and observers of a drama whose plot is being created as it is being played. No one is singularly responsible for its development.

However, some aspects of what is happening can be identified. Our culture is in a state of disequilibrium. Individually, we are unable to assimilate impending change quickly enough.

In a recent three-year period, 66 of the top 100 companies reported major re-organizations. The need for more

information quicker has undermined traditional structures. The stable organizations of the past have been unable to remain the same.

CHANGE, STRESS IN PHILOSOPHIES

Changes in the thinking of society at large have affected the thinking or people inside the organization. New management philosophies are emerging to combat traditional ones. Are at least six theories worthy of mention contribute to our "jungle."[5]

1. *Management Process school:* This theory speaks of functions required for effective management—planning, organizing, staffing, directing and controlling. The idea here is that if you teach and execute these functions well the enterprise will be successful.

2. *Decision Theory school:* This school says that management practice rests in making good decisions. The best decisions are based on the rational choice from among alternatives. If people are trained in decision-making, the whole organization will function more effectively.

3. *Mathematical school:* The key to effective management is to produce mathematical models and processes which indicate the way an organization should move. Operations research has gained prestige because of this emphasis.

4. *Empirical school (reconstructionist):* Effective management of any organization can be best accomplished by identifying and implementing the successful practices of the past. The organization is preserved by maintaining the style management that made it what it is.

5. *Social System school:* This theory views the organization as a social system comprised of various groups working toward common purposes. The task of

[3]Bennis, Warren G., *Organization Development: Its Nature, Origins, and Prospects,* in Addison-Wesley Series on Organization Development, eds. Schein, Edgar, Bennis, Warren, and Beckhard, Richard, 6 vols., Addison-Wesley 1969.
[4]*Ibid.*

[5]Kuriloff, *op. cit.*

management is to develop a macro-system unique to its organization. In this way coordination, open communication, and effective personal transactions will be assured.

6. *Human Behavior school:* This is in contrast to, but not in conflict with, the social system approach. This school is a micro-approach focusing on the quality of relationships among the members of the organization. Good managers are expected to develop interpersonal competence and utilize this in increasing collaboration at all levels and groups throughout the organization.

The first four theories—management process, decision theory, mathematical, and empirical—are of classical derivation. They express the values of "scientific management." The last two—social system and human behavior—are based on recent insights gained from the social and behavioral sciences, primarily sociology and psychology. The former group attempts to achieve a neat, orderly, predictable management climate. The latter two value open, democratic, participative methods that are typically not very neat or as predictable.

The crisis all organizations are facing can be directly attributed to the internal and external forces we've mentioned briefly. The challenge is to attain a balance which enables the best insights from each approach to influence the organization. The *prevailing management style*, its values, *the structure of the organization*, its assumptions, and the *quality of personal relationships*, their effects, all determine the viability of any organization. The task then is how to understand the environment, the organization, and the human system to determine *what is* and *what ought to be* and to find an effective way to make the transition.

THE SYSTEMS CONCEPT

Thus far we have looked at how things got to be the way they are from one person's perspective. We've referred to the typical hierarchical organization (functional or divisional) as being traditional and based on the classical assumptions about the nature of organization and the nature of man. We've also examined some of the threats these established views are experiencing in terms of changes in societal values.

Let us now look at an approach to understanding organizations that appears to deal with rapid change more effectively. It is based on some different assumptions and allows for the existence of varying values inside and outside the system.

CLOSED AND OPEN SYSTEMS

Developments in the biological sciences and electronics have made it possible to adapt some of their models for organizations. Systems theory as applied to organizations can classify organizations as closed or open systems. A simple system's model consists of input, processing, and output. If you add a feedback mechanism from output to input, you have an example of a *closed system* (e.g. thermostat).

Traditional organization models (functional, divisional) are examples of closed systems. The adaptive organization models are examples of open systems.

Closed systems are described in terms of the *second law* of *thermodynamics.* The system moves toward equilibrium. It tends to run down. Its differentiated structures tend to move toward dissolution. A second descriptive term identified with a closed system is *entropy.* Entropy increases toward a maximum. Equilibrium occurs as the system attains the state of the most probable distribution of its elements.

In other words, the structure of the organization becomes increasingly fixed and rigid, more difficult to change. *A priori* assumptions go unchallenged. The *Peter principle* unconsciously affects manpower planning.

OPEN SYSTEMS' CHARACTERISTICS

At this point it is probably helpful to investigate the concepts of open systems theory.[6]

1. *Importation of Energy:* Every individual is dependent on the continuous inflow of stimulation from the external environment. Likewise, organizations must draw energy (human and inanimate) from outside sources in order to perform their tasks.

2. *Through-put:* Open systems transform the energy that is available to them. The organization creates a product, processes materials, trains people, or provides a service (i.e., some work gets done).

3. *Out-put:* Open systems export some product into the environment.

4. *Systems as Cycles of Events:* The pattern of activities of the energy exchange has a cyclic character. A system can be identified whenever an interrelated set of events returns upon itself to complete or renew a cycle of activities. Events rather than things are structured, so that the organization structure is *dynamic* rather than *static*. Activities or behavior are structured so that they comprise a *unity in their completion or* closure.

A single cycle of events of a self-closing character gives a single form of structure. Single cycles combine to give a larger structure of events or an *event system*. Event systems may be composed of smaller cycles which are intergral components of other systems not a part of the particular event system under consideration.

5. *Negative Entropy:* To survive, open systems must arrest the entropic process (i.e., acquire negative entropy). The entropic process is a universal law of nature which says that all forms of organization move toward disorganization or death. An open system can im-

port *more* energy from its environment than it expends, and thus can store energy and acquire negative entropy (e.g. manpower planning, management development, recruitment).

6. *Information Input, Negative Feedback and the Coding Process:* Inputs into living systems consist of more than energy. Information furnishes signals to the organization about the environment and about its functioning relationship to the environment.

Negative feedback is the simplest form of information the system receives. It enables it to correct its course. Without negative feedback there is no corrective action taken. Lacking this, the system will expend its energy, or ingest too much energy and the system will terminate.

The *coding process* of the system selects which inputs will be absorbed into the system. This mechanism is determined by the nature of the functions performed by the system.

7. *The Steady State and Dynamic Homeostasis:* The importation of energy to arrest entropy operates to maintain some constancy in energy exchange, so that open systems that survive are characterized by a steady state.

A steady state is a continuous flow of energy from the external environment and a continuous export of the products of the system, but the character of the system, the ratio of energy exchanges, and the relations between parts remains the same.

Any internal or external factor which disrupts the system is countered by forces which restore the system as quickly as possible to its previous state.

Homeostasis is apparently contradictory to the tendency of living systems to grow and expand to counteract entropy. The basic tendency of the system is homeostatic in that it will *preserve its character*. Under stress the system will import more energy than needed for preserving its character. It acquires a margin of safety beyond the immediate level of existence. Social systems tend to incorporate within their boundaries

---

[6]Katz, Daniel and Robert L. Kahn, *The Social Psychology of Organizations,* John Wiley and Sons, Inc. 1966.

the external resources essential to survival (i.e., the expansion of the original system;) (e.g., hoarding, over-staffing—as an Amoeba).

At the simplest level, the steady state is homeostasis over time. At complex levels, the steady state is maintained by preserving the character of the system through growth and expansion (e.g., adding more units of the same essential type it already has).

8. *Differentiation:* Open systems move in the pattern of differentiation and elaboration. Diffuse global patterns are replaced by more specialized functions. Sytems are first governed by dynamic interaction of their components; later on, fixed arrangements and conditions of constraint are established which render the system and its parts more efficient (e.g., policies, procedures).

9. *Equifinality:* A system can reach the same final state from differing initial conditions and by a variety of paths. As open systems move toward regulatory mechanisms to control their operations, the amount of equifinality may be reduced.

IMPLICATIONS OF SYSTEMS THEORY

Some subtle distinctions are to be made if systems theory is to be applied to organizations.

Closed systems are by definition those which tend to concentrate on its own internal functioning as if environmental changes were largely independent of the productivity, morale, and motivation of the organization. Coordination and control become ends in themselves rather than means to an end. Internal changes are viewed more in terms of attaining desired organizational goals rather than adjusting to the environment in order to achieve its objectives.

Closed systems tend to prescribe one best way for behaving because the conditions are already established each time a known problem occurs. Variances tend to call for full-scale investigations of the organization with incidental reference to environmental influences. *Open systems* on the other hand give extensive consideration to the interface between the organization and its environment. They are evolutionary, dynamic systems which adopt a positive stance on change.

THE SOCIO-TECHNICAL SYSTEM

Let us now shift from the theoretical underpinnings of systems theory to some applications of the theory for purposes of organization planning and development. In this context an industrial organization can be viewed as a socio-technical system. The simple input-process-output model is made more definitive. Systems processes are further delineated into transformation subsystems—goals and values, technology, structure, psycho-social, and managerial.

Each subsystem is essential to the successful accomplishment of the organization's mission. Subsystems can be defined with sufficient properties that the internal processing of inputs can be improved so that eventual outputs can be affected.

1. *Goals and Values subsystem:* Organization norms and personal values can be integrated by process interventions into the system (i.e., how things are done is important).

2. *Technology subsystem:* The technology of an organization refers to its knowledge and skills utilized in performing its tasks. This subsystem converts spontaneous and unreflective behavior into deliberate and rationalized behavior according to the technology the business employs.

3. *Structural subsystem:* Structure is the established pattern of relationships among the components or parts of the organization. This is designed according to the concepts utilized by the organization. Traditional organizations

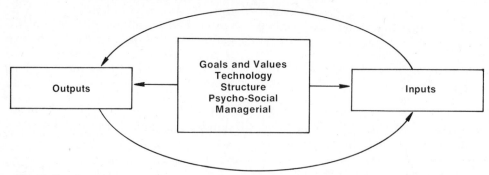

Figure 5. Organization as a socio-technical system. (From Schmuck, Richard A. and Matthew B. Miles, *Organization Development in Schools,* National Press Books, 1971.)

focus on line/staff, span of control, chain of command and other classical principles of organization. A systems approach would design the structure according to the unique properties of the system under consideration.

4. *Psycho-social subsystem:* This system refers to the individual in social relationships. It can be understood in terms of the motivation and behavior occurring in environment which includes: status and role systems, group dynamics, influence systems, and leadership.

5. *Managerial subsystem:* This system views the ways managers coordinate work 1) through people, 2) via techniques, 3) in the organization, and 4) toward its objectives. It is the process by which human and material resources are integrated into the organization for accomplishing its objectives. This can be viewed in terms of 1) decision-making, 2) control and influence, 3) recruitment processes, 4) orientation processes, 5) reward systems and 6) leadership.[7]

A SYSTEMS CHANGE AND ORGANIZATIONAL RENEWAL APPROACH

If one can accept a systems model of an organization, there are some logical extensions of this approach which affect the means by which systems are to be changed and renew themselves.

One of the basic assumptions regarding all organisms is that they remain healthy and survive to the extent that they develop the capacity to develop effective integrations with their environments. This is especially important in the social context organizations are in today.

Following are requisites of a systems approach to change and renewal:[8]

1. *Determining environmental influences:* This is a repetitive process for helping the client group develop a contextual mapping of the manner in which it is currently interacting with its environment.

2. *Systems planning:* The main aim of this procedure is to recognize the demands of the environment and identify the responses the organization makes based on its value system.

3. *Systems design or redesign:* The purpose of this task is to help the client system organize itself so that it has the inbuilt dynamic capacity to make continual integrations with its changing environment.

The result of this approach is that the client develops an integrated sense of what its present engagement with its environment looks like.

[7]Schmuck, Richard A. and Matthew B. Miles, *Organization Development in Schools,* National Press Books, 1971.

[8]Krone, Charles G., unpublished paper presented at the NTL New Technology in Organization Development Conference, New York, 1971.

IDENTIFYING PROCESS

The process of identifying and defining the appropriate systems model is as follows:[9]

1. Identify the system's *core process.* What is the system trying to do? What is the nature of our business? What is the character of what we're trying to create or produce? What needs in the greater environment are we trying to answer?

The core process contains the essential properties of the system.

2. The next stage is *environmental scanning.* This is identifying the external forces influencing the system. It is a process of making judgments about the realities at work in the interactions between the external environment and the internal world of the system.

This should be done as objectively as possible, while realizing the innate subjectivity of the identification process.

3. Identify demands made on the core. When done in a group, the demands vary—shared, conflicting and independent. These "demand domains" define the requirements of the system.

4. Map out the inside responses to the system to each of the demand domains.

For every demand there is a response. The task is to identify particular responses. Frequently there are incongruities between the demand and the response. The effect on the client group is one of increasing self-awareness.

5. Identify ways to increase the congruity between the demand and the response.

Steps 1–4 are definition stages. Step 5 is a planning phase.

Responses to the demands can be prioritized to the values of the system. Temporary teams can be formed to develop plans for dealing with discrete processes within the system.

Here in capsule form is a technique for identifying the components of a system. The system can be the total organization, a major unit, or a unit of any scope depending on how the system is defined.

This approach offers flexibility in organization planning and development. It is contextual, uniquely suited to the system under study. The process has the added benefit of involving the client group in the system design and the planning it requires. It develops insight into the nature of the organization and its environment. During the process, values and norms of the organization are surfaced and accounted for in any strategies that are taken.

EMERGING PERSPECTIVES

The open systems approach seems to effectively answer the fluctuating, often conflicting demands made in today's social climate. Alvin Toffler documented some of these in his book *Future Shock.*[10] He noted forces which have deluged every human institution. With regard to organizations, two significant changes can be mentioned: 1) increased transiency and 2) changed views of the nature of human resources. The effects of changes in both of these realms are indicative of a need for an open systems approach to viewing organizations.

The effects of *Future Shock,* the disequilibrium found in persons influenced by change quicker than they can assimilate it, have created an ideology of *transience.* Social mobility has made it possible for people to move quickly, frequently, and great distances. Recruitment and employment efforts are vital to an organization's survival. Frequent job changes are not viewed as about career development and self-fulfillment than to organizational loyalty.

[9]Krone, *op. cit.*

[10]Toffler, Alvin, *Future Shock,* Bantam Books Inc., 1970.

HUMAN RESOURCE FACTOR

Views toward *human resources* are also being affected. The "organization man," though once desired, is no longer a realistic expectation in most companies. People themselves are coming to accept employment changes as being inevitable. Frequently, these changes are made in order to do more interesting work than for financial considerations alone. This suggests increased independence on the part of the worker.

It appears that the values and assumptions of a closed, traditional system cannot long survive in the emerging social system. Organizations will be forced to become more participative. An open systems theory of organization planning and development is suited to meet unexpected demands in an efficient and effective manner. It has the capacity for enabling the organization to realistically view itself and its environment and start the long process of becoming what it wants to be, must be.

SECTION C

Management of Human Assets

A firm's most important resource is its human assets. If the company's personnel are properly trained and developed, the net worth of the organization is increased. Conversely, if the firm's personnel are treated poorly, performance will decline and the company may cease to exist. The articles in this section illustrate the importance of both developing and measuring a firm's human assets.

In the first article, James Waters describes a process known as human resource accounting. This process represents an attempt to make a total evaluation of a firm's human assets. In the article, the author describes human asset investment based on costs incurred. These costs include recruiting, acquisition, training-orientation, informal training costs and supervisory time. These are expenses that are incurred within the first two years. In addition, there are costs incurred during an employee's career: investment building experience costs and development costs. The knowledge and measurement of these costs allows the manager to evaluate the impact of layoffs, attrition rates and rehiring. It can also be an aid in conducting a cost-benefit analysis of training.

In the second article, Arthur Beck and Ellis Hillmar discuss another technique for managing human assets: management by objectives (MBO). The authors contend that MBO and other organizational development (OD) programs must be implemented simultaneously if they are to be successful. They present a model that demonstrates the interrelationships between MBO and OD. The article illustrates the complexity of MBO and OD variables and their interrelationships to the development of a firm's human assets. The article also points out that motivational tools and leadership styles should be developed on the bases of what is best, given the parameters of each situation, and not simply categorized as good or bad based only on broad generalizations.

In the last article in this section, Professor Fred Luthans and Mr. David Lyman describe a process for training supervisors to utilize organizational behavior modification or O.B. Mod. as it is popularly known. The steps involved in this process are identifying behavioral events, measuring frequencies of behavior, functionally analyzing behavior, developing intervention strategies, converting to positive reinforcement and understanding the importance of contingencies, i.e., the relationship between the managers' behavior and that of their subordinates. The authors note a number of benefits to be derived from O.B. Mod. training. First, training is highly job-oriented, thus providing a high degree of transferrability. Second, the approach lends itself to individual development and therefore can alter organizational parameters to allow for more effective management. Third, the O.B. Mod. approach utilizes a scientific methodology. However, there are also three disadvantages to this type of approach, including complexity of organizations, negative connotations concerning manipulation of people, and general resistance to change. The authors feel that the advantages far outweigh the disadvantages, however, and they describe the future use of O.B. Mod. as highly deterministic of efficient human resource allocation.

19   A Practical Application of Human Resource Accounting Techniques

James Waters

The annual reports of many corporations and the statements of numerous nonprofit organizations maintain that employees are their most important asset. These organizations point out their payroll costs and extensiveness of their human resource programs. However, they invariably understate the costs associated with this asset. While they quickly recognize the obvious costs of payroll, the less obvious costs entailed in the acquisition and development of human assets are not as carefully analyzed and measured as payroll costs. Consequently, they cannot completely control the costs and measure the benefits returned by their human assets. Lacking complete cost data, they cannot make sound decisions about their human resource programs and policies.

To remedy this situation, a research team has recently done work in the field of *human resource accounting*. This research involved personnel from the University of Michigan and the R. G.

This article originally appeared in *Personnel Administration* (May–June 1972), pp. 41–46, 70. Reprinted by permission of the International Personnel Association.

Barry Corporation, a manufacturing company with 1,700 employees. Over a period of years, human-resource accounting has been operational in the Barry organization, and has enabled it to better manage its human resources.[1]

Human-resources accounting provides a new conceptual framework to evaluate the real costs and benefits of a firm's human assets. It is an attempt to quantify costs that presently are not recognized under traditional financial and accounting treatment. These costs, such as acquisition and development costs, provide long-term benefits and thus are investment costs, consistent with the treatment of capital assets.

Simply stated, the objective of human-resource accounting is to make human-resource management more effective by assessing the real costs and benefits of this asset.

This article, however, extends its application to the measurement of both costs and benefits. It builds upon the foundation developed by the Michigan-Barry research team and provides a new application of the work they have done. The case study discussed below analyzes the costs and benefits of human assets through the same techniques used with conventional capital assets. The objective of the study is twofold:

to present a *different way of thinking* about an organization's human resources, and
to measure the *total costs* associated with these resources.

Specifically, the use of present value analysis in the study evaluates human assets as if they were capital assets. This process—*human resource investment evaluation*—gives the manager more information on which to base such decisions as whether or not to hire additional employees or institute a new training program—that is, whether or not to invest more in human assets.

Human resource investment evaluation is most appropriate in organizations that are human resource intensive, such as consulting, legal, and marketing firms, and governmental service organizations. In such organizations, the costs and benefits of human assets are relatively more important for their overall welfare. It is with such an organization, the Initial Corporation, that this study deals. The Initial Corporation markets both computer hardware and software and assists customers in designing and implementing computer systems. The high level of sophistication of the firm's products and services and the competitive nature of the industry require that the salesmen be well-trained and highly competent. Consequently, Initial Corporation incurs extensive human resource costs to recruit and select high potential salesmen and to develop their capabilities.

While the company's identity has been disguised, the data used were obtained through interviews with Initial personnel. The costs used in this study are based on 1970 data and represent the cost to Initial in that year to recruit, acquire, and develop its salesmen. The specific costs identified for the typical salesmen are average costs. They are based on total expenditures for all salesmen and then allocated on a per capita basis. For example, training costs are apportioned among all salesmen in the training program for 1970. This study analyzes the human resource investment in a typical salesman at Initial. This typical salesman is assumed to have been hired directly upon graduation from college. He begins as a sales

[1] For more detailed discussion of their work, see the following articles:

R. Lee Brummett, William C. Pyle, Eric G. Flamholtz, "Human Resource Accounting in Industry," *Personnel Administration,* July-August, 1969.
Rensis Likert and William C. Pyle, "Human Resource Accounting, A Human Organizational Measurement Approach," *Financial Analysts Journal,* January-February, 1971.
Eric G. Flamholtz, "A Model for Human Resource Valuation: A Stochastic Process with Service Reward," *The Accounting Review,* April, 1971.

trainee and progresses normally throughout a ten-year career at Initial. The study measures the different investment costs incurred by the salesman during his career and determines the expected benefits resulting from the investment.

These costs and benefits are calculated as to amount and timing. They are then compared using present value analysis. The total present value of the investment costs is determined and from it is subtracted the total present value of the benefits associated with the investment. The result is the *net* present value of the resource investment.

The cost figures used in this study are conceived of as investment costs. As such, they are depreciated over their useful life, a period which is assumed to extend from the year they are incurred to the end of the salesman's employment with Initial. The yearly depreciation charge is then assumed to produce a tax savings that lowers the net investment cost each year.

Obviously, this assumption of yearly depreciation charges related to human assets is not consistent with present tax and accounting treatment. The depreciation assumption is used only to show how human resource investment analysis would proceed if human assets were conceived of and treated in the same terms as other assets.

This study separates the various investment costs associated with Initial salesmen into the six categories developed by the Michigan-Barry team. The six categories, representing costs that are probably not considered by many managers, follows.

The first of these costs is *recruiting outlay costs*—cost of locating and selecting new employees; including costs incurred for unsuccessful candidates. These costs include both out-of-pocket and opportunity costs. The out-of-pocket recruiting outlays were costs for transportation and meals for successful recruits going to the home office for interviews.

The opportunity costs of recruiting represent the time spent by Initial employees—salesmen and staff (personnel and clerical)—in recruiting. These costs equal the value of this time to Initial. This value is the expected hourly income of the salesmen or staff person used in recruiting. The value of staff time is proportionately less than that of salesmen because staff employees are not expected to be as productive in generating income. The total per capita recruiting outlay costs were $5,558 and were assumed to be incurred at the beginning of the sales trainee's first year of employment.

The second category of investment costs is *acquisition costs*—costs of bringing new employees into the firm. These are essentially processing costs and include both out-of-pocket costs and opportunity costs. The out-of-pocket costs include those of the pre-employment medical exam, moving costs to bring the new salesman to his location, and temporary housing costs incurred while the individual is arranging for a permanent residence. The opportunity costs include the time spent by the personnel office in processing the new sales trainee through filling out employment and benefit forms, etc., and by other staff and sales personnel in informally orienting him. The total acquisition costs were $2,136 per capita and again were assumed to be incurred at the beginning of year one.

The third category of investment costs that are incurred early in the salesman's career are *formal training and familiarization costs*—formal orientation and training program costs incurred immediately after the employee joins the firm. Most of these costs are incurred during the basic orientation program through which all sales trainees must pass. This three-month program involves both out of pocket and opportunity costs, including the cost of the trainee's time since he is now a full-time member of the firm. The time spent by the sales trainee in the training program deprives the company of his productivity in the field.

The out-of-pocket costs are similar to those in the acquisition category —entailing travel expenses to bring the sales trainee to the training site and living expenses once he is there. The company must pay the costs of housing and meals for out-of-town trainees.

The opportunity costs involved are twofold in nature. First, there are the costs of the time spent by Initial employees in the training program —salesmen and company staff people who teach various sections of the program. The faculty time is the sum of actual time spent in the training session plus the time spent by faculty members preparing their presentations. The staff time involves that spent administering the program and assisting faculty members in their preparation. The total cost of this time was then distributed over the members of the training program, to give a per capita cost.

The second opportunity cost involved is that of the individual trainee's time spent in the program. Although his expected hourly income is low at this point in his career there is still a significant cost to Initial Corporation during the thirteen weeks of the program. The total per capita formal training investments are $8,552 and are assumed to be incurred at the beginning of year one.

The fourth category of investment costs encompasses *informal training and familiarization costs*—costs associated with the process of integrating the employee into the organization and teaching him to adapt his existing skills to the job requirements so that he is fully effective. These costs result from the time spent by the trainee in learning the policies and objectives of the company, determining the communication patterns and practices in the firm, and understanding the people with whom he regularly deals. Essentially, these costs are related to the trainee's learning the ropes.

The informal costs have two components. The first is the trainee's relative ineffectiveness because of his lack of training and experience. This cost equals the difference in the total hourly sales income (productivity), including actual sales, promotions, and business-getting time, between salesmen and sales trainees. The lower productivity of the trainee is evidenced by his lower total income and represents a cost to Initial. If the company employed only experienced salesmen and did not bring new talent into the organization, it could avoid the cost.

Added to the cost of informal training as the trainee develops his skills on the job are the write-offs of customer charges that the sales trainee incurs during his first years with the firm. These write-offs result from the trainee's taking more time than an experienced salesman to complete a customer assignment. This extra cost comes from the time involved in advising the customer in designing and installing a computer system. The redundant time of the trainee cannot be charged directly to customers he serves.

A final cost in this category is that of the time spent by senior salesmen giving advice and informal guidance their first year of employment. This alternative use of salesmen's time is a real cost to Initial because it is time that is not spent selling. The total per capita informal training and familiarization cost is $37,127, assumed to be incurred at the beginning of the second year of the trainee's career.

Beyond the investment costs incurred during the trainee's first two years with Initial, two types of costs are undertaken throughout the rest of his career. The first of these is *investment building experience costs*—on-the-job learning costs incurred after the initial training and familiarization period and increasing the employee's total capabilities. These costs aim at developing the salesman beyond his normal technical abilities so that he is a more effective salesman, more able to keep up with the rapid changes in computer technology and meet the competitive pressures of the computer industry. These costs are measured by the time spent in direct and indirect promotion and business getting activities which include presentation of papers to professional societies and solicitation of new accounts. These activities increase the range of the salesman's abilities and sharpen his skills. However, since it does not produce sales income this time is an investment cost for Initial. This investment cost is approximately $4,053 annually and is assumed constant over the salesman's career. It is incurred at the beginning of the third through tenth years of the salesman's employment with Initial Corporation.

The last of the investment categories is that of *development costs*—costs of seminars and university courses aimed at increasing the employee's abilities beyond the specific skills required by the position. Technical expertise is a definite requisite for success in the computer industry, both for the individual and the company. But it is not enough. The salesman must be well informed so that he can anticipate customer needs, needs that vary by size and type of organization and by industry. He must be able to relate Initials products and services to the rest of the economy. This broadening of the salesman's abilities and skills is the objective of development programs.

These development costs are the formal counterpart of investment building experience costs and encompass the costs of yearly seminars held by Initial, both at corporate headquarters and at other training sites. Again, out-of-pocket and opportunity costs are involved. The out-of-pocket costs include travel expenses for the salesmen and the cost of accommodations during the program.

The duration of the programs represents only about half of the formal development time of the salesman. An equal amount of company time is spent by the salesman in various modes of self study. The formal programs of study and the self study efforts comprise the salesman's opportunity cost—a cost which is much greater than the more obvious out-of-pocket costs. An additional opportunity cost is that of faculty time spent on the programs, both in preparation and presentation. The total annual development cost is $3,430 per capita, again assumed to be incurred at the beginning of each year.

PRESENT VALUE OF THE INVESTMENT COSTS

Having determined the total investment cost incurred each year by Initial in the selection, training, and development of a salesman, the *present cost* of the investment was calculated utilizing an after-tax cost of capital of 11% (a 22% pre-tax cost based upon the opportunity cost of funds for the company) and assuming a 50% tax rate to simplify calculations. The after-tax cost of the total human resource investment in the salesman was determined, using two approaches. The first approach (which is not permitted under present tax laws) calculated the tax savings resulting from depreciating each year's investment cost over the remaining years of the salesman's employment. The present value of each of these net costs was then determined.

The second approach calculated the tax savings resulting from deducting the full cost of each investment in the year in which it was incurred, as would be appropriate under current tax treatment. The present value of these savings represents the real world cost situation. Thus these net investment costs will be compared with the benefits resulting from the investment to determine its net present value. To highlight the investment nature of these costs under Approach II, the after-tax investment costs are allocated over the remaining years of the salesman's career (on a non-discounted basis).

CHART A
INVESTMENT COSTS

Yearly Cost	$16,246	37,127	7,483	7,483	7,483	7,483	7,483	7,483	7,483	7,483
Year	1	2	3	4	5	6	7	8	9	10

Total Present Value = $84,232

Approach I
TAX SAVINGS (REFLECTING DEPRECIATION)

Yearly Savings	813	2,875	3,343	3,877	4,501	5,299	6,185	7,422	9,303	13,044
Year	1	2	3	4	5	6	7	8	9	10

Total Present Value = $30,964

Approach II
TAX SAVINGS (REFLECTING NO DEPRECIATION)

Yearly Savings	8,123	18,564	3,742	3,742	3,742	3,742	3,742	3,742	3,742	3,742
Year	1	2	3	4	5	6	7	8	9	10

Total Present Value = $42,119

ALLOCATION OF INVESTMENT COSTS

	812	2,875	3,343	3,878	4,502	5,250	6,186	7,433	9,304	13,046
Year	1	2	3	4	5	6	7	8	9	10

Chart A shows the time distribution of the investment costs and the tax savings under both approaches. The top series of numbers presents the yearly investment costs (common to both approaches), and the total present value of each of the years' costs discounted to the first year of the salesman's employment.

Under Approach I, the total investment cost was adjusted for the assumed tax shield produced by the depreciation of these investment costs. Assuming straight line depreciation and a useful life extending from the year, the cost is incurred to year ten of the salesman's employment, the after-tax cost of the investment was calculated. The second series in Chart A shows the time distribution of these yearly tax savings (50% of the year's depreciation), and the total present value of the tax savings is $30,964, present value of these savings. The total giving an after-tax present investment cost of $53,268.

Under Approach II, the first series of figures shows the tax savings related to each year's investment cost, with full cost deducted each year. The present value of these tax savings is $42,119, resulting in an after-tax present investment cost of $42,114. The second series of figures allocates the after-tax investment costs on the same basis as depreciation in Approach I. The costs are apportioned equally over the years remaining in the salesman's career.

PRESENT VALUE OF THE INVESTMENT BENEFITS

The next step in the human resource investment evaluation is to calculate the benefits associated with human resource investment. The benefit that the Initial Corporation receives from its salesman is the profit he returns from his sales and systems consulting income. This benefit is measured by the difference between his sales and consulting income and the sum of his cash salary, fringe benefits, and allocated overhead costs. The latter total represents the current costs associated with the salesman's employment. This measure of return assumes that all of the salesman's profit results from the investment costs associated with him. (It should be noted that this measure relates to the total investment. Isolating the return on specific investment com-

CHART B

GROSS SALES INCOME ATTRIBUTABLE TO SALESMAN

	$21,000	38,640	38,892	43,548	52,257	56,061	65,181	69,092	73,238	75,435
Year	1	2	3	4	5	6	7	8	9	10

TOTAL SALARY, BENEFIT AND OVERHEAD COSTS ATTRIBUTABLE TO SALESMAN

	14,000	25,760	25,921	29,032	34,838	37,384	43,454	46,061	48,825	50,290
Year	1	2	3	4	5	6	7	8	9	10

AFTER TAX PROFIT ATTRIBUTABLE TO SALESMAN
(Return on Investment)

	3,500	6,440	6,481	7,258	8,710	9,344	10,864	11,516	12,207	12,573
Year	1	2	3	4	5	6	7	8	9	10

Total Present Value = $47,307

ponents would be an extension of the present analysis.)

At Initial Corporation gross income for its salesmen is a given multiple of the salary, benefit, and overhead costs associated with the individual. This multiple reflects both value received by the customer as perceived by Initial Corporation and the internal pricing mechanism of the firm.

The cash salary of the salesman is the starting point in generating the needed current cost data. With an assumed starting salary of $14,000, the salesman's benefit and overhead costs and his gross income could be determined. These figures are compounded at a growth rate of 9% per annum, representing expected salary increases over the salesman's career. These figures are then adjusted by yearly percentage factors that represent the proportion of the salesman's time in each year that he is expected to generate income. For example, vacation and sickness time are not included as productive time for the salesman. With these adjustments the yearly profit earned by Initial from its salesmen could be determined.

The yearly distribution of these figures is shown in Chart B. The top series presents the gross income attributed to the salesman for each year of his career; the middle series shows the salesman's yearly salary, benefit, and overhead costs (including an adjustment for the 50% tax shield resulting from these chargeable expenses); and

the third series presents the yearly after-tax profit attributable to the salesman. The total present value of the salesman's career profit is $47,307 (after tax).

The benefit from the human resource investment must now be compared with the net cost of the investment. From Chart A, the present value of the investment cost (using the currently acceptable tax savings of Approach II) is $42,119. With the benefit amount from Chart B, the net present value of the investment is:

$$[\text{Benefit } (\$47,307) - \text{Cost } (\$42,119)]$$
$$= \$5,188$$

Based on the assumptions and data presented in this case, Initial Corporation is recouping its human resource investment costs, and then some.

Human resource accounting has much practical value for today's manager—whether in a profit or nonprofit organization. Possibly its greatest value is that it pinpoints an organization's investment in human resources. This facilitates a manager's analysis of each human resource cost applicable to the employees in his unit. This analysis can indicate not only where changes are needed (diagnosis), but also where they are needed most (action). Those human resource programs with the lowest return on investment probably require most immediate attention. This type of analysis will give the manager better control over the resources for which he is responsible. It will also permit the organization to hold its managers more accountable for the use of all the resources they control.

Human resource accounting can be helpful in many ways. A manager whose unit faces widely fluctuating demand can better decide whether to lay off employees during slack periods and hire others when volume increases or to maintain an inventory of existing employees. The costs (recruiting, training, etc.) of replacing employees can be compared with the salary costs of holding onto employees during the slack period. Further, a manager who faces the loss of a valuable employee being lured away by a competitor can assess how much he can afford to offer him to stay. The higher costs of an increased salary or improved benefits can be compared with the investment costs needed to replace him.

Similarly, an organization that offers its employees higher wages or better benefits than its competitors can determine the value of this policy. The increased expected tenure of its employees resulting from higher wages will presumably lead to savings in replacement costs which can be determined through human resource accounting. Finally, another use of this technique, possibly of more interest to organizations with fast track management development programs is to calculate the cost advantages of hiring an MBA as opposed to a BA. Because of the advanced education of the MBA, the organization should have to incur less training costs with him. This savings can be compared to the higher salary that must be paid the MBA, and the net value of the investment in him can be determined. These examples indicate only a few of the many ways an organization can use human resource accounting to more effectively utilize its most important resource.

CONCLUSION

The foregoing analysis of human resource investments at the Initial Corporation and the discussion of alternative uses of human resource accounting present some of the practical applications of the concept. The organization with a large investment in human resources seems well advised to explore human resource accounting. As the economy becomes more service-oriented and human resource intensive and as the work force becomes more sophisticated and more expensive to train and develop, human resource accounting will become more valuable and the costs of ignoring it more pronounced. Human assets involve many costs that currently are not explicitly recognized or controlled by management. If properly applied, human resource accounting can heighten awareness of these costs and make their control more effective.

20 OD to MBO or MBO to OD: Does it Make a Difference?

Arthur C. Beck, Jr. and Ellis D. Hillmar

Is it possible to have management by objectives and results (MBO/R) without organization development (OD)? Is it possible to have OD without MBO/R? We believe that the answer to both questions is: NO! If you are implementing either concept successfully, you are probably also implementing the other satisfactorily whether you put a label on it or not.

Richard Beckhard said very much the same thing in his recent book on organization development: "One of the major assumptions underlying organization development efforts and much managerial strategy today is the need to assure that organizations are managing against goals. Healthy organizations tend to have goal setting at all levels. As a cornerstone of their practices, individuals engage in systematic performance improvement and target-setting; groups and teams periodically and systematically set the work goals and plans for achieving them; the organization as a whole engages in systematic goal setting activities.[1]

Many of the attempts to implement the MBO/R system have been less than successful. Some who say they are using the MBO/R concept really are not; objectives they may have, but management by objectives and results they do *not* have. To successfully implement MBO/R it is necessary to have essentially the same organizational norms and values functioning as for implementing OD. Neither can be successful without the other.

[1] Beckhard, Richard, *Organization Development: Strategies and Models,* Addison-Wesley, 1969.

OD-MBO/R MODEL

The model in Figure 1 is an attempt to show how MBO/R, meaningful work and the OD process are all interrelated. This model was developed for the book, *A Practical Approach to Organizational Development Through MBO/Selected Readings,*[2] from the following three models utilizing behavioral science concepts to deal with the process of managing:

1. The "Conditions for Human Effectiveness" model, developed by Dr. M. Scott Myers of Texas Instruments, Inc.[3]

2. "The Goal-setting Process" model developed by Dr. Charles L. Hughes of Texas Instruments, Inc.[4]

3. "The Meaningful Work" model also developed by Dr. Myers.[5]

The conditions for human effectiveness diagram is an OD model that covers four basic conditions for motivation: interpersonal competence, meaningful goals, helpful systems, and achievement/self-actualization. These are overlapping, reinforcing, mutually dependent variables.

The goal setting process becomes functional as part of an organizational development process. It has a direct re-

[2] Beck, Arthur C., Jr. and Hillmar, Ellis D., *A Practical Approach to Organization Development Through MBO/Selected Readings,* Addison-Wesley, 1972.
[3] Myers, M. Scott, *Every Employee a Manager,* McGraw-Hill, 1970, pp. 53-4.
[4] Hughes, Charles L., *Goal Setting,* American Management Association, 1965, pp. 31-2.
[5] Myers, M. Scott, *Every Employee a Manager,* McGraw-Hill, 1970, pp. 96-103.

This article originally appeared in *Personnel Journal* (November 1972), pp. 827–834, and is reprinted with permission.

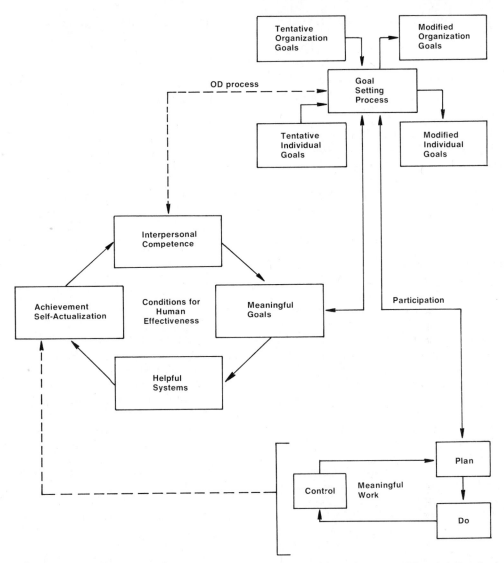

Figure 1. OD—MBO/R model. (Reprinted from A. C. Beck, Jr., and E. D. Hillmar, *A Practical Approach to Organization Development Through MBO,* 1972. Addison-Wesley, Reading, Mass.)

lationship to meaningful goals as well as less obvious impacts on helpful systems and achievement. The two-way arrows between the goal setting process and meaningful goals denote this relationship with the constant changing and interaction aspects of the process.

The goal setting process also provides a means for the development of interpersonal competence. A broken two-way arrow between these two boxes shows this relationship.

The meaningful work model be-

comes functional in a highly evolved organization which is practicing MBO/R. At that point there is a functional participative management style which allows for that model to be implemented in conjunction with the goal setting process. The functioning of the meaningful work model bears a direct relationship to the goal setting process (shown by two-way arrow). It results in a realization of a high level of achievement and self-actualization at the individual level and also contributes to organizational achievement. This payoff is indicated by a broken arrow by-passing helpful systems to show that it is possible to enjoy results before the helpful systems are developed. There can be a lag in system changes up to a point.

Conditions for Human Effectiveness

The four variables in the conditions for human effectiveness—inter-personal competence, meaningful goals, helpful systems and achieve-ment—were described earlier as overlapping, reinforcing, and mutu-ally dependent. Any attempt to create a motivating climate must include a ba-lanced effort to maximize each of the four conditions. At Texas Instruments these became prime concerns in its ap-proach to managing growth and change in a way that retains innovation, flexibility, open communications and individual motivations.

Scott Myers describes interpersonal competence as having high expecta-tions, respect for the individual, honest relationships, freedom to act and a team orientation.

He states that meaningful goals must be understandable, desirable, attaina-ble and synergistic and that there needs to be the opportunity for the individual to influence them.

The helpful systems must be under-stood by the user, goal-oriented, con-trollable by the user, adaptive to and by the user and provide him feedback.

The resultant achievement/self-actualization condition yields profitable organizational growth, profitable indi-vidual growth, commitment to goals, high motivation, minimal dissatisfac-tion and high trust.[6]

The managerial skills and organiza-tional processes by which these condi-tions are realized is a function of what is now identified as OD. The movement from knowledge and acceptance of the theory to application activities will be dealt with later.

Management by Objectives and Results

Management by Objectives and Re-sults is a management concept that has had increasing acceptance since Peter Drucker wrote about "Management by Objectives and Self-Control" in his 1954 book *The Practice of Management.*[7] Six years later Douglas McGregor, in his book *The Human Side of Enterprise,*[8] described two sets of assumptions about individuals—Theory X and Theory Y.

In the Theory Y set of assumptions, he emphasized that "men will exercise self-direction and self-control toward achieving objectives to which they are committed," and that "commitment to objectives is a function of the rewards associated with their achievements."

These two classics provided the foundation for the development of this innovative management concept.

Drucker also wrote about the neces-sity of having a true team and welding individual efforts into a common ef-fort. He pointed out that each member of the team, regardless of where he is in the organization, needs to understand the objectives of the whole organization and to see how his performance is con-tributing to these over-all objectives.

Both Drucker and McGregor, when writing about objectives and self-control, are also describing the total or-ganization process necessary for a goal/results oriented system to be suc-cessful. Thus, we find the OD process a necessary support to enable the MBO/R system to become successful.

The crucial factor of the goal setting process is to get results oriented in-teraction while providing for more than simple participation. But interac-

---

[6] Rush, Harold M. F., *Behavioral Science —Concepts and Management Application,* National Industrial Conference Board, 1969, pp. 142-3.

[7] Drucker, Peter F., *The Practice of Management,* Harper and Row, 1954.

[8] McGregor, Douglas, *The Human Side of Enter-prise,* McGraw-Hill, 1960.

tion will be achieved only if management's guiding philosophy permits. In describing the goal setting process and the necessary managerial climate for its successful implementation, Charles Hughes identifies the need for a goal setting "umbrella" where management (1) makes company goals known to the employees and (2) provides opportunities for employees to participate meaningfully in meeting these objectives (3) in a way that gives employees a chance for identifying personal goals so that (4) the motivation to work which results will achieve (a) company goals as well as (b) personal goals.[9]

At Texas Instruments humanism is not the only consideration behind such a concept. One executive was quoted: "No program, no job, or no person ought to exist within the company except in pursuit of company goals." [10]

Meaningful Work

The meaningful work portion of the model shows how the doer is involved in all aspects of the job. He is involved in the problem-solving, goal setting, planning, scheduling, etc. In doing this he also sets up the standard of measurement by which he will be evaluated. A means of feedback that allows him to evaluate his performance is necessary so that the individual can make corrections and continue with the doing. This concept, of course, requires that the supervisor be willing to give up considerable "turf" to his employees so that *they* can manage their jobs.

This meaningful work process should take place in conjunction with the goal setting process which ties into the OD model at the meaningful goals point.

The role of the manager also will change considerably if this concept is implemented. In his new role he will find himself making fewer decisions and doing more of:

1. Assuring that decisions are made by those who have the information to make the decisions and are closer to the organizational level where the decisions will be implemented;

2. Assuring that those making decisions know the limits within which they operate, such as finances, resources, legal implications, etc.;

3. Assuring that decisions made are supported;

4. Assuring that *all* results are evaluated. It is just as important that we know why we achieved as why we did not achieve. With this feedback we can do a better job next time. Without this final step there would be permissiveness, for there is no accountability in the situation—no need for results to be achieved.

It will also become obvious that many management systems will have to be changed to be supportive of the results orientation of the organization brought about by the implementation of the MBO/R and meaningful work concepts.

APPLICATION EXPERIENCES

The OD-MBO/R model has value in facilitating a cognitive understanding of some of the complex issues in organizations. In showing the relationship of their variables, it allows the management of an organization to become aware of what can happen if they do not consider the total process when they embark on a change in one variable.

The "acid test" of this model is its applicability in operational activities. Our OD-MBO/R model evolved from development activities with a variety of organizations in both government (state and local) and business. We believe that an understanding of the model by managers, trainers, and consultants will facilitate the implementation of both OD and MBO/R programs.

---

[9] Hughes, Charles L., *Goal Setting,* American Management Association, 1965, pp. 21-2.

[10] Levinson, Harry, *Management by Whose Objectives,* Harvard Business Review, July-August, 1970, pp. 125-134.

One of the first issues to be dealt with is: Do you start with OD or MBO/R? Our experience indicates quite strongly that OD is a better place to start.

STARTING WITH MBO/R

If you have already started with MBO/R, it might be helpful to check your experience against the model. Having determined where you are within this point of view, future directions might be indicated.

The MBO literature seems to support our position. The mechanics or techniques of MBO/R are relatively simple, but putting them into action is quite difficult. Inability to adequately deal with the human and system process issues leads to the ultimate failure. These experiences can create great tensions in the organization and can be extremely dysfunctional to organization development. For instance, we have seen numerous instances of managers returning from an MBO/R seminar and starting to implement the concept immediately. Shortly, many objectives, well written by the boss, appear. They are then given to the subordinate as his objectives. Quite often they are printed and elaborately bound. They usually find their way to the files and the conclusion is soon reached that it did not work. As one subordinate said to his boss, "They were your objectives, not mine." There was no commitment.

Another example of misuse is the boss asking the subordinates to set goals for their jobs for the year. When the subordinate submits them, he is then "hung" with them, and they are used as a club over his head. The negotiation aspect in the goal setting process is missing in both instances.

Harry Levinson criticizes the MBO/R process "as one of the greatest management illusions because it fails to take adequately into account the deeper emotional components of motivation."[11] If the intent in implementing MBO/R is to follow the Frederick Taylor tradition of a more rational management process or if it is being installed to bolster a sagging performance appraisal system where the manager continues to "counsel" the subordinate on his good and bad characteristics, then MBO/R is being used as Dr. Levinson describes it. We do not think this is management by objectives and results, but merely objective or goal setting, which may get an improvement in performance but not the management process. It is a directive-control system and should be recognized as such.

When considering MBO/R an organization should be able to answer the question, "Why?" If that answer is anything less than "to achieve more effective organizational results," you might do better without it. A second question should be: "What are we willing to commit as resources to achieve a functional MBO/R process—not just a program?" If all you want is an improved planning technique, or a better performance appraisal system, better look at other alternatives.

The MBO/R process has to ultimately become the total management process of the organization. It has to be the way you manage and not just a special technique. To achieve this as a total organizational process may take two to five years depending on the intensity of application.

Experience suggests that the organizational capabilities for a successful MBO/R process are essentially the same as those developed through OD. Therefore, we urge an organization to start there unless there is a valid need for MBO/R techniques in the short-term situation. Given that need, the organization must also have the commitment to concurrently work at these process issues.

This all takes time. Short cuts can be dangerous. An attempt to fully implement a MBO/R program immediately usually causes organizational "indigestion." The OD-MBO/R model is useful here to remind us that there are other

---

[11]Levinson, Harry, *Management by Whose Objectives,* Harvard Business Review, July-August, 1970, pp. 125-134.

variables that must be coped with simultaneously. If any one variable, e.g. meaningful goals gets out of balance, there is trouble.

STARTING WITH OD

Starting with OD means starting with the development of process (how we work together) and interpersonal skills. In the OD-MBO/R model this would be starting at the interpersonal competence point. No effort would be aimed at improving problem-solving, and decision-making skills and developing the abilities to work in groups within the organization.

The OD approach should be a systemic approach rather than just a human relations orientation. A systemic approach is one focusing on the organization as a social system, e.g., more concern with how one function relates to another and to the total organization, or how the total organization interacts with its environment and how the organization copes with changing market and social conditions. This approach is more task oriented —working on activities like job enrichment, changing the organization structure and how people interact in solving problems—as compared with the human relations approach when the chief focus is on people and small groups.

When starting with OD, it should soon become evident that you will need goals. The first goal that should be set is what results do you wish to achieve with OD. Consequently, the meaningful goals variable in the model become necessary. In establishing the goal of the OD program, the goal setting process needs to be worked to achieve the level of commitment and resultant motivation to achieve the long term goals of OD.

As the training/consultative OD activities develop, the interpersonal skills, the growing need for objectives should become evident. Without objectives it may be difficult for the participants to receive feedback on their performance and thereby fulfill the need to achieve.

The MBO/R process may start gradually as the need for it becomes evident. It may start formally and may start in different ways at different times in various segments of the organization. It is a helpful system and has to be developed within the organization so that everyone understands how it works, how it can be controlled, changed and adapted to achieve organizational goals and personal goals at the same time.

VALUES AND NEEDS OF PEOPLE

Too often, organization development is looked upon as developing participation, team building and the like, emphasizing the more democratic style of leadership as opposed to the autocratic style. Often, we find that the autocratic style is only viewed as theory X management and, therefore, "bad."

Clare Graves found in the research for his concept of levels of human existence that individuals at different psychological levels had different value systems, and needed and wanted different styles of leadership.[12] In other words some people preferred a more directive—"autocratic"—style, whereas others preferred a participative style. Some wanted more than just participation: they wanted a goal-oriented management style. In doing his research in work environments, he found that when individuals desiring a particular style of leadership were put with supervisors feeling comfortable with this style, there was a resultant increase in productivity. In other words, an individual desiring a "directive" leader can be just as frustrated with a leader forcing participation and involvement on

[12]*Clare W. Graves' Theory of Levels of Human Existence and Suggested Managerial Systems for Each Level,* Institute for Business and Community Development, University of Richmond, 1971.

him as the individual desiring participation being supervised by an autocratic supervisor.

It must be remembered that McGregor, in describing Theory Y assumptions, said "external control and threat of punishment are not the only means of getting them to work toward organization objectives."[13] Autocracy is a means and has a place in most organizations when used appropriately with individuals desiring direction. The sensitivity of a manager to the needs and values of his people is necessary in determining when, where and with whom a particular style of leadership is used.

Consequently, in an OD program, managers need to be developed so that they can manage in a way that meets the needs of the people, while at the same time satisfying the needs of the organization. MBO/R is a process that helps the manager achieve this integration of individual and organization needs so that both are satisfied. In using this system it will become evident that some people will want objectives set for them. If this is their need, this the manager will have to do, but frequently repeat the offer that he is willing at any time to explore their personal goals with them and negotiate with them on both their personal as well as the organization goals. This is, we believe, the true commitment to the personal growth process inherent in Theory Y *assumption* about the nature of man as a growing being.

It may be a while before some people will accept participation in the goal setting process. In some cases it may be a year or more, and in other cases it may never be accepted, depending on the particular individual's openness to change. The manager has to be patient and ready to change his leadership approach to an employee as that employee shows a desire for a different style.

TRAINER/CONSULTANT ROLE

There needs to be someone who is constantly keeping the organization's progress along the OD-MBO/R route in perspective. We believe this model will be helpful from a cognitive standpoint in keeping all of the variables in balance.

This trainer/consultant role is best handled by someone inside the organization who uses the services of outside consultants as needed to achieve a specific result. In all probability an outside consultant will be needed more in the early stages of the implementation process and less later as the internal OD manager or department develops the organization's competence. The internal trainer/consultant's role should be filled by an individual or individuals with high competency and should be placed high in the organization structure—outside the president's office is not too high.

Neither OD nor MBO/R is a panacea, of course. If they are implemented slowly, but deliberately, with objectives which you wish to achieve, the result can be increased satisfaction and achievement on the part of both management and labor. Furthermore, they can be and usually are very profitable; or in nonprofit organizations show an increase in results and greater cost effectiveness. They will go a long way toward making work fun!

[13]McGregor, Douglas, *The Human Side of Enterprise*, McGraw-Hill, 1960, p. 47.

21   Training Supervisors to Use Organizational Behavior Modification

Fred Luthans and David Lyman

The contingency theory of management as applied to leadership and organizational design has already been well validated, and in mental health and education, contingency-based behavior modification approaches are also being widely used. Largely overlooked, however, has been the potential of these concepts and principles in the overall management of human resources. This article points out how contingency management in general and behavior modification techniques in particular can be taught to and successfully employed by supervisors in managing workers in modern organizations.

The authors, along with Robert Ottemann, all of the University of Nebraska, recently completed a training program for a group of supervisors in a medium-size manufacturing plant. (There were ten foremen in the initial program; subsequently, 17 more first-line supervisors, five general foremen, and two plant managers went through it.) In ten weekly, 90-minute sessions, the trainers used a process, rather than a lecture, method to teach the supervisors how to use the principles of operant psychology/behavior modification in analyzing and solving human performance problems in their departments. This new contingency strategy for managing human resources is called organizational behavior modification, or O.B. Mod.

THE O.B. MOD. TRAINING PROGRAM

There are several identifiable steps in training supervisors to utilize O.B. Mod. effectively. Here we shall briefly summarize some of them and how they were actually implemented in the training program for the manufacturing plant.

Identifying Behavioral Events. The early sessions in the program were spent teaching the foremen to pinpoint employee problems in terms of observable, measurable behavioral events. This meant taking constructs such as attitudes or values and defining them in a manner that would allow them to be observed and measured. Initially, this was no small task, because the men spoke only of problem employees as having "bad attitudes" or being "unmotivated."

Measuring Frequencies of Behavior. After the supervisors were able to identify an employee's problem behavior, they were taught to keep records of how often and/or when this behavior occurred. Since it was often impossible to keep track of every instance, time sampling methods were worked out. For example, one foreman observed a particular employee twice an hour on a random basis. By observing their subordinates at random intervals, the foremen were able to get an overall picture, or baseline measure, of the

Reprinted by permission of the publisher from *Personnel*, September/October 1973, © 1973 by the AMACOM, a division of American Management Associations.

frequency and circumstance of the problem behavior.

Making Functional Analyses of Behavior. In addition to keeping records, the supervisors were shown how to observe the events immediately preceding a pinpointed behavior—its antecedents—and the events immediately following the behavior—its consequences. By observing these before-and-after circumstances, they were able to make a functional analysis of what cues, or stimuli, elicited the behavior and what kinds of things reinforced or maintained that behavior.

Developing Intervention Strategies. Once the foremen were able to analyze functionally, they were ready to devise strategies to encourage desirable behaviors and discourage undesirable behaviors. These intervention strategies took many forms, but the essential goal was to reinforce appropriate behaviors and extinguish inappropriate behaviors. Extinguishing meant ignoring or providing no gratifying consequence for an undesirable job behavior. To encourage desired behaviors, the foremen had to determine what sorts of events were reinforcing to their workers, often a trial-and-error process. When a reinforcer was found, the desired behavior often increased dramatically. Reinforcers that were found to be effective included social approval, additional responsibilities, rescheduling of breaks, job rotation, special housekeeping or safety duties, positive feedback, and more enjoyable tasks upon completion of less enjoyable tasks. All the reinforcers used in the program lay within the normal pattern of the organizational environment; no artificial or contrived reinforcers were necessary. (For cost-conscious management, this is one of the most persuasive aspects of the program.)

Converting to Positive Reinforcement. Adopting a positive, rather than punitive, reinforcement strategy at first was not easy for the foremen, because even though they all believed in reinforcement, punishment was a consequence they had traditionally resorted to in order to change behavior. The trainers stressed the point that punishment would, indeed, suppress unwanted behavior, but seldom permanently, and would often create counterproductive hostility and resentment toward the supervisor. Having adopted a positive reinforcement intervention strategy, the foremen implemented it on the job and recorded the results.

Understanding the Importance of Being Contingent. By keeping records the supervisors were able to compare the rate of behavior occurrence prior to the intervention strategy with the later rate. Not all of the foremen met with success in their first attempts, but by analyzing what happened in the training sessions and modifying their behavior or their strategies, all of them were eventually able to effect some change. This was a crucial learning step, for it dramatically showed the power of being contingent, the relationship between the worker's behavior and their own. The supervisors found that by setting up "if-then" contingencies with their people, they could effectively manage behaviors toward improved performance: *If* the worker evidenced certain desirable, productive behaviors, *then,* and only then, was he reinforced by the supervisor.

THE TRAINING EXPERIENCE: PRACTICING WHAT WAS PREACHED

Some familiar problems were encountered in the training program. At times, attendance was one of them, even though top management "highly recommended" the program. The noncompulsory attendance policy, plus daily "brush fires" to put out, worked against perfect attendance. And some of the supervisors didn't always complete their "homework" assignments (recording behaviors on the job), largely because of the minor crises and poor management of time. This problem lessened, however, when they learned better use of time sampling and were themselves reinforced when they began to see the results of record keeping. The trainers also helped alleviate this situation by paying attention to participants who had their data and, to a degree, ignoring those who had not carried out their assignments. Since the trainer was a source of social reinforcement, his ignoring those not prepared was a negative consequence and his attending to those who were was a positive consequence. In other words, the trainer himself was being contingent with the trainees. As a result, data collection improved.

Again, when the group discussion during a session was moving in a productive direction, the trainer would give his attention to those who were contributing; if they digressed, he would bring the verbal interaction back on track and ignore inappropriate comments. Thus, group participation was encouraged and reinforced during the sessions, while general conversation and banter were held to a minimum, so that each participant had a chance to make suggestions and provide alternatives or interpretations to the problem situations being discussed. Since those who made contributions experienced social reinforcement from the trainer, the foremen came to understand firsthand how O.B. Mod. might have an effect on their subordinates.

All in all, the training experience was very successful. Every supervisor in the program was able to improve the performance of at least one worker in his department, and most were able to effect change on the part of several workers. And these changes were reflected in the supervisors' effectiveness ratings, which were calculated daily. The foremen boosted their individual effectiveness ratings at least 5 percent, an increase that represented a considerable cost saving to the company. In general, the foremen reported that the training they received was very useful and that they would continue using the O.B. Mod. techniques learned in the program.

EVALUATION OF AN O.B. MOD. APPROACH

A program to train supervisors to be contingency managers offers several advantages. It also has its problems, but let's consider the advantages first.

This approach deals only with behaviors that can be tied to job performance. Unlike training programs that attempt to change vaguely defined internal states of employee attitudes and values, this program precisely measures whether or not an observable job behavior of an employee has been changed. The measures may take the form of units produced, tasks completed, orders filled, or even the number of words typed. When a daily performance record is kept, a change in the rate of behavior change becomes immediately apparent. This feedback is continuous and can be used as a learning device and source of reinforcement. Thus, performance feedback is one of the biggest pluses of O.B. Mod.

A second advantage of O.B. Mod. supervisory training is the assumption that if an employee cannot currently perform a particular task, he can be taught to do it. Of course, this does not imply that employees can perform *all* jobs in the organization; it would be foolish to expect key punchers to solve engineering types of problems or personnel managers to take on maintenance of machines. On the other hand, through the process of shaping behaviors, where successive approximations of desired behaviors are selectively reinforced, new behaviors can be effectively learned and maintained and the job can be enlarged in scope, or the employee can be moved to a more demanding one.

A third advantage is that O.B. Mod. is an effective means of altering organizational environments to prevent or solve employee behavioral problems. This entails altering some behaviors in the environment, including those of supervisors, to maintain others. It is unrealistic to assume that as a result of several traditional human relations training sessions supervisors are going to change their ways; changes in supervisory behavior will come about only when the actual job environment changes, and the O.B. Mod. approach is meant to do just that—alter environmental situations to allow and encourage people to perform in a more productive manner.

Perhaps the most important advantage of O.B. Mod. is that it is based on a rational, scientific methodology. It requires the collection and analysis of data, decision making on the basis of the data, implementation of the decisions on the job, and assessment of results. More specifically, this means pinpointing problem behavioral events, observing and recording the frequency of this behavior, carrying out a functional analysis by examining antecedents and consequences of the behavior, devising an intervention strategy utilizing positive reinforcers, implementing the strategy in practice by being contingent, and observing and measuring the results. These O.B. Mod. techniques for managing human resources lead in no haphazard way to improved performance and greater satisfaction.

Now we come to the problems and criticisms that an O.B. Mod. training program is likely to run into.

Probably the most frequently encountered reason for reluctance to use the approach has to do with manipulation of people. Critics contend that changing behavior in this way is "using" people, making them do things against their will, or perhaps even exploiting them. What the critics overlook is not only that control of behavior is inevitable, but that it can be desirable. When a job requires a person to wear a suit and tie (formally or informally), the job is controlling certain behaviors. Schedules, time clocks, appointments, and even daily memos are only a few of the everyday controls found in all organizations. The O.B. Mod. approach is merely a systematic way of changing behaviors so that desirable, productive behaviors occur more often, as they are systematically reinforced. Indeed, the person whose behavior is being changed is "manipulating" the behavior of the modifier, too. One is reminded of the old cartoon about the rat in the Skinner box, with the caption reading, "I really have the experimenter conditioned. Every time I push the bar he gives me a reward." The accusation of manipulation can be countered by a clear explanation of the content and purpose of O.B. Mod.

Another negative element is the complexity of the modern organizational environment. Unlike a research laboratory, mental hospital, or classroom where behavior modification has been successfully carried out with experimental subjects, patients, and children, a manufacturing plant or business office has many distractions that can disrupt the use of any technique. During a typical day in a business organization, there are phone calls, hastily called meetings, special orders, machinery breakdowns, to name but a few of the noncontrollable events that occur. An O.B. Mod. approach must be able to try to deal with these events so that the intervention strategy being employed is not damaged or misleading. To write off the business organization as being too complex an environment does not seem justified.

A third obstacle to overcome is plain, old resistance to change. Managers —and training directors—are naturally hesitant about launching new techniques that they do not completely understand. In this case, they should spend as much time as is needed to find out what O.B. Mod. is based on, what it can and cannot do, how it can and cannot be used, and how long it would take to get it going in a supervisory training program of their own. This and subsequent articles should be useful in this respect and in breaking down resistance to change. The authors and their associates in the department of management at the University of Nebraska are actively involved in expanding the theory, research, and practice of O.B. Mod.

IMPLICATIONS OF O. B. MOD. FOR THE FUTURE

As modern organizations become more automated and productivity-conscious, workers seem to become more dissatisfied, and some, apparently, deliberately do not perform anywhere near their potential. The experience of the Vega plant at Lordstown, Ohio is an extreme case in point, but every day newspapers, television specials, and formal and informal discussions focus on the management (or mismanagement) of human resources vis-à-vis the productivity concern. To turn the trend around, or even turn it in another direction, managers of all organizations must look to new approaches. One thing they can do immediately is provide a more reinforcing organizational climate for their employees.

There are many reinforcers readily available to any supervisor. The tried-and-true pat on the back for a job well done is one, but it soon gets to be old-hat to an employee, and other means of reinforcement must be found. Money is definitely a reinforcer, but it is unrealistic to propose that every time a worker does a good job he should get a monetary reward. It is necessary, then, for supervisors to make better use of the reinforcers that are already at hand on the job. Through O.B. Mod. supervisors can be taught how to be contingency managers. If they understand that behavior depends on its consequences and if, on this premise, they utilize the steps of O.B. Mod. to change behaviors, they should be able to manage their human resources more effectively, with lower cost to the company and greater satisfaction to its employees.

There is no reason that O.B. Mod. should not work just as well with personnel in other situations as it did with workers in the plant we have talked about. Actually, applications of O.B. Mod. seem limited only by the creativity and ingenuity of those who study it and recognize the capacity of contingency management to direct human effort toward, instead of away from, organizational objectives.

SECTION D

Social Responsibility

Business has many responsibilities. It must provide a fair wage to its workers, a fair return on investment to its owners and a good product or service to its customers while being responsive to the needs of the general community. In recent years, the community has received a great deal of emphasis as people have begun asking, what is business' social responsibility? The answer, of course, is going to depend on the company. Some firms have greater social power than others, so they must assume greater social responsibility. One thing, however, is clear. Today the public is demanding that business assume a social-responsibility role. The articles in this section were chosen for the purpose of presenting a picture of some of the major variables that management must consider when fashioning its social-responsibility strategy.

The first article, by Michael Mazis and Robert Green, describes a number of social factors that concern businessmen. These include consumer interests, pollution and general economic conditions. The authors illustrate the ways in which firms tend to deal with these social issues, including the ad hoc and permanent committee. They feel, however, that the present approaches to dealing with social problems are just not sufficient. As a result, a new structure called a "department of social affairs," which would forecast as well as react to social needs, is suggested. The authors describe this department as a viable alternative to the current methods of dealing with social problems.

The second article, by Mildred Buzenberg, examines a problem currently receiving a great deal of attention, namely, the lack of women in management. In particular, Ms. Buzenberg attempts to explore some of the mythical stereotypes of women such as women are content with intellectually undemanding jobs; women work for pin money; women have a higher turnover rate and a higher absentee rate than men; and women are not emotionally capable of management. Since these stereotypes are based on myth and not fact, the author points out that the only way to explode them is to employ more women as managers. As this is done, it will become evident that business has been overlooking a major pool of managerial manpower—its women.

The final article in this section deals with business and ecology, a subject that has been the center of much controversy. In this selection, Ms. Hazel Henderson reviews a group of books which provides an indepth look at this area. In addition, she discusses the implications of this ecology-economist controversy as it relates to both businessmen and the economy as a whole. As she notes in her article, "Any assault on economics, sooner or later, is an assault on the mandate of corporations, and it behooves management to understand the rational basis of the ecologists' criticisms."

22   Implementing Social Responsibility

Michael Mazis and Robert Green

In the past few years businessmen have become increasingly aware that they have social responsibilities which should be considered in the operations of their firms. This message has been propagated by business leaders such as George Champion[1] and Henry Ford,[2] high ranking government officials,[3] and myriad critics which include radical political groups and social crusaders. The recurring theme of these messages is that business, as a social institution, cannot operate solely in its own interests, but also must consider the interests of the society in which it functions.

Some of these societal interests consist of areas in which business is directly involved. For instance, business is told that it must be cognizant of the interests of the consumer in the formulation of marketing policies. The spokesmen for consumers, spearheaded by Ralph Nader, have become some of business' most constant critics in the drive to make business more responsive to its immediate environment. A second environmental element with which business is directly involved is pollution. As one of the primary polluters of the environment, business is expected to work in the interests of the larger soci-

[1] George Champion, "Private Enterprise and Public Responsibility in a Free Economy," *Conference Board Record,* June 1966, pp. 18-22.

[2] Henry Ford II, "The Hidden Revolution," a speech delivered at the 21st Los Angeles Regional Brotherhood Testimonial Dinner of the National Conference of Christians and Jews, Los Angeles, California, June 5, 1969.

[3] Maurice Stans, "Business Involvement in Helping to Solve Our Great Social Problems," a speech given before the 38th International Conference of Financial Executives Institute, Chicago, Illinois, October 2, 1969.

Michael Mazis and Robert Green, "Implementing Social Responsibility," pp. 68-76, *MSU Business Topics,* Winter 1971. Reprinted by permission of the publisher, Division of Research, Graduate School of Business Administration, Michigan State University.

ety to "un-pollute" both its products and production methods. Much the same is true in the case of the conservation of our natural resources.

The idea of the social responsibility of business goes further than concern over only those issues or areas in which business is an active participant. It is said to involve other elements where current business involvement is, at best, indirect. The most obvious examples are the intertwined issues of the economic advancement of minority groups and urban redevelopment. In general, it cannot be said that business has been a primary cause of the present state of minorities or the cities, but it appears to be widely accepted that business does have a major responsibility to participate actively in the solution of these problems. A more recent issue which falls into this category is the relationship of business and crime; one executive recently has expounded the view that business has a definite responsibility in the battle against crime.[4]

Actually, the current fervor over the social responsibility of business is not a new issue to most firms. Companies always have been concerned about serving the communities in which they are located, and the idea of conservation of natural resources has been an issue facing business since the time of Theodore Roosevelt. Furthermore, appeals for social responsibility have been made for several years in areas such as the hiring of the handicapped and ex-convicts.

However, today's demands for environmental concern can be differentiated from those of the past by their scope, magnitude, and the manner in which the demands are made. Today, business is confronted with a varied set of social demands which are primarily national rather than local in scope. Furthermore, previous business concern for its environment was consi-

dered to be completely voluntary, and, when actions were taken, they were viewed as being highly benevolent. Now, similar actions are regarded as requirements and the firm which is not active in social affairs is looked upon as misanthropic.

In addition to these differentiating factors is the fact that today business is facing coercion, both overt and covert, to become socially concerned. The most obvious coercive instrument has been the government, which has become increasingly vigilant in the areas of consumer protection and pollution control. Other forces at work include influential interest groups such as consumer groups and local committees of black citizens, which attempt to change business behavior in some manner. Finally, there are other, more subtle, pressures being applied to business. The one which probably has received the most publicity has been the rejection of business careers by growing numbers of college students. This has occurred for a number of reasons, but major among them have been the charge that business lacks social values and the concomitant view of the corporation as a social parasite.

It is possible to argue the validity of these issues and the degree to which business should become involved. Debates of this nature have been raging for the last few years with no consensus in sight. However, quite aside from these normative considerations is the practical fact that these social issues are having a direct impact upon business. When problems have arisen, they generally have demanded some response on the part of the firms involved. Whether because of an accusation by Nader, a riot in the city where the firm has facilities, or an indictment by the federal government, business has been forced to react. A hardly profound prophecy would be that the demands for environmental concern on the part of business are likely to continue to intensify rather than to recede.

---

[4] "Business Has a Responsibility in the Battle Against Crime," *Steel*, 7 July 1969, p. 38.

RESPONSES TO SOCIAL PRESSURES AND PROBLEMS

The manner in which to respond to social pressures appears to be a major problem to most businesses. To date, a variety of approaches have been taken, with different degrees of success. These responses can be categorized into three classifications which permit analysis and evaluation: the task force approach, the permanent committee, and the permanent organization structure.

Apparently, the most common approach in dealing with social problems is to establish a temporary task force of top executives to deal with a critical issue when it arises. Usually, such action is prompted by a specific event, such as a riot or an accusation that the firm is polluting the environment. The common course of these committees is to adopt certain policies relevant to the immediate issue and to delegate their implementation to middle management. The task force then disbands or disintegrates when the problem begins to appear less critical. This approach was taken by Kodak when pressed to hire and train several hundred unemployables in 1966.[5]

While a response of this nature typically is well intended, many problems exist which negate its effectiveness as a tool for dealing with social issues. One major drawback of this method is that it only deals with social problems as they arise. The firm is placed in the position of "fire-fighting" or operating under crisis conditions and is unable to anticipate future areas of concern. As a result, the committee does not have sufficient time to study a problem or formulate viable solutions, and the decisions emanating from it often are not optimal. From the standpoint of those making the demands, the hasty formation of an ad hoc committee may appear to be an insincere effort at appeasement. In most cases, social concern on a broad scale among the executive elite has been lacking for decades,[6] and it is assumed that any current actions are taken only because of coercion. Because there is doubt about the genuine concern of a committee of executives, mistrust and hostility result.

Another problem with the task force approach concerns the capability of top executives to cope directly with social problems. Most managers do not have the time or expertise to deal with current problem areas. This is not to say that the role of top management is unimportant in the firm's social course. However, the specific environmental problems with which the firm is faced generally are extraordinarily complex and incapable of being understood in the relatively short period of time in which management has to act. Furthermore, the executive's lack of time intensifies management's inability to deal with social problems.

A third drawback to executive task forces is the lack of established channels of communication between executives and those lower-level managers charged with making the committee's decisions operational. A poor communications flow has the potential consequences of increased distrust and hostility between the firm and the groups pressuring it. This situation occurred at Kodak where the top management committee delegated bargaining powers to an assistant vice-president without clearly spelling out its position. When the bargainer signed an agreement which was unacceptable to the committee, Kodak reneged on the agreement, an action which fostered a period of ill will and unfavorable publicity for the company.

[5] "Fight That Swirls Around Eastman Kodak," *Business Week,* 29 April 1967, pp. 38-41.

[6] Theodore Levitt, "Why Business Always Loses," *Harvard Business Review,* March-April 1968, pp. 81-89.

THE PERMANENT COMMITTEE

The ad hoc top echelon committee is not highly functional, but a variation of this approach, with which some firms have claimed a measure of success, is the permanent committee of senior officers supported by a full-time staff. This mechanism, used by John Hancock to cope with its problems,[7] overcomes some of the problems of the ad hoc committee. The major improvements offered by this arrangement are the level of expertise brought to bear on the problems and the likelihood of establishing better channels of communication. Expertise develops primarily from the fact that there is a group, the committee's staff, which is solely devoted to understanding and dealing with these problems. Given a permanent position in the organization, the group is likely to develop efficient channels of communication to the rest of the firm.

Several difficulties still remain. Permanent committees also tend to continue to be firefighters, dealing with problems only as they arise. This is largely because the staffs which advise the committees generally are of minimal size, and because these staffs are incapable of acting except through the committees. It is doubtful that such high level committees would meet except in response to a pressing problem. The issue discussed in relation to the ad hoc committees, that of direct top management participation in a firm's social responsibility programs, again is raised. Undoubtedly, the enthusiastic backing of management is necessary if the firm is to be active in social affairs, but other responsibilities and a lack of expertise severely constrain top management's potential contribution. The utility of their direct participation is highly in doubt.

MORE ADVANCED MECHANISMS

Perhaps in response to the problems of top management participation, many firms have gone one step further in their social responsibility program and have instituted a permanent individual or device to handle recurring social problems in a specific area. For example, James Patterson suggests a Customer Review Board composed of consumers which would evaluate the firm's products, supposedly from the standpoint of consumer interests.[8] By maintaining constant contact with its customers, a firm would avoid inciting their wrath and indignation. E. B. Weiss suggests that firms create a vice-president of consumerism,[9] whose duties would be to present the consumer viewpoint to the firm and the firm's viewpoint to consumer groups, legislative committees, and others. Occupying a high rank within the organization, such a person would possess the authority to make his views felt in corporate decision making.

Similar suggestions have been made in regard to corporate devices to deal with urban problems. In fact, Jules Cohn discovered that several firms recently had incorporated an urban affairs group into their structures. The status and responsibilities of these groups varied considerably, ranging from a complete department to an advisory committee to a single individual. Urban affairs arrangements of these types were found in fifty-six of the 247 firms surveyed. They primarily were concerned with hiring the hard core unemployed, organizing and implementing programs to train and upgrade Negro workers, and, on occasion, participating in ghetto economic development programs.[10]

[8] James Patterson, "What Are the Social and Ethical Responsibilities of Marketing Executives," *Journal of Marketing*, July 1966, p. 15.

[9] E. B. Weiss, "Marketers Fiddle While Consumers Burn," *Harvard Business Review*, July-August 1968, p. 53.

[10] Jules Cohn, "Is Business Meeting the Challenge of Urban Affairs," *Harvard Business Review*, March-April 1970, pp. 68-82.

[7] Robert E. Slater, "An Industry Responds to Urban Problems," *The MBA*, February 1969, p. 32.

THE NEED FOR INTEGRATION

The formation of special departments to deal with certain types of social issues appears to be the most advanced formal status yet conceived for handling a firm's social responsibility issues. Although these departments overcome most of the drawbacks of the committee systems, such as those of time and expertise, they do not appear to be the best means of coping with social problems. These departments are capable of responding to and anticipating one type of problem, such as urban crises, but their very structure makes them incapable of dealing with other, equally important, social issues. There would be no serious difficulty if the various issues were independent of each other, but there is a great deal of interrelationship between most of them. Consumerism does not exist independent of the student revolt, and pollution is not separate from urban redevelopment—all these issues are intertwined.

Furthermore, while an urban affairs department or a department of consumerism may function efficiently to manage or guide corporate response to a specific set of problems, their focus is limited. For example, an urban affairs department often is organized as a result of continued demands by the black community for greater sensitivity to its views and by the government for a more integrated work force. While this organizational device is symbolic of the corporation's recognition of the recurring nature of an important social issue, it is only the first step in the process of enlarging the firm's capacity to respond to the social environment. Many other social problems, involving stockholders, consumers, ecologists, youth, education, foreign countries, government, charities, and others have consequences for the modern corporation.

After developing an organizational device to respond to one social problem, firms often discover that issues emerge which heretofore were considered insignificant. For instance, five years ago, beer and soft drinks companies never would have considered their products a controversial social problem; today there are massive advertising campaigns designed to assuage the critics of the disposable aluminum can. To cope with the changing nature of the environment it faces, the corporation needs a new organizational structure, which can anticipate as well as react to a variegated set of societal needs.

DEPARTMENT OF SOCIAL AFFAIRS

A possible answer may lie in the establishment of a department of social affairs. This department, with top management support and commitment, would function on the corporate level and assist operating divisions and departments in the formulation of plans to implement social responsibility programs. By taking a corporate view, the department would be in a position to assess company resources and market opportunities and design programs to maximize profits and social contributions. An important aspect of such a department is its interdisciplinary character. Representatives with marketing, manufacturing, finance, research and development, personnel, and legal experience would be supplemented by full-time individuals or consultants with expertise in problem areas such as ecology, urban affairs, and consumerism. This interacting body of individuals, working and discussing social concerns which affect the firm, could aid in anticipating the effect of future environmental developments.

A department of social affairs in its early stages probably would be organized on a functional basis and staffed by individuals knowledgeable about the major functions of the firm but still possessing sensitivity toward social affairs. The department would serve in a staff capacity to encourage line departments to set specific social goals and coordinate social programs so that all elements of the firm would function together to achieve social objectives. The major focus of the departmental members would be toward motivating the line managers to integrate social concerns into the planning process. Eventually, social affairs might become more important to the corporation and necessitate an expansion of the department. Sections of the department probably would become problem centered, and perhaps divisions of urban affairs, environmental affairs, and consumer affairs would develop. However, since social problems are dynamic in nature, it is ex-

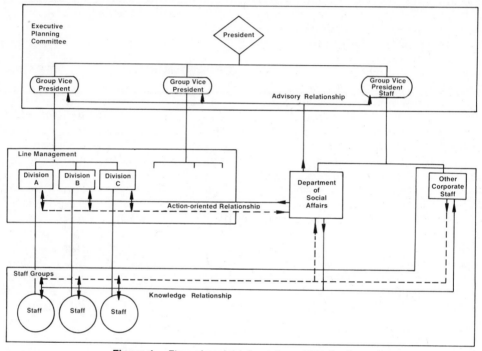

Figure 1. Flow of social information within the firm.

Interfaces of Department of Social Affairs
Advisory Relationship—Top Executive Committee
Input from department of social affairs:
—recommendations of social objectives and goals
—evaluations of social consequences of corporate actions
—information on social affairs
—report on firm's social performance

Action-Oriented Relationship—Line Groups (day-to-day working relationship)
Input from department of social affairs:
—information on social affairs
—social audit
—assistance in information to formulate programs to meet social goals
—aid in design of programs to monitor social aspects of operations (consumer re-

view board, ecological testing, pollution control, community participation)
Output to department of social affairs:
—dissemination of programs to department
—social performance plans

Knowledge Relationship—Staff Groups (two-way flow of information)
Input from department of social affairs:
—information on social affairs
—advice to staff groups on desirable social actions
Output to department of social affairs:
—notification of department about staff efforts which could affect social affairs
—dissemination of information which may have social consequences
—performance of special projects (market research, financial analysis, and so forth) for department

tremely important to have a group of experts continually assessing the environment to anticipate new areas of concern. These individuals would function in a manner similar to new product researchers by evaluating the external forces which could affect the firm and discovering new ways to capitalize on those changes.

A department of social affairs would serve the firm's need for a flexible organizational structure to aid in the adaptation of the firm to society's changing expectations of business. The department could perform several functions which the previous single orientation departments or crisis management techniques could not. First the department of social affairs could develop a system for processing information concerning the environmental forces which might influence corporate activity. Second, the department could help the firm plan realistic responses which would result in a congruity between long-term profits and benefits to society. The interjection of social concerns into the planning process necessitates recognizing corporate social objectives, setting social goals, and establishing a control mechanism for measuring social performance. Figure 1 illustrates how the department of social affairs might accomplish these functions and explains the interrelationship with other elements of the firm.

SOCIAL AFFAIRS INFORMATION REPOSITORY

As social responsibility issues have become more critical to the firm's operations, managers increasingly have found difficulty in gathering information; typically, a manager is forced to react to a situation with inadequate preparation. Several informational problems can be identified:

Most Social Affairs Information is not Recognized by Management. Since line managers generally are concerned with meeting sales or production goals, they usually are unaware of the social consequences of their decisions and the possibility of actions which may have social as well as profitable benefits. Most managers selectively view the environment from insulated perspectives, which is reinforced by the corporation's stress on profits.

Social Information is not Received on a Systematic Basis. Information which is received usually results from some group placing demands at the corporation's doorstep. What is needed is an orderly and continuous flow of social responsibility information from external sources.

Social Information Received by One Individual in the Firm Rarely is Transmitted to Other Individuals. Three explanations may account for this state of affairs. First, no formal mechanism exists for processing social information. Second, managers have not considered this information essential to the firm's operations. Rather, social problems and the information about these problems have been viewed as a nuisance to normal corporate functioning. Third, the meager amount of information transmitted often is distorted as a result of continual encoding and decoding. In addition, social problems, which often are emotionally laden, sometimes are distorted due to a great amount of ego-involvement. In today's environment, social information no longer can be ignored. A systematic procedure for collecting and transmitting social information within the firm also is needed.

The Accuracy of Social Affairs Information, Coming from Diverse Sources, Often is Questioned. Under this cloud of suspicion, managers cannot be expected to use such information as a basis for decisions. Expertise is clearly needed to evaluate the source and content of the information. A department of social affairs is designed, in part, to correct the aforementioned impediments to the systematic flow of social information.

With one central processing unit, social data can be collected, analyzed, and disseminated as an interacting body of information, a system which can be managed to facilitate consideration of social concerns in the planning process (see Figure 2).

The gathering of social information requires great sensitivity on the part of the department. Individuals involved in the collection phase must be oriented principally to the external environment, but with an awareness of company operations. In addition, finely tuned communication channels must exist for internal transmission of information within the firm. Personnel managing this information flow must possess great sensitivity to people in the firm.

The analysis of social information consists of validating, screening, and synthesizing. Validation of social inputs requires expertise and experience in evaluating external events, screening and synthesis demand greater awareness of the corporate decision processes since social information must be abstracted and prepared for transmission to management. The dissemination phase is the most critical aspect of the department's information processing activities. Social developments must be transmitted to the proper individuals in the firm in manageable form; if too much data is received, much that is important will be overlooked.

While it is important to have a continuing source of social information, the firm ultimately should strive to actually integrate social concerns into the planning process. In this way, the company will be able to plan for recurring environmental problems rather than have to deal with them after they have reached the crisis stage. Social affairs then can be considered on a routine basis like sales or production goals. This integration means that the firm should formulate overall corporate social objectives. In other words, it needs to recognize societal concerns in its corporate mission and philosophy.

Many firms already have included

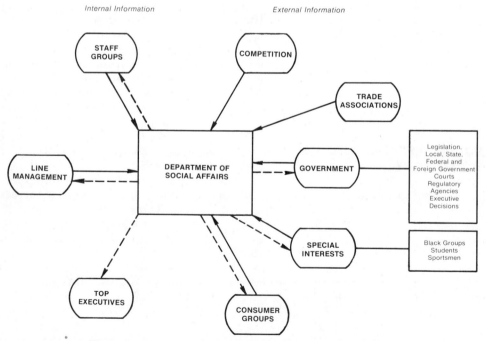

Figure 2. Informational interfaces of social affairs department.

social goals in their statements of corporate purpose. For example, General Electric has specified that its corporate objectives include "a greater social content" by bringing its technological strengths to bear on urgent problems of society.[11] Ford has defined four "challenges" which will be prominent in the firm's thinking in the 1970s: reduction of environmental pollution, provision of full equality of opportunity for minority groups, reaction to consumerism, and creation of safer automobiles.[12]

While statements of social objectives are important, they only can establish direction for the firm. Specific social goals, which are specific in the sense that they are to be obtained by the firm over the planning period, are useful for guiding corporate activity. In the past, firms always have set specific goals, such as return on investment, sales increases, market share, and so forth, but rarely have set similar social goals. Pfizer is one company, however, which has established an overall corporate goal: 12 percent of its work force in 1969 was to be from minority groups.[13] Top management also should charge the line functions and divisions with setting a series of goals throughout the hierarchy which will lead to the achievement of overall corporate social goals.

Once corporate objectives are defined and specific goals are set, a firm should establish targets or standards of social performance for each of its departments in much the same way sales or profit targets are assigned. A program for achieving these targets should be developed and a system for measuring actual results, comparing results against targets, reporting deviations, and taking corrective action also should be established. In this way a company can be said to be controlling social performance.

Control of social performance is the key to truly integrating social concerns into corporate functioning. If there is no control mechanism, social affairs will not be taken seriously by line management. No matter how well intentioned line management may be, they always will place objectives they are held accountable for ahead of social goals. To encourage accountability for social goals, top management must examine performance which deviates from them and base rewards on social performance as well as on the traditional indices of competence.

The department of social affairs, which would serve as a full-time monitor of the environment, could play a major role in integrating environmental affairs into the corporate planning process. With its understanding of both the environment and the firm, it would be able to recognize salient issues and opportunities for corporate action and could interpret social happenings and aid top management in establishing social objectives. Lower levels of management also must set social goals which are consistent with overall corporate goals. The department of social affairs could supply information to these managers to assist them in this process, and once targets for social performance are set, the department could collect information about the social effects of corporate programs. It then would report the performance of the firm to top management and would note any significant deviations from goals.

BENEFITS FROM A DEPARTMENT OF SOCIAL AFFAIRS

A department of social affairs could benefit a firm in several ways, some of which are enumerated below. A department of social affairs would be an integrative department which could deal critically with the interacting nature of social problems. Since environ-

[11] General Electric Company, *Annual Report* (1968), p. 5.
[12] Ford Motor Company, *Annual Report* (1969), p. 3.
[13] Charles Pfizer, *Annual Report* (1969), p. 7.

mental issues often affect many functional areas of the firm, the department could aid in assigning responsibilities to specific departments. Actions by various elements of the firm may conflict and retard positive action. For example, while a personnel department may be desirous of infusing the firm with black employees at all levels, certain areas may be better served through black consultants. A coordinated program is needed to assess the needs of the functional departments and the personnel available to meet these needs. Many personnel departments are infused with a unidimensional view since they are under pressure to hire more blacks and often do not have the responsibility to deal with the larger problem. Compounding this dilemma, the firm may seek to encourage black-owned business or subsidiaries to meet black needs. Responsibility for these actions often is housed in finance, manufacturing, or a new department. Both internal and external responses may be employed exclusively or simultaneously, but rarely does the firm make a thorough review of the alternatives and undertake the action which will enhance long-term corporate profitability and societal growth as well. A department of social affairs would promote the development of a planned, integrated approach to handling social issues which confront the firm.

An integrative department of this nature would provide tangible evidence to middle management that top management has a serious desire to meet social commitments on a recurring basis. A new department, placed in a meaningful position in the corporate hierarchy and staffed by well-paid key performers, could give social performance a prominent position in the firm's actions.

A new department concerned with the humanistic aspects of corporate activity would be far more flexible to changes in the external environment. An environmental sensitivity and formal information processing capability could be developed which could be useful to all divisions of the organization. If such information was integrated with other, profit-oriented information, it could serve as the basis for injecting social concerns into the planning process. Only when social concerns are integrated into the planning process will consistent corporate action result.

A department of social affairs also would serve to warn a firm against any actions which could have negative social consequences. The societal implications of major corporate decisions would be considered rationally as a result of evaluations supplied by an informed body of individuals.

Finally, as a result of its interdisciplinary character, with knowledge of corporate activity, and possessing social sensitivity, a department of social affairs could specify profitable social actions. For example, the lumber industry's policy of promoting conservation of resources falls into the dual maximization realm. Walgreen Drug Stores' promotion of "child-proof" medicine bottles is useful to society and the corporation as well. The recent advertising campaigns by several beer companies to reduce the pollution of our highways is likely to benefit the firms by possibly forestalling legislation affecting the disposable can and the advertising may help the pollution problem in some small measure.[14]

This is not to say that all social actions must have a direct payoff to the firm, but many actions may aid society and benefit the firm as well. There is no reason for the firm not to cultivate profitable social activities. As Henry Ford II has stated, there is "the growing understanding that the profit motive is not an antisocial force acting against community interest, but a very practical reason why business should help solve the social as well as the economic problems which beset our nation."[15]

---

[14] See *Time* 24 August, p. 37, for an account of the Bowie, Maryland, ordinance prohibiting the sale of nonreturnable containers.

[15] Henry Ford II, "The Hidden Revolution."

23 Women in Management— Good Business in the 1970's

Mildred E. Buzenberg

WOMEN ARE AN UNDERUTILIZED RESOURCE

An increasing number of large businesses are changing their policies toward women in management. Title VII of the Civil Rights Act made discrimination illegal and more recently the revised U.S. Department of Labor Order #4 requiring affirmative action programs by all government contractors made changing policies the expedient thing to do, but more than that; it is good business. A chief executive of one of the largest U.S. corporations said recently, "In the decades ahead any organization which ignores or underestimates the potential of women—or overlooks any source of talent for that matter—will be making a fatal mistake."[1]

Arch Patton, Director of McKinsey & Co. predicted that the low birthrate of the 1930's will cause 1974 to be the lowest point in what has been a steady decrease in the number of men in the 35–45 age group. This age group provides most of the departmental and functional heads in the average company.[2] This shortage can be avoided or eliminated by firms alert enough to hire or promote women into management positions.

Now in the 1970's a growing women's movement is demanding equal treatment in employment practices. The impact of this movement is reflected in the following directive distributed to all managers of the General Electric Corporations.

This movement is not a fad or an aberration, but a major social force with great and growing impact on business and other social, political, and economic institutions. As such, it must be taken seriously by business managers; its future potential must be foreseen and constructive responses must be designed to meet legitimate demands.[3]

This paper will focus on the myths which keep women out of management positions, refuting them with facts, in the hope that this information will encourage employers to re-examine their own preconceptions and thus develop hiring and promotional practices which will benefit both women and business. Women have the ability and training to handle management jobs and to limit them to low level positions is wasting our country's resources.

MORE WOMEN ARE AVAILABLE AND QUALIFIED FOR MANAGEMENT JOBS

Between 1947 and 1968 the number of women in the work force increased dramatically. Figure 1 shows by index number the relative growth of the labor

---

[1] Barbara M. Boyle. Equal Opportunity for Women is Smart Business., *Harvard Business Review,* May-June, 1973, p. 85.

[2] Rosalind Loring and Theodora Wells, *Breakthrough: Woman into Management,* 1972, p. 34.

[3] *Op. cit.:* Boyle.

---

force by sex. This represents a 75% increase (from 16.7 to 29.2 million) while the number of men increased only 16% (from 42.7 to 49.5 million). Since 1968 this trend has accelerated, demonstrated by the fact that by 1970 over 31 million women were working, representing about 40% of the total civilian work force. Furthermore, it is estimated that between 1970 and 1980 the female labor force will increase by about 6 million.

Not only is it possible to hire more women at all levels of employment, but more women are becoming educated and rapidly gaining the training to make them valuable as managers. Perhaps nothing documents this more dramatically than the statistics on educational achievement. Today there are about 15 million females who have had at least some college training—which is more than twice as many as two decades ago. Figure 2 shows women with a College education by age, for three years; 1950, 1972, and 1980. The average American woman today is far better trained than her mother. For example,

some 30% of all females 25–29 have continued their education beyond the high school level, but among those 45–64 the comparable figure is 17%. The educational level of the males has also increased during this time span, but there are indications that the educational gap between men and women is narrowing. In 1960, of all persons 25–29 with a college degree only 36% were females, but by 1970 the proportion had grown to 40%, and based on recent trends in college enrollment it is projected to reach almost 45% by 1980.[4]

These national figures are reflected in the experience of Kansas State University. Not only is the proportion of women to men enrolled in the University increasing but the College of Business Administration has experienced a dramatic increase in the number of women students enrolling in Management, Accounting and other profes-

[4] Fabian Linden. Women a Demographic, Social and Economic Presentation. Published 1972 by the CBS Broadcast Group, pg. 19.

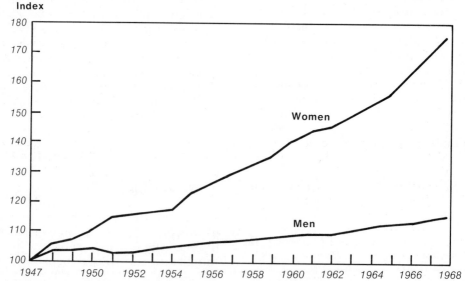

Figure 1. Relative growth of the labor force, by sex, 1947–68.* Index 1947 = 100. (From U.S. Department of Labor, Bureau of Labor Statistics.)

*Annual averages.

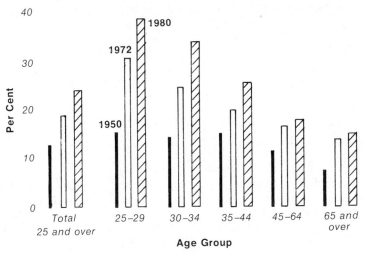

Figure 2. Women with a college education by age. Per cent each age group having any college. (From *Digest of Educational Statistics*, Office of Education, Department of Health, Education and Welfare.)

sional business courses. Between 1969 and 1973 the number of women enrolled in the College of Business increased by 89% (from 119 to 225) while the number of men enrolled in the College increased by 35% (from 728 to 984). The total number of women students majoring in Business Administration is still less than 20% (18.6%) but with dramatic increases like those of the last four years, we would expect to reach 30% by 1980 or before.

Although there are more women being educated for management today, they are not being employed in positions which fully utilize their capabilities and training. This fact was verified by a recent survey of women graduates from Kansas State University with Bachelor of Science degrees in Business Administration.

All women graduates with addresses on file who graduated between 1967 and 1972 were sent questionnaires. From the 71 questionnaires sent, 51 responses were received. In response to the inquiry about their employment status, 9 indicated they were full time homemakers. This represents 18% which is very low by national standards, and may be biased somewhat because

the mailing was unable to reach all women graduates. Nevertheless, it is a sign of the 1970's that 82% of these women reported they were working. They held a broad range of jobs from secretary (10 graduates) to Broker-Registered Representative. The salaries ranged from $200 per month to $2500 per month. The largest number were employed at jobs with the title of Accountant (14 graduates) and the most frequent income interval was $400 to $599 per month.

The measure of job level can be partially determined by the job title and the salary. By both measures many of the women graduates are employed where their education is not being used. They probably are capable of handling higher level positions, since their education has prepared them for the same kinds of jobs the men graduates hold. Tables 1 and 2 compare salaries and job titles of men and women graduates. The men graduates are a random sample drawn from the December '70, May '71 and May '72 graduating classes. Table 2 shows a random sample of job titles held by the men and women graduates who answered. These women have the same education as the

TABLE 1. STARTING SALARIES OF MEN AND WOMEN GRADUATES, COLLEGE OF BUSINESS ADMINISTRATION, KANSAS STATE UNIVERSITY, 1969–72

MONTHLY SALARY INTERVAL	48 WOMEN GRADUATES	48 MEN GRADUATES
$ 200–399	5	0
400–599	16	5
600–799	14	22
800–999	9	16
1000 and over	4	5
	48	48

men and in many cases their grade point averages are higher. This last fact is demonstrated by a study of the final grade point averages (G.P.A.) of the May, 1973 graduates from the College of Business Administration. Forty-two percent (6 out of 14) of the women graduates earned a cumulative G.P.A. above 3.3 while fourteen percent (19 out of 128) of the men did. Only one woman earned a grade point average below 2.4, while 31 or 24% of the men did. Employers may indeed be overlooking good executive talent when they hire these bright young women as secretaries and bookkeepers.

The women graduates were also asked, "Would you need to be a college graduate to hold your present position?" One-half of the respondees answered "No" to this question. Evidently they are underemployed by their own analysis and are undoubtedly employed in positions which a high school or business school graduate could fill. Giving these women access to positions where they can use their full education to help make business decisions is not only beneficial to the firm, but it is just plain good business to use fully the abilities of all employees.

In the last decade the number of working women has increased and society has generally accepted the working wife. In addition, women in positions of responsibility and authority are also being accepted. The women's movement has created an awareness of the possibilities of employing women in formerly all male occupations. Perhaps a customer or a salesman might be initially surprised by a woman sales executive, but if she does her job well, she will be accepted. An article in Sales Management magazine entitled *Women in Sales—Ms. is a Hit!* has this to say:

Top sales managers who have pioneered in employing women are finding that it pays to include females in jobs ranging from field representative to sales vice president. They believe that in the long run the recruitment of women will mean better hiring practices and more professional selling. . . .[5]

[5] Sally Scanlon, "Women in Sales—Ms. is a Hit.", *Sales Management*, February 5, 1973, p. 22.

TABLE 2. RANDOM SELECTION OF JOB TITLES HELD BY MALE AND FEMALE GRADUATES, 1969–72

FEMALES	MALES
Computer Programmer	Staff Accountant
Accounting Clerk	Internal Auditor
Assistant Credit Manager	Gamble Store Manager
Legal Secretary	Auditor
Office Manager	GMC Management Trainee
Cost Accountant	Tempo Store Management Trainee
Executive Secretary	Bell Telephone Installation Foreman
Accountant	Kroger Management Trainee
Secretary	H. O. Lee Co. Analyst
Staff Accountant	State of Kansas Financial Examiner

The article cites numerous examples of women in selling jobs, traveling jobs, and sales executive jobs. The women are quoted as well as their employers. One woman says, "I want what a man wants from a job: money, accomplishment, and challenge."

Men may accept a woman peer, but would they accept a woman in authority over them? Yardley of London's national sales manager, Bill Spiegelberger answers with an emphatic "yes".

"We've had no problems whatsoever with the men accepting Karen Hall." Hall became Cleveland District Sales Manager late last year after 2½ years on the force. "If any of the men resent her, that's their problem," he says. "None quit or asked for a transfer." Spiegelberger says he's delighted that women are now interested in sales careers. "Ten years ago, gals didn't apply for sales jobs," he says, "their current interest makes the labor pool a lot bigger, and that certainly makes my life a lot easier." [6]

EXPLODING THE MYTHICAL STEREOTYPES ABOUT WOMEN

Mythical Stereotype No. 1

Women are Content with Intellectually Undemanding Jobs. In the past, employers have not used women as executive talent. This oversight was accepted and approved, as long as society in general accepted the sexual stereotypes about women. The present generation is not accepting these stereotypes. As a matter of fact the young people today (and many not so young) are vehemently denying the sex-typed roles attached to both men and women.

Employers have said, "Women don't want positions of authority—they invest their energies in the roles of wife and mother and hence aren't interested in challenging work. They prefer not to

---

[6]Joan E. Crowley, et al., Seven Deadly Half Truths About Women, *Psychology Today,* March, 1973, p. 94.

think and make decisions." If this statement said "Some people don't want positions of authority," it might be closer to the truth. Undoubtedly, in our society there are both men and women who avoid positions of responsibility, but to apply this indiscriminately only to women and not to men is patently unfair.

A study made by Joan Crowley and others and reported in the March, 1973 *Psychology Today* proved the falsity of the undemanding job myth. The data was obtained through a nationwide probability sample of 539 working women and 933 working men. They determined which persons in the sample actually held intellectually demanding positions by asking them to rate their jobs according to such criteria as "requires that you keep having to learn new things," "requires that you do a lot of planning," and "allows you a lot of freedom and creativity." As expected, they found women were underrepresented in intellectually demanding jobs. Only 37% of the women indicated that they held such jobs in contrast to 55% of the men. They next asked all the workers how satisfied they were with their jobs, and, again women were less satisfied than men. But this sex difference disappeared when they controlled for the intellectual requirements of the work. Those who answered yes to the three questions above were equally satisfied with their jobs whether they were men or women. Women with college educations and working experience are just as unhappy with a dead-end job as a man with the same qualifications. Educated women enjoy intellectually stimulating jobs. Therefore, the fact that she is a woman does not justify passing her up for a position of responsibility.

Mythical Stereotype No. 2

Women Work for Pin Money. Many employers believe that women work not from necessity or career commitment, but because they want some pin money for a few extra luxuries.

There are two aspects to this myth. The first is that women don't need the money—their husbands provide the basics and they are working for the extras. The men's earnings are more critical—their need is greater. The other justification for the pin money myth is the claim that women's achievement is less so they naturally should be paid less.

There are data available to refute both these points. Information on family incomes indicate that a significant portion of the working women work out of real economic necessity. Of all working women, close to 40% are either over 25 and without husbands or are married to men who earn less than $5,000 annually. The pin money myth does not apply to them nor does it apply to the college educated woman who has spent four or more years and much money to prepare herself for a career. To her the salary she earns is a measure of her success on the job just as it is for the male employee. She "needs" the income as much as her husband "needs" his.

The most damaging aspect of the pin money myth is the belief that earnings should be based on an employer's concept of need rather than on merit or productivity. The economic system as we know it emphatically denies this concept. Employers pay male employees on the basis of their contribution to the business and almost never on need. If they mistakenly assume all women "work just for pin money" they will be less likely to pay an equal salary to a qualified woman who is capable of handling a job as well as a similarly qualified man.

The belief that women should be paid less because they achieve less is rationalized under the assumption that unequal pay is legitimate where there is unequal achievement. This assumes that when achievement is equal pay will be equal. Again data are available to show that this is not true. A study by the Survey Research Center of the University of Michigan concluded, "We have clear evidence that women *do not* receive pay and benefits commensurate with their achievement. They are far worse off than equally qualified men." [7] The study attempted to measure worker qualifications and performance that, according to the achievement ideology should legitimately be related to a person's income and quality of work. The six major factors measured were: 1) education, 2) tenure with one's employer, 3) tenure on one's specific job with that employer, 4) number of hours worked each week, 5) amount of responsibility for supervision and 6) occupational prestige. When these six factors were equal for a particular job classification for a man and a woman worker, the achievement was assumed to be equal and therefore based on the above assumption, the pay should have been equal. Their findings were that on the average the women workers actually earned $3,458 less than they should have, and the median woman would have to earn 71% more than her current salary to equal the income of a man with her achievement scores. It is obvious from this study that women are not currently being paid for their achievement.

Further support for this contention is found in Table 3 which shows the median income by occupation and sex in 1971. The median income of male full-time workers is $3,930 more than the median income of female full-time workers. This sex differential in income is due in large measure to the level of occupation of women compared to men. Table 3 shows that 39.3% of the full-time female labor force is engaged in clerical work while only 6.9% of full-time male labor force is clerical. The term clerical workers can include a large number of specific jobs, and apparently the males in this occupation hold the higher paying ones

---

[7] Teresa E. Levitin, et al., "A Woman is 58% of a Man," *Psychology Today*, March, 1973, p. 89.

TABLE 3. MEDIAN INCOME BY OCCUPATION AND SEX—1971. CIVILIAN YEAR-ROUND. FULL-TIME WORKERS*

Occupation	Median Income in Occupation	Male Median Income	Female Median Income	Per Cent of Full-time Male Labor Force	Per Cent of Full-time Female Labor Force	Female Workers as Per Cent of Occupation Group
Managers, Officials, and Proprietors	$12,192	$13,087	$6,970	15.8	6.4	14.6
Professional and Technical	11,395	12,842	8,515	15.7	18.6	33.4
Sales Workers	9,683	11,122	4,681	6.2	4.2	22.3
Craftsmen and Foremen	9,664	9,779	5,493	21.6	1.4	2.7
Operatives	7,274	8,069	4,884	17.7	13.9	25.0
Laborers (except farm)	6,932	7,063	4,486	4.8	.6	5.1
Clerical Workers	6,904	9,512	5,820	6.9	39.3	70.6
Service Workers	6,090	7,484	4,375	6.9	13.3	44.8
Farmers and Farm Managers	n.a.	4,915	n.a.	3.4	.2	2.2
Farm Workers	n.a.	3,806	n.a.	1.0	.3	10.8
Private Household Workers	n.a	n.a.	2,328	n.a.	1.7	n.a.
	n.a.	9,631	5,701	100.0	100.0	29.8

*Source: U.S. Department of Commerce. Bureau of the Census: Money Income in 1971 of Families and Persons in the U.S. Series, p. 60, No. 85.

because their median income is $9,512 compared to $5,820 median income for the females in the same occupation. This is the pattern for every occupation in the study.

Although this has been the pattern, employers should be aware that the bright young woman of today expects to earn the equivalent salary of a similarly qualified man today. If pay and position do not live up to her expectations, she will look elsewhere for employment, just as any bright young man would. If employers really need that person's talent, the pin money myth should be avoided. This is good business in the 1970's.

Mythical Stereotype No. 3

Women Have a Higher Turnover Rate and a Higher Absentee Rate Than Men. A U.S. Department of Labor comment says "Labor turnover rates are influenced more by the skill level of the job, the age of the worker, the worker's record of job stability and the worker's length of service with the employer than by sex." [8] If this is true

of the whole gamut of job levels it is even more true of management level jobs. Other labor department data show that voluntary "quit" rates for the sexes are not very different—2.2 per hundred male employees per month and 2.6 per hundred female employees per month in 1968. Furthermore, the labor department asserts that about one half of this quit rate differential is attributable to the greater concentration of women in occupations where quit rates for both men and women are above average. [9]

Despite data that refutes the myth of higher turnover rates for women, employers continue to believe that there is a greater risk in investing in on-the-job training for female workers. Employers in the past have refused to interview women graduates of the Kansas State University College of Business Administration because they said they didn't want to hire a woman only to have her get married and leave in a few months. In 1963 they may have had a justifiable argument. In 1973 it is not justifiable nor is it legal.

[8] Handbook on Women Workers, U.S. Department of Labor, Wage and Labor Standards Division, Women's Bureau Bulletin 249, 1969, p. 76.

[9] Barbara R. Bergman, "The Economics of Women's Liberation," in Economics: Mainstream Readings and Radical Critiques, ed. by David Mermelstein, 1973, p. 331.

The women graduates today are career motivated.

If marriage is in their plans it does not preclude a career. When both marriage partners are equally qualified by education for managerial level positions they no longer automatically assume the man's job is the more important. Books that are popular among the young people such as the *Two Career Family* by Lynda Holmstrom and *Open Marriage* by Nena O'Neill and George O'Neill express the new philosophy of career and marriage. The employer's concern should always be the potential contribution of the individual employee for this is how he maximizes the efficiency of his business. He may penalize himself and deprive his business of talent by operating under misconceptions and outdated premises of female behavior.

A corollary of the turnover myth is the belief that women have a higher absentee rate than men and therefore are less productive. As in the case of turnover rate, the statistical data do not support this contention.

Government research indicates that age, occupation and salary may be more important determinants of absenteeism than is sex. In 1967 men between the ages of 24 and 45 lost 4.4 days per year due to illness, while women in the same age bracket lost 5.6 days—a difference of but 1.2 days per year. In the 45 and over age bracket, female employees lost *fewer* working days due to illness than men, making the overall averages 5.3 days per year for men and 5.4 days per year for women.[10]

Another part of the absenteeism myth states that women will be absent more because of family responsibilities. This, too, is shown to be false by the facts. Labor Department data show that during an average week in 1971, 1.4% of women and 1.2% of men did not report to work for reasons other than

illness or vacation. This is a very slight difference. The myth that women are poor risks due to turnover and absenteeism became entrenched when women held only low level, uninteresting and low paying jobs. Women today in positions of responsibility have basically the same rate of absenteeism and turnover as men, therefore women should be as employable as men.

Mythical Stereotype No. 4

Women Are Not Emotionally Capable of Management. The myth that women are not emotionally capable of management is accepted by some women as well as men, and as long as both sexes in any business firmly believe this myth, for that organization it is *true*. No woman can become a manager or make managerial decisions as long as she is convinced she cannot. Where did this myth come from? It came out of the 19th century when the wealthy and would-be wealthy business tycoon liked their women delicate, ineffective and hobbled in bustles and high buttoned shoes. It became the fashion for women to faint easily, cry a lot and giggle nervously at any provocation. This was the fashion, it became the socially desirable way to act. People came to believe it was the inherent nature of women. A large portion of society today still accepts the 19th century stereotype.

At this same time in history, the woman on the farm was a different type of individual. In a paper presented at a conference entitled "Women's Challenge to Management," James W. Kuhn, Professor at the Graduate School of Business, Columbia University had this to say:

. . . through most of history woman's place has not been in the home, since the home as we know it today hardly existed. Even in agrarian America, which dominated all of the United States until the 1920's and some areas until World War II, women did not simply serve their husbands

---

[10] Mary Hamblin and Michael J. Prell, "The Incomes of Men and Women: Why do they Differ?" Federal Reserve Bank of Kansas City *Monthly Review*, April, 1973, p. 3.

and their children, tending the housekeeping chores, cooking meals, mending, and rearing children. They carried out those activities, but they did much more besides. They were *full* partners in the economic undertaking of the farm.

For example, they were the major suppliers of the family food . . . raising cash crops, preserving, tending and harvesting the garden, raising chickens, and selling produce. In fact, I came to the conclusion that the major portion of the family food came from women's work and effort. The wife on the farm helped not only in providing the food but also in various other farm routines: milking cows, harvesting fruit or vegetable crops and helping to pack them for the market, helping to manage harvest hands and to oversee their work, and acting as paymaster and foreman.

Later, when the families left the farm to move near the city or town, the wife was left with the children to tend for there was no new economically significant work to replace her accomplishments on the farm. The result is that the nation now has a large sector of the population, mostly women, who cannot easily find socially useful and satisfying employment.[11]

Are women emotionally capable of management? Some women are, (as

some men are) and men who have worked with career women attest to their effectiveness. Men who have worked only with women in subservient roles may see women as not capable of making the tough decisions of a manager, but this is not the experience documented by a study made by Dr. Eleanor B. Schwartz of Georgia State University.[12] She conducted a survey by sampling big businesses who have women in management jobs. Among other questions asked was the results of their experience in utilization of women in management. Table 4 shows the result.

Answers of yes to questions A, B, and C all seem to show women to be successful as managers. These answers represent 95% of the companies responding to the survey. The level of the management job held by women in these businesses is not specified and probably very few were top management jobs, but nevertheless if women are really not emotionally capable of management, as the stereotype claims, would 95% of them be designated good, very good, or excellent by their

[11] Eli Ginsberg and Alice M. Yohalen, editors, *Corporate Lib: Women's Challenge to Management,* 1973, p. 64.

[12] Eleanor B. Schwartz, *The Sex Barrier in Business,* 1971, p. 72.

TABLE 4. EXPERIENCE OF RESPONDEE COMPANIES IN UTILIZATION OF WOMEN IN MANAGEMENT

Statement Describing Experience	Businesses N	%
A. "Excellent. Women in general perform very well in management, often better than men."	2	2.5
B. "Very good. Women do a fine job—equal to men."	47	58.0
C. "Good. No real problems or complaints."	22	27.1
D. "Poor. Women just don't adjust to responsibilities of management."	4	4.9
E. Companies not responding to this question.	6	7.5

firms? It is obvious that the broad generalization about women's emotional inability to develop into good managers is badly in need of re-evaluation.

There are some women who are not capable of handling management jobs and who are not interested in having management jobs; there are also some men for whom this is also true. There are probably more women in this category because women have been socialized to believe that it is not in their nature to be leaders or to hold positions of responsibility. Education and the Women's Movement are changing this. Over 700 universities in the country are now offering courses developed specifically for women. Many of these courses directly or indirectly will encourage women to develop their full potential and no longer passively to accept societal and traditionally accepted behavior patterns. Some of these courses are aimed specifically at upgrading women's skills for management-type jobs.

As more women are hired for management positions, hopefully, the sexual stereotypes held by both men and women will disappear and eventually women will be accepted equally with men for their contribution to the business community. This will give women freedom to choose management as a career and the businesses that make use of this new source of management talent will be the beneficiaries.

24   Ecologists versus Economists

Hazel Henderson

All the talk of the "energy crisis," zero population growth, the need for a new "steady-state economy," the ecological limits to growth, and the inadequacy of the gross national product (GNP) as a measure of progress signals a growing debate between ecologists and economists. In the months ahead, businessmen will need more than a superficial familiarity with this debate, because it not only raises issues that question some very fundamental economic assumptions but also generates serious criticisms of corporations as allocators of resources.

In the United States, even ordinary citizens have become aware that, by and large, economists tend to ignore those social and environmental realities that do not fit their theoretical models. Economists also frequently avoid such issues as the distribution of wealth, accepting it as a given. And they perpetuate the classical concepts of the free market and the all-knowing, ever rational "homo economicus," ignoring ways in which these concepts are distorted by the wielding of power, the manipulation of information, the speed-up of technological change, and the human needs and motivations that lie beyond the marketplace.

In addition to this list of indictments, economists are embarrassed by the persistence of both unemployment and inflation that culminate in the need for wage and price controls. Arthur F. Burns, the chairman of the Federal Reserve Board, was prompted to note in July 1971: "The rules of economics are not working quite the way they used to." [1] And Milton Friedman was even more frank in his speech given at the American Economic Association's annual meeting in January 1972: "I believe that we economists in recent years have done vast harm—to society at large and our profession in particular—by claiming more than we can deliver." He added, "We have encouraged politicians to make extravagant promises which promote discontent with reasonably satisfactory results, because they fall short of the economists' promised land."

As these issues develop and the debate becomes more sophisticated, there will be a growing need for economists and ecologists to clarify their positions. Exaggerated, simplistic polemics between those environmentalists who cry for "halting economic growth" and those economists and businessmen who vilify environmentalists as "elitists who care nothing for the poor," previously characteristic of the debate, will no longer suffice.

My aim in this article is to review a group of books that provide a glimpse beneath the surface of such generalities and to discuss the implications of the ecology-economics controversy for businessmen and for the economy as a whole. First, I shall discuss a recent book by Carl H. Madden that assesses the current context of the debate and its meaning for corporations. Then I shall assess the key ecological, economic, and social issues that have been raised by various parties in this new controversy.

SETTING THE STAGE

Carl Madden, an economist, puts the issues in perspective in his insightful

new book, *Clash of Culture: Management in an Age of Changing Values*.[2] Madden finds the current argument over societal goals and priorities rooted in rapidly shifting values as people make painful mental adjustments to the twentieth century scientific revolution.

Business planners, he feels, should consider the impact on marketplace values of such scientific achievements as knowledge of the chemistry of life's origin, space exploration, medical triumphs, developments in cybernetics, and other seemingly esoteric advances. The new concern for the quality of life is based on the wide dissemination of information about these godlike new capabilities and the resulting changes in perception. This concern encompasses a powerful new sense of the nation's ability to achieve advances in human welfare and of its recognizable shortcomings that can be remedied.

Madden, who also serves as the chief economist for the U.S. Chamber of Commerce, believes that the new value shifts are now challenging traditional concepts of what is rational. Since corporate management of economic resources derives its political and social legitimacy from the presumably rational allocation of resources, disputes over the nature of rationality itself are bound to affect corporate strategies, management, markets, and products.

This book, which Madden prepared for the National Planning Association's Business Advisory Council, outlines many possible ramifications of the new consumer values and places them in a historical, political, and economic context that is both satisfying and coherent. He believes that corporations are gradually changing from a "Cartesian view," in which products are seen as separate parts determining overall strategy, to a "holistic view," in which situations and patterns are seen as de-

---

[1] Arthur F. Burns, statement before the Joint Economic Committee, July 23, 1971.

[2] Carl H. Madden, *Clash of Culture: Management in an Age of Changing Values* (Washington, D.C., National Planning Association, Report No. 3, 1972).

termining products. This latter perspective, for example, is helping Detroit's auto companies to understand that they are in the transportation business, rather than just producers of automobiles. Such an approach should aid corporations in finding new market opportunities by fulfilling functions rather than by turning out an increasing welter of uncoordinated, ill-adapted, separate products which may not mesh with the market or the environment.

Madden also discusses the current renegotiation of the corporate mandate as citizens and stockholders confront management in the legislature and at the annual meeting. And he sees the questions that arise over the definition and goals of economic growth as embodying a very real challenge to conventional economic thinking.

Such new challenges to economics will of course concern business. Economic data determine both individual corporate decisions and the national policies of resource allocation within which companies must operate. Moreover, this attack on conventional economic practice as the basic tool for managing national resources is coming not only from an increasingly skeptical public but also from other disciplines, such as physics, the life sciences, anthropology, and psychology.

THE ECOLOGICAL BROADSIDE

Strangely enough, it was the environmentalists, normally chided for their lack of realism, who began to question the premise that an economy could continue helter-skelter growth without eventually incurring severe environmental losses. The appearance of John Kenneth Galbraith's *The Affluent Society* [3] in 1958 augered much of the new debate. This book ques-

tioned why the U.S. economy seemed so well-supplied with hair oil, tail-finned cars, and plastic novelties in the private sector while cities decayed, air and water became polluted, and land was despoiled in the public sector.

Elaborating on this theme, economist Kenneth E. Boulding attributed much of man's despoiling of nature to his inadequate frame of perception. In *Beyond Economics,* written in 1968,[4] he claimed that man still saw his natural resource base as a limitlessly exploitable frontier. This "cowboy economics," as Boulding termed it, did not account for environmental costs—i.e., "externalities" which are part of the true cost of production. Boulding predicted that, with the growth of air and space travel, we would finally come to realize that we live on a vast spaceship which is a closed, rather than an open, system.

I should note that the English economist, Alfred Marshall, introduced the concept of externalities as far back as 1890. He showed economists that they should be concerned with forces outside conventional economic activities. But the externalities of which Marshall wrote were mostly positive and included the rising levels of education of workers and the public services provided by government, from which the entrepreneur of that time had profited but to which he had made no contribution. His younger contemporary at Cambridge University, A. C. Pigou, became interested in the notion that there could also be negative externalities, as he watched smoke and sparks pour out of an English factory chimney.

But this concept remained a theoretical abstraction—an empty box on economists' diagrams—until K. William Kapp published his *Social Costs of Private Enterprise* in 1950.[5] Kapp

---

[3] John Kenneth Galbraith, *The Affluent Society* (Boston, Houghton Mifflin, 1958).

[4] Kenneth E. Boulding, *Beyond Economics* (Ann Arbor, University of Michigan Press, 1968).

[5] K. William Kapp, *Social Costs of Private Enterprise,* revised edition (New York, Schocken Books, 1971).

documented the environmental and social effects of business activities. His basic thesis was that the maximization of net income by micro-economic units (entrepreneurs, corporations, and so on) was likely to reduce the income or utility of other economic units and of the society at large. In short, he claimed that conventional measures of the performance of an economy were misleading, since they ignored social and environmental costs.

An Environmental Price Tag. The issue of the ecological price of industrial activities took another 20 years to emerge. But, by the first Earth Day in 1970, these environmental costs had broken through the threshold of sensory awareness for millions of Americans. In 1971, systems analyst Jay W. Forrester's *World Dynamics* [6] appeared. This book attempted to develop a computer model, on a world scale, for the interactions over time of population growth, food supply, capital investment, geographical space, pollution, and resource depletion. By a different route, Forrester came to the same conclusion as had Kapp in 1950: in complex, nonlinear systems the optimization of any subsystem will generally conflict with the well-being of the larger system of which it is a part.

Most economists scoffed at *World Dynamics* (and also at the later study, *The Limits to Growth*,[7] prepared by Forrester's colleagues at the Massachusetts Institute of Technology). They argued with the very large aggregations of data and other methodological approaches used by Forrester and his colleagues. But it soon became necessary for economists to address population, resource, and distribution issues, because Forrester's work had created such an impact that these issues had entered the realm of political debate and action.

Economists React. Gradually, economists with intellectual investments in economic "growthmanship," such as Henry C. Wallich and Walter Heller, began to deal with the problems raised by Forrester and others. Their first evaluations were that these were new Malthusian scares. Since Thomas Malthus's grim predictions of overpopulation and food shortage were made 150 years ago and had not yet occurred, except in localized regions, economists argued that they would be unlikely to occur in the future (a somewhat shaky linear extrapolation). Resource shortages were discounted because, as in the past, prices would rise and encourage innovation.

The environmenal view, however, was that, while technological innovation is vital, it would be foolhardy to place faith in technology as the infinite source of salvation. It might be just as likely for a technological plateau to occur, as has happened in so many other civilizations in the past, and for research investments to yield diminishing returns. The United States could, for example, be forced to extract minerals from increasingly low-grade ores at higher cost.

Moreover, although prices will undoubtedly rise to reflect specific scarcities and encourage substitution in the prescribed manner, environmentalists pointed out that prices are merely subjective expectations of availability and are not based on objective scientific research. There are often severe time lags between the scientists' warnings of increased resource depletion or major ecosystem disturbances (e.g., accelerating water eutrophication rates) and the point at which security analysts, bankers, corporate financial officers, and economists digest this new knowledge and crank it into their forecasts. Even Henry C. Wallich, who had at first derided *World Dynamics* and *The Limits to Growth*, later wrote in *Fortune* [8] that

---

[6] Jay W. Forrester, *World Dynamics* (Cambridge, Massachusetts, Wright Allen Press, 1971).

[7] Donella H. Meadows, et al., *The Limits to Growth* (New York, Universe Books, 1972).

[8] Henry C. Wallich, *Fortune*, October 1972, p. 121.

such lags might not provide enough lead time to change pricing policies accordingly.

In addition, correct pricing must reflect information on environmental externalities. Although such information can be obtained or approximated in many cases, few social institutions support its collection or back campaigns for its dissemination. An obvious example of such pricing lags is U.S. electricity-rate policy, which still reflects earlier assumptions of continued abundance. Thus major users of electricity receive subsidies while the nation is in a power crisis.

THE DEBATE SHIFTS

The controversy over the environment not only continues to expand but also has led to what is becoming the real nub of the ecology versus economics debate: the distribution of wealth. While environmentalists maintain that economic growth must be curtailed in the name of ecological sanity, most economists hold that economic growth (presumably as currently defined by GNP) is the only way to ensure that increasing shares of wealth trickle down to the poor. Here their Keynesian premises are revealed.

Such a plea for the inflation-prone, trickle-down Keynesian model of economic growth forms the basic argument of *Retreat From Riches: Affluence and Its Enemies.*[9] Just published, and written by Peter Passell and Leonard Ross, this book is only passingly concerned with the ecological limits to growth, which it dismisses in one chapter with routine Keynesian arguments that growth is the only means of increasing the lot of the poor. Like most economists, they see environmental protection largely in terms of correct

effluent taxation. While environmentalists agree that effluent taxes are a useful "fine-tuning" tool for reducing pollution, they argue that such taxes do not serve to reduce resource-depletion rates or improve energy-conversion efficiencies, where the real economic and ecological payoffs lie.

The authors devote most of their effort to a well-meaning attempt to deal with intractable distributional issues. Unfortunately, they never get below the surface of the maldistribution-of-income problem, since they accept current distribution of wealth as a given. They say, in essence, that, although we know that economic growth does very little for the poor, it is still more feasible than any other form of redistribution yet devised. The bulk of the authors' argument is concerned with other influences which are "the enemies of affluence"—namely, inflation and balance-of-payments problems. Their prescription: keep on the same track, supporting economic growth policies and full employment, while cushioning the effects of inflation for those who are most burdened (e.g., people on fixed incomes).

New Ammunition. Beset by Keynesian arguments for growth and by charges from economists and corporate executives that, in their ecological zeal, they wished to stop economic growth now that they had achieved middle-class comfort, environmentalists were at first baffled about how to respond. But when Barry Commoner, in his 1971 book, *The Closing Circle,*[10] zeroed in on the distribution question, he provided the environmentalists with both new direction and new ammunition. Commoner's argument was three-pronged:

1. He noted that, if economic growth would have to be stabilized at some future point, then there could be no further moral justification for the Keynesian "trickle-down" theory of

[9] Peter Passell and Leonard Ross, *Retreat From Riches: Affluence and Its Enemies* (New York, Viking Press, 1973).

[10] Barry Commoner, *The Closing Circle* (New York, Alfred A. Knopf, 1971).

growth and distribution. The earth's resources would give out long before such uneven economic growth could ever provide for the millions still waiting in poverty. Those unlucky enough to be traveling in steerage class on "Spaceship Earth" would never even make it to the second-class deck.

2. He declared that excessive consumption by rich nations not only condemned the third world of less-developed countries (LDCs) to poverty, but also caused most of the environmental devastation. These "over-developed" nations were disrupting the environment because of their increasingly capital- (i.e., resource-) intensive production methods. They used highly profitable but polluting technology to synthesize artificial rubber, fibers, and plastics in place of naturally produced commodities with low profit margins. Moreover, since such commodities (e.g., wool, cotton, sisal, hemp, leather, and latex rubber) comprised a large proportion of most third world exports, the rich nations were decimating the export markets, and thus the economies, of LDCs.

3. He maintained that the over-developed nations, whose populations had stabilized in step with their rising standards of living, had achieved this stability through colonial exploitation of LDC resources. Continued heavy resource consumption by the over-developed countries, he argued, would prevent LDCs from achieving their own "demographic transitions" to stable populations. Hence his conclusion: ecological sanity now *requires* social justice.

In addition to Commoner's analysis, which was widely accepted by environmentalists, two recent studies further question the Keynesian assumptions about growth and redistribution.

Many economists who argue for growth cite studies by Robert J. Lampman [11] that relate economic

growth to increased welfare by showing a 37% gain in real per-capita consumption between 1947 and 1962. But, according to a study by Lester Thurow and Robert Lucas of M.I.T.,[12] during the years of economic growth between 1947 and 1970, the relative income shares of different groups in the economy remained essentially unchanged. Even more disturbing is a second study by Peter Henle of the U.S. Department of Labor,[13] which notes a persistent trend in the U.S. economy toward actual inequality. Henle shows, for example, that from 1958 to 1970 the share of aggregate wage and salary income earned by the lowest fifth of male workers declined from 5.1% to 4.6%, while the share earned by the highest fifth of male workers rose from 38.15% to 40.55%. Henle does not visualize a nefarious plot against the poor, but he does argue that the structure of the U.S. economy is such that it produces more high-paying, high-skill jobs while low-skill employment remains constant.

A WIDENING DIALOGUE

Commoner's analysis and the growing evidence that conventional arguments for trickle-down distribution are open to question turned the environmental movement toward a much more radical critique of economic and social arrangements. In addition, the movement had been stung by barbs from industry and confronted with corporate tactics designed to put environmentalists in conflict with labor (e.g., over a few highly publicized plant closings) and with the poor and consumers (e.g., by warning of astronomical price rises due to environmental controls).

These conflict situations further impelled environmentalists to examine the issue of distribution of wealth and

---

[11] See, for example, Walter H. Heller, "Ecology and Economic Growth," *Economic Impact*, Spring 1973, p. 37.

[12] Reported in *Business Week*, April 1, 1972, p. 56.
[13] Reported in *The New York Times*, December 27, 1972.

income. In the process, they discovered the influence on distribution of scores of weightier factors in the U.S. economy. For example:

National policies to control inflation.

Taxes and subsidies.

Discrimination.

Technological change.

Public works projects.

The wide prerogatives of large corporations to invest in other countries and to deploy freely their facilities and resources.

It was obvious that all of these factors had infinitely larger impacts on jobs and the distribution of income than did the environmental control measures that business leaders were fighting. Moreover, the environmental control sector was becoming an increasingly important part of the economy and had indeed added 850,000 new jobs, even though labor markets could not always match these new jobs with the people left unemployed by the closing of an obsolete facility.

The 'Stock of Wealth.' A key element in the environmentalists' growing concern over the distribution of wealth and income is related to contentions by several authors that many environmental problems result from the increasing production, consumption, and waste caused by planned obsolescence and the creation of wants by advertising.

For example, Herman E. Daly asks in his new book, *Toward a Steady-State Economy,* "Why do people produce junk and cajole other people into buying it? Not out of any innate love for junk or hatred of the environment, but simply in order to *earn an income.*" [14] Daly believes that we need some principle of income distribution that is independent of and supplementary to the income-through-jobs link.

The ethic of distributing the "flow of wealth" through jobs is at the heart of the Keynesian growthmanship effort, and was institutionalized in the

Employment Act of 1946. This "flow fetishism" of standard economic theory holds that everyone gets part of the flow—call it wages, interest, rent, or profit—and everything looks rather fair. But, Daly asks, what about the stock of wealth (capital)? Not everyone owns a piece of the stock; yet its distribution is usually accepted as a given—and that does not seem so fair.

If, as Robert J. Lampman has reported, the stock of wealth is held so tightly, with 76% of all corporate securities owned by 1% of the stockholders,[15] then most people must rely for survival on the flows it engenders (i.e., jobs or welfare). And, because of a growing population, the flow cycles must be continuously increased by whatever means possible. The results are built-in obsolescence, waste, creation of new wants through advertising, government pork-barrel projects, and burgeoning bureaucracy.

Environmentalists ask, "Why are we so dependent on the production of goods in the private sector to maintain employment, goods that are ill-matched with such new human needs as mass transit and clean sources of power? Why, in fact, can we not restructure our corporate and governmental institutions to meet new and future needs instead of continuing to address past conditions?" And they point to the encrustation of the federal budget with dozens of obsolete programs, such as the stream channelization projects of the Soil Conservation Service and many projects of the U.S. Army Corps of Engineers, that cost the taxpayer dearly and exact a terrible toll on the environment.

Labor and Capital. This crazy-quilt of government policies and projects is identified by Louis O. Kelso in *Two Factor Theory: The Economics of Reality* [16] as being rooted in the same prob-

[14] Herman E. Daly, editor, *Toward a Steady-State Economy* (San Francisco, W. H. Freeman, 1973).

[15] Robert J. Lampman, *The Share of Top Wealthholders in National Wealth, 1925–1956* (Princeton, Princeton University Press, 1962).

[16] Louis O. Kelso, *Two Factor Theory: The Economics of Reality* (New York, Vintage Books, 1967).

lem described by Daly. He argues that ever-increasing numbers of latter-day "Works Progress Administration-type" projects will be needed if society cannot grasp the fact that, as long as capital (the stock of wealth) is concentrated in the hands of the few, the many are condemned to rely for survival on the flows from income and welfare payments.

Kelso maintains that capital produces wealth just as labor does. And in advanced, highly industrialized economies, it produces an ever-increasing portion of wealth without much human intervention (e.g., in such capital-intensive, automated industries as oil refining and petro-chemicals). He claims that, to mask this disturbing and politically explosive fact, economists attribute productivity advances not to the increasing sums of capital used to increase the efficiency of each worker, but rather to the worker's own increased effort, i.e., "labor productivity."

Kelso argues that labor productivity advances are actually the result of additional capital placed at labor's disposal. And he notes that much labor strife in highly automated industries, where capital plays the major role in production, is due to the workers understanding that they need only be present *at the scene of production* as members of a well-organized pressure group in order to derive an income from automation.

Similarly, Kelso interprets all the paraphernalia of Keynesian redistribution. Jobs have become the nation's chief device for distributing income in a thinly disguised mélange of what he calls "warfare," "workfare," and "welfare." What is archcapitalist Kelso's prescription? Spread the ownership of corporations among their workers by means of his tax-deductible employee stock ownership trusts, as increasing numbers of corporations are now doing.

Environmentalists find analyses such as those of Daly and Kelso supportive because they highlight the propensity of the private-sector economy to con-

tinually substitute capital for labor. This, of course, taxes the environment and increases rates of resource depletion through the massive-scale, centralized operations it allows. As Arthur Pearl of the University of Oregon put it in a recent article in *Social Policy*, "In essence, we now have a surplus of human beings and a shortage of nonrenewable resources: thus we have to reverse our historical view of efficiency." He added, "It is only in a human services society which is labor-intensive rather than capital-intensive that the resources of the earth will be conserved and human resources be expended for the benefit of human beings." [17]

The Integrated Economy. While Kelso's treatment of the capital-labor issue was important, his most useful insight for environmentalists was his underlining of the political nature of all economic distribution.

This issue was first raised by John Stuart Mill in 1848 in *Principles of Political Economy*. Mill held that, once goods or any form of wealth had been produced, society, by its laws and customs, could place this wealth at the disposal of whomever it pleased. He added that even individual wealth could not be kept without society's permission and without society's willingness to employ police to guard individuals from thieves. In this regard, the criminal justice system in the United States employs some 1% of the labor force, and in fiscal year 1969–1970 expended $8.57 billion.[18]

In *Beyond Economics,* Kenneth E. Boulding elaborates on the politics of economic distribution. He claims that there are three basic modes of human transaction:

1. The primitive threat system (e.g., "Give it to me or I'll kill you") with its

[17] Arthur Pearl, "An Ecological Rationale for a Humane Service Society," *Social Policy*, September–October 1971, p. 41.

[18] Joseph F. Coates, "Urban Violence: The Pattern of Disorder," *The Annals of the American Academy of Political and Social Science*, January 1973.

more sophisticated "blackmail" variation (e.g., "How much will you pay me to stop harming or annoying you?")

2. The exchange system of market economies.

3. The maturing, integrative system in which increasing interdependence is necessary for the viability of the whole economy.

In his forthcoming book, *The Economy of Love and Fear: A Preface to Grants Economies,*[19] Boulding contends that the U.S. economy is moving (in spite of policy lags and distributional errors) toward such an integrative system, which he terms the "grants economy."

As evidence, Boulding points to ubiquitous grants and income transfers and increasing acceptance of responsibility for the disabled, unemployed, aged, and poor. He also points to the public services and amenities, which provide a viable context for market activities, and to "positive externalities." By the latter, he means commodities that benefit the society as a whole yet represent investments that are not fully recapturable. Knowledge and the flow of information, for example, play an increasing role in advanced production, innovation, technological change, and economic development but receive less than their share of attention from economists.

A recent book, *The Economics of Information and Knowledge,*[20] edited by Donald M. Lamberton, surveys some of the crucial knowledge and information issues raised by Boulding. Contributions by social choice theorists Kenneth Arrow (recent Nobel Prize winner in economics) and Gordon Tullock, labor economist Albert Rees, and information theorist Jacob Marschak focus on such topics as uneven information availability and how it can distort the labor market, prices, and political and corporate decision making. Other papers consider optimum public investments in research that advances knowledge, the patent system, and international trade and technology transfer.

While this book of essays is somewhat technical, it contains many readable pieces and a superb bibliography for anyone wishing to pursue this interesting field.

One Versus All. Also, the Lamberton book is an important one for environmentalists because it underscores that, without vastly more information between buyers and sellers in this complex age, the uncontrolled aggregation of small decisions (on which market economics rests) could add up to large-scale ecological chaos.

The way such chaos evolves is described by ecologist Garrett Hardin in his now-famous treatise, "The Tragedy of the Commons."[21] In feudal England, Hardin points out, all the farmers grazed their flocks in a large communal field (the commons). Some farmers realized, however, that they could maximize their advantage by grazing more animals than their neighbors. It was only a matter of time before the idea caught on and the commons was destroyed by overgrazing. Likewise, if we arbitrarily designate a jointly shared resource—such as air, water, or even whales—as a "free good," then no individual is responsible for its overall protection. As a result, it is likely to be destroyed completely.

The anthropocentric markets of conventional economics cannot provide much information on how to cope with such free-goods problems, in which public resources can be depleted and public services jeopardized by the temptation of each individual to avoid paying his share or restraining his greed. Moreover, argue the environmentalists, economics is ill-suited to

[19] Kenneth E. Boulding, *The Economy of Love and Fear: A Preface to Grants Economies* (scheduled for publication by Wadsworth Publishing Co., Belmont, California, in 1973).

[20] Donald M. Lamberton, editor, *The Economics of Information and Knowledge* (Middlesex, England, Penguin Books, 1971).

[21] Garret Hardin, "The Tragedy of the Commons," *Science,* December 13, 1968, p. 1243.

dealings with value preferences that cannot be assigned monetary weightings. Such qualitative value conflicts must be left to the political arena, where they face a key axiom of Kenneth J. Arrow's "general impossibility theorem." Arrow states flatly that, in democracies, individual preferences cannot be logically ordered into social choice.[22]

In dismay the environmentalist must ask, "If economics cannot yet provide a sufficiently rational system for public decisions, and if Arrow is right that democracies cannot order individual preferences into logical social decisions, where do we go from here?" To the rescue come many scholarly responses to Arrow's dismal prognosis for democracy, including Gordon Tullock's rebuttal, "The General Irrelevance of the General Impossibility Theorem"; [23] Duncan Black's argument that reiterates the theorem's irrelevance to an understanding of how social choices are actually made in committee situations; [24] and Edwin T. Haefele's contention in his paper, "Environmental Quality as a Problem of Social Choice," [25] that Arrow's conditions for ordering individual preferences into social choice can be met by representative governments with a two-party system.

The Steady-State Economy. The foregoing debate over social choice theory, however abstract it seems, is vital because it concerns the structuring of orderly societies that seek to optimize the general welfare without individual repression. Herman E. Daly sheds light on these issues in *Toward a Steady-State Economy.* He believes that both radical institutional changes and a paradigm shift in economics are required for a society to achieve a political economy of biophysical equilibrium and "nonmaterial" growth in areas such as knowledge, leisure, and the arts. Daly advocates a steady-state economy, with constant stocks of people and physical wealth maintained at some chosen level by a low rate of throughput (i.e., flow of goods, services, resources, and so on). He suggests these key steps for achieving this goal:

First, Daly endorses a plan by Boulding for issuing each individual a license at birth to have as many children as correspond with the dictates of replacement fertility; the licenses could then be bought and sold on the open market.

Second, he argues for transferable resource-depletion quotas, based on estimates of reserves and the state of technology; these would be auctioned off annually by government.

Third, he advocates a distributive institution that would limit the degree of inequality in wealth and income.

TOWARD PRAGMATIC ECONOMICS

Once more we come to this recurring theme in environmental thinking—the distribution of wealth and income. On what basis might a new formula for such distribution be justified? Might such a new rationale lie in the growing interdependencies of advanced production processes?

As many of the papers in *The Economics of Information and Knowledge* suggest, production has now become so complex, based increasingly on such abstract commodities as knowledge, that it is no longer possible to neatly formulate the rewards due to labor and the rewards due to capital. Neither the Keynesian labor interpretation of value

[22] Kenneth J. Arrow, *Social Choice and Individual Values,* 2nd edition (New York, John Wiley, 1963).

[23] Gordon Tullock, "The General Irrelevance of the General Impossibility Theorem," *Quarterly Journal of Economics,* May 1967, p. 256.

[24] Duncan Black, *The Theory of Committees and Elections* (Cambridge, Cambridge University Press, 1963).

[25] See Allen V. Kneese and Blair T. Bower, editors, *Environmental Quality Analysis* (Baltimore, Johns Hopkins Press, 1972).

nor the Kelsoist capital view of value is persuasive in resolving this point. Production of wealth in advanced economies is fast becoming a social enterprise, based on a tangled web of interrelationships. The old formula—— —with land, labor, and capital as factors of a production process that leads to a logical distribution of wealth—is no longer adequate.

The inadequacy of this traditional distribution formula concerns environmentalists for another crucial reason. It is precisely these knowledge inputs to production which increase energy-conversion efficiencies and reduce resource-depletion rates—the only other routes to environmental sanity besides that of more equitable distribution.

The fuel cell is an example of such a knowledge-intensive, resource-conserving product, the value of which is difficult to distribute via the traditional formula. The fuel cell's energy-conversion potential is some 60% (compared to 12% for the internal combustion engine), and it is largely this advance which represents its greater value. To whom does the fuel cell belong and who shall share in its rewards? The operators? The man who invented the fuel cell? Or the taxpayers whose government grant supported the university which supported the research? The pathways through such a system of infinite interdependencies are unchartable by current economic methods, unless many arbitrary weightings and assumptions are inserted into those economic models which attempt the task.

This and other problems make it increasingly difficult to design accurate economic models and to avoid the dangers of forcing public decisions into the straightjacket of cost/benefit analysis. Paul Streeten illustrates this point by noting that cost/benefit analysis has the tendency to convert political, social, and moral choices into pseudotechnical ones; hence its psychological appeal to administrators, but also its logical flaw.

"If two objectives conflict," argues Streeten, "say the requirements of industrial growth and protection of the environment, someone will have to choose. The choice may be democratic, dictatorial, or oligarchical, but choice it must be." Streeten holds that cost/benefit analysis, using the economist's often highly arbitrary weightings, conceals such value-conflicts, which can only be resolved politically.[26]

In addition, the welfare economists, however well meaning, are busy trying to examine the costs and benefits of pollution control. Using marginal analysis, they are attempting to evaluate environmental goals in terms of the willingness to pay for some standard of environmental quality or the willingness to accept compensation for damage. As K. William Kapp notes, this economic "compensation principle" as a criterion for environmental quality leaves no doubt in anyone's mind that the common denominator is going to be money. Kapp continues. "The basically questionable point of departure consists in the fact that original physical needs for rest, clean air, nonpolluted water, and health, as well as the inviolability of the individual, are being reinterpreted in an untenable way as desires or preferences for money income."[27] He also maintains that the compensation principle does not take income distribution or information requirements into account, and does not lead to systematic research into alternative policy options.

The growing list of shortcomings in current economic concepts and methods was summed up in a witty broadside by economist Alan Coddington, who believes, with Kapp, that the main body of economic thought is ill-suited to coming to terms with ecolo-

[26] Paul Streeten, *Cost-Benefit and Other Problems of Method* (Paris, Mouton, 1971).

[27] K. William Kapp, *Social Costs, Neo-classical Economics, Environmental Planning: A Reply* (Paris, Mouton, 1971).

gy. "It may even be the case," Coddington wrote, "that the greatest service economists can render to posterity is to remain silent." [28]

If money is an inadequate measure for harmonizing economic activities with the ecosystem, what new criteria might be devised to evaluate the policy decisions which will face citizens in some future steady-state economy? As a few daring economists begin to respond to this question with new concepts which more accurately match new realities, we will see their discipline incorporate more hard data on resource factors.

Kenneth E. Boulding and Barbara Ward, for example, first drew their fellow economists' attention to the unrewarded chemical work of natural ecosystems powered by the sun, which should provide all baseline data for economic models. In 1971, Howard T. Odum's book, *Environment, Power and Society*,[29] noted the inadequacy of economic models in capturing the value of such energy cycles and chemical exchange work (for example, in changing carbon dioxide from combustion back into usable oxygen). In a new, unpublished paper, Odum has devised a "value system" that converts kilocalories to dollars and permits a cost/benefits analysis to credit work performed by the natural systems on which all economic activities eventually rely.

The Entropy Concept. Economist Nicholas Georgescu-Roegen's new book *The Entropy Law and the Economic Process*[30] sets the problem of inadequate economic paradigms in a heroic spacetime context. In what may be the most important recent book on the ecology-economics debate, Georgescu-Roegen notes in sympathy that

economic activity is an evolutionary process which generally changes faster than economists can keep up with it.

He maintains that the overarching paradigm of economics pictures economic activities as analogous to Newtonian concepts of locomotion——that is, linear, arithmetical, and reversible. But economic processes themselves are not reversible because they are a part of the irreversible process of evolution and they operate within two basic laws of thermodynamic physics:

The first law states that matter cannot be created or destroyed within our planetary system.

The second—the dismal entropy law—states that all matter and energy in the system are in an inexorable process of degradation, decay, and dispersal into an eventual thin gruel of undifferentiated molecules.

For example, once a piece of coal is burned and its energy has been used and dispersed through friction as waste heat, that particular piece of coal can never be reconstituted or burned again. Matter can be recycled, but only with inputs of energy, which can never be recycled. Thus the process of energy utilization is always associated with entropy (i.e., frictional energy losses, such as waste heat).

One despairing physicist, after failing to get this concept across to a group of economists, related his favorite example of unnecessary entropy in a market economy. He asked them to consider the almost sinful dispersion of the valuable resource, chromium, collected and used to face the edges of razor blades, which are then irretrievably pushed down those little slots in millions of U.S. bathrooms.

Georgescu-Roegen not only challenges the quantitative assumptions of the locomotion model of economic processes but also suggests that economics has fallen into what Alfred North Whitehead called "the fallacy of misplaced concreteness." Because the qualitative changes associated with the greater entropy levels of all economic

[28] Alan Coddington, "The Economics of Ecology," *New Society*, April 1970, p. 595.
[29] Howard T. Odum, *Environment, Power and Society* (New York, Wiley Interscience, 1971).
[30] Nicholas Georgescu-Roegen, *The Entropy Law and the Economic Process* (Cambridge, Massachusetts, Harvard University Press, 1971).

processes are not easily modeled, economists ignore them in favor of the easy processes that can be expressed arithmetically. As a result, argues Georgescu-Roegen, economists address increasingly irrelevant, simplistic problems, excluding all those stubborn and intransigent variables, so the model can "work" in the approved Newtonian style.

He states flatly that the low entropy (i.e., ordered matter containing high energy potential) represented in finished goods is always less than the sum of the naturally occurring low entropy in the resources used to fabricate them. And he adds that in entropy terms all recycling is equally fruitless, because it consumes more energy, and that cannot be recycled. It may be amusing to note at such a depressing juncture that both economists and ecologists have always cheerfully agreed on one basic proposition: *there is no such thing as a free lunch.* Now the dismal entropy law is forcing both groups to recognize an even more dismal proposition: *each lunch costs more than the last.*

One implication of the entropy law is that all economic processes must be modeled in their entirety, from extraction to fabrication to distribution to consumption to waste to recycling. This is necessary to pinpoint any hidden energy subsidies along the way and compare the energy-conversion efficiency of each part of the production cycle. Thermodynamicist Stephen Berry has prepared such a model of the life cycle of the automobile, which leads him to conclude that the largest energy and "thermodynamic-potential" savings can be achieved in the basic method of metal extraction and fabrication, which could, in principle, reduce the "thermodynamic costs" of automobiles by factors of five, ten or more. By comparison, extending the life of the vehicle could realize savings of 50% to 100%, whereas recycling could achieve a saving of roughly 10%.

Questions of Value. All of these new issues lead environmentalists to call for a reexamination of cultural notions of "value." The economic impact of these qualitative concepts surrounding the concern for "quality of life" is discussed by Walter A. Weisskopf in his new book, *Alienation and Economics.*[31] He notes that economics, once based on the ethic of thrift and self-denial, now requires an ethic of "utilitarian hedonism" if it is to justify mass consumption, mass production, and advanced market economies. Yet this very hedonism, promoted by corporate advertising, is now leading to the breaking down of industrial discipline and cries of dehumanizing, boring jobs.

Weisskopf stresses that notions of value are arbitrary and culture-bound. For example, he holds that the U.S. economy overvalues material wealth while dismissing psychic wealth. Similarly, we overvalue competitive activities and undervalue cooperation and social cohesion.

The real dimensions of scarcity are not economic, claims Weisskopf, but existential. Time, life, and energy are for man the resources that are ultimately "scarce," because of his mortality. Such psychic needs are similar to those described by psychologist Abraham Maslow: love, peace of mind, self-actualization, companionship, and time for leisure and contemplation. These needs can never be satisfied by purely economic means, although economic activity that satisfies lower-order survival needs permits them to emerge. In short, humans tend to assign values arbitrarily and then pay measures to collect only those data which conform to prevailing assumptions of "value." The hypnotic circle is complete.

Environmentalists have intuitively come to the same conclusions as has

[31] Walter A. Weisskopf, *Alienation and Economics* (New York, E. P. Dutton, 1971).

Weisskopf. They note another example: people in the United States overvalue property rights and undervalue amenity rights, with which property rights often conflict. One can find hundreds of examples in the courts today in cases involving the conflicting interpretations of these two sets of values and rights. In such cases amenity rights are beginning to win (e.g., recent court awards for noise damage).

On this issue of value clashes, Benjamin Ward shares Weisskopf's view. Ward's book, *What's Wrong With Economics*,[32] questions the avoidance in economics of efforts to study the moving target of constantly changing human values and preferences. While acknowledging the difficulties, he takes issue with arguments that such studies are beyond the scope of rigorous, scientific methods of inquiry. Ward feels evasions of such problems have caused economists to retreat to easier, but less-relevant problems. He notes that a sister discipline, the law and the judicial process, does embody an often highly satisfactory system for empirically validating the changing values of consumers. Through the continuous building up and reinterpreting of legal precedents, changing consumer values and preferences become codified in law and custom. Economists must seek to capture this type of dynamic process in their analyses.

---

[32] Benjamin Ward, *What's Wrong With Economics* (New York, Basic Books, 1972).

CONCLUSION

Many of the environmentalists' indictments of economists may seem esoteric or even "un-American." Yet some of them are spurring more openminded economists into new efforts to create fresh concepts and paradigms, such as those discussed in this article. After all, economics is still the discipline concerned with scarcity, choice, and the behavior of equilibrium systems, all of which are still central concerns for the future. Although many of the young, radical economists in the United States have criticized their colleagues' overwhelming preoccupation with market economics and the elegant contours of the closed, equilibrium systems it hypothesizes, they are no happier with the bureaucracy that typifies so many centrally controlled socialist and communist economies. And five-year plans can be just as environmentally destructive as those plans of entrepreneurs or government agencies in market economies.

A review of the many new microeconomic studies now being undertaken by a few economic innovators is needed to supplement some of the broader concepts discussed here. But such a review would provide enough material for another article. Suffice it to say that any assault on economics, sooner or later, is an assault on the mandate of corporations, and it behooves management to understand the rational basis of the ecologists' criticisms.

International Management

The concept of multinational enterprises has engendered a more global approach to management; competition is no longer limited to national boundaries. The energy crisis has demonstrated the importance of this international market to American business. This section investigates the important variables that must concern a firm when it attempts to extend its activities beyond the boundaries of the United States.

The first article, by Professor Pieter Kuin, discusses how the multinational firm is able to build an effective, cross-cultural work team of managers. It has now been accepted that such teams are necessary. No longer are companies allowed to utilize only United States managers in foreign countries; the management team must be supplemented by nationals. Yet how can a multinational firm combine managers of widely differing cultures into effective work teams? In a manner of speaking, the "magic" rests in their ability to produce open, positive attitudes toward other nationalities and cultures. Specifically, the firms rely on certain policies of training nationals and expatriates to work together. On the basis of experience, they are learning how to balance local initiative with the need for central control and the need for understanding local ways with that of understanding company ways. In this article, Professor Kuin explains how multinational firms are accomplishing these things.

The next article, by Mr. James R. Piper, Jr., suggests that decisions related to foreign investments are far less refined than similar domestic decisions. International decision making assumes the same underlying basis as do less complex domestic decisions. This article reviews the decision process of 21 corporations regarding foreign investments. Basically, the results demonstrate that political, social and marketing variables receive little attention. U.S. firms generally seem to have a great deal of difficulty applying sound domestic concepts to the international market.

The final article, "The Multinational Enterprise and Nationalism," is concerned with the role that a multinational enterprise should play in a host country's economy. The author is particularly interested in problems generated by animosity toward foreign investment. He discusses a number of joint venture laws now existing in foreign countries. He also describes the reasons for the host country's fears of foreign investment. Once concern over the amount of investment arises, greater control is often sought by the host country. Domestication is described as one orderly process of giving greater control to the host country without losing foreign expertise. The author suggests a predetermined policy of domestication to protect foreign investments. Even though a firm may lose some control, it is worthwhile in terms of minimizing the risk.

25 The Magic of Multinational Management

Pieter Kuin

The executive development problems of the multinational company (MNC) are partly those of all large and diversified organizations: how to plan the required intake of new managers, how to train them for future positions, how to ensure fruitful cooperation among a variety of people.

But in the multinational enterprise such general problems have a particular edge. There is a variety not only of skills, personalities, and ages but also of nationalities. Moreover, in spreading its operations over the globe, an MNC meets problems and obstacles which companies working in one national market are spared. On the one hand, MNC executives have to cope with diverging national interests and government policies, and, on the other, with

such mundane things as national tastes and idiosyncrasies. Many of them may be torn by conflicts of loyalty or by tensions between instinct and reason when the objectives of the "foreign" company they represent seem to collide with national viewpoints or feelings.

How have the more mature multinationals learned to deal with these difficult management problems? And is there anything new to report from which beginners might benefit? I shall try to answer these questions from the viewpoint of executive manpower development, rather than organization, because having the right people is far more important than having the right organization. The people will adjust the organization to the requirements of place and time.

Reprinted by permission from the *Harvard Business Review* (November–December, 1972), pp. 89–97.

EXPATRIATES AND NATIONALS

Let us consider an initial problem of the typical MNC as it starts from a base in one country (which I shall call the "home" country) and spreads its operations to a number of other countries (which I shall call "host" countries). What is the proper ratio between the number of managers sent out from the home country and those recruited locally?

The need to combine different nationalities in the management of an MNC is now generally recognized. The time when practically all senior managers of an international company were citizens of the home country is past. Managers from the home country have one great advantage and a number of actual or potential disadvantages. Their advantage is that they know the traditions and policies of the corporation and therefore are likely to preserve its cohesion. As against this, they are aliens in the country in which they operate, liable to be resented or misunderstood, and possibly critical of national idiosyncrasies. Moreover, they are costly to the company, requiring regular home leave and allowances for educational and other family expenses.

Manning the boards of operating companies with nationals has definite advantages. Nationals possess cultural identification, easy understanding of local markets, distributors and consumers (as well as suppliers and bankers), and knowledge of "the ropes." Moreover, the policy helps the MNC better to identify itself with the legitimate aims and aspirations of the host country.

There are no general rules as to how to recruit and train local managers; so much depends on the state of the country and the nature of the operations. For example, in a country that has just started on the road to modern economic development, recruitment is harder and intracompany training periods are longer than in more sophisticated parts of the world. Neverthe-less, a few general observations can be made in light of the past experiences of MNCs.

Resisting Extremes

Until the middle of this century, it was usual for companies to man their operations abroad with trusted and experienced managers who had won their spurs at home. These men, without any qualms of conscience, became "expatriate" managers in foreign lands.

The tide began to turn very soon after World War II. National aspirations abroad had become stronger and national feelings more sensitive to dangers of domination. European multinational enterprises, which have longer experience with overseas operations than have most American companies, began to recruit, train, and promote national managers to positions of real responsibility. These companies led the way to what some have called "ization" (Africanization, Indianization, and so on) of management. In less developed countries during the last two decades, many MNCs have put all their efforts into replacing expatriate managers with nationals.

Recently, however, the tide seems to have turned again. Government and other political pressures for "ization" have become so strong—particularly in politically immature countries—that MNCs have been forced to put up some resistance. They feel that the quality of management and also the cohesion of the organization require at least a certain proportion of experienced men from home. The approach of some companies is to define a small number of "key positions" in a country, half of which should be held by expatriates. In this way they try to prevent centrifugal forces from gaining the upper hand.

The experience of Unilever, the MNC with which I have been associated for many years, mirrors some of the needs and compromises that multinational companies everywhere have contended with:

Decades ago the firms of Jurgens and Van den Bergh, out of whose union (after bitter strife) the Dutch side of Unilever eventually arose, would never have dreamed of manning all their executive posts abroad with Dutchmen. For one thing, there were perhaps not enough capable compatriots at hand to meet the needs. But more important, the experienced merchants who led these firms knew that for certain activities, such as marketing, personnel management, and external relations, almost any foreigner is at a handicap compared with nationals.

It is true that they trusted Dutchmen more than foreigners with one thing—money. The financial directors of their companies abroad were almost always Dutch, and so were the chief accountants. On the English side, Lever had a similar policy, and so it is no wonder that to Unilever, the merged organization formed in 1929, the need for multinational management was never in doubt.

After the Second World War, the policy of "ization" was deliberately pursued. In 1950, half of the management of Unilever companies outside Europe and North America was expatriate; 20 years later this figure was down to 10%. It would, however, be wrong to assume that this multinational company had decided to let its management consist of national blocs managing national chunks of Unilever business. On the contrary, a number of other nationals, besides the British and Dutch, were sent across the world to gain experience outside their own countries or help to fill posts for which they met the specifications.

And so today we find Belgians in Unilever's office in Austria and an Austrian in Greece, Spaniards in Germany and Germans in Portugal, a Frenchman in Italy and an Italian in France, and so on. At headquarters, more nationalities are found in one office—between 10 and 12, all holding fairly senior positions—than anywhere else in the company, except perhaps research. Even the stronghold of financial control is breached in places; some very trusted individuals, long steeped in Unilever traditions, have overcome the handicap of not belonging to the parent nations.

International Job Rotation

MNCs also must keep places open for foreigners in order to maintain job rotation across national boundaries. If all responsible positions in every country were to be held by nationals, no manager could ever be trained abroad. This would be unacceptable to the MNC for two reasons:

1. Job rotation is an essential element of executive training in general, and international job rotation is an especially valuable source of personal experience in MNC management.

2. The multinational company cannot allow nationals to attain the most responsible positions in their countries without first giving them experience abroad (and this experience should not be limited to a spell at headquarters or in an operating company of the home country). If it does not send them abroad, it creates an overload of high level "trainees" in the home country, resulting in frustration for all.

Some limitations to transferability are imposed by government. We tend to think of newly independent nations in this connection, but even mature and sophisticated countries can be very difficult about granting labor permits to foreign managers. Switzerland is a case in point; Japan is another. The situation in the United States has greatly improved these last few years. Eventually, MNCs based in the "difficult" countries, from the standpoint of transfer, may have to bring home to their governments the importance of the golden rule.

CORPORATE ACCULTURATION

Another reason why sufficient scope for international job rotation should be maintained is the need for what I would call "corporate acculturation." If a promising young manager is to rise to one of the highest positions in his country, he has to acquire understanding of the basic nature and policies of the company. This is not a matter of molding him into some uniform type, an "organization man"; he would be useless if he became one.

A large and widespread organization must function with a high degree of delegation if it is to avoid the rigidity of bureaucratic rules. This means a manager should possess a deep-rooted sense of what the company's policy would be in the case of a particular issue he has to decide. Such a sense can only be instilled by experience, instruction, and personal contact at headquarters or in parts of the organization thoroughly familiar with the policies and style of the corporation. Let me quote E. G. Woodroofe, Chairman of Unilever Ltd., London. He has stated:

The talents, the flair, the intuitive thinking, and the points of view of many different cultures can be brought to bear on a problem, whether it is one of science, management, organization, or consumer response. But, of course, it is not easy to do this, for if people from many cultures are to work effectively together, they must also acquire for themselves some common language of communication, some common culture.

For instance, it is not enough for Unilever to appoint Indians to manage our Indian business, as we have done with considerable success, or to bring Germans into head office jobs in London or Rotterdam. We must do this within the context of an overall Unilever way of doing things—what in America would be called a business philosophy. I must emphasize that the Unilever way is not an Anglo-Dutch philosophy, but one to which all nationalities have contributed: one which Englishmen and Dutchmen have to absorb just as much as do Brazilians or Swedes.

I mean that in giving advice, in setting out company policy, or in reporting on marketing campaigns, technical developments, or political changes, there is (or should be) an accepted way of doing things which is read-ily understood in *all* parts of the Unilever world. Moreover, this pattern of behavior is not simply imposed from the center. Rather, its elements have been drawn from all parts of the organization, and they have been crystallized by the center.[1]

In the absence of corporate acculturation, management has to maintain unity by a fairly high degree of headquarters control and expatriate management. These are poor substitutes for the free cooperation and easy understanding that can develop among men who are trained in the same corporate philosophy.

Key Role of Tenure

Of course, all of this presupposes a certain continuity in the careers of MNC managers. Long tenure has, in fact, been a tradition of European multinational management for many years. Basically, one became a Unilever man, a Siemens man, or a Volvo man for life—after the first trials and tribulations of choosing and changing careers were over. Getting the pink slip or resigning in mid-career usually meant that an accident had happened. Both the company and the man invested so much in a career that abrupt endings were viewed with regret. I should add that the investment was not in money alone. Much trust and loyalty were given and expected each way.

U.S. companies setting up shop in Europe—or in Asia and Africa, for that matter—have often caused harm by disregarding such feelings of mutual dependence. Many are the tales in Europe of an experienced executive giving up a position he has held for 20 or more years, only to be sacked on trivial grounds after a few months by his new American employer. It is, of

---

[1] See "Technology and Business Opportunity for the International Business," in *Technological Change and Management: The John Diebold Lectures 1968–1970,* edited by David W. Ewing (Boston, Harvard Business School, 1970), p. 96.

course, possible that in such cases the hiring, not the firing, was rash. But the result is the same.

This is not the place to discuss the pros and cons of executive mobility between corporations. Certain it is that high mobility is incompatible with the kind of careful conditioning to a company's style and policies that enables a manager to stand on his own, far removed from headquarters, and make the right decisions. A high rate of hiring and firing forces management to depend on standard procedures and tight control, rather than on delegation of power and initiative.

Fitting In

In an MNC the always-difficult process of executive development is complicated by three unique problems:

1. Most MNCs have one world language for communications at the head office, and between the head office and the operating companies or divisions in different lands. At the latter, however, operations usually are, and should be, conducted in the vernacular. The need to learn the local language may vary in importance for managers of different categories (accounting, marketing, production, personnel, and so on), but he who cannot or will not learn languages always remains a stranger in any part of the business but "home." From the viewpoint of job rotation, such a man needs a special tab on his card.

2. Some nationals are more deeply rooted in their culture, and therefore less transferable, than others are. While it is dangerous to generalize, more than one firm has found, for instance, that married Frenchmen, alive and well and living in Paris, can hardly be moved at all. Again, Italians and other Mediterraneans are strongly attached to relatives and may prefer to stay with them or move together. The Swiss however will put up with less well-organized societies than their own for a limited period of time only.

On the other hand, Germans are keen, and Dutchmen on the whole are willing, to work abroad. Scandinavians and Englishmen will accept transfer but want a "return ticket." Americans are often difficult to fit in, being used to a high standard of living and a homogeneous civilization.

Let me emphasize that the foregoing are only generalizations. People with experience in multinational business can usually think of exceptions.

3. Recently, there has been a change in attitudes among younger managers, particularly Europeans, with regard to international transfers. They have shown a declining willingness to accept a transfer just because it suits the firm. Managers of an older generation took pride in being "good soldiers" and went where the company needed them, whether they liked it or not. Saying *no* was not impossible, but was not considered prudent or quite loyal.

Today's more independent young managers raise all kinds of objections. Many of them plead family circumstances, a thing the old "toughs" would have been ashamed to do. Others consider every "proposal" in the light of their own careers. Transfers to less developed countries are sometimes resisted because the manager fears they may keep him outside the mainstream of his profession too long and impair his ability to cope with sophisticated markets or techniques. This could set him back in the promotion league. As against this, he is likely to gain in stature and ability to make decisions—an advantage which superiors proposing the change sometimes have to spell out. It means that he improves his position in the "general management" line.

Underlying such ructions is the general trend toward "participative management." Young people consider it a right to be consulted about a transfer—a situation rather new in international business. Personnel directors, making a virtue of necessity in preaching the gospel of consultation to impatient senior executives, often have a hard time making themselves understood. But, given a fair chance, the method works reasonably well.

REALISM IN PLANNING

The new tendency for young managers to be particular, if not difficult, greatly complicates the task of management planning. If managers cannot be relied on to go where they are needed, the numbers of those available may be misleading. If most managers want to return to home base fairly early, the recruitment of people of a certain nationality—Mexican, let us say—is limited by the capacity of the company organization in Mexico to employ managers.

In an "age of discontinuity," [2] the phrase "career planning" may soon be regretted by those who coined it and distrusted by those to whom it pertains. The only promise that really can be made is that every manager's position and potential will be considered periodically and that the company will do its utmost to match the one with the other.

The trend toward recognition of the younger men's personal rights and views involves a readiness on the part of seniors to make appraisals known to their juniors before they are put on record. The best practice is to have the younger men countersign the minutes of the appraisal talk. More and more, such talks include a statement by the candidate about the sort of career he would envisage for himself.

Not all expectations raised by recruiters or secretly cherished by candidates will eventually be met. As management education progresses, both inside and outside the MNC, the number of fully qualified managers available is likely to exceed the number of places in the higher ranks. I see this happening in the specialist service departments (law, economics, accounting, and so on)

at many MNC headquarters. I see it beginning to happen in the research laboratories of MNCs. And I believe it will happen later in marketing and other new fields of specialization, as well as in general management.

In short, the middle ranks will no longer be held solely by men who rose from modest beginnings, but also by those who started with high qualifications and ambitions. This may involve painful mental adjustment for men in the latter group. It also contains a warning for recruiters, planners, and superiors. They would be well advised:

Not to hold out high hopes to everyone.

Periodically to compare existing positions with available potential talent.

To give an early red light to people whose expectations exceed their foreseeable chances.

Estimating the Intake

How many recruits of each nationality should the multinational enterprise take in each year? This may appear to be an impossible question to answer—so many uncertainties exist with regard to growth or decline of branches, methods of planning and control, wastage through early departures, changes through acquisitions, losses due to political disasters, and so on. Yet some attempt at planning must be made to avoid embarrassing deficits and surpluses in the future.

Fortunately, an answer is not so impossible to obtain as it seems, particularly if one breaks it down—or rather builds it up—by starting at the periphery and working toward the center. Estimating future management requirements begins at the operating company level. It can only be done by making forecasts of the following factors:

Growth in volume.

Intended diversification.

Refinements of management methods.

Changes in organization.

---

[2] Peter F. Drucker, *The Age of Discontinuity* (New York, Harper & Row, 1968).

In practice, the management development officer from central or regional headquarters helps company executives by insisting on such forecasts, and, in particular, on an imaginary (but realistic) organization chart of the company five years hence. Such a chart, completed with personnel data of the present establishment, will bring to light the gaps that are likely to occur. In a multinational organization, it is important to remember those who are working abroad and expected to return; all too often, this group is "out of sight, out of mind."

At the central or regional headquarters, the figures of the operating companies should be grouped by countries, product divisions, categories of managers, age brackets, and so forth. The cumulative result is an estimate of the requirements for the next five years. It would be a bad thing if recruitment started only when this estimate was ready. Recruitment should be a continuous process. Often, therefore, the estimates will indicate only slight changes in quantity or composition that appear to be necessary. In other cases, quite alarming gaps will appear, and special recruiting efforts will be necessary.

Restraints on Mobility

One important factor in staffing is whether the lines of command are geographical or divisional.

In a geographical organization, operations tend to be grouped in international divisions or under regional chief executives, and transfers within a region are not too difficult. Litigations between area managers about the release of valuable assistants are decided by the regional head, who loves them all equally well. Difficult transfers from one region to another are settled between the regional heads, who are colleagues somewhat removed from the battlefield.

But in a divisional organization, the lines seem to be sharper. First of all, the candidates are trained and specialized in certain product groups and not in others. In a diversified company, the technical knowledge and skills may differ greatly from one division to another. Consequently, superiors are often unwilling to let go of an experienced man, the more so since product divisions seem to be clearer profit centers than regional groups are. This may explain the lesser indulgence of top people in a division to share in the give and take of executive exchange.

But the fault is not all theirs. Prospective candidates for transfer also resist change, sometimes for fear of the unknown (which means fear of personal failure), more often because they think some divisions are larger and more prosperous than others and offer better prospects of promotion and higher rewards. One result of this lower horizontal mobility may be somewhat more slack in the organization; another is the greater burden on personnel directors to maintain uniform policies with regard to training, transfers, promotion, and remuneration.

QUESTIONS OF PAY

Management remuneration is a difficult problem in any multinational enterprise, whatever its organization. It is impossible to do justice to this important subject in a short space. Here I shall discuss but one important trend.

Whereas American companies usually pay expatriate managers according to what they would earn at home (which makes them nabobs in poor countries), European firms for a long time adjusted the salaries of expatriate managers to the levels existing for nationals in equivalent positions in the countries in which they operated. Thus it was a windfall to be placed in a prosperous country or in a country with great economic inequality, and just bad luck to be transferred to a country with a low standard of living or an excessive sense of social justice. An imaginary "home salary" was registered as the basis for pension contributions and the level at which one would eventually repatriate.

The advantage of this system was that it avoided tensions and jealousies between national and expatriate managers in one country. Extra allowances for home leave and school fees might be granted, but usually they were not begrudged by the nationals. The disadvantage was that an expatriate in a privileged country was extremely hard to transfer, especially if he could not be compensated for the change by a rousing promotion.

This traditional policy of maximum adjustment to local levels is now being abandoned by European companies. More and more managers have resisted or even refused transfers which entailed a reduction in real net income. The rule now tends to be that the standard of living in real terms after tax should at least be maintained for an executive who is transferred to another country. The consequence is that a man transferred from, say, Paris to Oslo may rise considerably above his new colleagues salarywise. He must use a lot of tact to maintain the peace. For multinational enterprises, this new situation may well become a stimulus to top management to be very careful in its transfer policies and not to send young people to highly eligible countries too soon. A spiral-type movement up the scale of possible locations is preferable to a fast, direct rise.

In any case, comprehensive planning along these lines is never easy. As a young adviser, I once worked out a complete system for an executive placement policy in an MNC, and was rash enough to submit it to the board. It took me three years to live this down; my paper was torn to pieces by the very people it was meant to help—those in the personnel department who were in charge of transfers. They did not want to be tied to a system. Real life often consisted of filling one hole by making another. But who knows, I may still be vindicated.

TRENDS IN TRAINING

Intracompany training is an important part of the process of corporate acculturation. Its main purpose, however, is to improve the executive's managerial ability.

The general pattern, as I have seen it in European practice—particularly for graduates—seems to be something like this:

1. A manager receives a short introductory course after entering the company at around age 25.

2. Next he receives training on the job, possibly with some job rotation, for four or five years.

3. He gets his first command at about age 30.

4. He may enter a junior managers' course between age 30 and 35.

5. He receives a more important command at about age 35.

6. He takes a general course for managers when he is 40–45 years old.

Larger companies organize the introductory and junior managers' courses themselves; they also organize courses aimed at bringing specialists up to date with professional and technical information. The largest multinational enterprises even run their own general or senior managers' courses. But in this case they draw heavily on outside instructors, because the purpose of such courses is to widen the horizons of participants and perhaps extend their knowledge beyond what the company itself has to offer. This purpose is served even better by sending the most promising executives to such advanced management courses as the ones given at Harvard, Stanford, and Columbia in the United States, and at Geneva, Fontainebleau, Lausanne, and Rotterdam in Europe.

Emphasis on Utility

In the training of younger managers, the trend in Europe seems to be away from the general toward the particular. Young men and women who take fairly general courses can have difficulty in applying what they learn to their actual work and situation. The work is not always of the required level, and the environment, including superiors, is not always sympathetic. The result is a sense of irrelevance. Enlightened companies are counteracting this problem by concentrating on two types of courses for which a manager may be elected in the first ten years of his career:

1. Short courses that bring participants up to date with changes in professional skills and techniques. Usually, these courses do not last longer than one or two weeks.

2. Courses for members of a particular sector of the company, centered around a real problem of that sector. Participants and problems are chosen in close consultation with the senior management of the operating company or department, if it is a large one. The object is to develop managers' ability to define and solve problems as a team. In each group a psychologist or sociologist is available for advice.

Course meetings may be interspersed with periods of regular work. In some cases, the course is concluded by a short period of intensive instruction with outside teachers, treating some closely connected subjects that have been carefully chosen for their relevance to the work and problems of the group. The need for such tailor-made instruction offers an interesting prospect for business schools.

High-level, general management courses remain important for more senior managers up to the age of 45 or so. These managers will be able to make good use of broad concepts and principles in their present or future positions. Such courses should be long enough to let the daily job fade into the background and open minds to new and unaccustomed things. One month seems a bare minimum; three months is better, if combined with really hard work; a course of four or five months' duration offers more scope for going into depth, but also requires a bigger

sacrifice, in time and money, from the employer.

The Language Question

The training problems of the MNC are largely the same as those of any large and complex organization, with the added dimension of cultural and linguistic differences. If the company is large enough, it can organize its courses by geographical areas, with English, German, French, or Spanish as the leading language. If it has to send managers to outside courses, a good knowledge of English is practically always necessary, and this need may handicap otherwise able people—an additional reason for company- and problem-centered courses with tailor-made instruction in the participants' own language.

For training and development of personnel, there is no substitute for the vernacular—and not merely from the standpoint of fluency. Every leader and instructor of a multinational group should be aware of the influence of cultural backgrounds on the understanding of words and the perception of ideas. Lack of such awareness leads to many mistakes in training. To illustrate:

There is an important difference in meaning between "in principle" in English and "en principe" in French. The former refers to a basic tenet; the latter mainly serves to announce qualifications and exceptions.

A recommendation to "convince the government" has different connotations and may lead to very different steps in various parts of the globe.

CONCLUSION

To sum up, I find that the most important needs and trends in management development in MNCs are as follows:

No MNC can do without a generous number of nationals in charge of local operations. However, there is a limit to the efficacy of this policy. Companies that have had time to recruit and train ample cadres of nationals are now forced to insist that a number of key functions remain in the hands of expatriates—both for the sake of corporate cohesion and for training purposes.

In order to avoid the rigidity of bureaucratic rule in a worldwide organization, a high degree of delegation is necessary. In a multinational management this can be done only after careful corporate acculturation, particularly of foreign recruits. International transfers in the first five or ten years of managers' careers are part of this process, and long tenure is a condition for success.

In an "age of discontinuity," the idea of career planning has to be deemphasized. Career planning is being replaced by periodic review of a manager's performance and potential in the light of available opportunities.

In appraisals and proposed transfers, more and more attention is being paid to the young manager's own ideas and preferences. As in other matters, the need for openness and participation is gradually being recognized by superiors.

There is a conflict between the need of the enterprise for rapid adjustment and the stiffening of managers' resistance to frequent or "arbitrary" transfers. Horizontal mobility is also impaired by a trend toward divisional organization of MNCs. These problems increase the value of open, two-way communication between senior and junior managers.

Estimates of future management requirements and decisions about the desirable annual intake of trainees are becoming more systematic. They are being linked with the projected growth or change of the organization.

In management remuneration, it has become necessary to avoid reduction of real net incomes following transfers. In poorer or more egalitarian countries this necessity may give rise to tensions around managers with privileged posts abroad and induce multinational enterprises to be more cautious in their placement policies, particularly with regard to the young.

In the training of young managers on company premises, the trend is away from long general courses and toward short, specific, and personally relevant courses emphasizing teamwork on real problems. Outside schools can help with tailor-made additional instruction.

The successful multinationals seem to have almost magical powers to elicit employee loyalty and interest. What is their secret? I would say that it is not in the perfection of methods, nor even in the excellence of men—although the sheer bigness of the task requires extremely capable men, especially at the center. The basic ingredients are attitudes and time to inculcate them in at least two generations of managers. Attitudes of respect for other nations' talents and traditions, of fascination with the variety of other worlds, of readiness to revise one's own prejudices, and of adjustment to local tasks and circumstances—these are the elements of the basic formula for success in an MNC.

26 How U.S. Firms Evaluate Foreign Investment Opportunities

James R. Piper, Jr.

Despite heady references in the business literature concerning the trend toward corporate multinationalism, the fact remains that many U.S. firms—large and small—approach foreign investment opportunities with much less sophistication and confidence than they exhibit in the domestic environment. This is particularly true when the prospective investment relates to a less developed country.

A surfeit of conceptually glamorous models and approaches has poured forth in recent years claiming to offer the decision maker a more systematic approach to his foreign investment decision problem. But few such models have been preceded by an attempt to establish more precisely just what those problems are. In surveying a number of foreign investment and feasibility studies made by U.S. firms, this article attempts to identify some recurring soft spots and problems in a typical foreign investment analysis.

The concept of risk implies uncertainty about the outcome of an event, which is a function of the interaction of variables affecting the event. The intelligent risk taker is one who presumably has identified these variables, and has performed some kind of analysis upon the variables in order to predict how they will affect the outcome. The U.S. manager considering a domestic investment decision perhaps best fits this characterization of the intelligent risk taker. The nature of the immediate environment surrounding his potential investment (that is, the U.S. domestic economy) has reduced the number of variables in his risk analysis. In other words, the relative stability of the U.S. political, social, economic, and legal milieu reduces such factors to constants for all practical purposes. The decision maker thus begins with a smaller and less complex series of variables which he must subject to analysis. Moreover, since the social-legal-political environment is relatively constant, he is able to focus upon what are largely commercial variables. These often are relatively easy to quantify and to investigate from abundant and available statistical data. In short, the domestic investor, confronted with a relatively small number of decision variables and the prospect of being able to analyze those variables in a rational way, has a reasonably good chance of becoming an intelligent risk taker, that is, of identifying and measuring an investment risk.

The same chances of success, however, are most often greatly reduced when the manager considers expansion into foreign markets, particularly in the developing areas. Two factors complicate his risk analysis in this case: (1) the social, political, and legal variables dormant in the U.S. investment decision are activated. These are often difficult to identify and to deal with in quantitative form; and (2) the commercial variables become more difficult to quantify in the absence of sophisticated economic and commercial data.

James R. Piper, Jr., "How U.S. Firms Evaluate Foreign Investment Opportunities," pp. 11–20, *MSU Business Topics,* Summer 1971. Reprinted by permission of the publisher, Division of Research, Graduate School of Business Administration, Michigan State University.

Thus, in the absence of successful precedents or guidelines for a systematic approach to the foreign investment decision, the company's decision methodology may range from the rational to the emotional and irrational. *Business International,* for example, surveyed a large number of U.S. firms of diverse background concerning their primary motivation for making an investment commitment abroad. Four principal factors emerged:

1) an outside proposal that cannot be easily ignored, for example, from a foreign distributor or an existing or potential customer;

2) fear of losing a market;

3) the bandwagon effect, for example, "Everyone is investing in the Common Market, why don't we?"

4) an active search by the advanced international corporation planning to establish its most effective presence in every market of every size.[1]

The wide diversity of investment decision approaches which such influences suggest is apparent. As one corporate executive observed, "Indeed, at times it seems there is no path leading to a logical decision that an investment makes sense or that the project is worth the effort."[2] For many companies the criticism is well founded. Within such companies the absence of a widely accepted, systematic approach to the foreign investment decision often leads to an extensive commitment based upon what Robert Stobaugh has called "a combination of inadequate information and intuition."[3]

A seasoned executive might smile at Stobaugh's complaint and ask what else is new. The experienced manager certainly understands that information and unquantifiable judgment (or "intuition") are the ingredients of virtually every significant, real-world decision, foreign or domestic. He thus may be prone to dismiss any line of reasoning which argues for the unique problem of the decision maker in the international environment.

For some of the reasons suggested above, however, the analogy between the domestic and foreign investment decision problem may be specious. In the case of the domestic decision, while the information may be incomplete, the manager can insure that the collection and analysis of the data is thorough, and based upon the proven business principles which stem from a century of American industrial experience. In the case of the foreign investor, it is not only the information but also the analytical tools themselves which are inadequate. *The decision maker, by virtue of habit, custom, and training, is prone to analyze the foreign investment within the same framework as previous domestic investments, utilizing the same assumptions, analytical tools, and intuitions that have brought investment success in the considerably less complicated domestic environment.*

While a number of normative approaches and conceptual models have been suggested as a means of handling the foreign investment decision problem more systematically, little effort has been devoted to identifying more precisely current thinking and practice as exhibited by actual firms in an operating environment.

[1] "How Firms Make Decisions to Invest Abroad," *Business International,* 9 September 1966, p. 287.

[2] Simon Williams, "Negotiating Investment in Emerging Countries," *Harvard Business Review,* January-February 1965, pp. 89–99.

[3] Robert B. Stobaugh, Jr., "How to Analyze Foreign Investment Climates," *Harvard Business Review,* September-October 1969, pp. 100–108.

REVIEW OF CORPORATE INVESTMENT SURVEYS

This article summarizes a preliminary research effort concerning twenty-one corporations which addressed two questions: What kind of variables do companies attempt to analyze in evaluating foreign investment opportunities? Does the range of variables most often considered by a potential investor reflect an adequate, thorough approach to investment risk analysis in the foreign context?

Two complementary approaches to data collection were involved: The first was a sample of "fifty-fifty" pre-investment studies—actual feasibility studies as opposed to preliminary surveys—made by U.S. corporations under the sponsorship of the now superseded AID Foreign Investment Survey Program.[4] The second approach utilized follow-up personal interviews with selected international executives to determine the significance of the trends identified in the survey sample.

Until the beginning of fiscal year 1971, the Agency for International Development administered a program of assistance to U.S. companies seeking investment opportunities in underdeveloped countries. One service offered was the "fifty-fifty survey," whereby a qualifying company could undertake an investment study in any country designated by AID as underdeveloped. If as a result of the study the company made a positive investment decision, it then bore the full cost of the survey. If the company decided not to proceed with the investment, AID assumed half the survey cost, and the study became government property. The file of negative decision studies available at the agency and the questionnaire responses from firms which had made positive investment decisions were used to analyze the issues raised in the introduction to this paper.

---

[4]The "fifty-fifty" program was phased out at the end of fiscal year 1970. Under the administration of the new Overseas Private Investment Corporation (OPIC) a revised, more selective program has been initiated, with OPIC paying up to 80 percent of investment survey costs.

Two Criteria

In order to reduce the influence of irrelevant variables upon the analysis, an attempt was made to select a reasonably homogeneous group of investment studies from the diverse files available. The two criteria used in this selection were: (1) a food production-food processing-agricultural support investor; and (2) a Latin American investment opportunity. Although the use of these criteria limited the quantity of the available research data considerably, such a provision seemed necessary to support any conclusions based upon synthesis and generalization.

From 1962 through fiscal 1969, 317 "fifty-fifty" investment studies were conducted, forty-one of which resulted in positive investment decisions. Approximately 150 additional studies were terminated or withdrawn for unexplained reasons with no claims made against AID support. Of the remaining 130 negative decision studies, sixteen qualifying under the criteria discussed above were available at AID. These constitute a substantial part of the data base for this paper. In addition, firms which had made positive investment decisions as a result of pre-investment surveys sponsored under the AID program were solicited by mailed questionnaire to participate in the survey. Five firms responded to the questionnaire, leaving the total survey base heavily weighted (sixteen of twenty-one) in favor of negative decision surveys.

There is a possibility that a substantial difference in character exists between positive and negative decision surveys. In fact, the data presented later in this paper seem to indicate that investment surveys resulting in positive investment decisions were generally characterized by consideration of a greater number and variety of decision variables. The possible explanations for this are: (1) a more thorough approach to investment analysis by firms more seriously committed to the foreign investment idea; (2) questionnaire "noise" generated by five positive decision firms who were perhaps seeking to present a favorable image of their approach to foreign investment analysis. In this regard, it is most important to remember that while the actual studies were available for review in the case of the negative decision surveys, positive decision surveys were not available, and firms which had conducted such surveys were asked only to respond to a questionnaire regarding the variables analyzed in their surveys; and (3) some combination of these two.

Identification of Decision Variables

The investment survey program of AID took a flexible and open-ended approach to the individual investment study, providing no format, standards, or specific criteria by which the company must structure its research project. As a result, the sixteen studies of interest in this article varied in terms of individual character, format, style, and overall quality (the latter being a subjective judgment of the authors). Nevertheless, in characterizing the discussion and analysis contained in each individual investment survey in terms of specific decision variables, such diversity did not present a significant problem. A discussion of estimated return on investment, for example, was relatively easy to identify regardless of the specific context in which it was presented. Still, some interpretation and judgment were necessary in order to construct a useful framework for generalization.

In essence, an informal content analysis was carried out upon the texts of the sixteen surveys. This analysis led to the identification of thirty-eight deci-

---

TABLE 1. DECISION VARIABLES IDENTIFIED IN SIXTEEN INVESTMENT STUDIES

FINANCIAL CONSIDERATIONS
1. capital acquisition plan
2. length of payback period
3. projected cash inflows (years one, two, and so forth)
4. projected cash outflows (years one, two, and so forth)
5. return on investment
6. monetary exchange considerations

TECHNICAL AND ENGINEERING FEASIBILITY CONSIDERATIONS
7. raw materials availability (construction/support/supplies)
8. raw materials availability (products)
9. geography/climate
10. site locations and access
11. availability of local labor
12. availability of local management
13. economic infrastructure (roads, water, electricity, and so forth)
14. facilities planning (preliminary or detailed)

MARKETING CONSIDERATIONS
15. market size
16. market potential
17. distribution costs
18. competition
19. time necessary to establish distribution/sales channels
20. promotion costs
21. social/cultural factors impacting upon products

ECONOMIC AND LEGAL CONSIDERATIONS
22. legal systems
23. host government attitudes toward foreign investment
24. host attitude toward this particular investment
25. restrictions on ownership
26. tax laws
27. import/export restrictions
28. capital flow restrictions
29. land-title acquisitions
30. inflation

POLITICAL AND SOCIAL CONSIDERATIONS
31. internal political stability
32. relations with neighboring countries
33. political social traditions
34. Communist influence
35. religious/racial/language homogeneity
36. labor organizations and attitudes
37. skill/technical level of the labor force
38. socioeconomic infrastructure to support American families

TABLE 2. MATRIX OF INVESTMENT SURVEYS AND DECISION VARIABLES

DECISION VARIABLES

		A	B*	C*	D*	E	F*	G*	H	I	J	K	L	M	N	O	P	Q	R	S	T	U	Number of Times Considered
Financial	1	X	X		X	X	X	X	X	X	X	X			X		X	X		X				14
	2	X	X	X	X		X	X	X	X	X	X	X	X	X	X	X	X	X	X	X		19
	3	X	X	X	X	X	X		X			X	X	X					X	X				12
	4	X	X	X	X	X	X		X			X	X	X					X	X				12.
	5	X	X	X	X	X	X	X	X	X	X	X	X	X	X	X	X	X	X	X				19
	6		X		X	X	X	X	X	X	X													8
Technical and Engineering	7	X	X	X	X	X	X	X	X	X	X	X	X	X	X	X			X	X	X	X	19
	8	X	X	X	X		X	X	X	X	X	X	X	X	X	X			X	X	X	X	18
	9	X		X		X			X	X	X									X				7
	10	X	X	X	X		X	X	X	X	X	X	X	X	X	X	X	X	X	X	X	X	20
	11	X	X			X	X		X	X	X						X	X	X	X				11
	12				X	X	X	X	X								X	X						7
	13	X	X	X	X	X	X	X		X	X	X	X	X	X				X	X	X		16
	14	X	X	X	X	X	X	X	X	X	X	X	X	X	X	X	X			X	X		18
Marketing	15	X	X	X	X	X	X	X		X		X		X	X				X	X				13
	16	X	X	X	X	X	X	X		X		X		X	X				X					12
	17	X	X	X	X	X	X	X	X		X	X	X	X		X						X	14
	18			X	X	X		X	X						X	X			X					8
	19	X									X													2
	20	X		X	X		X							X					X		X		7
	21	X	X					X		X														4
Economic and Legal	22	X	X	X	X	X	X								X		X							8
	23	X	X	X			X	X	X			X	X		X	X								10
	24	X	X	X		X		X				X	X		X									8
	25	X	X	X	X			X					X		X	X			X					9
	26			X	X	X	X	X	X	X			X		X		X	X						11
	27				X							X					X							3
	28				X			X	X					X			X							5
	29	X		X	X		X	X	X			X	X				X	X			X	X	12
	30		X	X			X					X	X	X										6
Political and Social	31	X		X	X	X	X	X																6
	32	X			X																			2
	33	X			X																			2
	34	X	X	X	X	X	X	X		X					X						X			10
	35	X			X																			2
	36	X	X	X		X																		4
	37	X	X	X	X																			4
	38		X	X			X																	3
Management	39		X																					1
Total		29	28	26	26	25	24	22	19	17	16	16	15	15	13	13	11	11	11	11	9	9	

* Questionnaire responses

sion variables utilized in one or more surveys which were grouped into categories as indicated in Table 1.

The numerical indicators (1 through 38) in Table 1 represent their respective variables in the data presented in Table 2. It should be emphasized that Table 1 represents a complete list of the kinds of variables considered in the studies which were surveyed; it does not represent an attempt to develop an ideal, conceptual listing of most significant variables. Some items in Table 1 may appear only in a single study, and

may not necessarily be of great theoretical significance; conversely, there may be significant decision variables which all the studies overlook, and which, therefore, do not appear in Table 1. The reader should bear these considerations in mind when interpreting the data which follow.

The list of variables developed from the content analysis was sent to twenty-two companies which had conducted investment surveys resulting in positive decisions. These firms were asked to identify from that list the variables which they felt they had addressed in their surveys.

One additional variable was suggested among the questionnaire responses: "communication and travel 'distance' from the home offices." This item is listed as number 39 in the data matrix of Table 2.

Company names and dates and locations of investment studies are not listed in this article. The list of survey subjects and countries is representative of the character of both the survey and questionnaire samples:

Cattle operations	Honduras
Fertilizer plant	Dominican Republic
Juice concentrate plant	Argentina
Corn production and marketing	Central America
Wholesale produce marketing	Central America
Poultry plant	Brazil
Citrus fruit processing	Brazil
Vegetable processing	Brazil

The participating firms ranged in size and character from a $1.5 million grocery wholesaler to the agricultural chemical division of a *Fortune* "500" industrial company. The typical firm encountered in this survey was a medium-sized food packaging or processing company with sales in the $15-25 million range.

Table 2 represents a matrix of investment surveys versus the range of identified decision variables, indicating the frequency with which each decision variable appears among the entire set of investment studies.

Tentative Findings

The data in Table 3 have been arranged to assist the reader in understanding some of the generalizations we formed as a result of the analysis. The major tentative findings are discussed above.

TABLE 3. NUMBER OF VARIABLES CONSIDERED PER STUDY

CATEGORY	AVERAGE NUMBER OF VARIABLES CONSIDERED PER STUDY
Technical and Engineering	5.5
Financial	4.0
Economic and Legal	3.3
Marketing	3.0
Political and Social	1.6
Management	0
TOTAL	17.4

With Very Few Exceptions, Political and Social Considerations (Variables 31–38) Received Only Slight Attention. In actual fact, these variables received even less attention than Table 3 indicates. For example, although the table shows that investment survey *A* addresses seven of eight political-social considerations, it does not indicate that only four out of approximately 160 pages of text were devoted to these factors. The sole negative decision survey with an in-depth analysis of legal-social-political considerations devotes approximately 100 pages out of 362 to a discussion of issues which fall within the framework of political and social consideration. All questionnaire respondents however, indicated a relatively high degree of interest in economic, social, and legal and political variables. The contrast with negative decision surveys is interesting in this regard.

Finally, although survey *H* contains no explicit discussion of political considerations, variables 31, 33, and 34 are so checked because the firm imposed a moratorium on its study in the spring of 1966 pending the outcome of the national election in the Dominican Republic in June. One can only suppose that management would have considered the return to power of a Bosch administration as an unhealthy investment signal (Bosch lost the election, but the company decided against investment for other reasons). Thus, the study implicitly acknowledged the importance of socio-political considerations.

In sum, the data seem to support the hypothesis that social and political factors tend, in general, to be treated with the same lack of concern in the foreign context as they are in the domestic. The reasons for this unconcern are open to conjecture, but it does not seem reckless to suggest that a combination of procedural inertia (that is, the habit of ignoring political and social considerations in the domestic environment) and lack of expertise is a prime cause in the neglect of such factors.

Marketing Considerations Received Relatively Little Attention. This is perhaps the most surprising generalization to be drawn from the data. Nevertheless, Table 3 clearly suggests that marketing is often a secondary, tertiary, or—in two cases—virtually non-existent consideration. Table 3 indicates that financial and technical-engineering considerations received primary attention, with marketing following a distant fourth.

What accounts for the apparent neglect of marketing considerations? The question is open to speculation, but a closer analysis of the survey suggests some clues which point toward at least one answer.

Each investment survey began with an objective which was limited by the national boundaries of the country in focus. For example, a study might be entitled *Feasibility of a Poultry Processing Plant in Argentina,* but no survey was entitled "Optimal Locations for Poultry Processing in South America," which would suggest a range of alternative locations by country, and so forth. It is also worth noting that a number of companies identify their original source of interest in a country. One cites a general interest article in a popular magazine as the source of its interest in cattle ranching in Brazil; another says it merely "heard" from business associates about the potential fertilizer market in the Dominican Republic. In other words, the one-country orientation of all these studies, the absence of comparative data, the often superficial or negligible market research contained therein, and the tendency toward exclusive interest in financial and technical feasibility suggest that market existence is largely a presumed postulate *before* a study ever begins.

There is little evidence in most of these studies of the influence of the kind of sophisticated marketing viewpoint which increasingly has characterized American domestic commerce since World War II. The approach might be characterized in general, perhaps, as the early-twentieth-century view of marketing: "Let's build a plant, make a product, then worry about selling it." It is difficult to accept what appears to be such a primitive approach to marketing considerations in the underdeveloped environment. Yet, there is ample evidence elsewhere of the same kind of phenomenon occurring within the management structure of top U.S. corporations. The collapse of Litton Industries' twelve-year-old, $240 million investment in Greece is partially explained by one Litton executive as being just such a case:

Litton just plain didn't know too much about the facts of life in Greece. They hadn't done their homework. Their advertising was way out of proportion. . . . In other words, Litton should have studied Greek customs, history, economics, . . . and other pertinent structuring before going out to sell.[5]

The corporate behavior pattern thus far discussed, that is, the emphasis on financial and technical considerations to the relative exclusion of socio-political and economic and legal considerations, and the neglect of marketing factors, poses an interesting

5 "The Litton-Greece Nation-building Experiment—Why Did It Go on the Shoals?" *Government Executive,* February 1970, pp. 58–59.

paradox. On the one hand, evidence points toward the tendency of many firms to adhere closely to domestic decision-making patterns in excluding consideration of socio-political and economic-legal variables; on the other, the same evidence tends to suggest that a number of firms diverge markedly from their domestic patterns of thoughtful market research and analysis. Perhaps further study will suggest a comprehensive explanation of such paradoxical behavior. At present, one hypothesis offered earlier suggests a partial explanation: in many developing countries firms lack the kind of sophisticated, empirical statistical data about commercial, economic, and marketing factors which they are accustomed to in the domestic environment. Companies are thrown into an unprecedented, procedurally ambiguous situation with regard to marketing research and analysis. In short, they simply do not know how to begin to do the same kinds of things which are almost mechanical in the domestic environment. One common reaction to this situation seems to be to avoid the problem by rendering only superficial or casual treatment to many marketing considerations.

In General, Investment Surveys Tended to Emphasize Those Variables Which Fell Within the Specific Professional Competence of the Survey Team. Lack of complete data regarding this observation makes it less susceptible to generalization, but the relationship is clear in those studies which do identify the professional status and background of the researcher. Surveys R and S (Table 2), for example, were conducted by engineering consulting firms; the decision variables (as well as total textual materials) are significantly weighted toward technical-engineering feasibility considerations. On the other hand, survey Q is the only study reflecting a really comprehensive investigation of the tax, legal, and investment aspects of its proposal (a cattle project in Brazil)—

the study was managed by a team of the firm's lawyers. Finally, the surveys evidencing some breadth of interest in the economic, social, and legal and political aspects of investment decision making (surveys A and B) were directed by international economists claiming some competence in the evaluation of social, political, and economic factors. These relationships suggest the necessity of careful design and selection of the survey team to insure balance, objectivity, and breadth of consideration in the survey.

A Group of Decision Variables Representing Some Specific International Business Considerations Received Little Attention. Variables ignored included monetary exchange (variable 6), import-export restrictions (variable 27), and capital flow restrictions (variable 28). Again it seems that lack of competence on the part of the survey team may have been a major reason for their apparent ineffective treatment of these issues.

Most Firm's Pre-Survey "Homework" Appeared Spotty at Best and at Times Totally Absent. While overall quality appeared to vary widely over the range of surveys, in the majority of cases there was little evidence to sustain our preliminary assumption that the typical firm would have conducted a thorough, pre-survey, secondary research effort in order to maximize the value and effectiveness of expensive on-site survey time.

Six Generalizations

In summary, six tentative generalizations were developed from the analysis of investment surveys and questionnaire responses:

1) inadequate treatment of economic, political, and social variables;

2) inadequate analysis of marketing variables;

3) lack of comparative (multi-country) analysis;

4) survey team professional bias;

5) inadequate treatment of international business considerations; and

6) poor pre-survey homework.

In formulating these generalizations, focus was on the primary objective of the study, that is, to identify some *potentially* significant problems confronting firms involved in foreign investment studies. These findings then were subjected to more intensive analysis through in-depth interviews.

INTERVIEWS WITH INTERNATIONAL EXECUTIVES

In an attempt to elaborate upon the list of generalizations formed as a result of the analysis of investment surveys, unstructured personal interviews were conducted with three top international executives: (1) the executive vice-president for international business of one of the 100 largest U.S. manufacturing corporations; (2) a senior vice-president of a top U.S. bank, formerly senior vice-president for international business; and (3) the marketing manager for an international subsidiary of a *Fortune* "500" corporation. Each executive was presented with the list of findings discussed earlier in this article and was asked to comment upon each.

Inadequate Treatment of Economic, Political, and Social Variables. All three executives unanimously agreed that there was a significant problem concerning the treatment of socio-politico-economic variables. All seemed equally convinced that there was no practical way to systematically evaluate such issues; what is necessary, instead, is a general feel for the socio-political risk environment in a country, the kind of feel which requires the assistance of a trusted native of the country. One executive pointed out that U.S. government or Department of State assistance in social and political analysis was not necessarily reliable, and might even be counterproductive. He cited as an example Egypt and the Soviet Union, whose close relationship in matters

of military technical assistance makes the investment environment high risk in official eyes. In reality, the investment climate in Egypt is probably among the most stable and advantageous in the underdeveloped world, at least in this executive's view. In other words, official analysis may be vulnerable to ideological bias.

None of the executives indicated an awareness of current efforts in social science research to quantify and measure social and political variables with a view toward providing a more rational, analytical approach to the evaluation of political and social stability.

Inadequate Analysis of Marketing Variables. The consensus was that criticism of marketing analysis was not valid if applied to Europe and Japan, but was relevant to market research problems in some of the less developed areas. As one executive noted, the potential market size in an underdeveloped country may be too small to warrant extensive market research. Inadequate census and commercial data and cultural obstacles to standard market research techniques (interviews, and so forth) were also cited as influencing the de-emphasis of marketing considerations.

Lack of Comparative Analysis. All three executives expressed an awareness of attempts to structure and conduct market research and investment analysis in terms of criteria other than national boundaries. Each executive, in varying degrees, seemed pessimistic about the "real-world" usefulness of such approaches. In the absence of an operational approach to answering the question "Do we invest in country *A, B,* or *C*?" each executive seemed to feel that single-country analysis, based upon some internal corporate lead or special interest, offered the most practical solution.

Survey Team Professional Bias. One executive believed that team bias was no more a problem in the international than the domestic context, and that as such it required no unique attention. The others thought this could be a significant problem for a company which lacked a specific survey plan, or had not formulated a set of precise survey questions covering the entire range of investment issues. One executive noted that despite a well-defined survey approach a team might significantly warp its report because of conscious or unconscious bias on the part of the members. He suggested an outside (contracted) survey team under the leadership of one or two corporate officers as the best approach.

Inadequate Treatment of International Business Considerations. None of the executives believed that poor treatment of international business considerations was a significant problem, at least in terms of their own experiences. One interviewee pointed out that such things as exchange controls, transfer pricing regulations, capital export restrictions, and so forth, were a constant part of the daily decision environment for the international executive, and that no investment opportunity could be given serious consideration without confronting such issues. He suggested that these matters may have been so obvious, so commonly understood by the individuals conducting the survey in question, that they were merely overlooked in many of the survey summaries. It may be useful to note, however, that while the three executives interviewed were all members of large, sophisticated U.S. corporations, many of the firms conducting investment surveys were not so large, and perhaps not so sophisticated.

All Pre-Survey Homework. All three executives indicated that they had encountered or observed inadequate pre-surveys in the past, either within their own firm, or in others. One suggested that such an error is most likely to occur when the firm perceives itself to be under some time pressure—to precede a competitor; or

when the firm is unaware of the information and assistance provided by various agencies of the U.S. government in this regard.

During the course of the interviews, two further issues were raised in the comments of at least two of the executives.

There is not necessarily a relationship between the size of the firm, and the sophistication of its approach to foreign investment analysis and international business in general. One executive recalled with some humor the lack of detail in his president's directive to develop the firm's international division: "John, go out and get some international business."

Generalized country and area evaluations of the sort provided by the Department of State, the Department of Commerce, AID, and so forth, may be useful in stimulating investment interest, but are inadequate in terms of providing precise answers to specific questions from serious potential investors. A firm may find such agencies useful in performing background research, but it is making a mistake if it uses such a shortcut rather than its own on-site investment analysis.

CONCLUSIONS

Despite the small size of the research sample, this analysis does suggest some insights which may have applicability in a broader evaluation of the current status of foreign investment decision making. This research points toward a most important general conclusion for which ample other evidence exists, but which still is not widely accepted because it sharply conflicts with the traditional lore of American business efficiency. *In general, many U.S. firms' overall approach to foreign investment decision making is much less sophisticated than their comparable domestic approach.* The former is often characterized by a lack of breadth in consideration of important variables, a biased perspective, and by lack of adequate preparation.

In addressing these problems in more specific terms, at least three areas seem to require particular emphasis in the future: (1) the need to recognize and to develop acceptable methodologies for the evaluation of important political, social, legal, and economic variables; (2) the need to develop effective substitute approaches to the market research and analysis requirement in light of the frequent irrelevancy or inapplicability of domestic approaches; and (3) the need to build balance and breadth into the structure of the study of investment possibilities.

Moreover, a final issue suggests itself in considering the noncomparative, one-country approach which still seems to characterize foreign investment analysis. Despite the contrary opinion of the executives interviewed in this study, it still seems defensible to argue that the studies reviewed here only touch on the most significant phase of the study—comparative analysis of alternative investment locations. Popular magazine articles and hearsay from friends hardly seem appropriate bases for narrowing a range of investment choices to a single country, yet the practice, apparently, is not uncommon. In any case, a major step in the development of a more sophisticated approach to foreign investment analysis is the necessity for American business to overcome, or at least become aware of, the limitations of the single-country conceptual framework.

The key to future improvement of investment decisions in foreign markets, particularly in the Third World, may lie in the motivation generated by the inevitable increase in competition. In the past, the sheer power, dynamism, and momentum of U.S. business virtually insured its success in almost any underdeveloped foreign environment. As competition, particularly from Europe, becomes more significant, the recognition of shades of difference and finer distinctions with regard to investment alternatives becomes more important as well. Yet, if the investment studies reviewed in this paper are representative, it seems fair to suggest the capabilities and methodologies necessary for making such distinctions have not kept pace with the need.

27 The Multinational Enterprise and Nationalism

Philip R. Cateora

This article reviews the growing trend of nationalism with its implications for multinational enterprises. Nationalistic sentiments expressed by a desire for greater economic self- sufficiency frequently inhibit and restrain the operations of multinational firms. The growing animosity toward foreign investment (especially U.S. direct investment) is apparent in both in-

Philip R. Cateora, "The Multinational Enterprise and Nationalism," pp. 49–56, *MSU Business Topics,* Spring 1971. Reprinted by permission of the publisher, Division of Research, Graduate School of Business Administration, Michigan State University.

dustrialized and less developed countries. This increased concern over foreign economic domination will be the most challenging problem facing the multinational businessman in the 1970s.

In order to grow, multinational firms must be able to profitably develop foreign markets, and direct foreign investment is necessary if the less developed countries are to achieve forecasted rates of economic growth. Although the mutual need is obvious, there is increasing evidence that recent events in Peru, Bolivia, and Chile are only harbingers of prevailing attitudes among underdeveloped nations, as well as many developed countries. As president of Chile, Salvadore Allende's proposed expropriation of most of the $965 million U.S. investment would only be one item in a long list of difficulties the foreign investor faces with host countries.

Just weeks before the Chilean election, the Peruvian government announced the development of a new industrial law which provides that the government buy control of all basic industries and sell the equity to nationals. Preliminary reports indicate that the government intends to buy at least two-thirds control of most companies in basic industries over a ten-year period. Foreign owners of companies in other industries will have to sell 51 percent control to Peruvians within a fairly short period, and eventually divest themselves of all but 25 percent ownership. Further, each company will be required to reinvest 15 percent of its net profits annually in company shares for the account of its employees until the employees own 51 percent of the concern. One could proceed in this vein as Latin American history is a continuous account of entanglements with foreign investors; however, uncertainty about multinational investors is by no means limited to Latin America or other under-developed countries.

In Great Britain, one industrialist apprehensive about increased foreign investment warned that "Britain might become a satellite where there could be manufacturing but no determination of policy." [1] While the British government generally has viewed foreign investment favorably, there is sufficient anxiety over possible U.S. domination that strict guidelines have been set for joint ventures between certain British and U.S. firms. For example, Chrysler was required to make assurances of the reinvestment of a large percentage of profits in Great Britain, to insure increased exports, to guarantee the number of nationals on the boards of directors, and to purchase components in the United Kingdom before the acquisition of Rootes Motor, Ltd., was approved.[2]

In Canada, a similar concern about the size of foreign investment has led the Royal Commission on Canadian Economic Prospects to recommend that foreign-owned subsidiaries must "Canadianize," that is, appoint Canadians to companies' boards of directors, staff key positions with Canadians, insure that a sizable minority of equity stock be sold to Canadians, purchase supplies in Canada, and aggressively seek export markets.[3]

In the EEC (European Economic Community), fear of U.S. business domination continues to smolder and is expected to flare up when the Common Market Commission makes public a report on the strong position of U.S. investment in common market countries. Among the highlights which are expected to increase qualms about the "American challenge" are such facts as:

---

[1] "Industrialist Warns Against U.S. Role in U.K. Economy," *Wall Street Journal,* 20 January 1969, p. 6.

[2] Reed Moyer, "British Attitudes Toward U.S. Investments," *MSU Business Topics,* Summer 1970, p. 65.

[3] I. A. Litvak and C. J. Maule, "Guidelines for the Multinational Corporation," *Journal of World Business,* July-August 1968, p. 36.

The amount raised by U.S. companies for investment in Europe rose from $477 million in 1959 to $2.6 billion in 1967.

U.S. companies reinvested 16 percent of profits in their operations in Europe in 1959, but only 9 percent in 1967.

By the end of 1968, American-controlled assets in the Common Market totaled $36 billion.[4]

Even Australia, one of the most open countries to foreign investment, is questioning the control of basic industries by foreign investors.[5]

What creates concern among developed nations depends upon the country and situation, but misgivings center around the following points:

1) Foreign companies will draw skilled personnel from national companies.

2) There often is a lack of congruency between the policy of foreign company operations in the host country and host country governmental policy.

3) Global planning of foreign companies may adversely affect national interests.

4) The viability of native research and development effort could be affected should the host country become too dependent upon foreign manufacturers.

Among the less developed countries, mistrust of economic and industrial domination is intertwined with a nagging doubt of whether the foreign investor has been making every possible effort to spur total economic and social growth. There is much accord with Augusto Zimmerman, spokesman for President Juan Valasco of Peru, who remarked in response to questions about the motives behind the recent foreign investment law: "We have had massive foreign investments for decades, but Peru has not achieved development. Foreign capital will now have to meet government social goals."[6] There also seems to be a combined fear of foreign investment and the multinational organization as an entity. An editorial in a Mexican newspaper states:

The question arises as to why the upsurge in Mexicanization continues to gain momentum. Nationalism is not the answer even though nationalists have been the most vociferous about the subject. What is of extreme issue is self-protection from the giant complexes of multinational corporations.[7]

The freewheeling ways of multinational companies are creating misgivings among labor unions and governments. Conflicts grow out of problems with job security, taxation, antitrust regulations, security issues, and trading with enemy nations.[8]

Even in the United States, when the dominance of basic industries is threatened, we become defensive toward foreign involvement. The Mills Trade Bill, presently pending in Congress, is evidence of this. It will impose quotas on imports of shoes, textiles, and other items. For that matter, restricting foreign business operations is not new in the United States; public broadcasting, banking, coastal shipping, and exploitation of minerals on public lands have been limited to U.S. firms for a number of years.[9]

[4]"International Outlook," *Business Week,* 4 July 1970, p. 55.
[5]See Donald P. Brooke, "Australia as Host to the International Corporation," in Charles P. Kindleberger, *The International Corporation* (Cambridge, Mass.: The MIT Press, 1970), p. 293–318.

[6]"Social Reform Jolts the Mine Owners," *Business Week,* 29 August 1970, p. 26.
[7]"Case for Mexicanization," *The News,* Mexico City, 19 July 1970, p. 27.
[8]"International Outlook," *Business Week,* 8 August 1970, p. 48.
[9]Raymond Vernon, "Future of the Multinational Enterprise," *The International Corporation, ibid.,* p. 391.

CONCERN JUSTIFIED

Justification for concern over the position of foreign investment in a country may be easier to understand if the perspective of the host country is appreciated. Let us examine some of the facts which alarm countries with heavy foreign investments. By the end of 1968, American-controlled assets in the Common Market totaled $35 billion. More meaningful figures, however, show that 95 percent of all integrated circuit manufacturing, 80 percent of all computers, and 30 percent of all automobiles are American controlled. In France alone, 87 percent of safety razors, 70 percent of sewing machines, and 74 percent of calculators are manufactured by U.S. firms. In Great Britain, U.S. companies control over 50 percent of auto production, and over 50 percent of all drugs supplied by the National Health Service are manufactured by American companies, either from subsidiaries in Britain, or by imports from the United States.

In much of Latin America, such basic industries as automobile manufacturing, mining, communications, oil, and chemicals frequently are owned by foreign investors, or were before being nationalized. The Chilean copper industry was nearly 100 percent dominated by foreign investors before nationalization. The political and economic consequences of a country's economy being dominated by one or several foreign firms might well be just cause for apprehension. In their minds, it leaves too much of the national development and welfare to the uncontrolled and possibly unpredictable high-level executive who may be unaware and perhaps even unsympathetic toward local economic and social needs. Apparent support of these fears lies in the knowledge that host country nationals may not be integrated into top management levels of multinational firms. One study of 150 of the largest U.S. multinational companies found that only 1 percent of the senior executives at headquarters were non-American while income generated overseas by these same 150 companies was about 20 per cent of their total.[10]

Some distrust may result from "blind nationalism" but in most cases, aside from nationalism, there are, in the minds of those in the host country, sound economic reasons for controlling the foreign investor. If the foreign investment deals with natural resources or public utilities there is a natural tendency to worry over possible exploitation when a foreign power is in control of such vital segments of the economy. In other instances, there may be worry among those in government that too many small producers in a single industry hamper continued economic growth and development. For example, one probable reason behind the Mexicanization of the auto industry was to reduce the number of manufacturers to three or four strong ones in hope that this would strengthen each one's market position and enable them to more easily comply with other governmental directives. Those who were able to continue operations in Mexico had to:

increase Mexican ownership and hire more Mexican employees;

increase the share of corporate profits going to Mexican workers; and

import fewer components from other countries.

The government's intention also may have been to force a larger proportion of money spent by Mexicans for consumer products to stay in Mexico in order to provide jobs and development capital for Mexico's economic growth.[11] It seems that whether justified or not, a defensive response on the part of a country generally arises as

---

[10]Howard Perlmutter, "Geocentric Giants to Rule World Business," *Business Abroad,* April 1969, p. 12.

[11]"Yanks in Mexico," *Wall Street Journal,* 27 January 1962, p. 1.

foreign investment grows in relative importance to its basic industries and establishes itself in more sensitive areas of national life.

A PREDICTABLE PATTERN

There appears to be a predictable pattern. Countries typically looking for capital, managerial know-how, technological capabilities, and/or markets, welcome and encourage foreign companies to invest. Specific provisions for repatriation of investment capital and profits, and special provisions for import taxes on raw materials and supplies may be provided as incentives but, once companies are established, it seems almost inevitable that concern will be expressed over the extent of economic influence. One international authority sees this concern as a natural misunderstanding resulting from corporations responding to the normal demands of business while governments of developing nations must react to political realities:

The company often conceives the scope and nature of its activities differently than the host government. It often views its profit needs differently. So the two find themselves talking at cross purposes, even to the point of reciprocal accusations of subversion and sabotage.[12]

GREATER CONTROL SOUGHT

Once concern is aroused, there are demands for greater control over the foreign investors. These demands for control may be little more than discussions in the press, or they may culminate in expropriation, the severest form of repression. With the exception

---

[12]A. T. Knoppers, "A Multinational Corporation in the Third World," *Columbia Journal of Business,* July-August 1970, p. 35.

of some undeveloped countries, most shy away from expropriating foreign investments. Their reason is very sound: once a country has shown a pattern of expropriation, investment tends to dry up quickly. Latin American nationalism has caused a great deal of pessimism among U.S. investors because of the fear that existing and future military regimes may resort to expropriation. Recent events in August and September of 1970 in Peru and Chile seem to bear out these fears.

Rather than outright confiscation, or expropriation, concern over foreign investment generally is manifested more subtly in the gradual encroachment on the freedom to operate within the country. In essence, governments seek to *domesticate* the foreign investor rather than expropriate.

DOMESTICATION—A MEANS FOR CONTROL

Domestication may be defined as the process of transferring the control of a foreign investment to national hands and bringing the firm's activities in line with national interests. Domestication entails:

a transfer of ownership in part or totally to nationals;

the promotion of a large number of nationals to higher levels of management;

greater decision-making powers resting with nationals;

a greater number of products being produced locally rather than being imported for assembly; and

specific export regulations designed to dictate participation in world markets.

Domestication differs from expropriation on several levels. Expropriation generally implies that the government takes over by decree, at an arbitrarily set price, the total ownership of the company. In turn, the company may be sold to private citizens or the government may maintain ownership, thereby nationalizing it. Domestication is that process whereby the government, by various means, forces a foreign-held enterprise eventually to relinquish control on several fronts to nationals.

Governments can force domestication through a variety of measures. They can resort to a national decree declaring that ownership must be passed to nationals, or they can be more subtle and suggest that greater local ownership will avoid unprofitable changes in import quotas and exchange rates. The government also may suggest that more supplies and component parts be purchased locally. Government intervention at the domestication level is one of persuading the company to meet certain domestication demands in return for the continuance of special concessions, or the right to continue operations.

WHY DOMESTICATION VS. EXPROPRIATION?

If greater control of the national economy is at issue, why does a country domesticate rather than nationalize or expropriate foreign businesses? The answer is that most foreign investors bring with them an expertise and capability on one or all of four levels; capital, managerial know-how, technical expertise, and access to world markets. If a country nationalizes or expropriates a foreign business, the invested capital is captured but the expertise, the managerial know-how, and access to world markets has escaped. Hence, after expropriation or nationalization, the host country quickly realizes that those factors which made the foreign investment important to them no longer exist. On the other hand, domesticating the foreign investment puts the country in a better position of continuing to benefit from the expertise and managerial know-how since the foreign investor still has some vested interest in the firm and can profit from maintaining a high degree of efficient production.

Thus, a country that domesticates an investment is able to secure basic control over it. This allays domestic fear of foreign domination, quiets political uproar, directs the firm's efforts toward national socioeconomic goals, and, at the same time, retains the other contributions the foreign investment makes. Expropriation gains total control but usually forfeits the elusive managerial and technical capabilities most needed by the country and can affect drastically future direct foreign investment. On the surface, domestication may appear to be desirable for both foreign investor and host country; indeed, in some instances it is, but it generally depends upon who initiates the domesticating action. Government-initiated domestication can be as drastic and disruptive for the foreign firm as expropriation, while company-initiated or predetermined domestication may result in an equitable position for both the host country and foreign company.

EFFECTS OF GOVERNMENT-INITIATED DOMESTICATION

The effects of government-initiated domestication of a foreign firm can be disastrous; in fact, the effect may be tantamount to expropriation. In addition to outright loss of investment, lack of control because of lost equity due to forced stock sales, lost management control because of forced hiring of nationals, and regulations requiring increased local supply purchases, government-initiated domestication can slow down or halt growth, limit markets or market expansion, decrease profits, and disrupt overall global marketing planning for the multinational company.

Consider an established foreign investor with 100 percent ownership of his firm facing an ultimatum to sell 51 percent of that ownership to local nationals by a specific date because political conditions and attitudes demand it. Even if local capital was available, it would be almost impossible to sell the stock at a fair and equitable price. Prospective purchasers realize that with the sale forced by a specific date, they can negotiate the price so low it could be at an expropriative level and the foreign investor has no recourse.[13]

In Mexico and other Latin American countries there have been numerous cases of companies being instructed to sell a percentage of ownership by a specific date with the result that the sellers were able to recapture only a fraction of the actual value of their investment. Even if equity is sold at reasonable prices, a basic conflict of interest between the foreign investor and the national stockholder frequently arises. When a forced sale is made it is generally to a small group who are interested in an immediate return on investment, rather than the reinvestment of profits necessary for continued market development and capital growth.

Equally calamitous can be government directives that require a certain percentage of top level management to be nationals. Unless adequately trained nationals who are willing to follow corporate guidelines can be appointed to fulfill these positions, companies find that they are unable to maintain control over their investments. In many instances when such decrees are issued, companies find that they have no adequately trained nationals within the company to transfer to higher level positions so they must seek others outside the business. They then find there are few available who have the depth of experience necessary, and the competition for those few is fierce.[14] Equally troublesome, the new owners may force the hiring of "loyal" nationals who have little capability for the position and who are more interested in protecting the personal interests of the national stockholder than implementing long-term corporate plans. In either case, they may have personnel in executive positions unable or unwilling to make decisions commensurate with the positions they hold. Further aggravation results when such under-trained managers are not given the responsibility equal to their positions and decision making reverts to the New York office. Unfortunately, even capable personnel in key positions often are not permitted to participate in major decisions. They are treated and feel much like one vice-president of a foreign subsidiary who noted to the author that, "I am just a *front office national* not too different from the *front office black* employed by U.S. firms."

Further complications and costly problems for the foreign investor come with requirements that supplies, raw materials, and perhaps component parts be purchased locally. In most cases, when a government requires that raw materials and supplies be of local origin, they are not readily or economically available. In fact, the intent of the government usually is to force the foreign owner to create local demand, thereby stimulating local production. The company then finds that not only are supplies unavailable, but, in order to create local supplies, the firm must provide the primary investment capital to develop local industries as well as to train and provide necessary expertise. With established supply sources, experience, and/or local financing usually completely lacking, the foreign investor must find ways (at enormous expense and time lapse) of producing locally.

ALTERNATIVES FOR THE FOREIGN INVESTOR

Certainly one way to sidestep the ultimate consequences of government-initiated domestication is simply to sell

[13]Louis J. Creel, Jr., "Mexicanization—A Case of Creeping Expropriation," *South-Western Law Journal* 22 (Spring 1968): 281–99.

[14]Sanford Rose, "The Rewarding Strategies of Multinationalism," *Fortune*, September 1968, p. 180.

out to other investors. This, of course, does not solve any problems nor does it generally fit into the long-range plans of most multinational firms. If a firm does not want to sell out, it must develop strategies to lessen the long-range effects of expropriation or domestication. Once expropriation or domestication are imminent, efforts may be made to negotiate, exert political or economic pressure, seek legal remedies, or, if nothing else works, to surrender and salvage whatever is salvageable.[15] Another avenue open to the foreign investor is simply to ignore the problem hoping he will not be seriously affected. One lawyer involved with a company caught in the recent Peruvian move to expropriate foreign investments admitted that as early as December 1968, the military regime outlined precisely what it intended to do. "We all heard it," he said, "but nobody was listening."[16]

An interesting alternative proposed by Albert O. Herschman is for a supra-national agency to be established which would stand ready to buy partial ownership in foreign investments on the behalf of the local government. This agency would create a market for companies that wanted to divest themselves or were forced to divest themselves of ownership.[17] Certainly this is a workable concept if properly financed, but until such an institution is created the multinational firm still is faced with the problems of government-initiated domestication and all the negative ramifications. If the foreign investor of the 1970s is seriously intent upon developing and maintaining an economic foothold in another country, other ways of operating must be found. They must be politically acceptable as well as profitable to the host country, and profitable and operationally feasible to the foreign investor. *Predetermined domestication* is a move in that direction.

PREDETERMINED DOMESTICATION: AN ALTERNATIVE

Predetermined domestication is, in essence, a gradual, planned process of participating with nationals in all phases of company operation. Initial investment planning would include steps to:

sell equity to nationals at fair prices over a number of years;

prepare nationals for top decision-making positions;

integrate local companies (where feasible) into world-wide marketing programs;

develop local companies as sources of supply; and

put on a sound economic base or make unnecessary any government concessions initially needed for successful investment.

The initial investment planning should contain provisions for eventual sale of a significant interest (perhaps even controlling interest) to nationals and incorporation of national economic needs and national managerial talent into business as quickly as possible. Such a policy would more likely result in reasonable control remaining with the parent company even though nationals eventually would have an important position in management and ownership. If company plans were to retrain and develop nationals to hold major positions in the investment, they would have the opportunity to insure that those who reached top positions would be qualified and in harmony with total corpo-

---

[15] For an interesting article on countering expropriations, see William R. Hoskins, "How to Counter Expropriations," *Harvard Business Review*, September-October 1970, pp. 102–12.

[16] "Social Reform Jolts the Mine Owners," *Business Week*, 29 August 1970, p. 27.

[17] See Albert O. Herschman, "How to Divest in Latin America and Why," *Essays in International Finance*, No. 76 (International Finance Series, Princeton University, Princeton, New Jersey), November 1969.

rate objectives. Such company trained nationals would be more likely to have a strong corporate point of view instead of only a country (national) point of view. If development of long-range plans provided for the use of local supplies there would not be sudden, short-term needs nor the necessity for crash programs to provide supplies. Local suppliers developed over a period of time ultimately could handle a significant portion of total needs. Further, if they developed a sound, sensible plan to sell ownership over a number of years, they could insure a fair and more equitable return on their investment in addition to encouraging ownership to be spread throughout the populace and thereby discouraging attempts by a few to exert undue corporate control. Finally, if government concessions and incentives essential in early stages of investment gradually were made economically feasible or unnecessary, the company's political vulnerability would be lessened considerably.

While predetermined domestication may not be the ideal investment plan, it is a practical, workable alternative to government-initiated domestication or expropriation. There is no doubt that more and more governments will establish policies for domesticating foreign investments; this policy is more palatable to all concerned. Domestication enables the host country "to have its cake and eat it too." Government-initiated domestication becomes one more condition which must be considered in developing an overall strategy for foreign investment.

The validity of predetermined domestication is supported by the Kaiser Corporation which has followed this policy for the last fifteen years, although not under that name, in its entire global empire. In their basic investment policy, they prefer a part interest in their foreign holdings with as many local managers as possible involved and, wherever possible, broad-based public ownership. Minority ownership can create some risk and some loss of control which many U.S. firms could not be comfortable with, but Kaiser's top management is inclined to take that risk in exchange for the better government relations which generally result. As a vice-president commented, "Where we have an assembly plant in which a local distributor is an owner, the government of that country isn't going to do anything to hurt our business . . . ,"[18] a statement typifying Kaiser's philosophy toward foreign partners. While some may quarrel with the success of Kaiser, they have managed to operate in countries (such as Brazil) noted for sporadic harassment and even expropriation of foreign investments with a minimum of risk or loss.

CONCLUSION

Foreign investors of the future face changing conditions directly affecting their interest in foreign countries. Unless the multinational investor of the 70s concerns himself with the host country's total economy, the growing animosity to U.S. dollars throughout the world will continue to show itself in government-initiated domestication and expropriation of U.S. investments. In order to avoid the economic pitfalls of these two policies, global investment strategies will have to include a social awareness of local needs and wants. The investment must be aimed toward becoming a fully-integrated part of the domestic economy. Such predetermined domestication seems to be the most workable policy for the coming years in light of the evolving hostile political atmosphere found in many countries around the world.

---

[18]"Kaiser's Global Empire," *Forbes,* 15 April 1968, p. 34.

IV MANAGEMENT IN THE FUTURE

This final part of the book is concerned with future developments in the field of management. Two subjects in particular are given attention. The first is the current trend toward professionalism in management, and the second is a profile of managers in the future.

The first article in this section, by Professor Robert Pearse, addresses the question of whether managers can be trained in a manner that will make professional certification possible. He specifies a number of criteria that are characteristic of professional management, including emphasis on short- and long-range goals, participative decision making, the management of human assets, and emphasis on self-development and career development. He also makes a number of suggestions concerning how management education must change if professionalism is to occur.

In the second selection, Professor John Mee describes the changes that have occurred in managers over the past 400 years. Beginning as office-holders and owner-managers, they were followed by captains of industry, corporate speculators and, now, professional managers. What does the future hold? Professor Mee sees a manager capable of coping with an environment in which human values are changing and rapid technological progress is occurring. In this article, he provides a profile of this emerging manager.

The last reading, "Reflections of a 21st Century Manager," presents some of the characteristics of the manager of the 1970s and 1980s, which reflect the opinion of its author, George Kozmetsky. Although his predictions may prove slightly inaccurate, he does provide the reader with a view of what the future may well hold. In particular, the author emphasizes on the need for the manager of the future to be a thinker and a planner capable of handling nonroutine jobs.

28   Certified Professional Managers: Concept into Reality?

Robert F. Pearse

"Although business management is not currently a profession as measured against the ideal model, the trend is in this direction. . . . There is a growing body of systematic knowledge concerning the management and administration of complex organizations; the authority role of the manager has been legitimized in our culture; this role has the sanction of the community; there is a growing number of professional management associations, particularly in the various specialized aspects of business; and finally, there is a nucleus of the development of professional self-control."

—Kast and Rosenzweig, *Organizations and Management: A Systems Approach*

The above observation, made in 1970, brings us in 1972 to a direct question: Can managers now be trained and developed in a way that will make professional management certification possible and desirable? Certainly, the concept of a professionally managed organization exists, having been developed by both university business schools and management organizations. This concept of professional management has these characteristics:

Emphasis on planning for both short- and long-range goals.

Participation and involvement of people at all levels in goal setting, planning, and motivating individual and team progress toward goals.

A systems and computer-applications orientation in forecasting and simulation.

Awareness of the importance of the human resources model of manpower utilization and development.

Emphasis on individual self-development and career development.

Understanding that social control of business involves both possible increased governmental regulation and more stringent consumer demands.

Anticipation of the impact of "future shock" on technological and human aspects of organizational life.

A question not covered in this definition of professionalism has to do with the functional skills required——expertise in the departmentalized areas, such as finance, marketing, manufacturing, purchasing, and so forth. These are, of course, taken for granted. But what of managerial skills referred to implicitly in the definition—skills associated with planning, organizing, supervising, controlling, and motivating people? These managerial skills all fall within—and are dictated by—managerial styles, although many maintain that they are quite separate entities.

Reprinted by permission of the publisher from *Personnel*, March/April 1972. © 1972 by the American Management Association, Inc.

FOCUS ON MANAGERIAL STYLES AND SKILLS

Like the blind men in the fable who seized different parts of the elephant and felt that they had each discovered the "whole truth" about what an elephant is like, some protagonists of the styles or the skills schools proclaim that theirs is the whole truth when it comes to professional management.

In the 1950s and 1960s management training programs featured a variety of styles, in the belief that self-understanding, sensitivity to others, and "authentic" interpersonal relationships on the job would solve most of management's people-in-organizations problems. So far, this kind of training has not brought about the expected reformations, but it has enabled many individual managers to improve their personal communications and awareness of the needs and feelings of others. It has also improved their interpersonal effectiveness in dealing with problems that involve perceptual distortion, negative or hostile attitudes, and situations of intragroup or intergroup conflict and competition.

More recently, university business schools have begun to place equal emphasis on styles and skills training in their required courses. Thus, there are required courses in human behavior (including self-concept, self-understanding and interpersonal dynamics) and in organizational behavior (small-group processes, organizational conflict, competition, and collaboration) offered along with courses on financial planning, marketing, production management, and other technical skills.

For the certification of managers as professionals, however, the curriculum would have to be more formalized and more elaborate, in both managerial styles and managerial skills.

Certified professional manager training in management styles might cover the following areas:

Understanding the effects of individual personality variables, such as ways of approaching problem solving, decision making, interpersonal interaction, and small-group leadership and membership.

Understanding individual differences in human needs patterns and how they affect both work and nonwork motivations, with awareness of different perceptual modes (in receiving signals and interpreting them, for example) and how these differences influence individual definitions of situations.

The effects of values, attitudes, prejudices, and other biases on behavior; ways in which self-image and the role of unconscious processes—such as rationalization, projection, and denial—can influence the individual's managerial behavior.

Role behavior, role expectations, role enactments, and role conflicts in terms of what other people in the organization expect from the individual in their role interactions with him.

Effective communications and the problems involved in transmitting clear messages from sender to receiver, plus the negative effects of inaccurate communications on people and organizations.

Individual power strivings, competition, cooperation, and collaborative behavior, with emphasis on helping managers maximize their individual satisfactions along with maximum contribution to organizational effort.

Those aspiring to become professional managers would also get intensive feedback and analysis regarding their own current managerial style. They would be encouraged to maximize both their capacity to behave flexibly with changing situations and to enhance their potential for further growth in their personal managerial style. Along with self-understanding would come an appreciation of individual differences in life styles, motivations, self-concept, and achievement expression. This knowledge, it would be shown, is not for oneupmanship competitive strivings of the may-the-best-man-win variety, but rather for leading to the positive behavior appropriate to a dynamic company.

This kind of company is concerned with the maximum utilization of human resources in the broadest sense. Meaningful career progression is encouraged, rather than the self-seeking opportunism sometimes found in the entrepreneurial or bureaucratic firm. Job enhancement and job enlargement as personal challenges are substituted for the grinding impersonality and rigid role expectations that are often hallmarks of the large, bureaucratic organization.

TRAINING IN MANAGERIAL SKILLS

Training in managerial skills for the would-be professional manager should relate to the following areas:

Personal Effectiveness. This skill includes the management of time and the ability to plan flexibly, to make either on-the-spot or long-range decisions as required. More broadly, it is the ability to harness both physical and psychic energy in organizational task accomplishment.

Interpersonal Effectiveness. Much of a manager's interpersonal effectiveness is a result of his individual managerial style. However, he can benefit from skill training that maximizes his personal style as he becomes more proficient in understanding factors such as the dynamics of authority relationships with superiors; successful collaboration with peers on joint tasks, even though they may ultimately compete for a limited number of higher positions; and the day-to-day responsibility of supervising, delegating, motivating, and developing those who report to him.

Administrative Effectiveness. Many managers have little or no technical training in administrative practices and processes, but the ability to understand and make intelligent use of the organization's administrative systems, rather than seeing them as a jumble of meaningless forms and paperwork, is an important ingredient of success as the manager moves up the line. This understanding and use can, and should, be learned.

Organizational Effectiveness. This area includes the ability to use procedures affecting the following areas:

Organizational direction—management by objectives; goal setting; and planning, forecasting, and measuring progress toward goal accomplishment.

Human resources utilization and development—management development techniques and programs, job enlargement and enrichment methods, and human resource accounting concepts.

Managing conflict and change—developing win-win, rather than win-lose or political-manipulative power play solutions to organizational conflicts; anticipating the impact of major technical, social, and economic changes on the organization, its customers, and its employees; involving employees in decisions relating to changes that affect their lives and work; and adapting to new life styles of employees, to the aspirations of women and minority groups, to young people, and to the changing relationship between work and leisure.

Organizational development and organizational self-renewal—the ability to work creatively with O.D. specialists who have developed techniques to improve organizational functioning, effectiveness, and adaptability to change, or to apply those techniques directly.

INTEGRATING AND EXPANDING SPECIALIZED KNOWLEDGE

In the professional development of both medical and accounting specialists, internship and residency forms of postgraduate field training enable the practitioner to integrate his specialized learning into an overall view of the client's or patient's problem. Business schools have customarily used business policy courses as a synthesizing experience in which the student learns to apply functional skills (marketing, finance, accounting, production, and so on) to overall problems of the firm. Here, there are several goals:

Training in Strategic Thinking. A most important professional managerial skill involves training in strategic thinking. In the past, managers usually come up the narrow, functional specialist's route; only a few management training organizations offered them training from the general management approach. Books like Newman and Logan's *Strategy, Policy, and Central Management* point the way for training in the broader strategic thinking that puts "functional" thinking in the context of "company" thinking.

Training in Situational Thinking. The professional manager needs to learn to think situationally, too. Managers, like others, are inclined to apply a limited range of techniques to a variety of problems. The ability to analyze situations and to modify behavior and decision making according to the aspects peculiar to a given situation is essential to a professional manager's "stretch."

Training in Creative Problem Solving. If business problems in the future are going to be without precedent because of rapid changes in technology and society, professional managers should have training in creative problem solving and in the encouragement of creative problem solving among their subordinates. The works of Gordon and Prince on Synectics and of Norman Maier on creative group problem solving at The University of Michigan are examples of this type of training.

CERTIFICATION IN OTHER FIELDS

For many years, the accounting profession has conferred the C.P.A. designation on accountants who pass professional examinations and who also have internship experiences in professional accounting firms. Similarly, the insurance industry designates as Certified Life Underwriter (C.L.U.) those who have demonstrated both technical training skill and on-the-job expertise in specified areas of insurance at a required degree of excellence. And, of course, the legal and medical professions have long had ways to measure competency and other credentials. Here, we might briefly consider how the medical and accounting professions go about it.

The Medical Model. The medical certification model currently involves the following elements:

1. Training directed by established professionals at a certified medical training institution, usually affiliated with a university.

2. Internship and residencies wherein the practitioner develops skills in applying theory to practical, real-life cases and patients.

3. Passing state licensing examinations developed by medical boards directed by members of the profession but controlled by the state.

4. Affiliations with hospitals and/or clinics controlled by senior members of the profession plus (generally) affiliation with a county or city medical society.

5. Indoctrination in codes of professional ethics and expected conduct, which the future professional is expected to internalize and use as behavioral controls in his professional life.

The Certified Public Accountant Model. Accountants typically go through the following steps in qualifying as C.P.A.s:

1. Formal training in university programs conducted by specialists in accounting and finance, customarily C.P.A.s and/or D.B.A.s. (Whether a D.B.A. should also be required to have a C.P.A. to teach advanced accounting is a current bone of contention among accounting faculties.)

2. A supervised internship under the direction of C.P.A.s, in which the aspirants work on real-life client problems.

3. Passing certifying examinations developed by members of the profession, under state control.

ISSUES AND PROBLEMS IN PROFESSIONAL MANAGER CERTIFICATION

Some of the issues and problems involved in setting up formal certification of professional managers revolve around key issues reflecting procedures adopted by the medical and other professions:

Who Should Do the Training? Should training be conducted at university business schools at the B.A. or M.B.A. levels? If so, should the training be done by academicians holding the Ph.D. or D.B.A. degree in specialized subjects like finance, accounting, economics, or marketing? Should successful practitioners who do not hold advanced degrees also be involved in this training? If so, should they be involved in classroom theory training, or field internship training, or both?

What Should Be the Content of Professional Management Training Courses? Should business school deans appoint committees to develop a model curriculum? What voice should the successful business practitioner have in curriculum determination? (This question is particularly relevant, since he will probably hire and supervise graduating business students, and it is equally pertinent in the next point.)

Who Should Control the Certification Process? Should control of professional manager examinations be left in the hands of business school academicians and researchers? Or should successful practitioners be members of such bodies?

What Voice Should Professional Associations Have in Certification? Do they have the capabilities and are they otherwise suited to developing an overall plan for professional manager training?

What Should Be the Role of Professional Management Training Institutions? From 1950 to 1970, both university business schools and large professional management training organizations were the two major forces in the evaluation of professional management training. Many successful entrepreneurs received university training in science, engineering, or business. Armed with these skills, they set up effective organizations, and as their companies grew they were able to send some of their top and middle managers back to the campus for advanced professional management training.

Though university-based M.B.A. and D.B.A. training programs are growing, it has been estimated that by 1980 only one out of seven practicing managers will have had either business- or engineering-degree training in college. If this is true, the professional management association will be called on to do much of the training of the six out of seven managers whose college background did not include business or engineering training.

WHAT ABOUT IN-COMPANY PROFESSIONAL CERTIFICATION?

Using currently available tools and concepts, can and should top business executives realign their in-company management development programs along lines that could lead to in-house professional manager certification? Such certification could be given after individual managers had successfully completed both formal course work and had demonstrated capacity to manage effectively field operating situations with the application of professional management skills.

The principles set forth in George Odiorne's recent book, *Training by Objectives,* coupled with those of the dynamic or professionally managed company described by Blake and his associates in *Corporate Darwinism,* plus the work of Harold Koontz (*Appraising Managers as Managers*), offer one composite model for setting up a pilot in-house professional management certification program for companies that would like to explore the possible benefits of a C.P.M. approach to manager development.

The training-by-objectives model supplies a practical, real-world method for setting up and evaluating training programs in terms of their contribution to corporate growth and profit. The *Corporate Darwinism* model outlines the characteristics of the professionally managed (or dynamic) organization, as contrasted with both the entrepreneurial and bureaucratic-mechanistic models. Last, the *Appraising Managers as Managers* model offers a technique for evaluation in terms of their effectiveness.

A number of top-level professional managers who are also graduates of business schools and management associations are ready to explore the in-house certified professional manager concept as a possible evolutionary step in management development programs. At this stage, such a C.P.M. program would include the following steps:

Defining the certified professional management skills required for successful managerial performance in the company at the present time.

Developing in-house management training courses to meet these training needs.

Surveying currently available professional management association and university executive training programs that can be used to supplement in-house training.

Setting up a training and development program based on the career plan and personal growth interests of each participant.

Setting up methods of measurement, including ability to pass formal training course examinations in subjects relevant to professional management, and

demonstrated field performance in applying professional management skills and techniques to actual management situations.

Developing methods of recognizing and rewarding the certified professional manager for having attained this level of personal development.

MANAGEMENT AS A PROFESSION—ON THE HORIZON OR HERE?

In the early 1900s, American education and accreditation in the medical and other professions were amorphous local efforts and regulations, but, as we know, nationwide reform programs vastly improved quality and made room for orderly progress, both internally, from the professional's point of view, and externally, from the public's point of view. If the parallel holds between that now-established kind of certification and the certification of the management profession, the practice of management will be vastly improved—if that C.P.M. concept is properly implemented.

That "if" means first, of course, the development of adequate training and certification programs for managers. The basis already exists, because over the past 20 years academicians, practitioners, and independent theorists have been developing and expanding a workable body of knowledge and technical skills applicable both in training and in measuring management competence. When the C.P.M.'s day comes —and it now appears to be imminent—more capable people will be attracted to the profession, and the broad road they travel toward professional status will block off some of the narrow paths of segmented group orientation that businessmen (and many professions-within-professions) now take. Finally, society itself will benefit, because the C.P.M. concept will encompass as prerequisites a concern for and commitment to an evolving social role for business.

29   The Manager of the Future

John F. Mee

Coming events cast their shadows before —if we study those shadows, we can observe the forces and factors that are shaping the manager of the future.

There will be managers in the future. The pathologists can predict with certainty that bleeding will always stop; managers can predict with certainty that the future will eventually involve them. Their concern is whether or not they are prepared for the changing social, economic, technological, and political environments that emerge as the future unfolds.

MANAGERS OF THE PAST

Managers of the past can be described and classified in relation to the environments in which they operated. The antecedents of the managers in our English-influenced culture can be recognized in sixteenth century Tudor England. They were the office-holders in the royal household, in the major departments of state, and in the army and the navy. They were men to whom administration and management was a professional life commitment, and their function was to administer the affairs of the state and the economy within the rules of the social order.

After the separation of the United States from England, our constitution provided that individuals might own private property. Our government, founded on the concept of government by law rather than government by men, established an environment of opportunity for the owner-manager in a private enterprise economy. For over a century, the owner-managers of small enterprises flourished, managing by right of ownership rather than by birthright in a predominantly agricultural society.

Some of those owner-managers thrived with the changing environment at the turn of the century, and, using their authority of ownership, developed our basic industries and promoted our industrial society. Facing death from the impact of the Sherman Act they resorted to corporate forms of business organizations to perpetuate their firms. The growth of large and complex organizations with the capability of generating a trillion dollar gross national product originated with these "captains of industry."

They were followed by a new breed of managers who are now classified as corporate speculators and exploiters. These managers, who had financial or legal backgrounds, gained control of the business organizations that they managed for corporate share owners. The era of the speculators and exploiters was rather short. They met with an ignominious end in the decade of the 1930s because they were unable to manage business organizations for the benefit of society through the intelligent use of human and capital resources.

During that decade the federal government set about helping managers with legislative guidelines and regulations. The health of the economy was deemed too important to trust to capricious managers with improper

This article originally appeared in *Business Horizons* (June 1973), pp. 5–14. Copyright, 1973 by the Foundation for the School of Business at Indiana University. Reprinted by permission.

human values and undesirable social ethics. The flow of legislation regulating business activities and the pressures for social responsibilities and objectives of business were initiated by the failures of these managers.

Following the debacle of the thirties, a class of managers known as professional managers appeared; most operating managers of business enterprise today are in this category. The term professional managers is used because these men manage for pay and do not own any significant share of the enterprises they manage. They profess to have the knowledge, the skills, and the value systems suitable for setting objectives and then attaining them through the utilization of other people's money, talents, and physical facilities. Some of them acquire professional manager citations from their professional associations to reinforce their image.

Evaluated by their records of economic progress and the creation of material wealth, our American managers have the best performance records in the history of the world. U.S. resources include 6 percent of the world's population and 7 percent of the land area of the world; with these, our managers have generated over half of the wealth of the world and about 35 percent of the world's annual income. They have achieved the world's first trillion dollar gross national product. The combined efforts of Russia, Japan, West Germany, and the United Kingdom—with double the population of the United States—would be required to equal that figure.

That is a formidable record of managerial achievement; why, then, are managers experiencing so much dissatisfaction with their performance? Why are today's professional managers, working on the objectives established for the decade of the sizzling sixties, absorbing attacks for matters that previously have not been considered germane to operating businesses? Despite the most outstanding performance of managers in all history, they are criticized and attacked by:

Consumer groups and regulatory agencies

Aroused antipollutionists who often press for hasty, costly, or sometimes unavailable solutions

Ecologists who are more concerned with preserving the wilderness than creating employment opportunities

Civil rights activists who demand more jobs for minority groups from top to bottom ranks

Naive and well-meaning activists who clamor for democracy on boards of directors

Employees who want relief from boring and monotonous work assignments.

Recognizing merit in some of the criticism, perhaps too many well-meaning people are finding themselves influenced by the extremists and activists who can proclaim without responsibility. James Roche of General Motors Corporation has tried to bring the extremist view into perspective: "Profits are the incentives, the driving force behind economic expansion and rising employment. It takes about $25,000 investment to create one new job opportunity. Just to keep pace with the rising labor force each year requires an opening of about 1.75 million new jobs."

Obviously, the managers of the future must be mindful of several worthwhile corporate objectives, but they had better not lose sight of the primary objective of a business, that of staying in business. No profits, no business. Survival is the first priority of managing.

Managers in the future will be expected to create wealth, generate profits, and provide employment for the fulfillment of the public policy outlined in the Employment Act of 1946. Furthermore, they will be expected to utilize the human resources of the nation in accordance with the spirit of equal economic opportunity, civil rights, equal employment opportunity, and, at the same time, adhere to the clean air and clean water guidelines of the Environmental Protection Agency within the Occupational Health and Safety Act standards. Managers will be challenged to create almost 2 million new employment opportunities a year with people working fewer hours per week. The four-day work week is on the horizon with "gliding work time" a probability. A 28-hour work week has been predicted for the turn of the century, compared with 37.3 hours in 1970, 49 hours in 1930, 57 hours in 1900, 70 hours in 1850, and 84 hours in 1800.

Future managers will be expected to create more goods and services with more profits and more employment, and to deal with employees' demands for more leisure, more services, and more conveniences in a technological economy in a scientific society. The role of future managers will be complicated further by energy and power shortages and pressure to guard the environment from damage.

Some of the most obvious and pressing factors and forces in the changing economic, social, and political situation have been cited to illustrate that managers of the future will be operating in an environment different from that in which managers of the past operated. The question of managerial concern is now posed. What knowledge, skills, and values will be required for the future manager's survival and success?

MANAGERS OF THE FUTURE

According to the time schedule, a new type of manager should now be emerging to cope with the complexity of factors and forces in a society that is struggling to adapt to changing human values and rapid technological advances. It is probable that the manager of the future will be classified as a "public manager" or a "public oriented executive." Harlan Cleveland, in his recent book *The Future Executive,* predicts the role of the future public executive and gives reasons for his or her emergence.

Today's professional manager will modify his style and begin the transition towards the era of the public manager; the potential managers among the some 8 million students in the universities today will complete the transition during the last portion of the century. The manager will develop from a hired man for private corporation shareholders into a business institutional leader who will manage enterprise for the best balanced interests of the state and the nation to preserve and maintain our private enterprise system. This development could be changed, of course, in the event of war, epidemic, depression, or some other unforeseen catastrophe.

The environmental factors and forces at work, such as changing human values along with the growing size and complexity of organizational patterns, are blurring the traditional lines between what is private and what is public. The future managers of private enterprise—profit or non-profit—will gravitate toward the concept that they are responsible for people in general and reluctantly accept the government as a monitor of business affairs. Concurrently, the government will contract to the private sector of the economy a growing proportion of the public business because public managers will be better qualified to achieve the results desired by the body politic.

The National Aeronautics and Space Administration is a prime example of this method of operation. No large business organization, whatever its formal ownership, will be able to escape social and public responsibility. Public managers will be faced with the major responsibility for merging human values with the potential from technological advances to conserve human energy in the creation and distribution of goods and services for improved life styles.

For the managers of the future, policies for the conduct of their firms will be formulated mostly by their sense of direction as modified by negotiation with their colleagues and peers. Private enterprise will prevail, but managers will be sensitive to the need to satisfy multiple claimants for the benefits flowing from national and multinational corporations.

Actually, it is the success of past managers that has developed this trend toward the concept of the public manager. The managers of our corporate enterprises have succeeded in creating most of the wealth of the nation; they also have attracted most of the nation's competent personnel into the work force of the corporations. Corporations, therefore, have the greatest capability of achieving state and national goals for economic and social progress. If the managers of private enterprise do not adopt the public manager concept, the alternative would not be acceptable to the advocates of the private enterprise system that has been the foundation of the American dream.

Future Managerial Situation

The first priority for managers of the future will be the survival of the companies that they manage and their own survival as managers. If present professional managers could send a scout into the future, receive reports, and ensure their survival by being prepared, such reports probably would include subject areas that already are discernible. The public manager in the future will perform functions with resources that may have names the same as or similar to present ones, but they will change in concept and nature in response to changing human values and environmental conditions.

The manager of the future will deal with highly complex organizations. The organizational vehicle will not be the hierarchical pyramid in which decisions are centralized and most of the planning and control are done at the top. The future manager's organiza-

tional mechanism will be in the nature of systems that will have interlaced webs of tension with loose control; power will be diffused among plural centers of decision. Decision making will become an increasingly intricate process of multilateral brokerage both inside and outside the organization.

As organizations become more horizontal and less vertical in structure, the style by which they will be governed will be more consensual, collegial, and consultive. The more challenging the objective and the more formidable the problems to be resolved, the more authority and power will be diffused so that a larger number of capable people can work toward achievement and problem solving. Collective leadership is not for the expression of democratic feelings; it is an imperative of size and complexity. The manager of the future must manage more complexity for survival.

Evidence of the increasing complexity of organizations is easily observable in the growth and influence of multinational firms, bank holding companies, and conglomerate corporations. Multinational firms already dominate much of the production of the world, and they are growing at a rate double the purely domestic companies. Some of them exert great influence on the world's financial affairs and have grown in economic size beyond all but the wealthiest nations. They are creating an economic and social movement that rivals the impact of the industrial revolution. Bank holding companies, as of mid-1972, held nearly 40 percent of all commercial banks in the nation with 58 percent of all deposits and 60 percent of all U.S. assets. The responsibilities of the managers of these complex organizations are greater than those faced by previous managers; the consequences of error and mismanagement could have serious negative impacts on the world economy.

Managers of these organizations have the opportunity to influence the peace of the world and the living standards and life styles of the peoples of less developed nations because the influence of their operations can transcend national boundaries more readily than that of governments or religious orders. However, they can only achieve their potential by managing with the concept and style of a public oriented manager. J. J. Servan-Schreiber, in his book *The American Challenge* paid tribute to the genius and viability of American managers: "American industry spills out across the world primarily because of the energy released by the American system—by the opportunity for individual initiative, by the innovative knack of teams, by the flexibility of business structure and by the decentralization of business decision."

The manager of the future will encounter an accelerating growth in the size and complexity of organizational systems that seem destined to move away from formal, authoritarian, and hierarchical managing. The trend is toward more informal, fluid ways of bargaining, brokerage, advice, and consent. Management will be practiced less as a system of authority and more as a resource in an organizational system to achieve desired results.

The view of William Blackie, the past chairman of Caterpillar Tractor Company, reflects the changing concept: "Insofar as authority has meant the power to order or command, its definition will be modified by the addition of some such qualification as 'but expect or deserve to be obeyed or followed only if you can satisfy those being ordered or led'." According to Blackie, the boss-man relationship will prevail and embrace both a superior and a subordinate. The gap will be narrowed, however, because of the rapidity with which the well-educated subordinate is acquiring skill and experience. The essential requirement is that both parties understand and appreciate the basic nature of their respective responsibilities.

The manager of the future will realize that employees will be more in-

clined to take authority from agreed-upon objectives and the nature of the work than from the dictation of an authoritarian boss. More than one mode of thinking can be utilized. The future manager will be a multiplier of the work of others; in the more complex organizations of the future, he will find it necessary to utilize the knowledge and skills that others possess. He will be responsible for results and for "getting it all together," rather than for preoccupying himself with individual processes.

Authority as used by the future manager will be modified by the changing values and motivations of university students as they populate the organizations of business. By 1985, college graduates will outnumber those without a high school education in the U.S. work force, and managers will have as a resource the most highly educated personnel in the history of the world. Employees will regard themselves as partners in management and expect to have their talents utilized for self-esteem and self-realization. The better educated young people today, especially those in the so-called new culture or counter culture, tend to demand their rights, resist authority and regimentation that try to put them into an organizational harness too tight for comfort, and search for their own identity instead of allowing themselves to be "house-broken" by endless procedures and processes.

Before anyone makes a quick decision that universities are subversive places and our young people have revolutionary ideas, it might be enlightening to read *The Unanimous Declaration of the Thirteen United States of America.* In this document, popularly known as the Declaration of Independence, one will find written:

> We hold these truths to be self-evident, that all men are created equal, that they are endowed by their Creator with certain unalienable Rights, that among these are Life, Liberty, and the pursuit of Happiness—That to secure these rights, governments

are instituted among Men, deriving their just powers from the consent of the governed—That whenever any form of government becomes destructive of these ends, it is the Right of the People to alter or to abolish it, and to institute new government, laying its foundation on such principles, and organizing its powers in such form, as to them shall seem most likely to effect their Safety and Happiness.

If a substitution of the words "management" for "government" and "employees" for "people" is made in the reading of that document, one can better understand why there is a trend in the concept of management by the consent of those managed. Of course, there is no reference to women. The proposed 27th amendment to the constitution might remedy this original writing. Some thirty states have ratified the amendment with thirty-eight required to provide equal rights for women by the enactment of an Equal Rights Act. Depending upon one's point of view, an equal rights act may be necessary to enlarge opportunities for women. With few exceptions, most professions and trades employed about the same percentage of women in 1970 as in 1950, twenty years previously.

Henry B. Schacht, commenting on the changing trend in organizational design and the use of human resources, has stated that managers must learn to handle both the underprivileged and the bright young people, especially those who are calling for a change [*Business Horizons,* August, 1970, pp. 29-34]. He adds:

What this means is shorter, flatter organizations; it means responsive management; it means a true willingness to allow people to participate in setting their own destiny; it means that the militaristically-oriented hierarchy that has characterized societies and most business enterprises is a thing of the past, and the quicker we recognize it the better. . . . all organizations will have to think of their key assets in terms of people and knowledge. People can be the most flexible of all assets; knowledge is the one thing that will give us insight into change and the consequences of change. Many

companies say that people are its most important resource, but few believe it. Many people say that they live or die with their people but then spend all of their time analyzing balance sheets and income statements.

Current professional managers who make the transition to public oriented managers will master the methods required to achieve objectives in organizations with more complex and decentralized relationships; they will develop the skills to use a modified concept of authority that will enable personnel to exercise self-commitment and self-control for the achievement of agreed upon results instead of emphasizing processes.

For the realization of high motivation and performance of personnel in more complex organizational relationships, authority must be applied with the consent and cooperation of those managed. Future managers will cope with the challenge of generating purposeful action while more and more employees demand the satisfaction of getting into the act.

Future External Forces on Managers

All organizations exist and operate in an environment of some kind. External forces and factors in the environment will complicate the work of future managers. Before the end of the present decade, for example, managers of all organizations in the United States will be faced with the problem of adapting their operations to the metric system of weights and measurements. (The meter unit of measurement was determined by measuring the distance from the North Pole to the equator and then dividing by 10 million. The meter is 3.3 feet or 1.1 yards in the English system.) At present, the United States and Burma are the only major nations still using the English system. Because of the world trend, Congress asked in 1968 for a sweeping investigation of the question. This investigation involved public hearings and surveys on almost every activity in our society—from education, manufacturing, and the consumer to international trade and national security. The recommendation of the Secretary of Commerce was that the United States should adopt the metric through a nationally coordinated program.

This conversion will affect all managers of business enterprise, especially the manufacturers. Temperature will be measured by Celsius instead of Fahrenheit; length will be computed by centimeters and kilometers rather than by inches and miles; mass weight will change from ounces and pounds to grams and kilograms; area will be determined by square meters and square kilometers instead of by square feet and square miles; hectares will replace acres; and volume will be measured by milliliters and liters.

Present managers are planning for the costs of conversion, which will be relatively greater in the manufacturing industry. The greatest burden of costs will be in production and industrial educational programs, particularly in the machine tool and automotive industries. The conversion will entail considerable costs for manufacturers during a time when costs will be increasing for pollution and environmental damage control.

The material wealth of the nation, measured by either the metric system or the passing English system, stems from the managerial use of the basic factors of production, land, labor, and capital. The manager of the future will be more restricted in his use of land than his predecessors. Managers of the past have enjoyed freedom of decision in the use of private land, regardless of whether or not it was devoted to its highest and best use. The market system prevailed. The future manager, however, will be confined to operating within federal and state land-use policy. A bill now in Congress (S. 268) will give grants to states for the development of plans for private land use.

J. Irwin Miller, a prominent Indiana industrialist, in a recent issue of *U.S. News and World Report,* expressed his views concerning corporate survival by serving effectively and well some real current need of society. He wrote:

We have a fixed amount of land in the continental United States. Contained in that fixed amount of land is a fixed amount of natural resources. On the fixed amount of land, then, with a finite quantity of resources, there exists a growing population of human beings. By the end of the century there will be somewhere between 50 and 100 million more people in this country. . . . Growing demand for a shrinking supply of land and materials can prudently be expected only to accelerate the rise in cost of capital construction despite the miracles that need performing in labor costs, regulations and design.

Land-use policy for the guidelines of the future manager stems from the growing population that requires more land for living, domestic and foreign consumption, recreation, and energy sources. Future managers will be expected to create the equivalent of a new city for a million people about every four months during the remainder of the century. They will also be expected to produce for a per capita consumption of some 700 British thermal units of energy by the year 2000, in comparison with 377 in 1970, and at the same time protect the environment from water and air pollution and trash.

Proposed legislation in Congress (S. 1283) will create a new federal agency with authority to relieve the fuel shortage. The legislation will create five "government-industry" corporations to develop technology to turn coal into gas, extract oil from shale rock, and harness geothermal energy. Soon legislation may be passed for the control of trash pollution in addition to water and air pollution. Currently we are producing enough trash annually to fill the Panama Canal four times over with a disposal cost of some $5 billion a year. This cost is exceeded only by that for schools and roads in the public services. Our trash volume will triple in the next decade to harass the future manager as increased demands will be made for the discharge of his social responsibilities.

Although the land resource is considered fixed for the future manager, he will have an increasing supply of labor flowing from the enlarging population. However, this labor resource will be different from that of the past and will require a different style of managing. This style must recognize the consent of the managed with an orientation around results rather than activities in more viable organizations. The members of the labor force of the future will be the best educated in history with knowledge and skills that many managers will need but will not possess. Furthermore, employees' expectations and value systems will be different.

Over 80 percent will be high school and college graduates who will expect managers to utilize their talents and abilities in interesting and challenging work opportunities with a minimum of boredom and monotony. Their work styles and life styles may be as important to them as their pay scales. They will resist being used as impersonal "inputs" in complex organizations under authoritarian supervisors. They will be products of the new knowledge industry that may account for half of the GNP by the end of the century, and they will expect managers to fulfill their responsibilities for both economic and social objectives.

In the future labor force, some will be specialists, others technologists, and many humanists. Some will have broad preparation, such as the proposed "poly-socio-econo-politico-technologist" background that has been conceived by Simon Ramo, vice-chairman of TRW, Inc. The manager of the future will be expected to utilize intelligently this highly competent labor force and avoid underemploying or wasting human resources. The wealth of the state and the nation will be measured more by the productivity of the labor force than by gold bullion, and future managers may be evaluated more on their abilities to skillfully utilize a growing labor force than to use capital equipment. The human asset will appear on the balance sheet of the future. Advancing technology will aid the future manager in his use of resources, but he will need to arrange a satisfactory combination of ethical human values with the flow of science and technology.

The capital resources available to managers in the future should be adequate if inflation can be controlled. National personal income in the United States has passed the lofty mark of a trillion dollars per annum for another historical first. No other nation has come close to this annual flow of personal income from wages, salaries (with fringe benefits), interest, rent, dividends, and social welfare, and the income to business proprietors and professional personnel. Reasonable savings and investment of a portion of this personal income can provide adequate capital resources for future managers to combine with land and labor resources for the maintenance of a healthy economy.

The public managers of the future will differ more in their values and attitudes than in their knowledge and skills. One can already discern in the United States that the line between public and private is narrowing because all private enterprise has some degree of public responsibility. The larger and more complex the enterprise, the more public responsibility it is expected to carry. Regardless of their personal values, more managers in private enterprise are serving more and more as public managers or executives.

If the manager of the future makes the transition from the firm-oriented professional manager of today to the public oriented manager, the business foundation of democracy and private enterprise can be maintained with managerial freedom to set objectives and policies for the best balanced interests of the economy. Furthermore, the future public manager can be recognized for making contributions to society as beneficial as those made by doctors, lawyers, ministers, engineers, educators, and scientists.

The public manager of the future can lessen the credibility gap in management that has widened since 1965. It is ironic today that our citizens want business to become more active in public leadership, yet believe that business is doing less than before, according to a recent Louis Harris survey. The future public manager will perform the essential managerial functions in society in a manner that will enhance his credibility. Alec Mackenzie, in his recent book *The Credibility Gap in Management,* states that "credibility is that quality, state, or condition that produces believability or trustworthiness." He comments that credibility depends more upon relationships with people than upon systems. Somehow, the public is inclined to believe that business is out of phase with current expectations and demands. It is not the capability and competence of business managers that are being questioned, it is their sense of priorities and good faith.

At a time when the public is crying for a new leadership style, some managers are retreating into fixed behavior patterns. They are charged with proclaiming a modern managerial theory but continuing to execute in antiquated managerial practices. Unless the manager of the future assumes a role similar to the public manager concept, there looms the possibility of the establishment of a public management commission because of the importance of managers in our economy and to prevent serious management failures in essential corporations that affect the public interest.

If governmental commissions are considered essential for the proper utilization of the resources of land, labor, and capital, it is not inconceivable that public pressures could develop for monitoring the application of the management resource in our society. Without the resource of management to utilize other resources, little is accomplished. Managers who learn to manage with a public orientation will obviate any need for a public management commission. Their value systems will embrace the service of multiple claimants in society by the setting and the achievement of both the economic and the social objectives of their firms.

The public manager of the future has the opportunity to achieve the prestige and the recognition that managers have earned but not received on the basis of contributions to society. Congress or a state legislature can recognize the importance of the future public managers by establishing a national or a state Management Day. For the contributions that managers make to economic and social progress, it would be suitable to have two holidays in one week, Labor Day on Monday and Management Day on Tuesday. This would focus attention on the relationship of both segments of our private enterprise society. Together they have produced the biggest national output, the highest personal income, and the highest standard of living in the world.

30 Reflections of a 21st Century Manager

George Kozmetsky

The end of the 20th century was duly marked by global celebrations. But for a relatively small group of Americans there were special satisfactions in entering the year 2001. They were the managers of various enterprises—in business, government and industry—whose careers extended all the way back to the late 1960s. Now in their fifties, they could look back on a period of extraordinary change. The manager's responsibilities had changed drastically while the composition of industry itself was marked by numerous stages of transformation.

Back in the early 1970s, they recalled, managers began to recognize new kinds of organizations. For convenience, these developing organizations were known as *nonroutine industries.*

Those nonroutine industries were made up of units of government, industry and education engaged in nonrepetitive or "nonroutine" pursuits. The education industry itself was a leading nonroutine industry. The defense and space industries were certainly nonroutine industries, and so were large segments of the medical, electronics, oceanography and "urban problem" industries. So were many areas of government.

The new industries had certain common characteristics. Often, for example, they were working on problems that required new orders of solutions. No textbooks held the answers to questions that arose in planning and building livable megalopolies, exploring the reaches of space or controlling the environment. Frequently, answers had to be improvised. The temporary solution to the problem of air pollution in Los Angeles, for example, was typically makeshift and typically "messy." When the pollution index struck a certain level, motorists were required to pull over to the curb and turn off the engine. As pollution grew worse, power plants were required to switch from diesel fuel to natural gas. Solutions to many such problems, ranging from garbage disposal to land pollution, were frequently patchwork and "messy," offensive to anyone who liked solutions to be "clean" and permanent.

Nonroutine industries were also technologically based; their products were the end result of much labor and thought by scientists, engineers and other technical and professional talents. Even as early as 1969, 70 percent of the available scientists and engineers were hired by the "nonroutine" industries.

Another characteristic of the new industries was that the number of units they produced was not very large. Sometimes, in fact, the "unit" consisted only of a program or a plan. If the "units" were products, they ranged from one-of-a-kind to small production runs. The computer industry, for example, produced only 14,300 units in 1968, after 20 years of existence as an "industry." In contrast, the old mass-production auto industry turned out 10 million units.

This article originally appeared in *Bell Telephone Magazine* (March–April, 1969), pp. 27–32, and is reprinted with permission.

Still another characteristic of the emerging industries was that their new products or proposals often required the cooperation and coordination of segments of government, education and industry. Problems associated with urbanization, for example, involved a large amount of interaction among public and private organizations. So did problems related to transportation, space exploration and health.

The rise and spread of such new industries gradually changed the nature of the manager's tasks.

In the old, mass-production industries, the manager was principally a supervisor of specialists. To his office came the experts in his company, the professionals in such fields as accounting, personnel, marketing, finance and production. But in the nonroutine industries, the manager had a different set of appointments. His office visitors were men in government, university professors, the many scientists and engineers within his own company, and numerous outside consultants.

More and more, it appeared, the manager of a nonroutine industry was not merely the supervisor and motivator of an assortment of talents; he was also a man with the ability to break across the artificial barriers among disciplines and professions. His experiences in education and government, as well as in business, enabled him to locate and tap expertise on short notice. He was, in fact, a manager of intellectual *resources*.

The ability to manage intellectual resources assumed overwhelming importance in the decades of the 1970s and 1980s. By then, education had unquestionably become America's leading industry. requiring a vast number of skilled managers. In 1980, college enrollments were three times higher than in 1970, and they advanced even faster in later decades. (In the year 2000, for example, the University of California had 275,000 students, compared with 99,000 in 1969, and that was fairly typical of the larger educa-

tional units. Education was a lifelong process of virtually all of America's 400 million people.)

Even as early as the 1970s, it had become quite common for a manager to leave The Company after five or six years in the demanding top echelons. Sometimes he went off to serve in government; often he joined a university. But in any kind of organization he was marked by his ability to tap intellectual resources, in the interest of solving problems and creating new knowledge.

The university was the ideal place for honing his abilities as a manager. The campus was obviously rich in intellectual resources. It offered him the chance to bring together different disciplines in an informal atmosphere and get them to work on a particular problem. The solutions they found—often unusual—could perhaps be applied in a few years to some industry, just as space technology and techniques had been adopted by industry in the 1960s.

Of course, the manager who could shuttle easily among government, industry and educational organizations was not particularly new. Such managers appeared noticeably in the 1960s. People like John Gardner, Robert McNamara, George Romney, Daniel Moynihan, Sol Linowitz, Dean Rusk, Orville Freeman and McGeorge Bundy were merely a few of the managers who could move gracefully—and successfully—from campus to a foundation, from business to government. Behind them were hundreds of lesser-known managers with similar adaptability. Increasingly, the business manager in most demand was one who could skillfully bring together experts of government and education into the planning stages of a project, drawing on *their* intellectual resources. But as the one-of-a-kind projects so typical of the nonroutine industries became more common in the 1970s and 1980s, the manager's tenure with a particular organization was significantly shorter than it was in the 1960s.

The need for managers of intellectual resources was intense, even in the 1960s. The shortage of such managers would have been worse, however, if the nation had not embarked on the era of manned space flight. With that era came the rise to prominence of the interdisciplinary scientists.

What America needed and got in that period was an increasing number of Leonardo da Vincis—people who could work across the sciences; people who could comprehend the subtleties of cellular biology and at the same time design the mechanical apparatus needed to keep living organisms alive and normally adjusted to the hostile environment of space. In addition, these same individuals were expected to manage and integrate their portion of the operation with the longer range objectives.

At the same time, a number of corporations—particularly those in the mass-production or routine industries—were themselves busily training future managers, even if they sometimes failed to realize the fact. It was occasionally noted, even in the 1960s, that systems experts quickly learned many of the essential details of running a company in the process of analyzing systems and structuring problems. As problem-solving by computer became more general in the 1970s, the systems experts were logical candidates for top management. It was they, after all, who could superbly perform what was to become the manager's chief function—the structuring of problems. And so, between the space programs and management training by computer, America had developed at least a stopgap supply of managers for the 1970s and 1980s. By this time, too, the leading university business schools had modernized their programs and were training many managers for the new-style enterprises.

One of the particularly vexing problems for nonroutine industry managers in this period involved an essential segment of their intellectual resources —the scientists and technicians. In the 1970s, most technically trained people had become even more mobile than managers.

The tenure of technically trained people on a project often lasted for just a few years. As soon as their specialized knowledge was exhausted, they found it necessary to acquire some other specialty—for their specialties were often usable for one project only.

For all the talk about shortages of engineers and scientists in the 1960s, for example, there began to appear a kind of occupational unemployment; like actors, scientists found themselves "at liberty." When England found it couldn't compete in atomic energy and in the aircraft industries, the requirements for technical people were cut back 50 percent. Job switches and "brain drains" became common.

Motivating people to do their best in short-term projects was particularly trying for managers in the 1970s. In those years, however, enormous strides were made in understanding how people store and process information internally—in other words, how they think. The psychology developed from research in that area also was applied to problems of human behavior; and by the 1980s, knowledge of learning and motivation was as advanced as were chemistry and biology in the 1960s. By the end of the century managers in both routine and nonroutine industries were superior motivators.

The motivation question affected entire organizations, of course. Back in the 1960s, corporations were becoming aware of what was popularly called "social responsibility." Many companies quickly laid claim to the virtue; others said they had it all along. In any case the question became increasingly academic as corporate policies and activities seemed increasingly to involve the public interest. By the 1980s and 1990s the largest corporations squarely identified their goals with social objectives, and the manager became concerned with developing industrial strategies that would mesh with the goals of raising the quality of life. The motivating force behind his company, as he saw it, was the need to furnish people with the things that gave full meaning to life. Philosophical questions found a permanent place on the agenda of board meetings, and the chairman was as concerned about them as about return on investment.

On the eve of year 2001, a manager could take some satisfactions in the ways that some of the fears of the 1960s and 1970s had disappeared.

In those years, he recalled, there had been widespread concern that automation would create disastrous problems of chronic unemployment. When it developed that computers could not only think but could also frame questions better than most humans, there was further alarm. And when automated equipment began to produce automated equipment—in effect, a machine with the human power of reproduction—there was something akin to terror. Was man becoming obsolete?

In retrospect, the fears were groundless. The machines were actually helping to open up new opportunities and force the continuous upgrading of tasks.

Some of the biggest changes of all had occurred within the old mass-production industries. A third of all working people were in these industries by the year 2000, and virtually all could be considered supervisors or middle-managers. The 40- and 35-hour work week had disappeared many years before; supervisors and maintenance workers were in the automated factory only four hours each day. A typical factory had six shifts, five days weekly.

The managers at middle levels handled actual operations of the factory. They turned their tactical problems over to self-organizing computers, which in turn put the solutions into automatic operation—subject, of course, to the middle-manager's veto.

The top manager had an enormous amount of authority, compared with the top manager of the 1960s. All lines on the organization chart led to his office. The trend really started in the 1960s with the centralization of certain operations like payroll and billing, that was made possible by computers. As computer applications spread during the 1970s, companies recentralized authority and control. By the year 2000, the top manager and the machines were directly responsible for virtually all decision-making. The authority of middle managers was severely limited.

A high percentage of the top manager's time was devoted to strategic planning. He was concerned with the day-to-day operations of the company only to the extent of monitoring performance—to make certain that decisions were in line with his company's goals and policies.

Top managers had ample time for such strategic planning. Committee meetings and routine briefings had long been eliminated. The chief executive carried out communications with a voice-writer, color TV-telephone and computer display board. In strategic planning, he concentrated on formulating specialized management principles which would eventually be built into the computer; the computer could then offer solutions to specific problems in line with management principles and company goals.

When he wasn't planning, the manager was studying. His administrative aide (upgraded from secretary) helped assemble research and study sources.

His study efforts were considered an essential part of his daily chores. For in the nonroutine industries, a manager needed a deep knowledge of the natural sciences, the arts, the social sciences and the physical sciences. All in all, he needed to keep abreast of 10 different fields in detail, and he needed a good conceptual knowledge of 90 others.

Other things had changed for the manager too. Communications had removed the necessity for most face-to-face meetings, and communicating itself was much briefer. And the proliferation of governmental authorities, with their overlapping jurisdictions, finally gave way in the late 1970s to a balance of federal and regional authorities, making communicating with government easier.

Solutions to problems were still tailor-made, but they were no longer "messy." With government, industry and education working toward the common goals of improving the quality of life, conflict of interest—that had made for patchwork solutions in the 1960s—had been largely eliminated.

Not all problems had been ironed out in the last third of the 20th Century, of course. The knowledge explosion, for instance, was never really tamed. Despite the compression and fast transmission of data in forms other than the old printed word, managers had still to find a way to keep completely current, because knowledge kept doubling at ever faster rates. The typical manager in the year 2000 was more or less resigned to the idea that he would never know all he needed to know.

But, on the whole, for the manager, the satisfactions in reaching the 21st Century far outweighed any yearnings for simpler times. His skills had played no small part in easing burdens so that people had more meaningful control over their lives, enabling them to manage their own destinies.